ECONOMY, SOCIETY AND WARFARE
AMONG THE BRITONS AND SAXONS

ECONOMY, SOCIETY AND WARFARE
AMONG THE BRITONS AND SAXONS

LESLIE ALCOCK

CARDIFF
UNIVERSITY OF WALES PRESS
1987

University of Wales Press, 6 Gwennyth St, Cardiff CF2 4YD
© Leslie Alcock, 1987

British Library Cataloguing in Publication Data
Alcock, Leslie
  Economy, Society and Warfare among the
  Britons and Saxons.
  1. Great Britain—History—Anglo-Saxon
  period, 449–1066
  I. Title
  941.01   DA 152

ISBN 0–7083–0963–1

Printed in Great Britain by The Bath Press, Avon

Preface

When the excavation monograph on Dinas Powys was published in 1963, it could reasonably be claimed that it was by far the richest site of the early post-Roman centuries so far excavated and published in western Britain. This remains true in 1987; but inevitably, in the meantime, the increase in available evidence, together with the movement of ideas, have rendered many of my earlier interpretations and generalizations inadequate, inappropriate, or simply incorrect.

As long ago as 1980, I circulated a revised *catalogue raisonné* of fortified sites in Wales and the Marches to interested colleagues; and in 1981, at the Silver Jubilee meeting of the Society for Medieval Archaeology, I presented a new list of defended settlements of the fifth to seventh centuries which extended to Dumnonia as well (D. A. Hinton 1983, 58–60). This was the primary element in the growth of the present book.

In addition to the lists of defended sites, in several lectures and papers I had discussed the warfare of the period; and continuing a central theme of *Dinas Powys*, I had attempted to relate weapons, defences, and warfare to social structure and its economic base. A selection of these papers forms the second element.

Finally, by 1983 the original print run of a thousand copies of the monograph was exhausted. Since the excavation had established itself as a classic of post-Roman Celtic archaeology, it seemed desirable that the basic evidence of structures, stratification and finds should be kept available in print. Data relevant to this period therefore comprise the third element in the book.

Fortunately, Mr John Rhys, Director of the University of Wales Press, accepted my proposals. I am deeply grateful to him for his encouragement, to the Press Board for undertaking the publication, and not least to Susan Jenkins for seeing the book through the Press.

While the book has been in preparation, the vigorous interest of scholars in post-Roman Wales has become increasingly apparent. At the broadest level, this is reflected in the formation of a Research Group on the archaeology of early medieval Wales, and the publication of summaries of papers given at its founding conference (N. Edwards 1984). As for Dinas Powys itself, the animal bones have been examined by Roberta Gilchrist, under the inspiration of Professor Philip Rahtz, and I am glad to incorporate her results in Chapter 3. In addition, Ewan Campbell and Alan Lane have been examining other classes of finds, especially the ceramics.

Without a doubt, when the work of all these scholars is fully available, it will lead to further major and exciting reinterpretations. Because, however, I do not believe in the possibility of definitive statements in a dynamic field of study such as archaeology, I have not delayed the book in order to await these potential developments. Whatever modifications the future will bring, the present synthesis has at least the advantage of first-hand knowledge of the major relevant excavations.

In 1963, I expressed my gratitude to Brasenose College, Oxford, to Glamorgan County Council, and to University College Cardiff for the financial support which made the original publication of Dinas Powys possible, and I wish to renew those thanks here. The present volume owes much to the assistance, most gratefully acknowledged, of the various bodies and individuals who have permitted the reproduction of material originally published under their auspices: the Board of Celtic Studies, Chapters 2, 5–9, 15 and 18; the Council for British Archaeology, part of Chapter 3; Exeter College, Oxford, and the Editor of *Antiquity*, Chapter 12; the British Academy, Chapter 13; the Cambrian Archaeological Association, Chapter 16; Professor V. I. Evison and Oxford University Press, Chapter 17; and Penguin Books, Chapter 19.

My chief thanks, however, lie at the personal level. In the preface to *Dinas Powys*, I wrote that my wife's active assistance and encouragement had sustained me at every stage: the whole venture had been hers as much as mine. This is every bit as true of the present book, both as a whole and in its several parts. Whatever merits it may be found to have are due as much to her contributions as to my own.

GLASGOW   L.A.
August 1985/November 1986

Contents

List of Illustrations

Introduction
The Growth of a Theme

The present book represents the core of my academic endeavour from the time of my appointment to the Department of Archaeology, University College, Cardiff in 1953, until my translation to the Chair of Archaeology in the University of Glasgow in 1973. That core contains certain interrelated elements. Firstly, in my fieldwork and excavation I concentrated on fortified and enclosed places, especially in Wales and south-west Britain, and especially those datable to the period from about AD 400 to 800. Secondly, I attempted to understand how such fortifications functioned in military terms, and I speculated on the social needs which they fulfilled. Thirdly, I sought for the social and economic interpretations which might be inferred from the archaeological evidence. Finally, I insisted that any attempt to derive social and economic inferences from the archaeological evidence needed to be both controlled by, and supplemented from, written sources.

Two elements of this core merit further exposition, because they help to explain how the theme which unites this book came into being. Such a concentration on a limited class of monument was unusual among the non-classical archaeologists of my Oxford generation. Unspecialized and untrained as I was—I have never attended an archaeological lecture as part of an academic curriculum—it might have been expected that I would become a general purpose digger, or 'jobbing excavator'. It was in fact Dinas Powys which generated my interest in Dark Age or early Christian fortification. An excavation undertaken in 1954, in the expectation that the site was a small multivallate promontory fort of the pre-Roman Iron Age, yielded instead a rich collection of artefacts datable to the later fifth to eighth centuries AD: a period virtually unrepresented at that time in the secular archaeology of Wales, but one which was currently receiving attention in Dumnonia, thanks to Radford's publication of the imported pottery from Tintagel, and Thomas's work in Cornwall, especially at Gwithian.

On the completion of the Dinas Powys excavations in 1958, it seemed desirable to look for contemporary fortified places elsewhere in Wales. Around this time, Savory and Hogg were exploring forts that were traditionally associated with Dark Age rulers, respectively at Dinas Emrys and Garn Boduan. I chose first to explore Castell Odo, because earlier work there had produced alleged post-Roman pottery: in 1958–9, however, it was possible to show that this really belonged to an early phase of the pre-Roman Iron Age. Subsequently, in 1961–6, I turned to Castell Degannwy, a manifestly defensible site which had a traditional association with the sixth-century ruler Maelgwn Gwynedd, as well as annalistic references in AD 812 and 822. Limited excavation did indeed yield pottery broadly contemporary with Maelgwn. It was presumably this record of excavation which led to an invitation to direct research at Cadbury Castle,

Somerset, a hill-fort with both Arthurian associations and pottery of around AD 500. The work at Cadbury–Camelot, in 1966–70 and 1973, was thus the continuation of a campaign begun by chance at Dinas Powys in 1954, but thereafter pursued deliberately.

It is easy to understand how the structural aspects of Dinas Powys had generated a long-term interest in Dark Age defences—as well as one in medieval ring-works, which is not, however, relevant to the present theme. In a no less compelling manner, the artefacts and other finds from the excavation fostered a concern for social and economic interpretations. I was already in some measure prepared for this. In my schoolboy dabblings in archaeological literature, I had been profoundly influenced by Grahame Clark's *Archaeology and Society* (1939), in which he had suggested that 'the object of locating, excavating and dating archaeological material was to interpret it in terms of societies that had once lived'; and especially so in terms of their economic activities. Later, reading for the Honours School of Modern History at Oxford, I had been enthralled by R. V. Lennard's newly-founded special subject on the manorial economy of medieval England. It became one of my ambitions to integrate the documentary and archaeological evidence from some area of medieval Britain into a social and economic synthesis. Dinas Powys provided the opportunity to realize that ambition.

In terms of sheer bulk, the most obvious finds from the site were the animal bones, coming from middens which also contained artefacts dating them broadly from AD 450 to 700. The bones could be studied, in the standard practice of the time, to give information about the species represented, and their age of slaughter. I then attempted to compare this information both with the expectations of medieval manuals of husbandry and also, nearer in time, with the food renders that were detailed in Welsh legal tracts. The great quantity of animal bones appeared to lend support to the traditional model of the early Welsh as a nation of pastoralists. But at the very time that I was working on the Dinas Powys material, this model was convincingly demolished by Glanville Jones, who was able to show the major role of arable farming in post-Roman Wales. It was gratifying that Dinas Powys could contribute to the debate by yielding evidence for the grinding of corn and the baking of bread. My conclusion was that the basic economy was one of mixed farming, in which stock-raising was balanced by a definite—though unquantifiable—arable component.

This basic economy represented the activities of a peasant class; but higher classes were reflected in other finds. The working of leather and bone might indeed be a peasant or cottage industry; so too might blacksmithing; but the occurrence of scrap bronze, some of it gilt, of scrap glass, of crucibles with globules of gold in them, and of the pattern-die for a penannular brooch, all denoted a higher class of craftsman: the jeweller. Moreover, there was literary evidence, of rather later date, to show that the appropriate milieu for a specialized craftsman was the hall and court of a prince. Here, then, by inference, was a yet higher social rank. The inference might be supported, moreover, by the abundant evidence that wine, pottery, and glass had been brought to Dinas Powys from the east Mediterranean, north Africa, and Gaul. The presence of defences argued in the same way.

In other words, the economic and craft activities at Dinas Powys were ineluctably related to social status. The site was pre-eminently one which revealed the chieftain, the craftsman and the woman at the quern. To that extent, my concern for social and economic archaeology has a certain Marxist flavour. This is scarcely surprising, since in the early 1940s I had studied—and rejected—dialectical materialism as a basis for understanding history; and I had read, with a qualified approval, Christopher Hill's interpretation of the English Revolution in Marxist terms. Today, it seems to me that it is not necessary to be a Marxist in order to believe that economic forces, social tensions, and class exploitation play large roles in human history. On the other hand, some present-day Marxist historians, at least in my own period of interest, have so far diluted the theoretical content of their writings that Marxism implies no more than a firm grasp of the obvious. Perhaps we are all Marxists now.

One final comment may be justified on the theme of social and economic archaeology. When I started to excavate at Dinas Powys, my training as a historian, as well as my readings in Clark, Childe and Collingwood, meant that I could have conceived of no significant basis for archaeological interpretation other than in economic and social terms. Manifestly the finds reinforced this view; and it is therefore implicit, and indeed taken for granted, in the section of the 1963 monograph which was expressly entitled 'Economic, Social and Political Aspects of Dinas Powys in the Early Christian Period' (below, pp. 31–66). It has therefore been a matter of mild surprise to learn that social archaeology and economic archaeology were actually invented at Cambridge (England) in the decade 1965–75.

I turn finally to some significant extensions from my theme of fortified sites. My concentration on the exploration of enclosed or fortified places had led me also to consider the character of the warfare which it might be presumed had called them into being. Among the pre-Roman Celts, I looked at this in a study of hill-forts in Wales and the Marches,[1] which is not reprinted here because it lies outside the chronological range of this book. In the fifth to eighth centuries AD, our best information comes from the conflicts between the Britons and the Anglo-Saxons, which are described, from the English point of view, in the *Anglo-Saxon Chronicle*, and from the British side, in the *Gododdin* elegies. These are represented here respectively by a discussion of the Chronicle entries (Chapter 15), and an archaeological appraisal of the 'Men of the North' (Chapter 16). The social structure of the 'Men of the North' had considerable influence on that of the Angles who supplanted them, and some archaeological evidence for this is therefore deployed in a study of the Anglian graves of Bernicia (Chapter 17). Finally, the wider relationships between the Britons and Angles were discussed in my University of Wales O'Donnell lecture (Chapter 18).

Several of the papers that are reprinted here were written, or at least published, after my translation to Glasgow. With the exception of passages in my reappraisal of Cadbury–Camelot (Chapter 13), they none the less derive directly from my fieldwork in Wales and Dumnonia, and are unmodified by my firsthand involvement in northern Britain. I had, however, been aware of the wider unity of western and northern Britain in my period ever since the exciting moment, in 1954, when R. B. K. Stevenson introduced my wife and myself to pottery from Dunadd, Argyll, which exactly paralleled that from Dinas Powys. This awareness of unity was formalized as the concept of an Irish Sea Dark Age culture-province in a paper to the Cambrian Archaeological Association in 1968;[2] but more importantly, it informed my synoptic essay, *Arthur's Britain* (1971; 1973). In Chapter 11 of that work I also returned to the interlinked themes of economy, society and warfare; and it is therefore fitting that this should round off the present work.

---

[1] L. Alcock (1965a).
[2] D. Moore (1970), 55–65.

Part One:
Dinas Powys—the Site

CHAPTER 1

Location, Stratification and Basic Interpretation

Prime place in this collection of studies must go to Dinas Powys itself, because it was the richness of the economic and technological information from that site which first led me to attempt a large-scale synthesis of the relevant historical and archaeological evidence for economy and society in early medieval Wales. That synthesis was originally published as Chapter III, Section 3, of *Dinas Powys* (1963): 'Economic, Social and Political Aspects of Dinas Powys in the Early Christian Period'. It is reprinted here as Chapter 2.

Before that chapter can be understood, however, it is necessary to set out briefly the structural and cultural history of the site, and, in rather more detail, some of the basic stratigraphic evidence for the early Christian phase, Dinas Powys 4. The earthworks to which I gave the name of Dinas Powys, by back-formation from the modern village, occupy a whale-back hill of Carboniferous Limestone, towards the eastern end of the Vale of Glamorgan (Fig. 1.1). The main work is centred on National Grid Reference ST 148722, with a minor work about 150m to the south (Fig. 1.2). Excavations by the Department of Archaeology of University College, Cardiff between 1954 and 1958 revealed six cultural phases, which may be summarized:

Phase 1: Iron Age pottery, together with flints and animal bones, occurred at the northern tip of the hill, but no associated structures were recognized.

Phase 2: an uncompleted hill-slope fort at the southern end of the hill.

Phase 3: represented typologically by the occurrence of rare Romano-British material, probably introduced in Phase 4.

Phase 4: datable to the fifth to eighth centuries AD (perhaps 450 × 500–650 × 750) on the evidence of abundant finds of Mediterranean and Gaulish pottery, Teutonic glass and scrap bronze, and metalworking debris. At this time, the northern tip of the hill was enclosed by earthworks, Bank II and Ditch II, within which two sub-rectangular dry-stone houses were built. It was argued that in Phase 4, Dinas Powys was the court (*llys*) and hall (*neuadd*) of a prince or chieftain.

Phase 5: after a lengthy abandonment, the northern end of the hill was defended by a massive ring-work, Bank I and Ditch I, with material of Phase 4 incorporated in the make-up of Bank I. The ring-work was considered to be Norman in inspiration, and late eleventh century in date.

Phase 6: the original ring-work was reinforced by the addition of the sizeable Banks III and IV and their accompanying ditches (Figs. 1.3, 1.4).

It should be emphasized here that no Iron Age structures were recognized at the main Dinas Powys site (though an incomplete hill-slope fort was postulated to the south in Phase 2). In other words, Phase 4 did not represent the re-use of a pre-existing Iron Age fort, but the founding of a defensive enclosure on a virgin site. This historical interpretation was set out clearly in the summary quoted above, and the evidence for it was fully discussed in the body of the report. Despite this, several commentators have treated Phase 4 as the reoccupation of a pre-existing fort, with obvious implications for

Fig. 1.1.
The environs of Dinas Powys (Based on O.S. 6″ sheet Glam. XLVII NW and SW,
with the sanction of the Controller of HMSO: Crown copyright reserved)

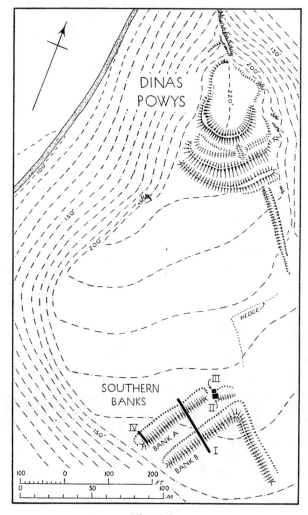

Fig. 1.2.
General plan of Dinas Powys and the Southern Banks, based on a survey by
RCAHM(W)

continuity in site location, and perhaps in social and military organization as well. No
new evidence or arguments have been advanced for this interpretation, which must be
decisively rejected.[1]

Turning now to the stratification of the site, this was only really present in and under
Bank I of Phase 5. In the interior of the site, humus, much disturbed by tree roots and
burrowing animals, lay directly on Carboniferous Limestone with occasional gullies
and pockets of red clay. Beneath Bank I, however, three groups of layers could be
assigned, on stratigraphic grounds, to phases before Phase 5: the O layers, spreads of

[1] L. Alcock (1980a).

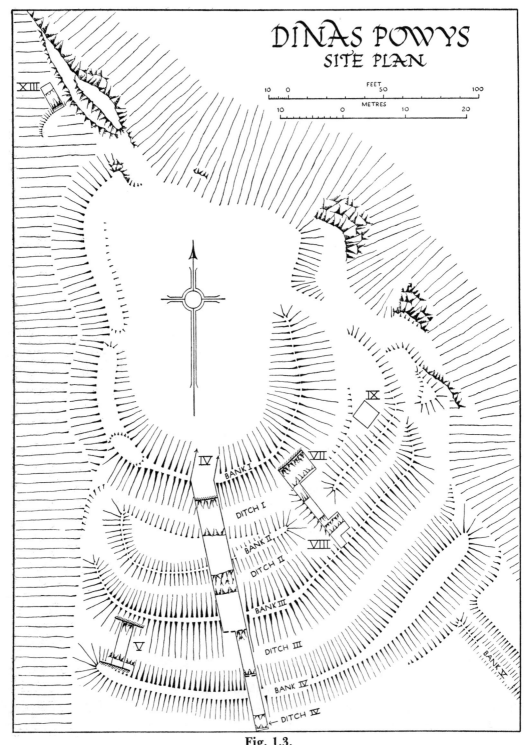

Fig. 1.3.
Site plan of Dinas Powys, based on a survey by RCAHM(W). For the interior, see 1.8

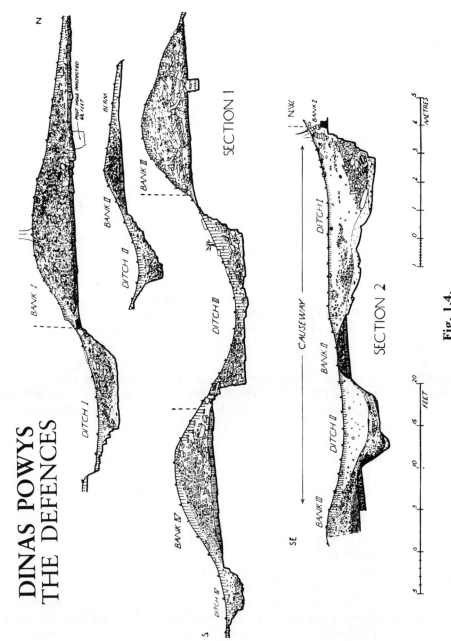

Fig. 1.4.

Section 1 across the ramparts, Section 2 along the causeway

ash and charcoal on the old ground surface, sometimes associated with built hearths; and above them the A layers, powdery soil with much animal bone and some charcoal flecking, representing human occupational activity. Both O and A layers contained pottery, crucibles and other objects of Phase 4. Below these, the N layer was a natural red clay, containing pottery and flints of Phase 1, probably the result of animal (including earthworm) burrowing and human trampling (Figs. 1.5–1.7).

The structure of Bank I was tripartite. At the base, and towards the scarp slope, the B layers consisted of reddish clay or soil with angular limestone rubble or gravel, all giving the appearance of being freshly quarried from Ditch I. The scanty finds were mostly of Phase 4. On the rear of this primary bank lay the C layers: a black, usually greasy, organically rich soil, with small angular rubble. Finds definitely attributable, on typological grounds, to Phase 4, were very copious and were accompanied by abundant animal bones and charcoal. It is suggested that this material had originated in middens of the Phase 4 occupation, which were tidied on to the back of Bank I in Phase 5. Finally, the construction of the bank was completed by placing large, often slabby stones, the D layers, on top of the C layers. In addition to a little Phase 4 rubbish, the D layers also contained a few sherds attributable to the late eleventh or twelfth century. It is these which date the whole structure of Bank I, and permit its interpretation as a Norman period ring-work (Figs. 1.5, 1.6).

Two other comments must be added. The stones of the D layers had a dirty, weathered look, in striking contrast to the reddish, freshly-quarried rubble of the B layers. It seems likely, therefore, that they had not come from Ditch I, but had been already present, as quarried rubble, in the interior of the site. From this it was further argued that they came from the walls of dry-stone buildings of Phase 4, long derelict by the beginning of Phase 5. The plan of these buildings is inferred from the drainage gullies which surrounded them. Secondly, while it is uncertain whether or not Bank I was continued above the steep northern slope of the Dinas Powys hill, excavations down this slope yielded a deep, organically rich soil, akin to the C layers, but with many weathered stones like those of the D layers: these are therefore cited as C/D layers. They were exceptionally rich in animal bones and in objects assignable to Phase 4. It is therefore suggested that the northern slope, which seems not to have been embanked at the time, formed one of the principal refuse tips of that Phase (Fig. 1.7).

This structural and chronological interpretation, fully documented and tautly argued in *Dinas Powys*, was not questioned at the time by reviewers. At a remove of a quarter of a century, however, it is necessary to reconsider one element in it: namely, the attribution of Bank I to Phase 5. When the finds which are assigned on typological grounds to Phase 4 are plotted[2] on the plan of the interior, it is evident that relatively few of them occur underneath Bank I. Those that do are concentrated at the north-east corner of the site, whereas few were recovered from pre-Bank I layers at the southern edge of the interior, in Cuts IV, XV, XVII and XXX (see Fig. 1.8). On the other hand, in this area, some 156 glass fragments came from the C and D layers of the bank. This distribution would be consistent with the hypothesis that, at the time when glass cullet was being used, Bank I bounded the settlement on the south, and the glass was thrown on to the back of an existing rampart. Bank I (and its accompanying ditch) would therefore belong to Phase 4.

[2] This exercise has been carried out on the basis of the stratigraphical information cited in *Dinas Powys* 1963, Part II: The Finds.

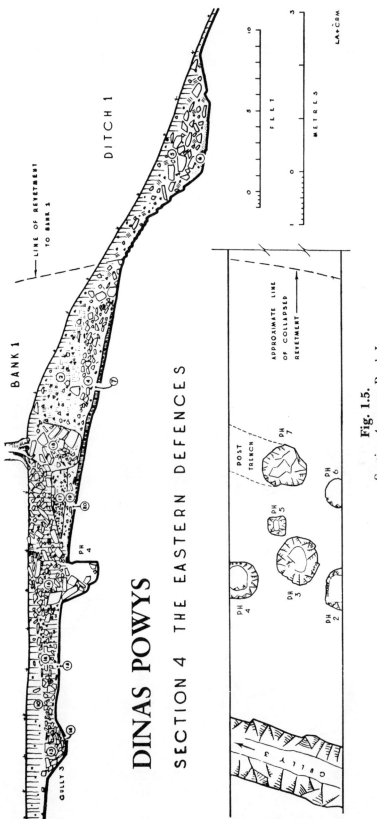

DINAS POWYS

SECTION 4 THE EASTERN DEFENCES

BANK 1

DITCH 1

LINE OF REVETMENT
TO BANK 1

GULLY 3

PH 4

0   5   10
FEET

0   3
METRES

LA·CRM

APPROXIMATE LINE
OF COLLAPSED
REVETMENT

POST
TRENCH

PH 7

PH 5

PH 6

PH 4

PH 3

PH 2

GULLY 3

Fig. 1.5.
Section 4 across Bank I

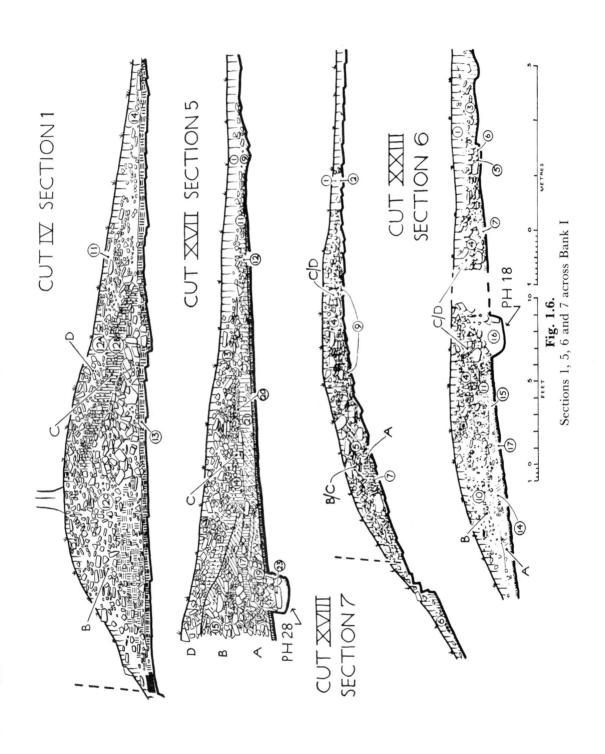

Fig. 1.6.

Sections 1, 5, 6 and 7 across Bank I

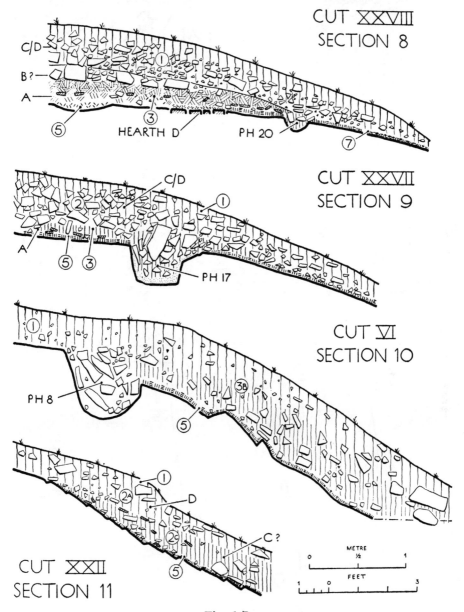

Fig. 1.7.
Sections 8, 9, 10 and 11 above northern slope

It must be noticed, however, that the occurrence of both objects and features—for instance, hearths and ash layers—beneath Bank I at the north-east corner (Cuts XII, XXIII, XXV–XXIX), demonstrates conclusively that all the activities and artefact-classes which characterize Phase 4 were already present before that bank was constructed. To list them: all classes of imported pottery, glass, bone (antler) combs, metal objects and metalworking are present in the O and A layers in that area. So, even if the

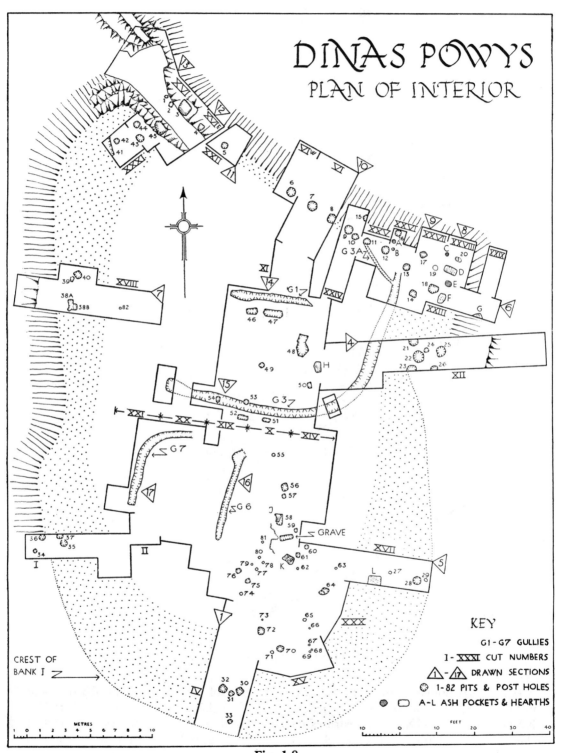

Fig. 1.8.
Plan of area within Bank I

conclusions of the preceding paragraph are accepted, Phase 4 was not initiated by the construction of the massive rampart of Bank I. Moreover, since the importation of pottery of Class E is later than that of Class A, and since Class E is already present in the A layers (for instance, in Cut XII, Section 4, layer (19)), it follows that a threefold chronological division would be necessary, thus:

4A—earliest imports; some metalworking: perhaps Bank II, House IA.
4B—Class E pottery; continued metalworking; perhaps House IB.
4C—construction of Bank I, with material from Ditch I; thereafter, refuse accumulates on the rear of Bank I in the C layers.

Apart from the application of Occam's razor, other criticisms can be levelled at this interpretation. The known disposition of structures, activities and artefacts in the interior makes it plain that these were not evenly or regularly distributed. Consequently, we have no basis for predicting what quantities should have been found underneath various segments of Bank I if it were a construction of Phase 5A rather than 4C, and no means therefore of assessing the significance of the scarcity of finds in Cuts IV, XV, XVII, and XXX. As for the character of the small but massive work defended by Bank I: in the light of further research, this still seems inappropriate for the fifth to eighth centuries AD, and altogether more appropriate to the late eleventh or twelfth centuries. This verdict will be endorsed in the forthcoming Glamorgan Inventory, Volume III,[3] in which Dinas Powys is classed as a castle ring-work. Finally, attention must be drawn to the conviction which grew up during the period of excavation,[4] that Bank I was a unitary work, to be dated, therefore, by the undoubtedly eleventh–twelfth century pottery from the D layer. This conviction could only be undermined by fresh excavations, for instance in the south-west segment of Bank I, between Cuts I and IV.

Turning now to the economic and social inferences which were put forward in 1963: these were largely accepted by reviewers. Hope-Taylor, for instance, fresh from the excavation of the Northumbrian *villa regia* ... *Adgefrin*, considered it to be 'a settlement of moderately high social status', and found it 'difficult to resist the conclusions that it was the *llys* of a local Celtic chief.'[5] Dissent was recorded, however, by Gresham, who could see 'nothing princely ... other than the finds' about this 'squalid and inconvenient eyrie'. He regarded it rather as 'a nest of robbers'; specifically, of Irish pirates who had settled down as immigrants.[6] Gresham's interpretation does not, however, seem to have won acceptance.

An altogether more searching review by Glanville Jones expanded on the interpretation of the site as a royal court.[7] Like Gresham, Jones was impressed by 'the squalor of the site, at variance with the princely quality of the finds, (and) far removed from the splendour of the timbered hall of heroic literature'. He proposed therefore, that Dinas Powys was 'a court occupied only in summer, the season of warfare', and he concluded that this would make it 'easier to understand why, at this inconvenient retreat, rubbish dumps, and industrial hearths should so closely adjoin the hall'. It may be doubted whether Jones was wise to seek his paradigm for a royal court in the heroic literature;

[3] RCAHM(W) forthcoming.
[4] *Dinas Powys* (1963), 9–10; 73–5; 147–8.
[5] B. Hope-Taylor (1965).
[6] C. A. Gresham (1965).
[7] G. R. J. Jones (1967).

and he may well have been over-impressed by the squalor and inconvenience of Dinas Powys. Other issues which he raised are dealt with later: the significance of the animals brought to the site as tribute in Chapter 3, and the much more important problem of administrative continuity in Chapters 4 and 11.

So much for the comments of the mid 1960s. What must now be asked is whether the major hypotheses and interpretations constructed around Phase 4 still stand up in the 1980s. Three major areas of interpretation demand consideration: the parallels that were adduced for Dinas Powys, especially among fortified sites in Wales and the Marches; the emphasis on romanized elements among the early Welsh dynasties; and the correlation of historical accounts based, on the one hand on archaeological evidence and on the other on literary documentation. The first of these forms the subject-matter of Chapters 10 and 11. The other two are considered, along with other lesser revisions, in Chapter 4.

Before the wider aspects of Dinas Powys 4 are discussed, however, this introductory account needs to be rounded off with some general comments on the excavations. These are put forward in the light of modern concepts of excavation tactics, and especially in response to discussions of sampling strategies. For medieval settlements, sampling was considered in broad terms at the Society of Medieval Archaeology's Silver Jubilee conference.[8] Specific examples have been analysed in relation to the Anglo-Saxon settlements at Chalton and at Wraysbury.[9] The recommendations set out here, however, owe more to my own training and experience of excavation than to these and other discussions of sampling.

In the first place, in the case of a defended or enclosed settlement, the defences themselves must be sampled on at least two transverse lines, by the cutting of substantive trenches. At Dinas Powys, these are represented by Cut IV and its extensions, and by Cuts VI and XII.

Secondly, if buildings are expected in the interior, as they normally will be, it is necessary first to recognize or discover them; and then to establish their constructional techniques, development, functions, and mutual relationships. The relationships of buildings and their functions are a major clue to social organization; the function of a building can only be established from its overall plan.[10] On a site where the floors of buildings are well preserved, quite small sampling cuts might reveal their presence. On other sites, where the evidence consists merely of tenuous ghost features, or intermittent lines of stones, only area clearance is likely to reveal the former existence of buildings. If resources are limited, however, a poor alternative to open-area excavation is a wide transect across the enclosed area. At Dinas Powys, Cuts X and XI (linking IV and VI across the interior) exemplify such a transect. In the case of both sampling cuts and transects, it is necessary, once a building has been located, to expand the area of excavation, so as to reveal the complete plan.

Thirdly, the range of varied activities—domestic, economic, industrial—represented within the enclosure needs to be established comprehensively. At Dinas Powys, despite the small extent of the enclosure, structures, artefacts and activities were not evenly or regularly distributed. To cite specific examples: analysis of the animal bones indicates that the head of the northern slope was a focus for the butchery of young animals,

[8] D. A. Hinton (1983), 5–7.
[9] Chalton: T. Champion (1978); Wraysbury: G. Astill and S. Lobb (1982).
[10] These last considerations are conspicuously ignored in G. Astill and S. Lobb (1982).

especially pig (Chapter 3.IV). On the evidence of the distribution of crucibles and glass fragments, jewellery making was concentrated in two limited areas; but since neither of these yielded moulds, there must be another, hitherto undiscovered, focus for jewellery making (Chapter 5). Fused glass, possibly implying the manufacture of bangles and beads, was concentrated in yet another area (Chapter 9).

In brief, the distribution of artefacts across the interior of the enclosure reveals considerable intra-site variability and specialization. In these circumstances, the digging of sampling cuts, located in terms of some approved sampling strategy, might have recovered evidence for all those activities which are known to have occurred in Dinas Powys 4; but inevitably any method would have been a hit-or-miss one.

It must also be recognized that, given the local specialization of activities, we have no basis for predicting what may lie in the unexcavated areas of the interior, and especially in the north-western quarter. To that extent, there are still discoveries to be made at Dinas Powys itself by a new generation of researchers.

CHAPTER 2

A History of Dinas Powys, Phases 3 and 4

This chapter is a reprint of the basic evidence from Dinas Powys in the fifth to eighth centuries AD, together with the historical, economic, and social interpretations which that evidence initially generated. In effect, it comprises those sections of the original Chapter III which are relevant to the chronological range and interpretative themes of the present book: a discussion of the artefacts of Romano-British date (Phase 3) and their implications; a detailed analysis of the structures attributable to the fifth to seventh or eighth centuries (Phase 4); and an extensive account of the economic, social and political aspects of the site in Phase 4. Apart from the excision of some nine lines, I have left the text as it appeared in 1963, and have concentrated such revisions as are now necessary in Chapters 3, 4, 10 and 11. Attention is drawn to these revisions in the footnotes.

PHASE 3—ROMANO-BRITISH; I–IV AD

The presence of Romano-British objects at Dinas Powys might seem to indicate a distinct phase of activity on the site. But before these finds are listed in detail, it would be as well to review in broad terms the problem presented by the occurrence of a scatter of Romano-British material on sites where the main weight of occupation appears attributable, on current systems of dating, to the post-Roman centuries.

In eastern England, for instance, T. C. Lethbridge has commented on the frequency with which Romano-British pottery is found in the huts occupied by the pagan Saxons; and he has not hesitated to claim this as evidence for the continuity of the Romano-British population, and for actual contacts between them and the pagan invaders.[1] At the Saxon village of Sutton Courtenay at least fourteen houses produced small quantities of Romano-British pottery, including six Samian sherds, six pseudo-Samian sherds, and nine bases which appear to have been trimmed for pot-lids. In addition, there are Roman coins, fragments of tiles, bronze brooches, and sherds of glass. It is not seriously suggested that the Saxon settlement of Sutton Courtenay had been preceded by one in Roman times; this material must have been brought in, whether for use or as curios, from some deserted Romano-British site. This is even clearer in the case of the Saxon homestead at Bourton-on-the-Water which yielded, in addition to handmade Saxon vessels, some fourteen Romano-British sherds, including sandy grey wares and pseudo-Samian. Here the Saxon pottery was dated not earlier than AD 600, thus precluding all possibility of continuity of occupation. The excavator suggested, indeed, that the Romano-British pottery, together possibly with a late Roman spoon, were loot from a nearby villa. Finally, the frequency with which Roman coins and bronze brooches are found in pagan graves serves to emphasize that such objects, picked up as curios on

[1] T. C. Lethbridge (1956), 118.

deserted Roman sites, were given a new currency by the invaders without implying any continuity of occupation.

Turning now to the Celtic West, we find for a start that there are sites like Degannwy (Caerns.) where the proportion of Romano-British material to that of post-Roman date is such that it is impossible to deny that an occupation in the fifth century AD had been preceded by one in the fourth and earlier; and where, indeed, the Romano-British material can be tied in on grounds of stratigraphy to definite building activities. By contrast, there are a number of sites where undoubted Roman material is scanty whereas pottery and metalwork assignable on current views to the fifth–seventh centuries are abundant. Such sites are Dunadd with four small fragments of Samian; Mote of Mark with one chip of Samian; Lough Faughan crannog with a Samian rim; Lagore crannog with three fragments of Samian; and other such sites. On none of them is the quantity of Roman material sufficient to mark a contemporary occupation; on none of them is the structural complexity such as to demand a period of activity prior to AD 400. In some cases the excavator has been led to suggest that the Samian sherds came in as strays along with the building material, especially of crannogs; in others, the reasonable suggestion has been made that these odd sherds of Samian had been picked up around the Mediterranean by pilgrims to the holy places and were brought back as curios. Used appropriately, such explanations are doubtless sound, but the evidence from Degannwy warns us that each case must be considered on its merits.

In the case of Dinas Powys, this is best done by listing all the undoubted Romano-British material from the site. Stress should be laid on the qualification 'undoubted', for there are objects, such as some of the composite bone combs, which could be as early as the third century AD, or as late as the tenth or eleventh century. These are here excluded, on the grounds that where the overwhelming mass of datable metalwork and glass belongs to the fifth to seventh centuries, it is most probable that objects which cannot be closely dated should also be assigned to those centuries. But it is freely admitted that this bias towards the post-Roman period prejudices from the outset any discussion of the Roman period at Dinas Powys.

With these comments in mind, the Romano-British material from Dinas Powys may now be listed:

A. *Glass* (p. 142)
Five sherds of glass vessels of various colours, all of I–II AD
One sherd of window-glass: I–II AD
One fragment of a counter: I–IV AD

B. *Pottery*
Eighteen sherds of Samian, from a minimum of six vessels, of which at least three are Drag. 18/31 and one is Drag. 33. All probably Central Gaulish: II AD
Ten sherds of coarse ware from six vessels, all too fragmentary for illustration or close dating: some probably datable late I–II AD, and none of them certainly later than II AD
One lump of Roman (?) brick.

C. *Metal*
Fragment of a La Tène III bronze brooch of Nauheim type: I AD (Fig. 5.1, 13.) Coin:[2]
Antoninianus of SALONINA; reverse, PIETAS AUGG; obverse, SALONINA AUG. AD 256–7.

[2] RIC V, part 1, 111, no. 33. I am grateful to the Ashmolean Museum for cleaning and identifying this coin.

D. *Shale*

Waste core from the lathe-manufacture of a Kimmeridge shale armlet (Fig. 8.4, 1).
With this may be associated a flint lathe-tool typical of those used in armlet manufacture
(Fig. 8.4, 2).

The distribution of these objects by layers is tabulated below:

Layer	Glass	Samian	Coarse ware	Brooch	Coin	Shale
N	—	—	—	—	—	—
O	—	1	—	—	—	—
A	—	1	1	—	—	—
B	—	—	—	—	—	—
C	1	1	1	—	—	—
C/D	3	6	4	1	1	1
D	—	4	2	—	—	—
H	1	—	1	—	—	—
U	2	4	2	—	—	Lathe-tool
G3	—	1	—	—	—	—

This list, extensive and varied as it is, compares well in quantity with the Romano-British material from some native hill-forts inhabited during the Roman occupation, such as Tre'r Ceiri in Caenarvonshire. At first sight, then, it would seem to necessitate the conclusion that Dinas Powys was inhabited during the first to fourth centuries, albeit less intensively than in the fifth to seventh centuries. But several considerations make this view appear unlikely.

Firstly, whereas much of the material assignable to Phases 1 and 4 occurs in distinct stratified layers, there is no one level which can be assigned to Phase 3 on grounds of stratigraphy, or which contains predominantly Romano-British material. Indeed, all the stratified finds assigned to Phase 3 were found in layers of Phases 4 and 5, mixed up with objects characteristic of Phase 4. Had the date of the Roman material not been known on typological grounds, quite independent of the stratification, it would all have been placed in Phase 4. Just as there are no levels distinctive of Phase 3, so too there are no structures which can be assigned to it; for by the time the defences and most of the traces of residential structures have been assigned to Phases 4, 5, and 6, there is little enough evidence for structural activity in Phase 1, and certainly none left over to place in Phase 3. This phase takes the form of a disembodied find list; and we must hesitate before we postulate a period of contemporary occupation to account for these finds.

A further examination of the find-list itself can only serve to increase our hesitation. Particularly striking is the preponderance of fragments of luxury articles—Samian bowls and glassware—over everyday items such as coarse ware cooking-pots. These are not the proportions which we should expect from a habitation site. As for the Kimmeridge shale core, it is difficult to imagine any purpose, whether of utility or luxury, which could have brought it to the site. Moreover, though the quantity of Romano-British material may seem adequate evidence for an actual occupation when compared with that from remote sites like Tre'r Ceiri, such comparisons are surely invalid in the highly romanized Vale of Glamorgan. Recent research has greatly multiplied the number of rural settlements in south-east Glamorgan;[3] and it is no exaggeration to say that some of these sites produce as many Romano-British objects from mole-hills as Dinas Powys has yielded in five years of excavation. Seen in its local context, the Phase 3 material can scarcely amount to a Romano-British occupation of the site.

Finally, the chronological isolation of Phase 3 must be emphasized. The bulk of the datable material, and especially the glass and Samian, is firmly placed in the first two centuries AD. This might suggest that it represents the continuance of the Iron Age occupation of Phase 1 into the Roman period; and the 'Nauheim' brooch, a native rather than Roman type, might support this hypothesis. But it is difficult to believe that the Iron Age pottery of Phase 1 could have lasted so late that its makers were the immediate ancestors of Phase 3. Moreover, the absence of Romano-British material from the N layers in which the Iron Age pot was stratified shows that there can have been no overlaps or even contact between Phases 1 and 3. At the other end of the Roman period, the scarcity if not complete absence of third to fourth-century coarse pottery and of late Roman metalwork combine to demonstrate that Phase 3 cannot be considered as a small-scale occupation of the site which was to develop, under the changed political and social conditions of the fifth century, into the intensive activity of Phase 4. In short, the early Christian occupation of Dinas Powys was not anticipated by a late Roman settlement.

Nonetheless, the presence of Samian and coarse ware sherds in the O and A layers of Phase 4 shows that Roman material must have been brought to the site in that phase. We have here, indeed, another instance of the collection of curios from deserted Roman sites in fifth and later centuries; sentimental mementoes, perhaps, of the happier days of Roman rule. This, at least, would account for the observed stratification as well as for the preponderance of luxury items.[4] Nothing demonstrates the nature of these curios better than the shale core and its accompanying flint lathe-tool. They have further interesting implications for contacts between Glamorgan and southern England, since they must come ultimately from a restricted area of Dorset. Waste cores are not known from Roman sites in south Wales, so there is no reason to believe that they were imported before AD 400. If, however, they were brought to Dinas Powys in the fifth to sixth centuries, it must be asked whether they came in the possession of a refugee from the Anglo-Saxon invasions.[5]

PHASE 4 A—EARLY CHRISTIAN 1; V AD

The earliest features which may undoubtedly be assigned to the early Christian period are the O layers on the north-east corner of the site, and especially hearths D, F, and G, and the

---

[3] RCAHM(W) (1976).

[4] Mr P. A. Rahtz has suggested to me another explanation based on his discoveries and observations in Somerset. In essence, he believes that as fine table- and glass-wares became scarcer, so the surviving pieces were used less and were hoarded more. When in the fifth century AD pottery and glass of any kind became absolutely scarce, the long-treasured heirlooms came into use again. Hence the appearance of early Romano-British luxury wares on Dark Age sites. This idea has much to commend it.

[5] A powerful contrast with Dinas Powys is now provided by the occurrence of Romano-British material at Cadbury–Congresbury: I. Burrow (1981a).

ashy pockets C and E and possibly A and B (Plan, Fig. 1.8; Sections, Fig. 1.7). The finest and best-preserved of the hearths is D at the extreme north-east corner of the site. It measured 3 feet 6 inches from east to west and up to 1 foot $7\frac{1}{2}$ inches from north to south. At either end was an orthostat up to 5 inches thick, set 4 inches deep into the natural clay and rock. Several thin stones had been laid on the natural surface to make a level surface. Partly on these and partly on the natural surface were laid the slabs of stone which formed the bed for the hearth. These had been so shattered by heat that it is impossible to say how many slabs had originally comprised the hearth. It is probable that there were at least three. The stones were overlaid by much black ash, and there were ash pockets and working hollows in the vicinity. None of the other hearths had been so carefully constructed. In general they took the form of one or more slabs laid on the natural surface or bedded on an accumulation of ash and refuse.

The position of hearths D and F, hard down on the limestone or with only 2 or 3 inches of natural red clay beneath them, gives a fixed point for the ground surface of the time and shows the thinness of the clay covering the bed-rock at this corner of the site. Around the hearths, and more especially to the south of them in Cut XII (Fig. 1.5), the surface of the clay was heavily flecked with charcoal. Here and there it bore patches of white ash up to 2 inches deep (Section 4, Layer 7). From among the ash came fragments of lidded crucibles of a distinctive early Christian type (Fig. 6.6), known also from Garryduff, Lagore, Iona, and Dunadd. These are important for two reasons: they show that the hearths were industrial rather than domestic; and they provide a date, admittedly rather imprecise, for Phase 4 A.

Only one other structural feature can be assigned to this phase on grounds of stratification, namely post-hole 28 under Bank I in Cut XVII (Fig. 1.6). The packing-stones of this hole were thrown down and its upper part was filled in during the deposition of the A layers (Section 5, Layers 19 and 17). In other cuts there are runs of post-holes parallel to the perimeter of the site. The stratification of these holes is ambiguous, for some, like post-hole 28, appear to have been filled in when the rampart was built, whereas in other cases the packing-stones project into the rampart material, suggesting that they are contemporary with Bank I. The most coherent explanation for these runs of post-holes is to take them as contemporary with the third phase of the building of Bank I—Phase 5 c. In some cases, however, the post-holes assignable to 5 c appear to duplicate other holes; for instance Nos. 35 and 37, 38 A and 38 B, 39 and 40, form pairs along the western side of the site. The possibility that one of each pair supported a fence in Phase 4 will be examined below.

There is also one defensive feature which may reasonably be assigned to Phase 4: Bank II and Ditch II. As Section 1 (Fig. 1.4) shows, these differ significantly from the defences of Phases 5 and 6, i.e. Banks I, III, and IV, and Ditches I and III. Whereas the banks of Phases 5–6 have well-built stone revetments, Bank II is an unrevetted dump. Ditch II is narrow and more or less V-shaped, but Ditches I and III are wide and flat-bottomed. In terms of stratification, Bank II is overlaid by the Causeway (Section 2), while the line of Ditch II is partly transgressed by Bank III; Bank II and Ditch II must therefore be earlier than Phase 6. They could, indeed, be considered as an outwork to Bank I and dated to Phase 5, but as the plan (Fig. 1.3) clearly shows, they do not run parallel to Bank I but diverge markedly from it on both east and west. This suggests that they are in no sense complementary to Bank I which was in fact erected without reference to them. For reasons already discussed, they are unlikely to belong to Phase 3.

Bank II overlies a number of Iron Age sherds, and apparently it did not form a boundary to the Phase 1 settlement since Iron Age pottery is also found beyond Ditch II. A Phase 1 date is thus most improbable, and Phase 4 remains the most likely period for the digging of Ditch II and the erection of Bank II. This attribution is supported by the discovery of a red ware sherd assignable to the fifth to sixth centuries under Bank II; but since the sherd was very small and came from an area much disturbed by burrows not much weight should be given to it.

If Bank II and Ditch II be accepted as belonging to Phase 4, then the defences of that phase may be described as follows. Bank II is about 10 feet wide and is preserved today to a height of little more than 2 feet. Originally, it probably stood about 5 feet high. It is a simple dump of clay and rubble, with no traces of revetment. Immediately in front of it, without any intervening berm, is a rock-cut ditch 11 feet wide by 4 feet deep. This, allowing for the nature of the rock, is V-shaped, with a very steep counterscarp. The section under the causeway (Section 2) appears to be a local anomaly, due to a gully or pipe of marl in the Carboniferous Limestone.

These defences marked the south-east and part of the north-east boundaries of a roughly trapezoid enclosure (Fig. 2.5), with its sides 190 feet long on the west, 100 feet on the north, 100 feet on the north-east, and 150 feet on the south-east. At the south-western corner the bank is heavily mutilated, but it clearly swings inward at a distance of some 10 feet from the head of the western slope. It is uncertain how far north this western arm of Bank II ran. It could have been truncated by the cutting of Ditch I, but this is unlikely because no signs of an earlier clay and rubble bank appeared under the Phase 5 bank in Cuts I and XVIII (Fig. 1.6). It seems most likely that Bank II stopped originally where it appears to end today. In that case, it is just possible that the entrance to the Phase 4 enclosure was here, between the inturned rampart and the western cliff. This is unlikely, however, because the surface indications are that Ditch II ran right through to the head of the slope.

On the west the enclosure may have been protected by a timber fence contained in holes 37, 38 B, and 40 (Fig. 1.8). We have already seen that these form pairs with holes 35, 38 A, and 39. One of each pair can reasonably be assigned to the timberwork which rose through Bank I in Phase 5; but the second can scarcely represent the replacement of a rotted timber later in that phase, because it would be very difficult to dig a new post-hole through the body of the bank. A clue to the chronology is provided by the relative depths of the holes. Nos. 35, 38 A, and 39 are only 9 to 10 inches deep and seem to require the body of the bank to be piled up round the posts as additional support. Nos. 37, 38 B, and 40, by contrast, are 1 foot 8 inches or more deep, and clearly could have supported free-standing posts. It is therefore reasonable to date them as earlier than the Phase 5 bank, and to interpret them as holding a fence or palisade at the head of the western slope in Phase 4.

At its south-eastern corner, Bank II turns sharply to run parallel to the eastern cliff for some 50 feet. At the corner, Ditch II is largely overlaid by Bank III, and it is not clear from the surface indications whether it runs out to the cliff or follows Bank II in a north-easterly direction. It seems certain that Bank II did not continue as far as the north-east corner of the site; but there is no sure evidence that its line was continued, as on the west, by a timber fence.

There may well have been an entrance into the enclosure round the north-eastern termination of Bank II. In this connection it may be significant that a sloping gangway has been quarried out of the hillside just below this hypothecated entrance. Since Bank I and Ditch I appear to run uninterruptedly along the north-eastern side of the site (Fig. 1.5), no access would have been possible on this side once they had been constructed in Phase 5. The entrance of Phase 5 was almost certainly at the north-western corner of the site. This quarried gangway can only have been of use in Phase 4, and it clearly implies an entrance hereabouts.

The slightness of these defences may seem out of keeping with the evidence to be adduced for the richness and importance of Dinas Powys in the early Christian period, but it is not inconsistent with other evidence from Welsh sites defended in the late fourth and succeeding centuries. At Dinas Emrys, for instance, a position of great natural strength was chosen, but the defensive wall was only some 8 to 10 feet wide. At Carreg-y-llam the enclosure walls had similar dimensions. On the other hand, the massive width of Bank I at Dinas Powys puts it quite outside the range of early Christian defences known in Wales (below, p. 60).[6]

Within the defences there may have stood a rectangular timber hall, House I A (Fig. 2.1). The suggested lines for the north and south walls are marked by holes 46, 47, 48, and 51–52, respectively. Hole 49, equidistant from both lines, might mark the central ridge of a house with its long axis running east–west, and extending to the west beyond the limits of the excavated area. It is difficult to go beyond these suggestions in attempting to reconstruct House I A. There can be no doubt that hole 49 was a post-hole; it was almost circular, 1 foot 4 inches diameter by 10 inches deep. Holes 46–48 and 51–52, by contrast, were rectangular or irregular pockets, roughly finished, and some 9 to 12 inches deep. In this form it is difficult to see how they could have supported posts, nor do they appear to be correctly spaced for any form of post-built house. When found, they were packed with stones, bones, and other rubbish, a filling very comparable to that in Gullies 1 and 3 (pp. 28–30). They were probably, therefore, standing empty, save for a little silting, when the gullies were filled in; and they were packed with stones and refuse in order to level off the site prior to building House I B. It seems most reasonable to suggest that holes 46–48 and 51–52 mark the first steps towards erecting a timber house, which was never completed.[7] Instead House I B was built in stone on the same axis but extending farther to the east and lying slightly farther north.

Other holes in the interior of the site may also belong to Phase 4 A, but no coherent pattern emerges from them. Hearths J and K could also belong here, but there is no positive evidence to support this attribution.

A reasonable case can, however, be made for attributing the grave and burial of a child to Phase 4 A, on the grounds that fragments of crucible in the grave-filling date the burial to Phase 4 at the earliest, whereas the un-Christian orientation of the body points to a date not later than the fifth century AD. The grave itself was 3 feet 6 inches long by 1 foot 2 inches or more wide, and was dug down into the rock for only some 6 to 9 inches. In it was laid the body of a child about five years old. The body was laid on its back, with the head to the east, and the face turned to the south, that is looking over the left shoulder. The legs were extended and may have been crossed, but they were missing below the knees. The arms had been laid down the sides, with the hands placed across the pelvis. The stones derived from digging the grave into the rock were placed over the

---

[6] The full argument for assigning Bank I to Phase 5 rather than Phase 4 will be found in *Dinas Powys* (1963), 73–5.

[7] The only associated find was an Iron Age sherd from hole 46.

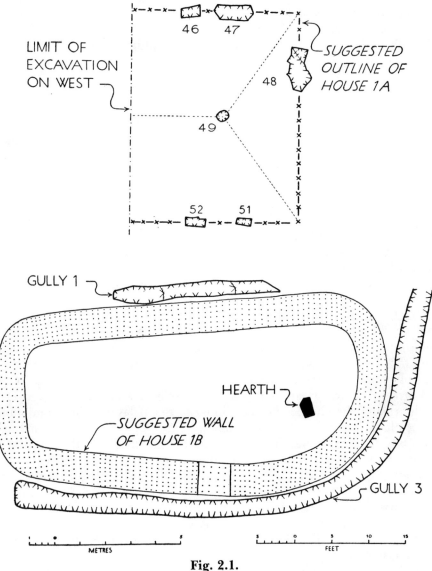

Fig. 2.1.
Reconstructed plans of Houses I A and I B

body, which was presumably covered by a low mound of earth. The skeleton was only about 1 foot below the modern surface, and can never have been much deeper.

Slight though the grave itself was, the body had obviously been laid out with care. It recalls the burials sometimes found within, or immediately adjacent to, Romano-British settlements,[8] and clearly looks back to native, pre-Christian traditions. It is tempting to

---

[8] e.g. Rotherley, Woodcuts. At Rotherley the extended burials seem to date to the third century and at Woodcuts to the fourth: C. F. C. Hawkes (1947).

wonder whether this child had been deliberately buried between hearths J and K if, indeed, these are also to be dated to Phase 4 A.[9]

The material remains of this phase cannot be distinguished from those of the succeeding Phase 4 B, and a general account of the culture of Dinas Powys in the early Christian period may best be deferred until the structures of the later phase have been described.

PHASE 4 B—EARLY CHRISTIAN 2; V–VII AD

The A layers were first recognized in Cut XII, where their content of early Christian pottery and metalwork, as well as bones, ash, and charcoal, suggested that they marked the refuse of a pre-bank occupation (Fig. 1.5, Section 4, Layer 4). It seemed likely that they had been heaped up to form the basal layers of the bank, thus sealing the industrial hearths of Phase 4 A (O layers; Hearths D and F). In that case, the material the A layers contained would have been contemporary with Phase 4 A, but piled up at the beginning of Phase 5 A when Bank I was begun. But A layers were not found to be present as the first stage of bank-building in all sections; and a further examination of them in Cut XVII (Fig. 1.6) and on the north-east corner made it doubtful whether they had anything to do with the construction of Bank I.

North of Cut XII the A layers thin out to such an extent that they look like refuse spread in the course of occupation rather than the first heaping-up of material for a bank (Fig. 1.6, Section 6; Fig. 1.7, Sections 8 and 9). Moreover they have rough stone settings, including possibly a hearth (hearth G) on top of them, again suggesting a phase of occupation rather than of bank-building. To the south, on the other hand, the A layers thicken up to a depth of about 1 foot 9 inches in Cut XVII, where they have the form of a complex of lenticular patches (Fig. 1.6, Section 5). If, as seems likely, Layer 21 in Cut XVIII is broadly contemporary with Layers 17 and 19, then here the A layers spread into the interior of the site beyond the limits of the B layers which undoubtedly do represent a phase in the building of Bank I. Hearth L, a rough stone setting with a spread of white ash, lies on the surface of Layer 21. Finally Layer 19 seals post-hole 28, so that if the latter does belong to Phase 4 A then Layer 19 must be assigned to Phase 4 B. The same applies to the A layers at the north-eastern corner, since they overlie the hearths (D and F) of Phase 4 A.

The principal mark of Phase 4 B in the stratification at Dinas Powys was, indeed, the accumulation of rich middens along the eastern side of the site. At the same time hearths G and L suggest that industrial activities were still being carried on in much the same area as in Phase 4 A.

It is probably to Phase 4 B that we should also assign the two stone buildings in the central area, Houses I B and II. No trace of the actual structure of these buildings was recovered, but their existence may be inferred from the patterns formed by Gullies 1 and 3, 6 and 7 (Plans, Figs. 2.1 and 1.8). These gullies are all dug down irregularly into the bed-rock to a width of 2 feet 9 inches and a maximum depth of 12 inches (Fig. 2.2, Sections 14–17). They form two pairs demarcating areas respectively some 27 feet and 22 feet wide. The area marked off for House I B is about 50 feet long, and has its long axis running east-west; that for house II is some 25 feet or more long, with its axis approximately at right-angles to House I. During the excavation of the gullies, it was thought at

[9] Anatomical details of the skeleton will be found in *Dinas Powys* (1963), 200–8.

first that they had served to hold either sleeper-beams or wall-posts, and that they marked the actual line of house-walls, but when their extent had been completely traced the plan showed that this explanation would not serve. At the same time, the irregular nature of the gully bottoms showed that they could not have been intended as open drains to take the flow of water. The nature of the fill suggested that their true purpose was as soak-drains to catch eaves-drip. In places the lowest fill was a reddish silt, scarcely more than might have been washed in by one heavy rainstorm. Above this, the gullies had been deliberately filled with stones and rubbish including animal bones and pottery. The stones were often large and were carefully packed lengthwise along the gully, so that a level ground surface was preserved. It might be thought that on a limestone site the provision of soakaways for the eaves-drip was unnecessary, but our experience during the excavations was that the natural clay of the site was relatively impermeable, and the enclosure itself became unpleasantly slushy after rain.

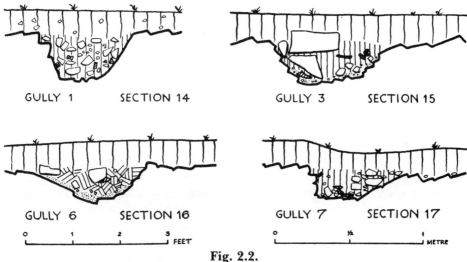

GULLY 1   SECTION 14   GULLY 3   SECTION 15

GULLY 6   SECTION 16   GULLY 7   SECTION 17

Fig. 2.2.
Sections across gullies 1, 3, 6 and 7

Gullies 1 and 3, 6 and 7 give us, then, the lines of the eaves of two buildings but tell us nothing of the actual nature of their construction. There are no post-holes to reveal the plans of timber buildings, and no stone-work remaining to suggest stone dwellings. It might therefore be suggested that the buildings were of timber, but frame-built rather than post-built. That is to say, instead of the uprights being set in post-holes, they could have been tenoned into massive sleeper-beams which would themselves be laid directly on the ground. Such an explanation would certainly fit the observed facts, for the sleepers, like the superstructure, would decay without trace. During the later Middle Ages, timber-framed buildings of this kind were doubtless pre-fabricated in carpenters' yards and erected where needed.[10] Rectangular timber-framed houses were certainly built up on sleeper-beams in Roman times,[11] and there are hints that the technique may

---

[10] P. Smith and D. B. Hague (1958).

[11] Well exemplified at Verulamium: S. S. Frere (1961, especially Pl. XX. see also I. A. Richmond (1961).

go back even earlier.[12] But the plan of the gullies at Dinas Powys, and especially the marked curve of Gully 3, suggest that the houses there were not rectangular but round-ended. It seems unlikely that curved sleeper-beams would have been used for the end walls, and it is therefore improbable that the Dinas Powys houses were timber-framed. Some other method of construction must therefore be sought.

A clue may be found in the make-up of Bank I, which can be attributed to Phase 5 and dated to the eleventh to twelfth century AD. The latest material to be added as a capping to the rear of the bank comprised medium to large slabby stones with very little rubbish among them (D layers). The stones are often dark, and have a weathered look, quite different from the reddish, freshly quarried material of the B layers, which was clearly derived from Ditch I. It seems unlikely that the D layers were derived from any contemporary quarrying; and since Ditch I had already been dug and the B and C layers piled up into a substantial bank before they were added, it is most improbable that the material for them came from outside the enclosure. The only alternative is that they derive from the demolition and robbing of stone structures already standing within the enclosure—in fact, from House I B and House II. The urgent need for stone to consolidate the defences led to the complete quarrying away of the walls of the two houses. This accounts for the absolute lack of evidence which is otherwise so puzzling a feature of the site. At the same time, of course, the demolition of these buildings left the interior of the Phase 5 defences free of encumbrances.

The demolition of the houses in Phase 5 c provides a *terminus ante quem* for their building. Since the gullies contain rare potsherds and other refuse characteristic of Phase 4, they cannot go back to the very beginning of that phase. It follows that the two stone houses belong to Phase 4 B, broadly datable to the sixth to seventh centuries AD.

The question now arises, can a reconstruction of these buildings be attempted? The plan of the two pairs of gullies shows that the houses were roughly parallel-sided, with rounded ends, evidently marking a hipped roof, not a gabled structure. The walls would have been dry built, with an inner and outer facing of roughly coursed slabs, and a core of smaller rubble. They would have been very thick, and the outer face at least would have been battered. There is, of course, no evidence for the location of the doors, but one in the south wall of House I B and one in the east wall of House II would not be unlikely. Hearth H, a carefully built structure, nearly on the axial line towards the east end of House I B, may well be contemporary, though there is no stratification to prove this.

The absence of rock-cut post-holes inside the buildings implies that they were not aisled structures like the Romano-British 'basilican' house, the fifth–sixth century palace at Castle Dore or the migration period dwellings at Vallhagar (Sweden); but this is not proven, for posts could perhaps have been dug down into the top soil and bedded on the rock without leaving any trace, or could have rested on stone bases at floor level. If, however, the apparent absence of roof supports is significant, then two alternative methods of roofing might be suggested. The first is with rafters of curved or cruck-like form, with the lower end lodged in the thickness of the wall. This method is known, for instance, from recent houses of primitive construction in Skye.[13] The second method

[12] e.g. in the Iron Age at Glastonbury Lake Village; in the Late Bronze Age at Ballinderry crannog, No. 2. It is inevitable that the evidence should come principally from sites where timber is well preserved, but the implication is that such buildings may have been widespread. For Glastonbury: A. Bulleid and H. St. G. Gray (1911, 1917); for Ballinderry No. 2: H. O'N. Hencken (1942).

[13] J. Walton (1957).

would be to use a king-post truss, with the tie-beams resting on the wall-tops. Beams about 25 feet long would have been needed for House I B, and their provision should have caused no difficulty. The roofing itself may have been of thatch or turf. The existence of eaves-drip soakaways implies that the roof itself did not rest on the wall-top, as that of the Hebridean black house commonly does, but projected beyond it. This consideration alone seems to preclude the possibility of a corbelled stone roof after the fashion of the Gallarus Oratory.

If hearth H is really contemporary with House I B, then it would seem that we have here the residential quarters of the settlement—a building which, considering the general richness of the material culture of Phase 4, should be dignified with the term 'hall'. House II, by contrast, produced no evidence of a contemporary hearth. It was probably there-fore a store-house or barn, though it is not improbable that servants or labourers and their families slept there. The lay-out of the two buildings is such that they frame two sides of a yard or working space, sheltered from the north and west, and open to the sun for much of the day. The concentration in this area of hearths and post-holes which cannot be attributed to any one phase on grounds of stratigraphy may reflect its convenience, in Phase 4 B, for the everyday activities of the homestead. Beyond this area to the east the middens of the period were piled up.

Economic, Social and Political Aspects of Dinas Powys in the Early Christian Period

From the middens of Phase 4 comes the largest assemblage of early Christian material so far recovered in Wales and the Marches. These finds are illustrated, catalogued and discussed in detail in Part Two. Their quantity and variety make it both possible and desirable to present here an extended account of the economic, technological, social and political aspects of Dinas Powys in Phase 4. This account is based primarily on the archaeological evidence, but I have also attempted to use relevant literary material to assist in its interpretation.[14] It will be appreciated that the literary evidence is of varied nature and date, and consequently of very mixed value; much of this excursus is therefore highly speculative. I believe the speculation to be justified, because this is the first time that it has been possible for an archaeologist with a wealth of material at hand to examine this period in Wales and the Marches. The cautious reader will discern how far the strictly archaeological material takes us, and where the realm of inference and specula-tion begins.

I have also attempted to compare Dinas Powys with other excavated sites of the period around the Irish Sea, especially in Wales and the Marches. Unfortunately no satisfactory general account of the Welsh sites is available, so it has been necessary to describe them in some detail. The richness of Dinas Powys makes it, in a sense, a touchstone for other early Christian settlements, and necessitates the rejection of the accepted interpretations of some of them. To this extent, even the archaeological content of this excursus is controver-sial. Nonetheless, I hope that it will be of some use to historians of the period, in showing them what material is available, and in showing them too that what passes for fact in archaeology normally contains a large element of inference.

To judge from the archaeological material which has been recovered, the main basis

---

[14] In documenting the literary evidence, I have not attempted to give exhaustive references, but have often allowed one witness to speak for several. This is particularly true of the Laws of Hywel Dda, where I quote only the most recent and accessible translation, M. Richards (1954), hereafter abbreviated LHD.

Fig. 2.3.
The Irish Sea culture province

of the Dinas Powys economy was stock-raising. The evidence[15] for this was provided by strikingly large quantities of whole and fragmentary animal bones found almost everywhere on the site, but especially common in the C layers of Bank I and in the mixed C and D

[15] For details and discussion, see Chapter 3.

layers of the northern slope. From the point of stratification, these bones belong strictly to Phase 5 when the bank material was piled up. But occupation material, and especially pottery, attributable to that phase is almost absent, whereas the C and D layers are rich in pottery, metalwork and glass appropriate to Phase 4. It is reasonable to attribute the animal bones also to that phase; and this attribution is given weight by the presence of a good quantity of bones in the O and A layers, too. All evidence points to Phase 4 as that in which the rich middens accumulated, however these middens might have been dispersed in later phases. The animals' bones from the middens are clearly from food refuse, for the long-bones and other bones had been split, and many fragmentary bones were burnt to some degree. Unfortunately, it is not possible to use the available statistics to give an account of the actual table meat at Dinas Powys. For reasons of expediency, only a small sample of the bones has yet been studied, and the method of selecting them has resulted in the identifiable bones being 'strikingly of the less edible parts of carcasses' (p. 69).

Nonetheless, crude figures may be presented to show the percentages among the identified bones of the various species represented, as some guide firstly to the order of frequency among the stock that was actually raised, and secondly to the kinds of meat which were chiefly favoured: in deducing the second from the first, it should, of course, be borne in mind that the meat available from one ox would be several times that from a pig or sheep. The percentages, reduced to the nearest integer, are: cattle 20 per cent, sheep 13 per cent, pig 61 per cent, horse (very rare), deer 1 per cent, birds 4 per cent. It would seem from this that pork, whether from wild or semi-domesticated swine, made an equal contribution to the table with beef; that mutton was little eaten; that game, whether wildfowl or venison, made only an insignificant addition; and that the horse was not eaten.

There are at present no comparable statistics from other sites in Wales, but it seems worth setting the Dinas Powys figures against those from some Romano-British farmsteads or hamlets in Wessex, and from three widely different Irish sites all broadly contemporary with our Phase 4. Lest too much weight be attached to the comparison, it should be pointed out that the sites vary markedly among themselves in both geographical location and social standing; and that the methods used to arrive at the figures also differ.[16]

Proportions of domestic animals on selected sites:[17]

	Cattle	Sheep	Pig	Horse	Dog	Wild
Woodyates %	37	33	2	26	2	+
Rotherley %	33	40	3	18	4	1
Woodcuts:	33	29	13	10	6	3
Lagore 1B: Skulls %	70	15	14	+	+	Fox
Lagore 1B: Bones %	85	6	9			
Ballyfounder: Bones %	58	12	27	+		Deer
Ballyfounder:						
Number of animals	15	3	7	1		1
Cahercommaun	97	1	1	+	+	Deer
Dinas Powys %	20	13	61	+		Deer

[16] A wider range of comparisons is now available in A. King (1978).

[17] The sources for these figures are as follows: Woodyates, Rotherley and Woodcuts are Clark's figures for 'occurrences of the various species shown as percentages of the total number of identifiable specimens from each site (J. G. D. Clark (1947), 123). Lagore bones are 'percentages of bones other than skulls by bulk' (H. O'N. Hencken (1950), 224–9). Ballyfounder figures are for percentages of total number of bones and for approximate number of animals represented (D. M. Waterman, (1958), 52–4). The basis for calculating the Cahercommaun figures are not stated H. O'N. Hencken (1938), 75–6).

The first point which emerges is the preponderance of cattle at all sites except for Rotherley (where they still form a third of the animals) and Dinas Powys; and, correspondingly, the uniqueness of Dinas Powys in its number of pig. At Cahercommaun and two of the Wessex sites the numbers of pig are insignificant, and only at Ballyfounder and Lagore do they preponderate over sheep. The numbers of pig at Dinas Powys would imply the existence of widespread forest in the vicinity to provide pannage in autumn and winter. The relative insignificance of sheep might suggest that the range of the Dinas Powys stock-raisers did not extend to the open moors, less than ten miles to the north.

The bones and teeth which have been studied also provide a basis for calculating the ages at which animals were slaughtered. No calves were represented, but 20 per cent of the cattle of which the age could be determined were yearlings, and most of the remainder appear to have been slaughtered before they were three years old. There were a few sucking pigs, doubtless a delicacy; of the pigs that could be aged, 20 per cent were piglets less than a year old, less than 2 per cent were definitely more than two years old, and most of the others had apparently been killed in their second year. Among the ageable sheep, 13 per cent are lambs under a year, and the bulk of the remainder may have been butchered as yearlings. These figures are of great interest. At first sight they bear out the commonly accepted view that before the Agrarian Revolution a shortage of winter feeding made it necessary to slaughter large numbers of animals in the autumn. Admittedly this generalization does not readily apply to swine, which could perhaps be fed more readily in autumn and winter than at other seasons. Further reflection suggests, however, that the figures quoted seem to represent a slaughtering policy so drastic that stock could not be bred. This is particularly true of cattle. The Laws of Hywel Dda,[18] in detailing how the value of a cow grows with its age, would suggest that the first calf should be produced at the end of the third year—by which time a majority of the Dinas Powys animals were dead. If we suppose, as is likely, that the Dinas Powys heifers calved at the beginning of their third year, most of them could still only have produced one calf each. When allowance is made for male calves, barren heifers, and lost calves, it is clear that this is quite insufficient to maintain the stock.

This is also true of the sheep. Few, if any, of the sheep appear to be more than two years old, so the ewes could have produced at most one lamb apiece. (Medieval manuals of husbandry clearly do not expect twinning.) On the Dinas Powys figures only the swine could be expected to maintain themselves. Walter of Henley thought that sows ought to farrow three times a year,[19] and an anonymous thirteenth-century *Hosebonderie*[20] claims that sows ought to farrow twice a year, having each time at the least seven pigs. These medieval manuals do not tell us how early the animals would begin to bear, and, of course, with the boars running with the sows, there would have been no control over this in any case. But it seems reasonable to believe that even if a majority of sows were slaughtered before reaching their third year, the stock of swine could nevertheless have been maintained. There is, however, another reason why the early slaughtering of pigs is remarkable. The farrowing sows could not have put on much bacon; Walter of Henley recommends that sows of inferior breed should be kept from farrowing so that their bacon might be worth as much as that of the males.[21] But even the boars at Dinas Powys are

---

[18] LHD, 87.
[19] Walter of Henley, 28–9: = E. Lamond and W. Cunningham (1890).
[20] Ibid., 74–5.
[21] Ibid., 28–9.

unlikely to have reached maturity if the evidence available from Saxon England is valid also for Wales.[22] In short, it is questionable whether these pigs were really ready for the table; certainly they were unlikely to measure up to the requirements of the Laws of Hywel Dda for the royal food gift (*gwestfa*): 'a bacon three fingers thick in its gammons, in its ribs and in its hams, or a sow of three years fattening'.

This last argument disposes of the possibility that the immaturity of the animals at Dinas Powys is due to them representing table meat paid as *gwestfa* to a lord, and therefore biased in favour of the young and presumably more tender. To what has already been quoted from Hywel's Laws it may be added that the fourth summer *gwestfa* comprised 'a fat wether three years old and a sow of three winters three fingers thick'.[23] Of course these regulations might have been incorporated in the laws at any time from the days of Hywel (*obit c.* 950) to the late twelfth to thirteenth century, the date of the manuscripts which we possess.[24] But the whole system of food-gifts implies so primitive a social organization that it may well represent one of the truly archaic elements in the laws. If this is so, then the emphasis was on maturity rather than on youth for table animals.

We are left, then, with the conclusion that the Dinas Powys figures are unlikely to represent the full age-range of the domestic animals of a viable stock-raising economy, simply because the cows and sheep could not have bred enough to maintain their numbers. Since we may reasonably take it that the bones which have so far been examined represent a fair sample of the total from the site, we must conclude that animals had already been selected by age before ever they reached Dinas Powys; but the reasons for this selection elude us. Considerably more comparative work on the domestic stock of the Celtic West will be needed before we can approach a solution.

So far these domestic animals have been considered purely as a source of table meat; but they had, of course, a wider importance. Fat, mature pigs would have provided lard for cooking, while both cows and ewes would have yielded milk for butter and cheese.[25] The importance of the milk of ewes (and, for that matter, of goats) in the medieval economy needs some emphasis. I have found no direct evidence for this in Wales, but analogies may be cited from Saxon England. There, according to Trow-Smith,[26] 'cows' milk was perhaps a somewhat rare commodity'; and, again, the evidence from certain marsh lands in Kent, 'leaves little doubt that dairying here was founded upon the sheep flock and not upon the herds of cows'. It seems clear (*pace* Trow-Smith) that by the thirteenth century the cow was regarded as the primary source of milk in England, for Walter of Henley[27] uses the cow's yield of cheese and butter as a standard, and then continues 'and twenty ewes ... ought to and can yield cheese and butter like the two aforementioned cows'. But Trow-Smith records that cheese was being made from ewe's milk in Breconshire as recently as 1954.[28] Cattle would be used, of course, as draught animals, for pulling ploughs and wagons. Sheep would yield wool; sheep, goats and cattle

---

[22] R. Trow-Smith (1957), 54.

[23] LHD, 73.

[24] As J. G. Edwards showed long ago (1929), the extant manuscripts are highly stratified documents. This must always be taken into account when attempting to use them as evidence for any particular period. Further discussion may be found, for instance, in *Welsh History Review, Special Number 1963: The Welsh Laws*, and in T. J. Pierce (1972).

[25] For a survey of the possibilities, M. L. Ryder (1983).

[26] R. Trow-Smith (1957), 58; 60–1.

[27] Walter of Henley, 26–7.

[28] R. Trow-Smith (1957), 74.

would produce skins and hides; and all domestic animals would be a source of bone, sinew and gut. Archaeological evidence for some of these by-products will be marshalled below in a discussion of the crafts practised at Dinas Powys (pp. 39–40). Finally, it should not be overlooked that pre-Roman farming practices in Wessex included the manuring of arable fields with dung from stalled animals, and this continued in the Roman period and doubtless later too.[29] This is not to say that cattle were stalled within the enclosure bank at Dinas Powys. The absence of a drain within House II shows that it can hardly have been a beast-house, and there are no other traces of buildings which might be interpreted as byres.

Hunting, fowling and fishing made only a slight addition to the table. The animal bones examined by Dr Cornwall included only 1 per cent of red deer, and even antler was very little used. The presence of wild boar has been suspected because of the size of some utilized tusks. But clearly neither animal was of great importance. This is the more surprising—if we are correct in interpreting Dinas Powys as a princely seat (below, pp. 55–6)—in view of the importance of the hunting of deer in Hywel's Laws,[30] or of the overriding interest which the boar-chase has in *Culhwch and Olwen*.[31] Even the charming lullaby 'Dinogad's Petticoat', incorporated by accident in the Book of Aneirin, glorifies the chase:[32]

> When your father went to the moor
> he'd bring back heads of stag fawn boar
> the speckled grouse's head from the mountain
> fishes' heads from the falls of Oak Fountain;

but Dinogad's father was clearly more successful than the lord of Dinas Powys. The archaeological evidence shows that he had birds 'of song-bird size' in addition to a fair number of domestic fowl. Shellfish[33] were collected from the coast, 2 or 3 miles distant; limpets were the most common, oysters were rare, and whelks were represented only by one or two shells. In any case, the total number of shellfish involved is minute when compared with the animal bones; all the limpets boiled together would scarcely make an appetizer by modern Breton standards. It is more difficult to judge of the importance of line or net fishing, for fish bones are notoriously fragile and unlikely to be preserved: but a dozen or so fish vertebrae were recovered, and show that salmon (*Salmo salar*), or less probably large sea-trout (*Salmo trutta*), was being eaten. In terms of habits, the distinction between these two species is probably of little significance, for both spend much of their lives in the sea but come into rivers and streams to spawn.

Two points of wider significance may be introduced here. Firstly, the evidence of the animal bones and molluscs may be compared with that from the Roman villa at Llantwit Major. The food animals are the same there as at Dinas Powys: ox, pig, sheep, and domestic fowl. Horse is more common; but the red deer is represented only by antlers,

[29] S. Applebaum (1954).

[30] LHD, 37–8 and 60–1.

[31] G. Jones & T. Jones (1949), p. 129 (the tusk of Ysgithyrwyn Chief Boar); 131–5 (the hunting of Twrch Trwyth).

[32] G. Williams (1950), 26–7.

[33] I am grateful to Dr T. E. Thompson of University College, Cardiff, for identifying the marine molluscs; and to Dr P. H. Greenwood of the British Museum (Natural History) for commenting on the fish vertebrae. It should be remembered that this material was collected before the introduction of flotation and wet-sieving techniques.

which may, of course, have been collected without actually hunting the stags. Sea shells were evidently both more numerous and more varied than at Dinas Powys for whelk, mussel, limpet, cockle, and winkle were all present, while oysters were common. Since the Llantwit villa is only slightly nearer to the coast than Dinas Powys, it would seem that we have here a definite change in eating habits. Secondly, the clear evidence for a vigorous stock-raising economy, and for the very slight role played by hunting at Dinas Powys, makes nonsense of Gildas's statement[34] that at some time before 446 *vacuaretur omnis regio* (or *insula*) *totius cibi baculo, excepto venatoriae artis solacio*.

Meat, butter, and cheese, then, were doubtless plentiful enough at Dinas Powys; but it is more difficult to write with assurance about bread, or to establish the place of arable farming in the economy. Since Gerald de Barri reported[35] that the Welsh of his day ate flesh plentifully and bread sparingly the view has been common among historians that bread played little part in the early Welsh diet. Thus Lloyd says[36] 'Let the Cistercian boast, quoth the witty Walter Map, his abstinence from flesh; I pit against him the hardy Welshman, who eats no bread'. Yet even from literary sources it can be shown that this view is, to say the least, unbalanced. Gerald himself, in writing of the hospitality and liberality of the Welsh, specifically mentions[37] thin and broad bread, baked daily, which was sometimes supplemented with pottage. The supposed bakestones from Dinas Powys (p. 137, Fig. 8.3, 13) would serve admirably for the baking of just such thin cakes of bread. Wheat flour obviously for bread, and even actual loaves, figure largely in the food gifts detailed in Hywel's Laws.[38] And when in the Laws we find[39] that the summoner 'receives a loaf with its relish' (*enllyn*: i.e. meat, butter, or cheese) 'in every house ...' we may believe that even for the middle ranks of society bread was the staff of life, supplemented though it undoubtedly was by animal products.

The literary evidence, then, hints that the role of bread was greater than has been allowed: archaeological evidence confirms this view. Fragments of three rotary querns, one of them of an elaborate form (Fig. 8.3, 11) were found at Dinas Powys, showing clearly that corn was being ground. The number may not seem large, especially when compared with the quantity of rubbing-stones (Fig. 8.1) used for leather-dressing, which demonstrates the importance of animal by-products: but it matches well the numbers observed on contemporary sites in the Irish Sea Zone. Incidentally, finds of rotary querns in the settlements of Pant-y-saer and Dinas Emrys, both to be attributed largely to the fifth century AD, reinforce the argument that bread-flour had a significant place in the diet of the early Welsh.[40]

It is one thing to show that grain was being ground at Dinas Powys and quite another to prove that it was being grown in the vicinity. We must therefore ask whether the site affords archaeological evidence of arable farming: and we must at once answer that it does not. Among a sizeable collection of iron objects, there is not one which can be

---

[34] *De Excidio Britonum*, chapter 19. Accessible edition: M. Winterbottom (1978).

[35] *Descriptio Kambriae* I, 8(= J. F. Dimock 1868); hereafter *Descriptio*.

[36] J. E. Lloyd (1911, 1939), 605. It should be noted that Lloyd's words are a colourful paraphrase, not a translation, of Walter Map's actual words.

[37] *Descriptio* I, 10: *pani quoque tenui et lato, quotidiano labore decocto, interdum pulmentaria supponunt*.

[38] LHD, 72–3.

[39] LHD, 43.

[40] Pant-y-saer: C. W. Phillips (1934); Dinas Emrys: H. N. Savory (1960).

connected with the tilling of the soil. At first sight this would appear fatal to any suggestion that Dinas Powys was a centre for arable husbandry. But when we take a wider view, the picture alters. Among contemporary settlements in the Celtic West very few have produced agricultural implements of any sort, and only Lagore and Ballyfounder have yielded plough-shares.[41] This, of course, could be interpreted as showing that arable farming played no significant role in the economy of the Irish Sea Zone as a whole. To check this hypothesis we may turn to certain Teutonic settlements whose inhabitants were undoubtedly tilling the soil. Among the published finds from the pagan Saxon village at Sutton Courtenay there are no agricultural implements, and certainly no plough-shares. The thoroughly excavated migration-period settlement at Vallhagar on Gotland—a village of twenty-four buildings, associated with a system of arable fields and yielding quantities of grain from the houses—produced one plough-share, one sickle, and four scythes, these last admittedly for cutting animal fodder. The excavation of farms of the migration period on Bornholm also uncovered actual grains in the houses, but yielded only sickles and scythes and no plough-shares. To sum up: plough-shares and other implements diagnostic of arable farming are found so rarely on settlements where such farming is known to have been practised that their absence is no proof that it was not. Nor can we adduce as evidence the absence of ancient fields around Dinas Powys, for these could well have been obliterated by more recent cultivation.

In default of any archaeological criteria, it is tempting to examine the literary sources for evidence as to whether arable farming was widely practised in medieval Wales. Gerald has been widely quoted as saying that the greater part of the land was used for pasture and little was tilled;[42] and from this it has been concluded that 'the economic basis of society was ... the pasturing of flocks and herds; agriculture held ... a quite subordinate position'.[43] Less attention has been paid to Gerald's references to the methods of ploughing,[44] or to the spring ploughing for oats.[45] Gerald's evidence may be supplemented from the Laws. In spite of this, until recently the conventional picture of Welsh society and economy in the Dark Ages and early medieval period has been of a society of nomadic freemen, wandering at will with their flocks and herds throughout the tribal territory, only rarely settled on the land, and sustained by an almost wholly pastoral economy. But now the whole concept of a Welsh 'tribal' society is rightly under attack. Certain salient points of great relevance to Dinas Powys must be brought out here.

Firstly, the Roman background in the Vale of Glamorgan, and especially in the area between the Thaw and the Taff, is one of intensive settlement. Recent fieldwork has identified a number of Roman sites, of which several, from their size, appear to have been villas.[46] To these must be added the well-known villa on the flood-plain of the River Ely. Though there is no archaeological proof of this, it is highly probable that these villas were the centres of estates engaged in mixed farming, with corn-growing playing an important role. What is more difficult to know is how far this agricultural system lasted into the fifth century. With the withdrawal of the Roman garrisons from Cardiff and Caerleon, and

---

[41] There is also a share of Roman date, but in a native context, from Dinorben hill-fort: W. Gardner & H. N. Savory (1964), 158–9; W. H. Manning (1964).

[42] *Descriptio* I, 17.

[43] J. E. Lloyd (1911, 1939), 605.

[44] *Descriptio* I, 17.

[45] *Descriptio* I, 8.

[46] RCAHM(W) (1976), Part 2, 110 ff.

with the progressive weakening of the central tax-collecting authority, the demand for corn would have been reduced: so a reduced acreage of arable might reflect no more than a slackening of demand. It is at least clear that no villa in Glamorgan has produced evidence of occupation after 400.[47] This would suggest that there was some change in farming practice, and perhaps also in tenurial arrangements, in the late fourth century. But it would be rash to assume that the unsettlement of Romano-British arrangements progressed so far that nomadic pastoralism became dominant. Indeed, it is perhaps more likely that in the decay of the villa system—considered as both an agricultural and a tenurial organization—lay the first seeds of growth of that system of bond hamlets, devoted to mixed farming with a definite emphasis on arable, which was widely prevalent on the eve of the Anglo-Norman conquest.[48] If, indeed, the *coloni* of the villas became the bondmen of the Welsh laws, then there is no reason to doubt that arable farming continued throughout the fifth and sixth centuries. We may believe, then, that corn-growing played some part in the economy of Dinas Powys in Phase 4.

There is, indeed, a further item of archaeological evidence which demonstrates that vegetable foods of some sort played a part in the diet of the times; namely the imported *mortaria* (p. 120). In a Roman context, it is believed that *mortaria* were used for 'grinding fruit, vegetables, and other foodstuffs, for soups, purées, etc. One complete specimen [from Silchester] still retains a consolidated mass of fruit-stones and pips from the last purée made in it'.[49] Their presence at Dinas Powys demonstrates the continuance, in an upper-class household, of romanized traditions of food-preparation.

Ancillary to farming in the economy of Dinas Powys were a number of domestic crafts or minor industries dependent on animal by-products for their raw materials. Foremost among them was the preparation of leather from hides and skins, and its utilization. The large number of animal bones from the site necessarily implies that hides of cattle and skins of sheep and goats were readily available. The Laws of Hywel show that skins were important perquisites for some of the royal household, and they hint at some of the ways in which skins might have been used.[50] That leather was in fact prepared at Dinas Powys may be inferred from the occurrence there of a number of utilized sandstone pebbles characterized by convex surfaces with a high gloss (Fig. 8.2). These are quite different from whetstones, which characteristically exhibit concave working surfaces, and it is suggested that they were used in some way for preparing leather, either for rubbing the hides to make them supple, or for polishing leather goods.[51] It seems likely that the supply of leather available would have exceeded the needs even of a princely household, and it is therefore probable that some was exported; clearly there must have been exports to pay for the imports of bronze, glass, pottery, and wine. Nonetheless, it may be suggested that some leather was being worked-up at Dinas Powys itself, for this is the implication of the relatively abundant iron awls and the two heavy iron needles with curving points (Fig. 5.4, 38–43). It is more difficult to say what kind of objects were being made of leather. We might expect shoes and hose for all classes; horse-harness, weapon-harness, and sheaths, and shields for the warrior; clothes for craftsmen and the lower classes; vessels and containers; straps and ropes for a variety of purposes; and tents and skin boats. Some of

[47] For the last phase at Llantwit Major, see now A. H. A. Hogg (1974).
[48] G. R. J. Jones (1963).
[49] G. C. Boon (1957), 166.
[50] LHD, 31, 36–7, 39–40, 42.
[51] Note the possibility that they may also have been used for finishing linen cloth.

these uses are to be found in the Laws of Hywel: 'the skin of a hart to make vessels to keep the horns of the king and his cups; halters for the king's horses, leashes for hounds; the king's leathern hose; untanned shoes not higher than the ankles for the summoner'.[52] The soil conditions at Dinas Powys were such that no leather was preserved, so that it is impossible to say which of these very varied objects might have been made there. But it is fair to point out that when leather has been preserved on contemporary crannogs such as Buiston, Lagore, and Ballinderry No. 2, the only identifiable objects have been shoes.

The animals slaughtered at Dinas Powys would also have provided sinew, gut, horn, and bone. Of these, horns are mentioned for both drinking and hunting in literary sources,[53] but they do not survive in the archaeological record; nor do sinews and gut. Bone objects, for use and ornament, are fairly common (pp. 126–8), but considering the great quantity of unutilized bones, it is clear that this was not an important raw material. The most interesting group of bonework comprises the composite double-edged combs (Figs. 7.1, 7.2), which stem from Roman prototypes in wood and bone, and which have widespread analogues in both Celtic and Teutonic circles. Their technical and functional aspects are discussed below (pp. 127–33). Among the other pieces, special attention may be drawn to the simple bone pegs (Fig. 7.1, 6), which appear to imply a game which involved the moving of pieces about a perforated board; and the segments of boar's tusk (Fig. 7.1, 12) which had been nailed as decoration to some large object—the curve of the tusk might best suit the rim of a shield, and the boar would be a fitting symbol of dashing ferocity. It is interesting to see that in spite of the evidence for metalworking there are no bone trial pieces or mould-stamps like the well-known ones from Ireland.[54]

Sheep and goats would also, of course, have provided wool. Evidence from Denmark suggests that sheep were being bred selectively for their wool even in pre-Roman times, while the mention of *birrus Britannicus* (a waterproof cloak) and *tapete Britannicum* (a plaid blanket) in the price-fixing edict of Diocletian suggests the general importance of woollen cloth in Roman Britain.[55] No shears were found at Dinas Powys, though these occur commonly on contemporary sites in Ireland and south-west Scotland. But spinning may be inferred from the presence of spindle whorls of bone (Fig. 7.1, 13–14), pottery, and possibly lead. Since some of the pottery ones are made out of sherds from class B amphorae, they are clearly dated to Phase 4. The only evidence for weaving is provided by a fragment of baked clay which may tentatively be interpreted as part of a clay loom-weight related to the pagan Saxon annular form. Slight though this evidence seems, it gains in importance when it is realized that loom-weights are almost unknown in the Celtic West. It is possible that wool was not the only material to be woven, for the Laws of Hywel mention flax and flax seed among the household property which particularly appertains to the wife.[56] This in turn suggests another possible use for the polishing stones, already discussed in connection with leather-working; for a similar stone from Clea Lakes crannog 'with a very high polish on both the flat sides may well have been used in finishing linen cloth'.

A subsidiary role in the Dinas Powys economy was played by metalworking. Some 50 lb of iron ore, slag, and cinder were collected during the excavations. It is not easy to

[52] LHD, 31, 36, 37, 40, 42.
[53] LHD, 33, 37.
[54] U. O'Meadhra (1979).
[55] A. L. F. Rivet (1958), 123–4; J. P. Wild (1963).
[56] LHD, 70.

find comparable figures for contemporary sites, but about 30 lb of slag was recovered during the excavation of Ballycatteen in which roughly one quarter of the interior of the site was cleared. More than 400 cakes and smaller pieces of slag were found at Lagore; the weights are not given, but it is probable that the total quantity does not differ greatly from that found at Dinas Powys. On the other hand, these figures appear insignificant when compared, say, with a single piece of iron cinder weighing 80 lb which had been built into the foundations of a Roman barn at Great Weldon, Northants;[57] or with a single piece of tapped slag from a medieval hearth in Weardale, which weighed 29 lb.[58] Even allowing for the two possibilities that much of the slag from Dinas Powys was thrown away down the northern slope and that much of the cinder was resmelted, it is clear that iron-smelting was not a major activity on the site. Most of the ore, slag, and cinder came from C and C/D layers; but enough sizeable pieces were stratified in O and A layers to justify the belief that iron-smelting was a feature of Phase 4.

No built furnaces were discovered; but this may partly be explained by the fact that if the bloom, slag, and cinder were completely removed from a simple bowl hearth after its last use it might well appear as no more than a fire-reddened scoop in the ground. At the north-east corner of the site, where much of the slag was found, there are indeed four ashy pockets which might be interpreted in this way—A, B, C, and E (Plan, Fig. 1.8). These are bowl-like depressions, 1 foot to 2 foot 3 inches in diameter, 3 to 5½ inches deep, filled with ashy or charcoaly soil; sometimes the rock or natural clay is fire-reddened. The ashy pockets C and E (Fig. 1.7, Section 8, Layer 5) may be associated with the well-built hearth D. The objection to interpreting them as the remains of bowl furnaces is that no slag was found in or around them. A better case can be made for hole 50, a shelving scoop 1 foot 7 inches long by 1 foot 1 inch wide, and up to 4½ inches deep. In and around this was a considerable quantity of slag, including large thin pieces adhering to highly-fired clay which is probably furnace-lining. None of this furnace-lining was in its original position; but it may well have been thrown back into a disused bowl-furnace which had been pulled to pieces to extract the bloom and cinder. In the absence of stratification in the interior of the site, it is, of course, impossible to say whether hole 50 was in use as a furnace while House I B was standing, in which case, of course, it would have been inside the building identified as a hall. At first sight this may seem unlikely; but that it is not impossible in a Celtic context is shown by the smelting furnace inside the principal house of the Iron Age settlement at Kestor.

In default of surviving furnaces, something can be learned about the technique of iron-smelting at Dinas Powys from a study of the ores, slags, and cinders. The ores used appear to have been principally, if not entirely, haematites which occur as large but irregular replacement deposits in the Carboniferous Limestone, principally between Llanharry and the River Taff: one such deposit has been mined within 2 miles of the site. One ore sample has been identified as limonite (or, more strictly, as goethite),[59] an ore which is found, for instance at Trecastle near Llanharry: and an analysis of ore from Trecastle agrees well with that of a sample from Dinas Powys, in having a low percentage of phosphorus and sulphur. Indeed phosphorus is completely absent from two of the slag and cinder samples that have been analysed. In the opinion of Mr H. H. Stanley[60] of the

---

[57] E. J. Wynne and R. F. Tylecote (1958), 339.

[58] R. F. Tylecote (1959), 32.

[59] Identified by Dr M. H. Battey, King's College, Newcastle upon Tyne.

[60] In a letter of 21 November, 1959. I am very grateful to Mr Stanley for having the slags and ores from Dinas Powys analysed. For detailed reports, see *Dinas Powys* (1963), 216–9.

Steel Company of Wales, some of the ores from which the slags originated must have been very pure and rich.

Something of the size of the furnaces used may be deduced from the examination of the plano-convex or concavo-convex cakes of slag and cinder known as 'furnace-bottoms'. O'Kelly, describing examples found at St Gobnet's House, Ballyvourney, says that 'they apparently form from the hot debris of smelting which falls into and fills the dish-shaped bottom of the furnace after the bloom of smelted iron has been removed. As the fire dies out the cake of material cools and solidifies taking the shape of the inside and bottom of the furnace. They therefore provide an indication of the size of the furnace used'. From the furnace bottoms at Ballyvourney (and from other pieces which he interpreted as furnace-covers), O'Kelly deduced that the diameter of the furnaces there ranged from $3\frac{1}{2}$ to 7 inches with a preference for 5 to 6 inches. Wynne and Tylecote, after referring to O'Kelly's work, considered that even a furnace 7 inches diameter 'would appear to be very much on the small size and it is considered that the assumption made in the estimation of hearth size is incorrect'. Their experiments in primitive smelting techniques used a simulated bowl furnace 9 inches diameter: and they suggested that 'furnace bottoms' did not form in the manner envisaged by O'Kelly.[61] Tylecote, referring to our material,[62] uses the term 'furnace-bottom' to describe 'the masses of material, part cinder and part slag, that are sometimes found in the bottom of bowl hearths after smelting. These are very much smaller than the furnace itself, since they formed underneath the bloom in the active smelting zone of the furnace. This zone usually forms quite a small proportion of the total furnace volume'. In short, the 'furnace-bottoms' provide only a minimum measurement for the size of the furnace. The four measurable examples from Dinas Powys ranged from $4\frac{1}{2}$ to $6\frac{1}{2}$ inches in greatest diameter, agreeing well in this with the examples from Ballyvourney and others from Ballycatteen, Garranes, Lagore and Cahercommaun. Such bottoms might well have come from furnaces 8 or more inches in diameter, like some contemporary bowl-shaped smelting hearths from Saxony which were 8 to 20 inches diameter.[63]

Two other comments may be made on the Dinas Powys material. Firstly, there appears to be no tapped slag, that is slag tapped from the furnace while still molten. This argues for a primitive form of furnace and a primitive technique of smelting. Secondly, some pieces of slag and cinder show casts or impressions of wood, presumably the charcoal used for fuel. These impressions must have formed while the slag was cooling down from its molten state.

Finally, it is of some interest to compare the evidence for iron-smelting at Dinas Powys with that from Glamorgan in the Roman period. It is clear, for a start, that Roman iron-working was on a large scale. 'Roman pottery is said to have been found in old workings at Ty-isaf and at Llechan, near Llanharry'.[64] Near Miskin in 1752 a bed of cinders was dug up and resmelted; it sealed a coin of Antoninus Pius and fragments of what sound like Castor ware beakers with hunting scenes.[65] Slag or more probably cinder

---

[61] E. J. Wynne and R. F. Tylecote (1958).

[62] In a letter of 18 December, 1959. I am grateful to Dr Tylecote for his comments on the slag, etc. from the site.

[63] G. Mildenberger (1959), 62–4, with Fig. 55.

[64] R. E. M. Wheeler (1925), 272.

[65] W. Harris (1773), 13–14. In Wheeler, loc. cit., and subsequent writers, the site of this discovery has been transferred to a hill-fort near Bonvilston through a misreading of Harris.

was used for paving the main streets of the Roman fort at Cardiff, and for paving a yard at the Ely villa. There is little evidence, however, for the technical processes involved. Hearths or furnaces allegedly for iron-smelting were found at both the Ely[66] and the Llantwit villas, but no wholly convincing account of them is available. That from Ely was stone-built and 9 inches internal diameter; that from Llantwit, which was inserted into the stoke-hole of the bath suite after AD 300, was 2 feet 6 inches diameter with a deeper cup only 9 inches diameter. In general, the evidence from other sites reveals that much larger furnaces were used in the Roman period; Wynne and Tylecote illustrate[67] one from Great Casterton well over 3 feet diameter. The use of local ores is reported from both Llantwit and Ely; but at Ely there was also a quantity of manganese ore, which was thought to have been imported from Spain. It has been suggested that this would have been combined with local ores to produce a steely iron of increased hardness.[68] Ely, Caerwent,[69] and more doubtfully Llantwit, have all produced evidence for the use of coal in addition to charcoal for iron-smelting. From all this, it seems clear that there was a marked regression in the scale and technique of ironworking in the post-Roman period.

Since iron was undoubtedly being smelted at Dinas Powys, it is reasonable to believe that it was also worked up into tools, implements, and weapons. There is no direct archaeological evidence for a blacksmith's forge, but it is probable that the establishment did include a resident smith. The social implications of this are examined below (p. 50). The surviving iron objects (pp. 104 f. with Figs. 5.3 and 5.4) give us some idea of his products; but it must always be remembered that serviceable implements would be removed when the site was abandoned, while broken pieces could be reforged, perhaps as something else. This may largely account for the absence of agricultural implements. The most important group of iron objects is the knives. These are of the kind found with both men and women in Teutonic graves, and it may be taken that they were normally carried by both sexes for a variety of culinary and domestic uses. At Dinas Powys it is perhaps worth noticing that the smaller ones would be particularly suitable for skinning knives. Second in importance to the knives are the awls which were doubtless used in leather-working. Drill-bits and a file for the carpenter, a farmer's bill-hook, fittings for buckets and harness: these are the kind of small items which the Dinas Powys smith was producing.

Another craft well represented in the debris of Phase 4 is that of the jeweller. The most conclusive evidence for this is provided by crucible fragments stratified in O layers towards the north-east corner of the site (e.g. Fig. 1.5, Section 4, Layer 7) where they are locally associated with quantities of fine wood ash. It is tempting to suggest that hearths D and F, both of them built on the natural ground surface, are the source of much of this ash. Hearth G, which was laid on an accumulation of ash and refuse, must be rather later, but all three hearths are contemporary with the crucibles. Whenever their form can be determined, the crucibles are all of a distinctive lidded type (Figs. 6.6, 6.7) which has also been found, though more rarely than at Dinas Powys, on other sites around the Irish Sea. It will be argued that crucibles of this type developed in Britain in the fourth to fifth centuries AD, and were then diffused to Scotland and Ireland by peripatetic craftsmen. Their invention and diffusion are symptomatic of the technological experiments of the time, which are witnessed in the archaeological record by a great variety of crucible forms. Most of the

[66] J. Storrie (1894).
[67] E. J. Wynne and R. F. Tylecote (1958), Fig. 1.
[68] *Cardiff Naturalists' Society Transactions* (1921–2), 38–9.
[69] J. Storrie (1894).

Dinas Powys crucibles had been used for melting copper or bronze, doubtless for casting brooches and other jewellery. One at least had traces of gold, but there is no evidence that any of them had served for melting enamel.

It is not easy to say just what trinkets were being produced at Dinas Powys, since much of the ornamental bronze-work found there was in the form of scrap-metal derived from a Teutonic source. Among the scrap only one piece (Fig. 5.1, 12), a silvered bronze strip with a repoussé scroll pattern, appears to be a Celtic product. But it is likely that a number of complete objects—a simple pin, a ring, and a gilt bronze stud (Fig. 5.1, 4, 3, 11)—do represent the work of the Dinas Powys craftsmen. There is also a hint that more elaborate jewellery was being made. From an A layer (Fig. 1.5, Section 4, Layer 4), immediately overlying an O layer rich in ash and crucible fragments, comes a lead object (Fig. 5.5, 2) decorated in a manner which recalls the Irish series of zoomorphic penannular brooches with champlevé enamel or millefiori ornament on their terminals. Because the Dinas Powys piece is of lead, it cannot possibly be part of an actual brooch, and it is most reasonable to interpret it either as a trial-casting or as a die for stamping the fine clay moulds in which zoomorphic penannular brooches were cast. The use of such a lead die for brooch-making can apparently be paralleled in the Roman period at Lydney; and in the Dark Ages by the bone models of pins from Dunadd, the bone stamps with linear and animal interlace from Lagore or the lead disc from Birsay. If our lead object is a die, or even if it is only a trial casting, then it implies at once that elaborately ornamented brooches were part of the repertory of the Dinas Powys jeweller.

It has wider implications, too. Firstly, although the known examples of this particular form of zoomorphic penannular brooch are exclusively Irish, we must now believe that they were also being made and worn in parts of Wales. Secondly, we have here an important pointer to the place of origin of that series of hanging bowls which has escutcheons richly ornamented in Ultimate La Tène or derived styles. Although only one escutcheon comparable to those found in fifth to seventh-century Saxon graves has yet been discovered in Ireland,[70] site evidence has seemed to favour that country as the place where the bowls were manufactured, for it was only at Garranes and Lagore that the technical resources need for champlevé enamel and millefiori work were known to be present.[71] Since our lead object bears a design which was intended to be reserved against a ground of red enamel, it is now clear that craftsmen in Britain were also capable of producing champlevé enamel as, of course, they had been in the pre-Roman Iron Age. The evidence of the lead die is reinforced by the discovery at Dinas Powys of a stick of millefiori glass (Fig. 9.2, 12) and of other glass fragments apparently intended for use in millefiori or enamel work. In short, it is now seen that Britain possessed the means of manufacturing the hanging bowl escutcheons; their known distribution may now be allowed due weight in suggesting that the main centres of manufacture lay east and not west of the Irish Sea.

From all this it becomes apparent that, despite the lack of distinctively Celtic ornaments or trinkets on the site, the Dinas Powys craftsman was fully competent to produce the range of jewellery decorated in Ultimate la Tène style that was current in the Irish Sea Zone in the fifth to seventh centuries AD. This makes it necessary to scrutinize the place of

---

[70] That from the River Bann: F. Henry (1956), 80. The other items in Mlle. Henry's list are either not from hanging bowls at all or do not belong to the period under discussion.

[71] This is the powerful argument advanced in F. Henry (1956), 76–9. More recently, the discovery of a mould far casting a hanging bowl escutcheon at Craig Phadraig, near Inverness, has demonstrated the manufacture of hanging bowls in Pictland: R. B. K. Stevenson (1976), 249.

the apparently Teutonic metalwork on the site. There can, of course, be no doubt about the Teutonic character of a gilt-bronze chip-carved disk, a bronze strap-end, or various bronze bucket fittings (Fig. 5.1, 1, 5, 9; Fig. 5.2, 14, 19, and 21). But the majority of the Teutonic pieces appear on the site as scrap; the embossed bronze strip (No. 21), which has been torn from a bucket and then folded up ready to go into the crucible, is particularly revealing here. It seems best, indeed, to regard these pieces merely as scrap brought to Dinas Powys to be melted down for their gold, silver, and bronze, which would then be recast as brooches and other trinkets in Celtic style. We shall see that the Teutonic glass from the site must be thought of in the same way as raw material for the jeweller. The cultural implications of this will be discussed below.

The presence of a jeweller seems to imply a relatively sophisticated technology, and it therefore comes as a surprise that flint-knapping was still practised in Phase 4 (p. 140). This is demonstrated principally by the numbers of worked flints present in C and D layers, and even in O, A, and B layers; for the number is too large to allow us to regard all these flints as rubbish survivals from Phase 1. Some, of course, must be that, but it is impossible to sort out the Iron Age flints from the later ones either on stratigraphical or typological grounds. It seems likely, however, that the principal implement used in the fifth and sixth centuries was a steep-nosed round-ended scraper which carried on Iron Age traditions. It is even possible that barbed and tanged arrowheads, typologically of a Bronze Age form, were still being used for hunting or fowling. It should be added that the evidence for post-Roman flint-knapping at Dinas Powys can be paralleled from contemporary sites in both Celtic and Teutonic circles. Other stones were also utilized, notably blocks of Old Red Sandstone for querns, carefully selected sandstone pebbles for whetstones and rubbing-stones, and lias pebbles for slingstones (pp. 134 ff.). These, of course, could be obtained locally, but it is interesting to see that jet or lignite was also being imported either as raw material or else in the form of ready-made ornaments.

One craft which might have been represented in the archaeological record was not, in fact, carried out at Dinas Powys: that of the potter. The reasons for this need to be considered against a wide background, bearing in mind the immaturity of both knowledge and hypothesis in this field. Throughout the Iron Age, both the coastlands and the inland Marches of Wales had been subjected to invasions by immigrants accustomed to the manufacture and use of pottery. As the evidence is read at present, however, the descendants of these immigrants abandoned these traits more or less rapidly, so that no abiding ceramic traditions were established. Under the Roman occupation, pottery in the form of both table ware and kitchen utensils must have been available, and site evidence shows that it was used in moderate quantities. The custom of using pottery vessels survived at least into the fifth century, but supply had by then become a major problem, for under the Romans manufacturing centres had only been established on the periphery of Wales, and there was no native tradition of pot-making as a village craft to survive the breakdown of the romanized pottery industry. It appears[72] that demand was then met in one of two ways, giving rise to two quite distinct groups of pottery on post-Roman sites (Fig. 2.4). Pottery of Group I is very crude, and is clearly the product of incompetent native potters: Group II, by contrast, comprises mass-produced wares of good quality imported from the Mediterranean or from continental Europe. The two groups are not

---

[72] The remainder of this, and the following paragraph, have been allowed to stand for their historical interest. For current views, see pp. 156 f.

known to occur on the same sites, but it is not clear whether this implies chronological or merely social differences between the sites where they are found. For our present purpose, a more significant difference lies in their overall distribution. Whereas the imported wares of

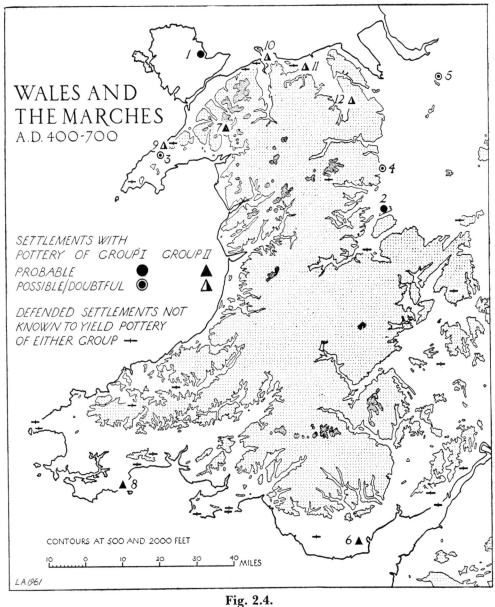

Fig. 2.4.
Settlements in Wales and the Marches, AD 400–700, as perceived in 1961;
1 Pant-y-saer; 2 The Breiddin; 3 Garn Boduan; 4 Old Oswestry; 5 Eddisbury; 6 Dinas
Powys; 7 Dinas Emrys; 8 Longbury Bank Cave; 9 Carreg-y-llam; 10 Degannwy;
11 Dinorben; 12 Moel Fenlli

Group II are found in both north and south Wales, especially in coastal districts, the native pottery of Group I has been found only in north Wales and the northern Marches. If we accept the crudeness of Votadinian pottery as providing a valid basis for comparison with that of Group I, then we might attribute its appearance to the settlement of the Votadinian leader Cunedda and his sons. This would explain why such pottery occurs only in the north.

Returning to Dinas Powys, we see that the absence of a native pottery industry in Phase 4 is merely one feature of a wider pattern. So, too, is the presence of the imported pottery of Group II. Its great importance is that it demonstrates the maintenance of romanized domestic habits and of explicitly Roman connections into the fifth century. There need be no doubt that all the pottery of Group II was imported. Of the classes into which it has been divided, Class D (pp. 120–1, Fig. 6.4) (fine grey dishes and bowls including *mortaria*) and Class E (pp. 121–2, Fig. 6.5) (hard, gritty kitchen wares) came from unknown centres of manufacture, but their forms and ornaments both reveal underlying romanized traditions. Class A (pp. 116–17, Figs. 6.1, 6.2) (red table wares) and Class B (pp. 117–19, Fig. 6.3) (amphorae) were not merely Roman in tradition; they came from Mediterranean sources.

The implications of these trade connections will be discussed below; here it is worth considering the uses to which this imported pottery was put at Dinas Powys itself. Amphorae of Class B, of course, appeared as containers, more significant for what they held than for what they were. In default of sediments or residues which might be analysed, their contents are really unknown; but it is very reasonably believed that they brought wines and oil from the Mediterranean. This in itself indicates the continuance of romanized tastes in drinking and romanized fashions in cooking. We have already seen that the Class D *mortaria* similarly imply that fruits and vegetables were being prepared in the Roman manner. The bowls and dishes of Class D and Class A would have been used as fine table ware, probably for the service of delicacies; some of the bowls could have been used for mixing wine. It is worth noticing that the grey D ware bowls with their blue-black wash are probably intended to imitate pewter, while the Class A bowls with their stamped ornament continue the long tradition of Roman sigillate pottery which itself owes something to gold vessels with repoussé ornament. Finally, Class E provided an eminently efficient kitchen ware which included small mixing-bowls, beakers, cooking-pots, and pitchers.

At first sight, it would seem that the Dinas Powys household was well provided. But it should be remembered that the total number of vessels present in Phase 4 was probably quite small. Minimum figures can be calculated from the sherds recovered by excavation. They are: Class A, nine vessels; Class B, ten vessels; Class D, nine vessels; Class E, nine vessels. These figures represent the minimum number of pots present in the excavated area. Allowing for the unexcavated pot-bearing levels, they could be multiplied by five, with the caution that in practice any expansion of the excavated area might yield more sherds of known pots rather than many new vessels. In any case it is clear that the number of table vessels is not large, nor does it cover all the requirements of a household. Bowls and platters, large and small, would have been needed for serving and eating meat, for instance; they could have been of wood or metal. Actual horns of cattle, or cups of wood, leather, or metal, would have been needed for drinking. In the kitchen, too, the Class E vessels must have been supplemented with iron cauldrons and pans, wooden dishes, and leather containers for liquids. The cooking pots would have served for porridge or stews of small game, but much meat was probable roasted on spits or baked in a clay wrapping. Bread and cakes, mixed in wooden bowls, would have been baked on the sandstone griddles, of which fragments have been found (Fig. 8.3, 13). This review shows that the imported pottery did not meet all the needs of the household, and that other materials could have been substituted for it without any practical disadvantage: it was in fact a luxury. This in itself only serves to emphasize the taste and wealth of the family which imported it.

Another luxury item which at first sight appears to have been imported for use at the table comprises the glass vessels (pp. 142 f., Fig. 9.1). More than two hundred and fifty sherds of glass were found, some of them very minute. They would seem to come from a minimum of thirty-three vessels, but the actual number involved may be considerably greater. The form and ornament of the determinate sherds show that they originate from a Teutonic source and may be dated in the fifth to sixth centuries. The cultural and chronological implications of this will be considered later. Here we must ask whether the glass found at Dinas Powys had ever been in use in the hall there for drinking wine, mead, or beer. The poem known as the *Gododdin* of Aneirin certainly suggests that among the northern Britons in the late sixth century feasting heroes might drink wine out of glass cups.[73] But it would be hazardous to use this poem as a sober statement about material culture and social customs. The warriors of the *Gododdin* wore gold collars or torques; yet these had disappeared from the archaeological record by the second century AD, and it is extremely doubtful whether British warriors were wearing such ornaments in the sixth century. In other words, the gold collar was merely a traditional poetic attribute of the hero, derived from the actual practices of the pre-Roman Celts. Any or all of the purported statements about material culture or equipment which are to be found in the early poetry may be subject to the same criticism.

In the present instance there are good reasons for believing that the sherds of glass from Dinas Powys do not represent glass vessels actually used for drinking on that site. Firstly Dr Harden, in commenting on the disproportionate number of sherds decorated with opaque white trails, suggests that 'it may be that these fragments were specially chosen for bringing to the west' (below, p. 143). Secondly, there is a striking disparity between the number of vessels represented by rim sherds, and those of which basal sherds were found. Given the thick bases of stemmed, claw, and cone beakers, one might have expected that when vessels were broken in drinking bouts their bases would be preserved very frequently, whereas rims would often be shattered to irrecoverable splinters; but in the Dinas Powys material there are rim sherds from some twenty-five vessels against only one true base and fragments from near the base of two other vessels.

It is therefore very difficult to suppose that these represent breakages on the site; and it seems reasonable to suggest, on the contrary, that the sherds came to Dinas Powys as so much broken glass to be melted down for making glass ornaments and inlays. If this is so, then it brings the Teutonic glass into line with the Teutonic metalwork, which was likewise imported as scrap metal for the jeweller. There is, indeed, other evidence that glass was being worked for decorative purposes on the site: the presence of fragments of emerald green (p. 145) and pale green (pp. 145–6) which appear to have been chipped off blocks of raw glass; the blue and chequer rods intended for millefiori work (p. 149, Fig. 9.2, 10–12); the fragment of yellow inlay; and the seventeen sherds of fused glass of which Dr Harden says that 'their very quantity suggests glass-working of some sort'. It should be remembered here that it is very much easier to reheat existing blocks of glass to make

[73] K. H. Jackson (1969).

beads, bangles, inlays, and enamels than it is to manufacture glass from its constituent minerals. It seems clear that the former process was within the technological competence of craftsmen in the Irish Sea Zone, whereas the latter was not. This, of course, would explain the fragments of Teutonic or even oriental glass which have been found on many western sites of this date.[74] In conclusion, it would seem that we must deny the Dinas Powys household the luxury of drinking wine out of glass vessels, at the same time adding glass-working on some scale to the repertory of their resident jeweller.

The importation of pottery, of wine and oil, of glass and of metal, in whatever quantity and for whatever purpose, implies that Dinas Powys was the centre of widespread trading connections. Imports were presumably paid for by the export of natural products and raw materials; principally livestock, hides, and other animal by-products, and also perhaps iron. These must have been exchanged on a barter basis, for the economy was clearly a natural, not a money, one. It can scarcely be maintained that the coin of Salonina (p. 21), minted in 256–7 and found in a worn, but not badly worn, condition, was still in circulation in the fifth and sixth centuries; and there are no other coins from the site. Here again Dinas Powys is typical of its date and region. How long coinage continued in use in England in the fifth century, and how soon the Anglo-Saxon rulers started to mint their own coins, are matters of numismatic dispute.[75] In Wales, however, the position is clear. Now that the Byzantine coins from Caerwent have been seen in proper perspective,[76] we can say that the earliest post-Roman coins known from Wales are a group from the Minchin Hole cave, Gower, deposited in the mid- or late-ninth century.[77] Next in point of time is hoard No. 1 from Bangor, deposited *c.* 930;[78] but it is only with the pennies of Eadgar (*d.* 975) that hoards and stray finds became more common around the Welsh coast.[79] Before the Anglo-Norman conquest, the only Welsh ruler known to have used coins was Hywel Dda; and even his coinage is represented by a single penny minted at Chester.[80] All this would suggest that currency played no part in Welsh economy in the early Dark Ages, but that its importance was increasing throughout the tenth century and later.

The coin evidence may be reinforced by that from literary sources. In *Culhwch and Olwen*, cattle provide the normal standard of value. Among the marginalia of the St Chad Gospel is a record of a lawsuit which had been settled on payment of a horse, three cows, and three cows newly calved.[81] In the Laws of Hywel, on the other hand, while there are still reminiscences of a system of values based on cattle, the majority of payments are reckoned in money. The process can perhaps be seen at work in the charters which formed the basis of the *Book of Llandaff,* for Morris has suggested[82] that 'seventh-century prices are

[74] Preliminary list in D. B. Harden (1956b), 149–51. To this may now be added Castle Hill, Dalry (J. Smith (1919), 127–8); Dinas Emrys (H. N. Savory (1960), 63–5); Castle Rock Dumbarton (L. Alcock (1976), 108–9), and unpublished sherds from Dundurn and Dunollie.

[75] In 1963 this seemed a reasonable comment; but see now the decisive statement of J. P. C. Kent (1979), 22, that 'there is no evidence that coinage was struck in Britain by any sub-Roman government'.

[76] G. C. Boon (1958).

[77] H. N. Savory (1956), 41–2.

[78] A. Fox (1946), 118.

[79] Hoards are listed in R. H. M. Dolley and D. M. Metcalf (1961), 162–5.

[80] G. C. Brooke (1932), 57 and 60, with Pl. XV, 1.

[81] J. G. Evans and J. Rhys (1893), xliii.

[82] J. Morris (1963), 231. But see now W. Davies (1978a), 60–1 for the limited use of both currency and precious metals in early Wales.

expressed as single objects—a chased sword-hilt, a "best horse", etc., in the eighth century they are calculated according to a uniform standard of value, the cow, but from the ninth century onward in gold and silver'.

This survey of the economic and industrial life of Dinas Powys prompts the question whether the site was primarily an industrial centre, occupied principally by craftsmen, and with little or no truly domestic activity. That craftsmen were working there is shown conclusively by the relics of iron, bronze, and glass-working. It is a reasonable inference that leather-workers were also present. The absence of domestic occupation is suggested by the paucity of relics connected with such feminine activities as spinning, weaving, and corn-grinding. It may be recalled that on similar grounds Ó Ríordáin suggested that while the triple-ring-fort of Garranes served as a place of refuge and a meeting place on social occasions 'in general, the site was occupied by a group of craftsmen' (pp. 141–2). But when Garranes and Dinas Powys are compared with other contemporary settlements in the Irish Sea Zone, it becomes apparent that querns and spindle-whorls are by no means common, and loom-weights are absolutely rare on these sites; yet it would not be reasonable to interpret them all as temporary refuges or industrial centres. Many, if not all, of them must have been occupied by ordinary households. At Dinas Powys itself the evidence for substantial buildings, and the presence of pottery and split or charred animal bones which were clearly kitchen refuse, all argue that the site was inhabited by a household carrying out a range of domestic activities. The imports show it to have been a wealthy household; and in this lies the explanation of the industrial activities. For within the social framework of the time only the household of a prince or magnate would have patronized its own jeweller and blacksmith. Conversely, these craftsmen would certainly have sought the patronage of such a person. In short, the evidence of domestic and industrial activities at Dinas Powys can best be reconciled if we interpret it as the *llys* or court of a local ruler, with its *neuadd* or hall (House I) surrounded by subsidiary buildings of stone and timber and forming the centre of a variety of agricultural, industrial, and domestic pursuits.

The cultural connections implied by the finds must now be examined. They lie in three directions: Roman, Teutonic, and Irish. The Roman connections themselves may be divided into those which are the result of tradition and those which are the outcome of trade. It is clear for a start that some attempt was being made to maintain a romanized way of life within a very changed architectural framework. Drinking imported wines, cooking in oil, having food prepared in *mortaria*, the lord of Dinas Powys was maintaining the traditions of the villa owners who had doubtless been his ancestors. In small things, too, some of his material equipment, like the querns and the composite bone combs, was based on Roman prototypes. It is this, of course, which makes the absence of mortared stone buildings, of locally-made pottery, and of a money economy so striking.

At the same time, the Roman trade connections, demonstrated by the importation of wine, oil, and pottery, show the lengths to which a wealthy household might go to maintain a tradition of good living. Significant also is the change in orientation of the trade connections. The road system of Roman Britain was focused on London and the short sea-route to Gaul: but in the fifth century the sea-link was severed by Saxon pirates in the narrow seas, by the barbarian invasions of Gaul, and finally by the English settlement itself. Thereupon a reorientation of trade took place in western Britain. The Irish Sea Zone is the natural terminus of direct sea-routes from Atlantic Europe and the Mediterranean. This had governed its cultural connections throughout prehistory—and it did so again in the fifth to seventh centuries AD. The best known evidence for this, of course, is the evangelization of western Britain and Ireland by missionaries from Gaul bringing a Mediterranean and specifically Roman religion. But the missionary field of the Celtic saints was at the same time a market for imports of wine and oil, and of Mediterranean and Gaulish pottery. This, then, was Roman trade with a difference.

More surprising than the evidence for Roman traditions at Dinas Powys are the relics which demonstrate Teutonic contacts. Some of the similarities with Teutonic material are admittedly very generalized, and relate to objects which were common to both the northern and western barbarians. This is the case, for instance, with the iron knives and the composite bone combs which are found in both Celtic and Teutonic circles. Here the principal value of the Teutonic parallels is that they come principally from burials where the grave goods were normally disposed about the dead person in the way that they would have been used or worn in life. These analogues, therefore, provide indications about the use of the objects concerned. But apart altogether from these generalized parallels, there are two important groups of finds at Dinas Powys which must have been manufactured in and imported from Teutonic centres. These are the glass vessels and many, perhaps a majority, of the bronzes. They immediately pose the question: do they prove a Teutonic settlement of Dinas Powys—and by extension of the Glamorgan coastal plain—by migrants hailing either from across the Bristol Channel or from Merovingian Gaul? The answer to this question must be found partly in historical sources, partly in the archaeological material itself.

It is well known that the anglicization of Morgannwg took place at a relatively early date, but it is generally considered that this was the work of English peasants following in the wake of the Norman conquerors. Immediately before the Norman conquest the Monmouthshire sea-plain had been penetrated by Swein and Harold Godwinson.[83] Somewhat earlier, there appears to have been some Scandinavian settlement in and around Cardiff.[84] All this, of course, is far removed in time from our Phase 4; but at least it indicates that the area came to lie open to various Teutonic influences. It is doubtful, however, whether this was so as early as Phase 4. It is generally accepted that there was no Saxon settlement as far west as the Bristol Channel until the battle of Dyrham and the capture of Gloucester, Cirencester, and Bath in 577.[85] If Phase 4 is correctly dated to the period of the fifth to early seventh century (below), then it is unlikely (though admittedly not impossible) that Saxon settlers could have crossed the Bristol Channel as early as that. It is equally unlikely that the glass could have been obtained either by trading or by raiding across the Channel.

In short, there is no historical evidence for a Teutonic settlement of our area, whether by a tribe or by a dynasty, at this date. This is in accordance with the archaeological evidence. We have already seen that both the bronzes and the glass came to Dinas Powys not as complete objects and vessels but as scrap, and as such they imply nothing more than trade. At present, unfortunately, it is not possible to locate the sources from which they came. When the other evidence for the trading connections of Wales at this time is taken into account, Gaul would seem as likely as England.

It is, however, the similarities with Ireland which are most evident in the finds from Dinas Powys. Some of these are due to the sharing of trade routes from western Europe

[83] ASC s.a. 1046, 1063, 1065.
[84] B. G. Charles (1934), 151–6.
[85] F. M. Stenton (1943), 29.

and the Mediterranean by both shores of the Irish Sea: this accounts for the presence of imported pottery of Classes A, B, and E in both Britain and Ireland. Others, like the continued use of flint implements, are part of a common barbarian heritage. Yet others are more specific. For instance, several of the iron objects and many of the bone pieces from Dinas Powys have good analogues on Irish sites: this is particularly true of the bone combs. Lidded crucibles of the type which is predominant at Dinas Powys are found widely in Ireland and in Scottish Dalriada. Finally, the lead die (Fig. 5.5, 2) for making zoomorphic penannular brooches is decorated in a style which hitherto has been found on penannular brooches only in Ireland.

Archaeological parallels as precise as these suggest very strongly that we have here evidence for an actual folk-movement from Ireland; that, in fact, the Irish pirates and slave-raiders of the third and fourth centuries had by the fifth become immigrants. This hypothesis must be examined with the aid of other evidence, both archaeological and historical. It cannot be doubted that the coastlands of east Glamorgan and Monmouth-shire needed protection against sea-borne attacks in the late-third and fourth century; this is shown by the building of a fort of 'Saxon Shore' type at Cardiff,[86] and less certainly by the addition of bastions to the walls of Caerwent and by the blocking of the north and south gates of that town.[87] But it may be suggested that the protection afforded, especially by the Cardiff fort, was more effective than previous commentators have allowed; or, at least, that certain other archaeological discoveries which had been interpreted as a reflection of Irish raiding will not bear that interpretation. In the first place, the banks and ditches with which the Ely villa was enclosed about 300 are no longer seen as implying the fortification of the house against Irish pirates; clearly a ditch 13 feet wide but only 2 feet deep is no military obstacle. Secondly, Nash-Williams's re-excavation of the Llantwit villa showed that the skeletons which had originally been interpreted as the result of a massacre at the hands of Irish raiders or migrants were 'in fact formal interments, possibly Christian, made on this part of the site, over a fairly prolonged period, after the final decay of the villa range'.[88] At present, there is no archaeological evidence of a successful Irish penetration of east Glamorgan in the fourth century.

Nor, it should be added, is there evidence for any substantial settlement in the fifth and sixth centuries. In the whole of Glamorgan, only two monuments with Ogam inscriptions are known, from Kenfig and Loughor; and there are none from Monmouthshire.[89] I have heard it argued that in these two counties agricultural development has led to a greater destruction of early inscribed stones than in south-west Wales, where Ogams are still common; but this is difficult to believe. In any case, the evidence of the Ogam inscriptions is powerfully reinforced by the distribution of place-names containing the element *cnwc*, 'hillock', which is considered to be borrowed into Welsh from the Irish *cnoc*. Such names are indeed not unknown in east Glamorgan and Monmouthshire; but their overwhelming concentration is in those parts of Pembrokeshire, Cardiganshire, and Carmarthenshire where the Ogam inscribed stones are also most common.[90] In broad terms, this was the kingdom of Dyfed, where the settlement of the Irish Dési is attested by historical evidence.

It is worth pausing to consider the date and nature of the settlement of the Dési, to point

[86] RCAHM(W) (1976), Part 2, 90–4.
[87] J. Wacher (1974), 388–9; D. R. Wilson (1972), 302.
[88] RCAHM(W) (1976), Part 2, 111–14 (Llantwit Major); 115–19, (Ely).
[89] V. E. Nash-Williams (1950), Nos. 198, 228.
[90] M. Richards (1960); A. C. Thomas (1972); M. Dillon (1977).

the contrast between the situation in Dyfed and that in south-east Wales.[91] A brief statement about the migration of the Dési to Demed (i.e. Dyfed) under Eochaid mac Art-chorp, together with a genealogy of the dynasty over fourteen generations to Teuder ap Regin, is given in an Irish tale, *The Expulsion of the Dessi*. The same tale includes an account of the slaying of Conn mac Cormaic and the partial blinding of Cormaic king of Tara by Eochaid's brother, Oengus mac Artchorp. This incident, allowing for some differences among the names, is referred to in *The Annals of the Four Masters*, sub anno AD 265. Meyer therefore suggested 270 as the date of Eochaid's migration to Dyfed, and in this he has been generally followed. 'Taking a generation as thirty-three years and starting with the year AD 270, a simple calculation brings us to AD 730 as the time when Teuder mac Regin must have reigned', and this date for Teuder is 'fully confirmed' by that of his son Meredydd who died in 796. Leaving aside the difficulty that thirty-three years would be an unusually long 'generation' for Dark Age rulers, there is another reason for doubting Meyer's date for the migration. A similar 'simple calculation' to that which he performed gives us a floruit *c.* 435 for Guortepir mac Aircol, who is fifth in descent from Eochaid. But this Guortepir is probably the Vortipor, tyrant of the Demetae, whom Gildas attacked in the sixth century. If we regard Vortipor as flourishing about 530, and work back from him using thirty-year 'generations' we arrive at *c.* 380 as the earliest possible date for the migration of the Dési to Dyfed.

That such a date might still be within the period of effective Roman control in south Wales is suggested by the coin series at the Cardiff fort, which runs down to Gratian (367–83).[92] This, in turn, would suggest that the settlement of the Dési may have been carried out not despite the Romans, but at their instance. The evidence of Vortipor's monument[93] at Castelldwyran confirms that this was so, for on it he is named as '*Protector*', that is as a member of the Imperial bodyguard. That this honorific title was hereditary in the family is suggested by one of the Welsh genealogies of the dynasty, for the genealogy in Harleian MS. 3859,[94] fictitious though it is before Vortipor's grandfather, yet remembered Protec and Protector as earlier members of the family. It is reasonable to conclude, then, that Eochaid and his followers were deliberately settled in Dyfed as *foederati*[95] and that Eochaid himself was the first to be styled *Protector*. Possible reasons for the need to plant *foederati* among the Demetae are not hard to seek. The scarcity of hill-forts in their territory suggests that they had never been a warlike people; they were therefore left largely ungarrisoned by the Romans; and this, combined with the geographical situation of their territory, left them peculiarly exposed to raiding and piracy. All this combines to suggest that the intensive Irish settlement of Dyfed was a special case, and that we should not expect to find similar settlements elsewhere in south Wales.

Seen against this background, the Irish connections exhibited by the material from Dinas Powys are best interpreted as the result not of folk-movement but of the movement of individual men of skill. That peripatetic craftsmen were a feature of the Dark

[91] I have left these two paragraphs as they were written in 1963; but see now M. Miller (1980a). For the Dessi, K. Meyer (1900).

[92] RCAHM(W) 1976, Part 2, 93 n. 8. For even later coins from Caerleon and Caerwent, J. L. Davies (1983), 90.

[93] V. E. Nash-Williams (1950), No. 138.

[94] Accessible in A. W. Wade-Evans (1938), 102–3.

[95] For a more cautious view, L. Alcock (1971; 1973), 123–4. I would certainly wish to withdraw the term *foederati* as based on no evidence.

Ages is well seen in *Culhwch and Olwen*, when Cei poses as a furbisher of swords to gain entry to the fort of Wrnach the Giant. The same source reveals the high status enjoyed by such men, for Glewlwyd, the porter of Arthur's court, in refusing to open the gate to Culhwch, declares that 'Save the son of a king of a rightful dominion, or a craftsman who brings his craft, none may enter'.[96] We have already seen that the lord of Dinas Powys was patron to jewellers, blacksmiths, and other skilled workers. We may now conclude that these were men who journeyed in search of patrons, whether permanent or temporary; and who doubtless travelled as widely as the contemporary Celtic saints.[97] Movement was easy across the Irish Sea; and it is indeed these journeys by craftsmen and missionaries which endow the concept of an Irish Sea Zone with a status comparable to that of the Lowland and Highland zones of Britain.

Here it must be emphasized that the movement of objects and ideas could proceed in either direction. Some of the connections between Dinas Powys and Ireland appear to be due to diffusion from Britain to Ireland rather than the other way round. Three classes of objects may be taken to illustrate this thesis. Firstly, the incidence of lidded crucibles, so far as it is known at present, suggests very strongly that the type was developed in Britain, perhaps in a late Roman milieu, and was then carried to Ireland and south-west Scotland. Secondly, if it is true that, so far as the British Isles are concerned, the composite bone comb originated as an imitation of imported Roman combs of box-wood, then it must have been developed first in Roman Britain and then carried to Ireland. Thirdly, the most reasonable explanation of the origin of the Irish zoomorphic penannular brooches with ornate terminals, enamelled or inlaid with millefiori (Fowler's type F 2)[98] is to derive them from a zoomorphic form in which the back of the animals' head is not yet used as a field for enamel or millefiori (Fowler type F); and this type itself had been developed in a Romano-British setting by a straightforward process of elaboration before the end of the fourth century.[99] Thereafter it may well have been diffused by the craftsmen who took the idea of the lidded crucible to Ireland.

Finally, in assessing the importance of the Irish analogues, due allowance must be made for the extent and nature of archaeological research around the Irish Sea. To the great credit of Irish scholars, sites of the early Christian period have received far more attention in Ireland than in any other region of the Celtic West. They have frequently proved rich in finds, and they have been published with a wealth of illustration. It is inevitable, therefore, that one turns to the Irish sites for parallels. More excavation of sites in Cornwall, Wales, and Scotland (to say nothing of the *terra ignota* of Britanny) is needed to redress the balance.

One aspect of the finds remains to be discussed: the evidence they provide for the date of Phase 4. Here it might be hoped that a precise chronology would be provided by the imported pottery, especially that which comes from the Mediterranean. The hope is vain. The amphorae of Class B will not be datable until their forms can be reconstructed

[96] G. Jones and T. Jones (1949), 122; 97–8.

[97] Note the suggestion of F. Henry (1956), 81–3, that the Irishman Fursey was accompanied by craftsmen on his mission to East Anglia. Dr M. Miller has pointed out to me that according to the Life of Cadoc, the Saint employed an 'Irish migrant, a truly skilful master-builder', *quendam Hibernensem advenam, artificiosum quidem architectum* (A. W. Wade-Evans (1944), 66–7). It seems unlikely that such a person would have been invented about AD 1200, when the Life as we have it was put together, so we may well believe in the existence of this Irish craftsmen in south Wales in the sixth century AD.

[98] E. Fowler (1960); H. N. Savory (1956). Now see also H. Kilbride-Jones (1980b).

[99] The chronology of Kilbride Jones (1980b) seems to me about a century too early.

and compared in detail with Mediterranean vessels. The evidence for the leading type of Class A bowl is conflicting; for while at Dura-Europos it may be as early as 256, at Antioch-on-the-Orontes it does not seem to occur before 425. The most that can be said of the importation of Classes A and B is that it must lie in the period from the fourth to the eighth century. For classes D and E there is, at present, no dating evidence which is independent of the insular sites on which they have been found. In effect, the importation of all four classes into the British Isles can only be dated by reference to site associations or to historical notices of questionable value.[100] At Dinas Powys other classes of objects must provide a date for the pottery.

For a start, we can say that the absence of late Roman pottery, metalwork, and coins indicates that Phase 4 did not start before 400. On the other hand, romanized traditions are still so manifest that an initial date early in the fifth century seems likely. The imported glass appears to date to the fifth to sixth centuries, but could possibly continue into the seventh (below, p. 144). The Teutonic bronzes, in so far as they can be paralleled, could belong to the sixth to early seventh centuries (below, pp. 99 f.). If we suggest that Phase 4 A should be placed in the fifth century and Phase 4 B, in the sixth to eighth centuries, this would not conflict with the dating of the Irish and Anglo-Saxon analogues of the iron and bone objects.

Finally, we must ask whether Phase 4 lasted long after 700, whether indeed Dinas Powys was continuously occupied until, in the eleventh to twelfth centuries, it was converted into a small but strongly-fortified ring-work. The pottery is no help here, for it is generally agreed that its importation came to an end about 700, and from then until the Anglo-Norman conquest many parts of the Irish Sea Zone made no use of pottery at all.[101] Fragments of a bone comb from Dinas Powys (Fig. 7.1, 23) are ornamented with bunches of diagonal grooves, a motif which occurs in levels of the Viking period at Lagore and Ballinderry crannog No. 1; but in any case the Dinas Powys example belongs stratigraphically to Phase 5. Since metal objects of the eighth to eleventh centuries have occasionally been found around the Welsh coasts,[102] their absence from our site is significant. Particularly important here is a metalworker's cache from the Lesser Garth Cave about 6 miles north of Dinas Powys. This included a slotted-and-pointed iron object of a type well known in Ireland and south-west Scotland, and a loose-ring pin which is a debased version of a common Irish type. These objects suggest that craftsmen were still moving freely between Ireland and Wales in the seventh to ninth centuries. The absence of similar metalwork from Dinas Powys argues very strongly that the site was abandoned around 700.

The evidence of the finds may now be combined with that of the structures to give a general picture of Dinas Powys in Phase 4 (Plan, Fig. 2.5). In the fifth to eighth centuries, the place was the seat of a princely household, wealthy enough to import wine and pottery from the Mediterranean in order to maintain a romanized way of life; wealthy enough, moreover, to patronize jewellers working in bronze, gold, and glass as well as blacksmiths and other craftsmen. In the archaeological record, the basis of the economy seems to be stock-raising and the utilization of animal products, but this was certainly supplemented

---

[100] This was written before the study of this pottery was much advanced. See now pp. 116–22 below.

[101] This is clear from a number of well-excavated Irish sites where metal objects suggest a date in the eighth to eleventh centuries, but pottery is completely absent, e.g. Ballinderry crannog No. 1 and the later levels at Lagore.

[102] Lists in A. Fox (1946), 121–2, and L. Alcock (1960b), 226–7.

by arable farming and to a lesser extent by the exploitation of local mineral resources. The lord of Dinas Powys lived in a hall which appears to have been a dry-stone building with parallel sides and round ends; there were subsidiary buildings of stone and perhaps of

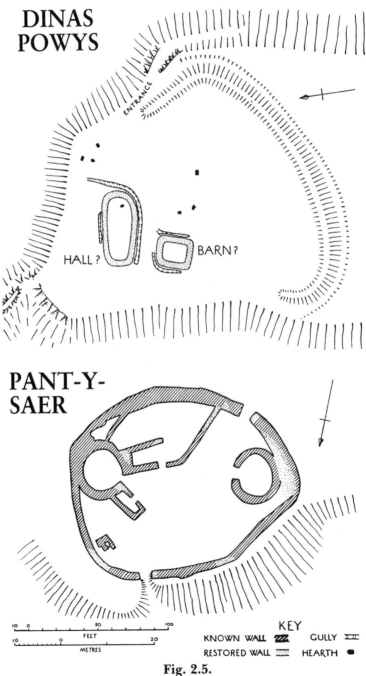

Fig. 2.5.

Comparative plans of Dinas Powys 4 and Pant-y-saer

timber. Striking features of the site were the industrial hearths, and the rich domestic middens which accumulated around the hall and on the northern and eastern periphery. The settlement was protected to some extent by steep natural slopes on the west, north, and north-east, and on the south-east and south by a rather feeble bank and ditch. Since the ditch was only about 11 feet wide by 4 feet deep and the rampart was of corresponding dimensions, this embanked enclosure cannot be thought of as a hill-fort; but within the framework of early Welsh society, it may conveniently be described as a *llys*.

It is now necessary to compare Dinas Powys with other excavated sites of the fifth to seventh centuries in Wales and the Marches. Before this can be done, the sites of that period must be identified. So far as settlements in the Roman manner are concerned—forts, towns, and villas—some in the area may well have continued to be occupied down to *c*. AD 400; and life of a sort may even have lingered on in the towns and in the vicinity of the legionary fortresses into the fifth century. There can be little doubt, however, that the villas and forts were deserted by then. Two special cases must also be examined. Firstly, at Caerwent we have the curious anomaly of hoards of the Theodosian dynasty, some of them containing thousands of coins, deposited in and among buildings which were often in ruins.[103] The only evidence of corporate activity which may reasonably be assigned to this late phase is the blocking of the north and south gates.[104] The coins certainly demonstrate that, decayed though Caerwent might be, it was in firm contact with the central authority in the last two decades of the fourth century. The discovery there of metalwork allied to the late Gallo–Roman bronzes from the Vermand cemetery prompts the question whether in the late fourth to early fifth century Caerwent was a garrison town.[105] The question is at present unanswerable; but at least it can be said that, on present evidence, Caerwent did not participate in the trade in Mediterranean pottery, wines, and oil which we have seen at Dinas Powys. Moreover, only one metal object attributable to the fifth to

[103] B. H. St. J. O'Neil (1935), 79–80, with refs.; also discussion in A. Fox (1946), 107–8.

[104] Two comments must be made here on the supposed church at Caerwent (V. E. Nash-Williams (1930), 235–7; (1953), 165–7).

(1) The attribution of the building to the late fifth to sixth centuries is based on the observation that its foundations 'were bedded at a height of a foot or more above the ruined remains of the colonnade' of the public baths (Nash-Williams (1930), 235). No section of this important stratification has ever been published, but photographs (e.g. loc. cit., Pl. LXXVIII) suggest that the colonnade had been carefully dismantled, so that we need not postulate a lengthy period of abandonment and gradual collapse between the disuse of the colonnade and the erection of this building. (Note that the south colonnade of the baths was infringed by secondary structures connected with the baths and unquestionably of Roman date; loc. cit., Pl. LXXVII). In any case, the foot depth of earth and rubble between the foundations of the building and the razed stumps of the colonnade may be deliberately-made ground rather than a slow accumulation of debris. The building may in part overlie a minor passage-way, but it is not certain that it infringed the main building-lines of its insula. In short, there is no cogent evidence, from stratification or structure, to demand a date later than 400 for this building; and the absence from Caerwent of relics of the fifth and sixth centuries makes such a date most unlikely.

(2) The identification of the building as a church (accepted by J. M. C. Tonybee (1953), 9) turns partly on the interpretation of a length of wall which does not bond with the main building as a narthex; partly on the description of the east end of the building as having a shallow apse. The plan (loc. cit., Fig. 1) shows that the inner face of this apse was not preserved, while a photograph (loc. cit., Pl. LXXVIII) shows that its outer face is in markedly different masonry to the remainder of the east wall. It may be doubted whether this feature will bear the weight of interpretation that has been placed upon it.

[105] On this metalwork, see now S. C. Hawkes and G. C. Dunning (1961).

sixth centuries is known: a double-spiral-headed iron pin of Irish or more probably Saxon origin.[106]

The second special case is represented by the temple of Nodens at Lydney and the earthwork within which it stands. If the ascription of Hoard II to the fifth century be accepted,[107] it is clear firstly that though the temple bath-house was in a dilapidated state by that date, it was, nonetheless, thought worth repairing the floor of one of the rooms; and, secondly, it was still possible to effect that repair in a cement of Roman character. This is the best, if not the only, evidence that we have for the late survival of Roman building techniques, and it is interesting to see it used in a Celtic religious centre. The earthworks at Lydney pose a more difficult question. It is indisputable that the original prehistoric earthwork was heightened at a time when quantities of late Roman builders' debris, potsherds, and coins could be scraped up to provide rampart-material. The effect was to produce a bank some 35 feet wide and standing 10 feet or more high, which enclosed an area 800 feet long by 300 feet wide. Wheeler argued that 'the contrast between the entirely un-Roman character of the earthwork and the elaborately Roman character of the temple-settlement is sufficiently striking to prevent us from supposing that the two works can belong chronologically to the same phase'. Consequently, the reinforcement of the earthwork must be ascribed 'to some period of recrudescent barbarism after the beginning of the fifth century'. Against this it may be urged that the cult centre is Celtic no less than Roman in character, and the deliberate placing of a Romano-Celtic temple within a hill-fort in the 360s or later can now be paralleled at Maiden Castle. That the rampart at Lydney should be reinforced in a specifically Celtic manner at some date before AD 400 may now seem less unlikely than appeared in 1932. It is at least clear that except for one bronze brooch which has no good parallels in Britain, there are no finds from Lydney, whether of pottery or of metal, which need to be ascribed to the fifth century or later. Moreover, an analysis of the earthworks of the fifth to sixth centuries in our area (below, p. 60) will show that Lydney differs from them because of the size of the reinforced rampart and of the area which it encloses. In view of this, it may be thought doubtful whether the heightening of the rampart at Lydney is really a work of the fifth rather than of late fourth century.

From sites which are Roman in style as well as in date we may now turn to those which represent a traditional Celtic way of life, little affected by Roman ideas of civil or military architecture.[108] There is a little evidence to show that sizeable hill-forts, founded in the pre-Roman Iron Age, were sometimes reoccupied in the fourth and fifth centuries. An acceptable instance of this is presented by the Breiddin, where a hill-fort, some 3,600 feet long by 1,000 feet across, produced wheel-thrown Romano-British pottery of the late third to fourth century associated with very coarse hand-modelled sherds of my Group I which may reasonably be interpreted as evidence of an occupation lasting into the opening decades of the fifth century. No structures of this late Roman and post-Roman occupation have been uncovered, and the only relics known are the potsherds, so it is not possible to say anything of the way of life which they represent. But it is important to notice that the ramparts, which had been slighted at the Roman conquest, were not

---

[106] A. Fox (1946), 108, with Fig. 12. The Irish examples are almost invariably more ornate than that from Caerwent, which stands close to the Anglo-Saxon series.

[107] In writing this, I had overlooked J. P. C. Kent's decisive rejection of such a date (1961), 7.

[108] The following paragraphs have an historical interest, as representing the synthesis which seemed reasonable in 1963. For a major revision, see now chapters 10 and 11.

refurbished at the time of the reoccupation. The Breiddin, then, represents the resettle-
ment of a traditional site, with only feeble fortifications. The suggestion has been
advanced that the same type of reoccupation of a hill-fort with ruined defences occurred in
the late fourth to fifth century at Castle Ditches, Eddisbury, and at Old Oswestry; but no
satisfactory evidence for this has yet been put forward, so judgement must be suspended.
An occupation continuing into the fifth century has been claimed for two other sizeable
and massively defended hill-forts. At Moel Fenlli, it has been suggested that the Nennian
attribution of the site to a King Benlli in the fifth century AD is reinforced by the discovery
of a sherd of Argonne ware; but if this had been found in south-eastern England it would
have been placed in the fourth. The second site, the hill-fort of Dinorben, was certainly
refortified, in the second century it would seem, and was then intensively occupied in the
fourth century. A group of flanged bowls from the site has been assigned to the fifth to
sixth centuries, though they have no parallels among the acceptable post-Roman import
wares. At present, neither Dinorben nor Moel Fenlli can be regarded as a proven example
of a hill-fort occupied into the post-Roman centuries.

A second class of native site which certainly lasted into the fifth century is represented
by Pant-y-saer (Plan, Fig. 2.5). This is one of the homesteads known as 'enclosed hut-
groups', which are common in Anglesey, Caernarvonshire, and parts of Merioneth. The
great majority of excavated examples have produced Romano-British pottery in sufficient
quantity to show that they were occupied in the second to fourth centuries AD;[109] but at
Pant-y-saer there are only meagre scraps of Roman pottery, and most of the sherds are
crude hand-modelled material of my Group I. The settlement-plan itself suggests that the
building of Pant-y-saer cannot be far removed from the Roman period, and a date in the
first half of the fifth century would seem reasonable. The primary settlement comprised
two round houses, each just under 30 feet in internal diameter, backing on to an enclosure
wall 5 feet or more in width and of uncertain height, which encloses a pear-shaped area
about 140 feet long by 110 feet wide. The settlement is placed in a semi-defensive position,
with steep descents on the northern and eastern sides, and the enclosure wall is widest on
the more gently sloping southern flank; but it would be wrong to think of the site as a fort.
After a quantity of Group I pottery and other refuse had accumulated within the
enclosure, two rectangular dry-stone buildings were butted on to the eastern round house;
the larger was 11 feet wide and of unknown length, the smaller 19 feet by 6 feet internally.
The combination of round and rectangular buildings within the same enclosure is known
in the Roman period at Dinllugwy and other enclosed hut-groups, but it is interesting to
see the rectangular plan surviving in the fifth century. The discovery of a silvered-bronze
penannular brooch at Pant-y-saer suggests that it was occupied by a household of
moderate wealth, well down the social scale compared with Dinas Powys. Further
comparison of the economic evidence from the two sites must be deferred until the other
settlements of the period have been examined.

Pant-y-saer appears to be the only true enclosed hut-group to survive into the fifth
century, but the same basic settlement plan, this time in a fortified setting, may be seen at
Carreg-y-llam. Here the crest of a craggy ridge, 110 feet long by 40 feet wide, was enclosed
by a dry-stone wall 10 feet wide. A round house, some 20 feet in diameter, was built
against the enclosure wall in just the same manner as the houses in the enclosed hut-
groups, but here the width of the enclosure wall, the presence of outworks, and the

---

[109] Best summary in RCAHM(W) (1964), lxxxvii ff.

naturally-defended situation, all demonstrate the defensive purpose of the site. It is in fact a small fort. The absence of Romano-British pottery and the presence of sherds which may possibly belong to my Group II argue for a date in the fifth century or later; but this should not be taken as established fact.

If this interpretation of the date and affinities of Carreg-y-llam is correct, then it provides a link between the enclosed hut-groups and the small- to medium-sized forts or embanked settlements. Next in size is the small fort, 220 feet long by 90 feet wide, with a dry-stone wall about 10 feet thick, which is set on the craggy summit of Garn Boduan. Inside are two round houses, respectively 12 and 22 feet in diameter; the smaller is free-standing, but the larger butts against the rampart, though not in the manner of the buildings in the enclosed hut-groups. Pottery which may belong to Group I suggests a date in the fifth century. More definitely dated to this period is the medium-sized fort at Dinas Emrys, where a wall varying in width from 3 to 11 feet encloses a very irregular and craggy area over 500 feet long by 300 feet wide. There are also two lower enclosures on the west. No complete building plans have been recovered. The site appears to have been fortified in the fourth or fifth century, and the quantity of Group II sherds makes it clear that there was an intensive occupation in the fifth century. Finally sherds of the Class B amphorae from Degannwy, the traditional seat of Maelgwn Gwynedd in the first half of the sixth century, suggest that this may have been a medium-sized fort like Dinas Emrys. There is tenuous evidence that a fairly level hill-top, some 300 feet long by 250 feet wide, was enclosed by a flimsy dry-stone wall; but excavation here has been limited to a brief reconnaissance, and far more work will be needed before we can speak with assurance of the nature of Degannwy in the fifth to sixth centuries.

We have, then, six wholly or partly excavated sites which can be assigned to the fifth to seventh centuries with reasonable assurance (Fig. 2.4). It must be admitted that generalizations based on so few examples can inspire little confidence; they must, none-theless, be attempted. We can say, firstly, that the majority of these sites are embanked or defended settlements—'hill-forts' in a very loose sense of the term. This does not in itself mean that the only or even the principal form of settlement in the post-Roman centuries was the 'hill-fort': it merely shows that such sites have attracted the attention of exca-vators, and that Dark Age material has been found on some of them in the course of excavation. Secondly, it seems that sizeable hill-forts with relatively massive ramparts were not being built in this period: when, on occasion, they were reoccupied, their decayed or even slighted ramparts were not refurbished. Thirdly, we can say that the only settlements which were demonstrably fortified in the fourth to fifth centuries were never more than $2\frac{1}{2}$ acres in area, and usually much less; their ramparts were not more than 11 feet wide and often narrower; and their sites were often defended by natural crags. This generalization fits the structures of Phase 4 at Dinas Powys to perfection. The settlement is protected on two sides by steep hillsides, and on the other two by a puny bank and ditch. The dimensions of the enclosed area, 180 feet by 140 feet, agree well with the range of examples quoted above. The only significant difference between Dinas Powys and the other sites is that they are defended by stone walls whereas it has an unrevetted earthen bank and external ditch. In short, Dinas Powys reinforces significantly the evidence that small settlements with relatively feeble defences were the rule in the fifth to seventh centuries.

This generalization has both politico–social and military implications which demand further examination. It seems reasonable to infer that the political situation and the social organization which on the one hand demanded the massive hill-forts of the pre-Roman Iron Age and on the other provided labour to build them no longer existed in the fifth to sixth centuries AD. The social organization must have changed markedly. This point is driven home by the siting of the small fort at Garn Boduan within the massive Iron Age defences. In particular, we may infer that the large hill-fort was the defence of a clan or other sizeable community: the small fort of the Dark Ages protected a single household. There is some evidence that these households were those not of ordinary folk but of persons of standing: the wealth of imports at Dinas Powys and Dinas Emrys, the brooch at Pant-y-saer, the traditional associations of Degannwy, the ostentatious fortification of Carreg-y-llam, all point in this direction. In short, within the framework of early Welsh society, most, if not all, of these sites represent the *llys* of a local lord.

What was the military role of these relatively weak defences in the dynastic struggles and the hostings of the period? Here we must turn to the literary evidence to see whether defended strongholds figure prominently in the battles of the time. The Welsh annals and *Bruts* are too sketchy to provide significant evidence here, though they leave an immediate impression of a difference between the methods of warfare practised before and after the coming of the Normans; in the later period attacks on castles are frequent, whereas, in the earlier, defended sites are rarely mentioned. The Irish annals are much fuller, and may be used with some caution for the fifth to seventh centuries.[110] Battles, sieges, and burnings at duns and raths do occur, especially in the last generation of the seventh century. There can be no doubt that these sieges and burnings involved actual attacks on fortified places; but the battles may have been in the vicinity of, rather than for the possession of, a particular fort. Thus the battle known in English sources as Nectansmere, and assumed to have been fought in a valley bottom, appears in the *Annals of Ulster* (s.a. 685) as *Bellum duin Nechtain*. Taking the printed text of the *Annals of Ulster* for the period 670–700, and omitting assassinations and slayings where there is no mention of a battle, we find that there are not more than ten burnings,[111] sieges, or destructions of fortified places (duns), perhaps another five battles in which a dun or rath is mentioned, and no less than twenty battles where there is no mention of a stronghold.

Turning now to the Welsh evidence, we find that attacks on forts have little place in the heroic poems. If the identification of Catraeth with Catterick is sound, then the objective of the expedition which forms the theme of the *Gododdin* was indeed a fortified place, but with its defences doubtless very decayed. One of the warriors of the *Gododdin* 'glutted the black ravens on the rampart of the city': but the general emphasis of the poem seems to be on cavalry warfare, which necessarily implies fighting in the open. Even the use of a fence of shields is more appropriate to a pitched battle than to the storming of a fortress.[112] The poems of Taliesin leave the same impression.[113] The 'low rampart' in the battle of Gwen Ystrat seems to have been a linear work thrown up, perhaps, at a moment of crisis, to defend a river crossing: it was certainly not a stronghold. The battle of Argoet Llwyfein

---

[110] Some of the chronological problems were discussed by T. F. O'Rahilly (1946), 235–59. See now K. Hughes (1972); J. Bannerman (1974).

[111] Some of the events took place at readily identifiable forts in Scotland: J. Bannerman (1974), 9–26; L. Alcock (1981a).

[112] K. H. Jackson (1969).

[113] J. Morris-Jones (1918); J. E. Caerwyn Williams (1968).

was clearly a pitched battle in which Urien had the advantage of high ground. There is the same emphasis on open warfare in the death-song of Owain ap Urien:

> Owein punished them grievously
> like a pack [of wolves] chasing sheep.

Finally, we may consider what the *Historia Brittonum*[114] says about the battles of Vortimer (cap. 44) and of Arthur (cap. 56). Out of fifteen battles for which a location is stated, one is *in urbe Legionis*; one is *in castello* or *iuxta castellum Guinnion*; two are on hills; one in a wood; one in a plain; and no less than nine are at rivers. It does not matter here whether these battles are historical or not; what is significant is that when the *Historia Brittonum* was compiled,[115] it seemed natural to locate battles most frequently at river crossings and only rarely at fortified places. In short, defended strongholds played no great part in the military activities of the Dark Ages, at any rate in southern Britain. This must largely account for the demonstrably puny nature of the defences of settlements in the fifth to seventh centuries.

Although the basic form of the defences at Dinas Powys agrees well with that of contemporary sites elsewhere in Wales, the internal buildings cannot at present be paralleled in the area. We have seen that the plans of the two houses of Phase 4 can be surmised from the lay-out of the drainage gullies which surrounded them. They had parallel sides with corners rounded externally and perhaps internally as well. The east end of House I B may have been a shallow apse, but the west end of House I B and both ends of House II were probably straight internally. It is likely that the walls were built in dry-stone rubble, wide at the base and battering to the top. Since the width of the walls is not known, the internal dimensions of the houses cannot be ascertained. There are no internal post-holes or other traces of roof supports. At present, these buildings have no acceptable prototypes or parallels in Wales, though it is possible that if the houses on Gateholm were properly examined some of them might be found to reproduce this sort of plan in turf with a facing of stone.[116] Elsewhere in Wales the commonest house plan in the fifth to sixth centuries is circular. Round houses may either be built against the enclosure wall as at Pant-y-saer and Carreg-y-llam, or stand free within the enclosure as at Garn Boduan. Both forms have an immediate ancestry in the enclosed hut-groups of the second to fourth centuries. Rectangular dry-stone buildings are also known at Pant-y-saer and, in an ecclesiastical context, in the supposed oratory of St Beuno at Clynnog Fawr. They differ from the Dinas Powys houses in that their walls are relatively narrow—only about 3 feet wide in each case—and the internal corners are right-angled: so too are the external angles of St Beuno's oratory, but at Pant-y-saer the outer wall-face is missing at the corners. This rectangular plan goes back into the Roman period in the enclosed hut-groups, and it can be found also in the hill-fort of Tre'r Ceiri, but in neither case are the rectangular buildings normally free-standing. In these buildings of Roman date but native construction the internal corners are frequently right-angled, but sometimes slightly rounded, whereas external corners, where they exist, are normally rounded.

This enquiry may be briefly extended to Cornwall and Ireland. At Gwithian very small dry-stone buildings of rounded plan were erected in the sixth to eighth centuries: the

---

[114] Accessible in J. Morris (1980).

[115] Recent discussion in D. N. Dumville (1976).

[116] This expectation has not been confirmed by further fieldwork: J. L. Davies, D. B. Hague and A. H. A. Hogg (1971).

internal dimensions of Hut 2 were 7 feet 6 inches by 8 feet 6 inches, and of Hut 3 10 feet by 11 feet. A larger building, which was rectangular with rounded corners, belongs to the ninth to tenth centuries. In Ireland circular dry-stone houses are found in early Christian contexts at St Gobnet's House, Ballyvourney, on Church Island, and at Leacanabuaile. One at Beginish had a slab with an eleventh-century runic inscription re-used as a lintel at the entrance, and this way of building must have continued down to recent times in parts of County Kerry. Strictly rectangular dry-stone building may occur in Ireland for ecclesiastical purposes as early as the seventh to eighth centuries, to judge from the Gallarus oratory and that on Church Island; these may be compared with the oratory of St Beuno at Clynnog Fawr. More important for comparison with Dinas Powys are the square or oblong houses, right-angled internally but with rounded external corners, which occur at Carrigillihy (Phase 2), Leacanabuaile, White Fort, House 2 on Church Island, and room II of House I at Beginish. Except for the last, which is unlikely to be earlier than 1100, all these belong to the second half of the first millennium, but they cannot be more closely dated. They resemble the supposed buildings at Dinas Powys in that they have thick walls, normally more than 5 feet wide. They differ in that they all have internal post-holes, which at White Fort may have supported an elaborate clerestory, but which elsewhere betoken rather primitive roofing arrangements. At Dinas Powys the absence of post-holes may imply the use of a king-post truss, a device which could have been learnt from the Romans. If this is so, then it is the only hint of a romanized architectural tradition which survives on the site. Since none of the Irish sites can be shown to be earlier than Phase 4 at Dinas Powys, and Church Island and Beginish are both certainly later, there is no need to derive the house-plan itself from Ireland. It is possible that it represents an experimental attempt to reproduce a romanized rectangular plan without the use of mortar.[117]

Only three contemporary Welsh sites have been excavated on a sufficient scale for their social and economic aspects to be compared with those of Dinas Powys. At Carreg-y-llam, the only signs of wealth were the ostentatious fortifications, and the importation of a little Group II pottery. The only other finds were utilized stones, including flints; but querns were absent.

At Pant-y-saer, on the other hand, there were both rotary and saddle querns. The grain implied by these was probably grown in small fields like those frequently associated with enclosed hut-groups, and there are slight traces of such fields below the site. Domestic animals—ox, sheep, pig, horse, and dog—were all kept, but the middens were not rich enough to reveal the relative frequency of the various species. Moderate quantities of shellfish were eaten. The only jewellery, and indeed the only remaining metal object, was the silvered-bronze penannular brooch which, as has been said, implies a modest degree of wealth. The only craft certainly represented was that of potting, but three fragments of what may be moulds hint at bronze-working either on the site or in its vicinity.

At Dinas Emrys there is clear evidence that iron-workers and bronze-smiths were patronized. The products of the latter may have included the 'Donside' terrets and the gold-plated strips and studs, discovered in 1910 and subsequently lost.[118] On the analogy of Dinas Powys, the fairly abundant fragments of late Roman or Dark Age glass, which

---

[117] For a recent discussion of round and rectangular houses in the period, C. J. Lynn (1978).

[118] C. E. Breese (1930), 350–4. One of the terrets is in the National Museum of Wales; W. F. Grimes (1951), Fig. 44. My suggestion that these 'Donside' terrets belong to the fifth to seventh centuries has been generally rejected: see H. Kilbride-Jones (1980a), 154–7.

include at least two fused fragments, may have been imported as scrap for jewel-making. Sherds of Class B amphorae, and a rim from a Class E cooking-pot, show that Dinas Emrys shared in the imports of Group II pottery and of Mediterranean wine or oil. Two fragments of querns of Romano-British or later types prove that grain was being ground, but there is no other evidence about either the arable or pastoral activities of the settlement. From all this, it appears that the range of economic activities at Dinas Emrys compares well with that at Dinas Powys. The presence of specialist craftsmen implies considerable wealth and social standing, and there can be no doubt that in the fifth to sixth centuries Dinas Emrys was by far the most important of the sites so far excavated in north Wales. Nonetheless, Dinas Powys appears to have been even richer, especially in imported objects. This in part reflects its situation near the coast in contrast to Dinas Emrys, which is about 10 miles inland.

It remains to ask what can be seen of the political background of Dinas Powys in the fifth and sixth centuries.[119] It appears, for a start, that the situation at that time was more obscure in the south-east than in other parts of Wales. In Gwynedd, for instance, in the early sixth century, we have Gildas's contemporary notice[120] of Maelgwn as king. According to Nennius he was a descendant of that Cunedda whose sons had founded princedoms throughout north-west Wales. If we accept the statement that Cunedda had come from Manau Guotodin one hundred and forty-six years before Maelgwn's reign, then the migration must have occurred before AD 400, and it is most reasonably explained as an act of Roman military policy. Even if we place the migration as late as 450, it would still seem explicable as a strategic manoeuvre in the Roman tradition.[121] In short, the dynasty that we find ruling in Gwynedd in the post-Roman centuries had been established by Roman or at least romanized authority. A reconnaissance excavation at Degannwy, one of Maelgwn's traditional seats, has suggested that this was already a strongpoint in Roman times.[122] The inscriptions of the early Christian memorial stones provide contemporary evidence for the romanized sophistication of Gwynedd in the fifth to seventh centuries. This is an area where horizontal inscriptions in the Roman manner (as opposed to vertical inscriptions in the Celtic fashion) are very common. The Venedotian stones themselves include almost all those which bear witness to settled political and ecclesiastical arrangements, with references to *Venedotis cives* (ECMW No. 103), *magistratus* (ibid.), *saerdos* (ECMW No. 33), and *presbyter* (ECMW Nos. 77, 78). The only use of the consular system of dating occurs here (ECMW No. 104). Finally, in the stone (ECMW No. 13) of Cadman, '*rex sapientissimus opinatissimus omnium regum*', we appear to have an echo of Byzantine court formulae.[123]

Dyfed is another kingdom whose ruler, Vortipor, was castigated as *tyrannus*, 'usurper' by Gildas.[124] But Vortipor's own memorial (ECMW No. 138) enables us to assess the rhetorical emptiness of Gildas's use of the term, for on it Vortipor's memorialist claimed a Roman title for him. Indeed, we have already seen that Vortipor's ancestors had probably been established in Dyfed by an act of military policy similar to that which planted the

[119] Latest account: W. Davies (1982), chapter 4.
[120] Gildas, chapter 33.
[121] See now chapter 4 and references.
[122] L. Alcock (1967c).
[123] ECMW = V. E. Nash-Williams (1950). On the stones, see further J. D. Bu'lock (1956); R. B. White (1978); M. Miller (1979).
[124] Gildas, chap. 31.

sons of Cunedda in the north-west. Dyfed lacks the other signs of political sophistication and romanization which are so plain in Gwynedd: the inscribed stones, for instance, show notably Celtic and specifically Irish influences. But we should not forget that this is the region in which Paulinus was celebrated in a very romanized metrical epitaph (ECMW No. 139).

For Powys we have no contemporary evidence, but the genealogies (for what they are worth) seem to imply that the area was ruled in this period by a dynasty which traced itself back to a certain Vortigern.[125] If we accept the traditions which lie behind the inscription on Eliseg's pillar (ECMW No. 182), then this Vortigern married the daughter of the usurper Magnus Maximus. Whether or not we accept the suggestion that Vortigern was a Roman official himself, it is at least a reasonable inference that the Powysian dynasty had its roots in romanized circles in the last two decades of the fourth century. In short, Powys resembles Gwynedd and Dyfed in that the dynasty which ruled in the post-Roman centuries appears to have been established with Roman authority by about 400.

In south-east Wales, by contrast, no clear dynastic lines are visible.[126] Dinas Powys lay in the princedom of Glywysing, which presumably had been founded by the eponymous Glywys, grandfather of St Cadog. The synchronisms of Cadog's life suggest that he flourished in the first half of the sixth century, perhaps towards 550, so his grandfather probably reigned in the second half of the fifth century. It does not seem possible to trace the dynasty back behind Glywys, for Nor and Solor, his immediate precursors in the traditional genealogy,[127] are not otherwise known and hence are probably fictitious; beyond them the genealogy goes back as a garbled list of Roman emperors and usurpers. If we were to accept the sequence Magnus Maximus–Owain–Nor–Solor–Glywys as genuine, then we might infer that Glywys, like his contemporaries, drew his authority ultimately from late Roman political arrangements. On balance, however, the genealogy before Glywys seems incredible, so it is probable that he had founded a personal kingdom and dynasty on the ruins of the Roman arrangements for the area. The dynasty may have been short-lived, for according to the Life of St Cadoc he prayed to the Lord to give him a king, and was given Meurig son of Enhinti.[128] Since there seems to be confusion here with the Meurig son of Henninni,[129] who was a remote ancestor of Cadog on his mother's side, it may be thought that no accurate tradition about the ruler of Cadog's day has been preserved. In the seventh century, it is believed, Glywysing was linked to Gwent under the dynasty of Meurig son of Tewdrig.

This sketch of the early dynastic history of the princedom in which Dinas Powys was situated does not attempt to solve the problems posed by the very unsatisfactory nature of the evidence. It cannot be denied that when the genealogies and the Life of St Cadog came to be written down, about AD 1200, in the forms in which we now have them the traditions about the rulers of the fifth to seventh centuries were already confused.[130] From this it

---

[125] C. A. R. Radford (1958); Radford's tabulation of the genealogies (loc. cit., p. 24) shows how unreliable they are in detail. J. D. Bu'lock (1960) presents a case for distinguishing two Vortigerns.

[126] For some recent attempts, not followed here, to write the early dynastic history of the area, see H. M. Chadwick (1954; 1959), 48–51; P. C. Bartrum (1948); and now, W. Davies (1982).

[127] A. W. Wade-Evans (1944), 118–19.

[128] Ibid., 80–1.

[129] Ibid., 118–19.

[130] Ibid., viii–ix.

seems not unreasonable to infer that the period had itself been one of confusion, with frequent changes of dynasty, influenced in part by equally obscure events in the neighbouring area of Gwent.

At first sight we are faced here with a paradox. In the relatively unromanized areas of Gwynedd, Dyfed, and much of Powys, we find in the post-Roman centuries relatively stable dynasties ultimately of Roman establishment. In the romanized south-east, by contrast, we have difficulty in discerning either a stable dynasty or an underlying Roman authority. Deeper reflection shows that this is a natural situation, not at all paradoxical. In abstract terms, we might say that the politico–military situation after 400 demanded un-Roman arrangements, and that these were most readily acceptable in unromanized areas. In more concrete terms, the unromanized areas were those which had presumably remained under military control: what happened in the late fourth century was that Celtic military power with Roman legal authority behind it was substituted for Roman military power; in the fifth century the power was consolidated while the legal backing became a fiction. But in the romanized area of the south-east there appears to have been a form of civil authority, the *ordo reipublicae civitatis Silurum*.[131] The precise structure and functioning of this body are not clear, and it is uncertain, for instance, whether it governed a tribal (or cantonal) area or was merely a town council.[132] It may at least be presumed that this was the sort of body to which Honorius referred when he ordered the cities of Britain to look to their own defences. The history of England shows that this was not the form of government best fitted to cope with the politico–military situation of the fifth century. On the other hand, the oligarchic nature of such a body would not lend itself to transformation into a monarchy drawing its authority primarily from military force. The transition from Romano-Celtic *civitas* to Welsh kingdom must have been painful, bloody, and confused: and it is this confusion that the records faithfully reflect.

This, then, is the background to Dinas Powys in Phase 4: the breakdown of romanized political arrangements followed by a period of conflict in which several short-lived attempts were made to found petty kingdoms. By the seventh century, it would seem, a degree of political stability had been secured. From this it would appear that Phase 4 corresponds with the period of conflict and confusion. Here we may recall the two principal features of the natural setting of Dinas Powys: its great natural strength and its seclusion. These must have combined to make the hill-top an ideal location for a princely household in the troubled times of the fifth to sixth centuries. On the other hand, as the political system became more stable in the seventh century, a more accessible site was probably needed, so the hill-top was abandoned until the military needs of the late eleventh to twelfth centuries once more called attention to its natural advantages.

---

[131] V. E. Nash-Williams (1954), 81–3, with Pl. II.
[132] J. M. Reynolds (1966).

CHAPTER 3

Dry Bones and Living Documents

I

In the original publication of Dinas Powys, considerable emphasis was placed on the potential economic evidence provided by the large number of animal bones recovered from the deposits of Phase 4.[1] A limited sample had been examined to determine the species present, and the age of slaughter, by Dr I. W. Cornwall and Mrs L. Haglund-Calley. The numerical information of their report is printed below as Table 1, p. 68. In 1963, I drew attention to some of the problems raised by the figures for age-of-slaughter. In particular, the cattle and sheep were killed so young that it would have been impossible to maintain the stock. To compound the problem, documentary evidence for the food renders due to the princes of medieval Wales showed that fully mature animals were favoured rather than calves or lambs. I developed this line of thought at greater length in a conference paper, which was delivered at Lancaster in 1974, and which is reprinted as Part II of the present chapter.

In 1974–5, archaeozoology could be described as 'a relatively recent and very much a cinderella field of study'.[2] Since then, however, there have been considerable advances in both methodology and interpretation. Relevant examples are surveyed in Part III. So far as Dinas Powys itself is concerned, however, the most significant advance has been, in effect, a response to Chaplin's further comment that 'the animal bones from Dinas Powys would repay further study', particularly so because Cornwall had only examined about a quarter of the bones that had been retained from the excavations.

While the present book was being written, and quite independently of it, R. Gilchrist analysed the hitherto unexamined bones as a dissertation topic in the Department of Archaeology, University of York. With the ready consent of the Head of Department, Professor P. A. Rahtz, Miss Gilchrist has made her analytical results and interpretations fully available to me. Part IV of this chapter, therefore, is based on her results, though she is not responsible for some of the interpretations which I have placed on them.[3]

II

The purpose of this paper[4] is to examine some of the ways in which documentary evidence can be used to breathe life into the animal bones found on archaeological sites, so that

[1] *Dinas Powys* (1963), 34–9; above, pp. 31–7.
[2] R. E. Chaplin (1975), commenting on my 1974 paper.
[3] The original dissertation is deposited in the Department of Archaeology, University of York, where it may be consulted on application.
[4] Delivered at the CBA Conference entitled *The effect of man on the landscape: the Highland zone*, held at Lancaster in March 1974: published in *CBA Research Report* No. 11 [J. G. Evans, S. Limbrey and H. Cleere (eds.) (1975), 117–22].

Table 1

Numerical analysis of animal bones (by Dr I. W. Cornwall and Mrs L. Haglund-Calley)

Group of bones	Cattle sum	Cattle 1–2	Cattle 2–2½	Cattle 2½–3½	Cattle sum	Sheep sum	Sheep 1	Sheep 1–1½	Sheep 1½–2	Sheep sum	Pig <1	Pig 1–2	Pig >2	Others	Remarks
Skull fragments					1		1			28	2			1	1 of horse.
Horn-cores	11				10										cattle: 5 long, 5 short.
Maxilla/mandible	23	5	5	10	39		4	9	16	228	8	106	4		pig: few worn, probably mainly *c.* 2 years old. sheep: the rest probably *c.* 2 years old. cattle: none very worn, adult, but young.
Loose teeth	126		7	2	132			1	6	435	72	100	3	16	4 of horse, very old. 12 of deer, adult. pig: 7 newly born. sheep: mainly young beasts. cattle: 1 calf, 2 very worn (probably one animal), the rest *c.* 2½ years old or less.
Axial skeleton	16				18										sheep: 15 caudal vert., probably sheep or cattle.
Shoulder and hip-girdles	6	1			5					1				4	4 of bird. cattle: 1 fragment, calf.
Long bones	12		2	3	6			1		11	3	2		29	28 of bird. 1 of deer, fairly young. pig: all young, 2 newly born. sheep: 1 lamb. cattle: 3 cut open with sharp tool.
Extremities	146	4	11		13					322		101		10	1 of Homo. 2 of deer (some under 'cattle' may be deer). 7 of bird (1 with spur). Cattle: the rest *c.* 1½ years old or more. 2 phal. fused through physical damage, not illness. 1 metapod., definitely calf. 7 metapod. out of 18 split open with sharp tool.
	340	10	25	15	224	5	11	22		1,025	85	309	7	+4	?
		2.94%	7.35%	4.4%		1.12%	2.46%	4.92%			8.71%	31.6%	0.72%	+21	other fragments of bird.
														+2	skulls of rodents.
														+1	concretion.
	340				224					1,025				88	
	21.5%				13.4%					61.2%				5.26%	

Grand total: 1,677

the zoological evidence from an excavation may be rescued from a specialist appendix, and integrated into the full historical account. The paper also looks at some of the problems which can arise when this integration is attempted—problems which concern the bone specialist as much as the economic historian. Its inspiration is twofold: an early training in the documents of medieval agrarian economy, and the discovery of well-preserved animal bones at the early medieval fortification of Dinas Powys, Glamorgan. This site also yielded a great variety of other evidence on which to base a picture of its economic life. Since medieval Wales has abundant documents to illustrate its economy, it therefore seemed worthwhile attempting a synthesis of the archaeological and literary evidence. What follows here is concerned only with the pastoral aspects of the economy at Dinas Powys.

The principal data, and some discussion of the problems which they raise, have been in print since 1963.[5] The reason for calling attention to them now is that the problems have been ignored by economic historians making use of the data, and both the data and the problems have been overlooked by students of excavated animal bones.

The most important period in the history of the Dinas Powys site fell in the fifth to seventh centuries AD. At this time, the place was a small and feeble fortification; but its middens yielded an extraordinarily rich collection of pottery and glass, silver, bronze and iron, worked bone, and utilized stone. The limestone bedrock favoured the preservation of animal bones, and consequently great quantities, principally from domestic animals, were recovered. Indeed, within the very limited resources of the excavation, these quantities were an embarrassment, and it was possible to retain only a portion of the bones. Although this was a matter of expediency, the actual selection was based on reasoned principles. Advice was taken from appropriate specialists, and questions about the animal husbandry of Dinas Powys, which the bones might serve to answer, were formulated as a basis for this selection. In particular, it seemed that we might hope to determine the order of frequency of species, the age of slaughter of the stock, and the stature of the beasts. With this in mind, we normally kept only jaws and teeth, and those long bones which retained their articular surfaces, a sample which amounted to about one-third of all the bones discovered.

Small though this initial sample was, in the circumstances of the late 1950s it was not possible to find anyone competent and willing to examine the whole of it. In the event, Dr I. W. Cornwall kindly agreed to examine some 1,600 bones, about one-seventh of those which had been retained on site. For this purpose, a further selection was a made on archaeological grounds. All the bones from one particular midden deposit, with much associated pottery of the fifth to seventh centuries AD, were studied as a group. It is believed that this represents a fair sample of the bones from that period. The remainder of the original sample still awaits identification.

One outcome of the original method of selection was to make it difficult to determine the actual table meat favoured at Dinas Powys. In his report, Dr Cornwall comments: 'Though the remains are clearly of food-animals in the main, the identifiable parts represented are strikingly of the less edible parts of carcasses. The few main long bones are almost all deliberately broken and many, even, of the vertebrae are caudals, representing, if anything, rather oxtail soup than sirloin cuts. The collection looks like waste from the kitchen thrown direct on to the midden, never having been to table at

[5] L. Alcock (1963a).

all'.[6] This may require modifying to the extent that oxtail—like cows' heels, pigs' trotters, or sheeps' brains—is perfectly edible in itself, without needing to be made into soup. Moreover, it is difficult to see how top-quality cuts of beef would be represented, except perhaps by T-bone steaks. Leg and shoulder of mutton were certainly present.

The numerical analysis of the animal bones by Dr Cornwall and Mrs Haglund-Calley is reproduced here as Table 1. This provides evidence for the interpretation of the age at which domestic animals were slaughtered, which is conveniently presented in a series of histograms for cattle, sheep, and pig (Fig. 3.1). What immediately emerges is the relatively early age of slaughter: all of the sheep, and all but 2 per cent of the pig, at under 2 years of age, and 70 per cent of the cattle at less than 30 months.

If these figures are accepted, they raise an immediate problem about the viability of stock-raising at Dinas Powys. Given such a drastic slaughtering policy, could the stock be maintained at all? It is not easy to determine the age of puberty, the minimum breeding age, for ancient domestic animals. Figures for modern methods of intensive breeding, from animals on a high-nutrition diet, may provide some kind of baseline, to which we must add an uncertain number of months or years (information from P. G. Hignett, MRCVS). In the case of sheep, it might be suggested that the ewes would normally lamb at the end of their second year, so each of the Dinas Powys sheep can have produced at best one lamb. When allowance is made for rams, barren ewes, and lost lambs, it is clear that this is quite insufficient to maintain a flock.

In the case of cattle, we may find some guidance on the age of calving in the early medieval Welsh Laws, which contain a great deal of virtually unquarried evidence for agrarian economy and farming practices. One passage details the rising value of a cow from 6 pence at birth to 30 pence towards the end of its third year. In May of the fourth year 'the attributes of a heifer are to be required of it . . . an increase of 16 pence is added, namely the value of her milk . . . and 4 pence for her calf'.[7] The implication would seem to be that, by May of the fourth year, the first calf had been weaned, the calf itself being born late in the cow's third year. By this time, according to Fig. 3.1., the majority of the Dinas Powys cattle were dead.

Only in the case of pigs does there seem some hope of maintaining the stock. Medieval writers on husbandry thought that pigs should farrow two or three times a year, having a litter of at least seven each time. Under modern conditions, puberty might begin at 5 months. Even if we adjust this to a year, it is clear that the stock of pigs could have been kept up, despite the fact that the overwhelming majority had been slaughtered by the end of their second year. But on the available figures, the flocks of sheep and herds of cattle could not possibly have been maintained.

Several explanations for this discrepancy may be offered and examined. The most obvious are: that some bias towards young animals was created by the method of sampling on the site; that there is some bias in the technique of ageing domestic animals from bones and teeth;[8] or that social choice had brought to Dinas Powys a collection of animal carcasses which in no way represents the normal age pattern of the stock or the normal pattern of slaughtering. These hypothetical explanations can be partially tested by comparison with the animals from other sites and by reference to early economic documents.

[6] L. Alcock (1963a), 192.
[7] M. Richards (1954), 87.
[8] I. A. Silver (1969).

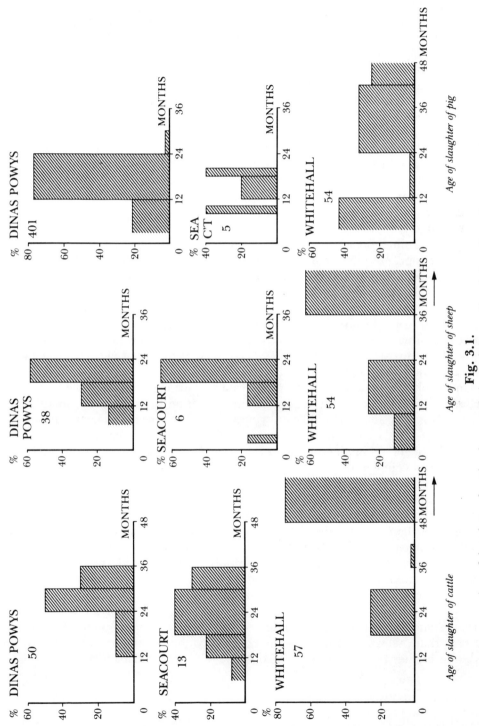

Fig. 3.1.

Age of slaughter of cattle, sheep and pig on three medieval sites. For references see text.
The figure below the site-name is the total number of animals represented. Note that
the method of calculating these numbers differs from site to site

Starting with the last of these hypotheses, there is a *prima facie* case that Dinas Powys was a special site. The existence of defences, combined with the site evidence for such prestige activities as fine metalworking, argue that it was a chieftain's or prince's defended homestead—a likely place, therefore, for specially selected cuts of meat. But before this line of thought is taken further, it is necessary to examine the evidence from sites for which no such claims can be made: more lowly farms or peasant villages.

Aldwick, Barley (Hertfordshire), would seem to represent such a site in the Iron Age. There 'some 65 per cent of sheep were killed at ages less than two years'.[9] Although this rate of slaughter raises problems about the maintenance of the flocks similar to those at Dinas Powys, it does not appear to have been questioned or commented on. A similar problem appears at Old Sleaford (Lincolnshire), in both the Iron Age and the Romano-British period. The sheep which can be aged to greater than 24 months comprise only about one-third of the specimens recovered.[10] Again there is a curious silence about the implications of this for the survival of the flock.

Even more directly comparable with Dinas Powys is the medieval village of Seacourt in Berkshire, where animal bones from the late twelfth to late fourteenth centuries AD have been studied by Jope.[11] A table showing 'approximate ages of animals based on average periods of eruption of teeth' may be converted into histograms which in their terminal ages parallel the Dinas Powys pattern almost exactly. This might suggest that we are observing a normal pattern of slaughter, common to both lords and peasants. If this were really so, it might well inspire serious doubts about ageing criteria. It might appear necessary to recalibrate the age scale on the histograms so as to allow the animals to breed sufficiently often to maintain the stock. As a corollary, it might be necessary for bone specialists to review their ageing techniques.

So drastic a solution may not, in fact, be necessary. Turning from the table of ages at Seacourt to the body of the animal report we find: in Period I, 'immature animals were present as well as fully adult ones. The only immature bone apart from jaws was one ox phalanx.' In Period II 'a sheep metatarsal was the only immature bone apart from jaws'. In other words, the use of tooth eruption as a principal criterion of age tips the interpretation in favour of young animals. But this observation does not provide relief from the dilemma at Dinas Powys. There, the teeth and jaws were examined for wear as well as for the degree of eruption. As the Remarks column of Table 1 shows, only two 'very worn' cow molars provide evidence for an animal that was older than 'adult but young'.

To emphasize the oddity of the Dinas Powys evidence, it is useful to consider the pattern of slaughtering at the early medieval farmstead at the Treasury site, Whitehall, London. Here the fusion of the epiphyses of the limb bones was used as the criterion for age at death, but tooth eruption and wear does not appear to have been taken into account. It is immediately apparent from the histograms that a goodly proportion of both cattle and sheep survived to breed more than once. With pig the proportion was smaller, but no doubt sufficient. It has been well observed that the marked peaks on the histograms demonstrate that 'selective killing on an age-related basis was practised on these animals'; and further 'the picture presented is one of rational husbandry'.[12]

---

[9] J. M. Ewbank *et al.* (1964).
[10] E. S. Higgs and J. P. White (1963).
[11] M. Jope (1962).
[12] R. E. Chaplin (1971).

Faced with the Whitehall evidence, it is necessary to reconsider the possibility that the explanation for the curious pattern of the Dinas Powys animal bones lies in the high social status of the site. A modern commentator, with a taste for veal or spring lamb, might expect the sixth-century lords of Dinas Powys to have had similar tastes, backed by the means to gratify them. The Welsh Laws suggest, however, that this expectation may not be justified. These Laws are preserved in manuscripts of the late twelfth to thirteenth centuries AD, but they claim to have been promulgated by King Hywel Dda (Howell the Good) who died *c.* AD 950. There is agreement that the Laws are in fact highly stratified, and that the earliest strata represent the customs of Wales in the centuries before Howell.[13] Among the more primitive elements are those which list the renders- (or taxes-) in-kind owed by both freemen and bondmen to the prince. If Dinas Powys was a princely homestead, these renders should be directly relevant to the animal remains found on the site. Some typical examples may therefore be quoted. It has been claimed that the bondmen 'were to present the king with young animals whenever he came to the court',[14] but the full text refers to sheep or lambs or kids or cheese or butter or milk, according to the ability of the bondmen.[15]

More generally in the Laws, however, the emphasis is on mature beasts, and sometimes the degree of maturity is spelt out with great care. For instance, the summer render paid by the freemen comprised four 'food-gifts'. Three of these included a cow—in one case, specifically the 'carcase of a fat cow without skin and entrails'—while the fourth included 'a fat wether three years old and a sow of three winters three fingers thick'. From the bondmen, the prince was to have two food-gifts a year, including 'a sow three fingers thick in her hams, her ribs and her gammons.' Another food gift included 'a bacon three fingers thick in its gammons, in its ribs and in its hams, or a sow of three years fattening'. For three winter food-gifts the carcass of an ox was to be paid.[16]

The wider aspects of this emphasis on mature beasts must be considered later, but first we must return to Dinas Powys. In an integrated account of the site, three elements should be capable of correlation: (a) the interpretation of the site as a prince's stronghold; (b) the documentary evidence for the character of food renders to a prince; (c) the interpreted age of slaughter of food animals. As we have seen, the expected correlation does not exist. It may therefore be necessary to question elements (a) and (c). As it happens, one reviewer has rejected the excavator's interpretation as the court of a prince and has suggested: 'if on this secluded and safe hill-top there was a nest of robbers, might not one find ... the bones of the most succulent animals belonging to the stock-breeding farmers of the district?'[17] It is difficult to believe that such a hypothetical robber-band would have preferred a scrawny lamb or calf to a fat wether three years old, or that young beasts are easier to rustle than mature ones. In any case, the interpretation of Dinas Powys as a nest of robbers has not found favour with other commentators, whereas the hypothesis that it was a prince's stronghold has been widely accepted.

It follows, then, that the apparent age of slaughter of the Dinas Powys animals cannot be reconciled with a reasonable interpretation of the social function of the site, nor with a sensible policy of animal husbandry. It is therefore necessary to ask again whether the

[13] H. D. Emanuel (1967), 82; G. R. J. Jones (1972), 300; T. J. Pierce (1972), 353.
[14] G. R. J. Jones (1967).
[15] A. Owen (1841), 95.
[16] M. Richards (1954), 73.
[17] C. A. Gresham (1965).

age-pattern has been distorted by the concentration on jaws and teeth as dating criteria. Table 1 shows that, out of 50 cattle for which an age estimate is given, only 20 are aged from the limb-bones, but there are no fewer than 138 limb-bones for which no age is given. Among the pigs, limb-bones account for 103 examples aged between 12 and 24 months, but there are also 227 unaged limbs. Could a significant proportion of these belong to mature beasts? At present this question can only be asked, not answered. But similar questions about the true age-span of domestic animals need asking about the stock at Seacourt, Aldwick, and Sleaford, and no doubt about other sites as well.

Turning now to the sheep, we may first recall the 'fat wether, three years old' of the Welsh Laws. He would have yielded three shearings of wool before he was brought to the prince's table. It used to be normal practice, at least in the upland regions of Britain, to keep the wethers for several years for the sake of their wool before they were slaughtered— the taste for lamb is a product of the affluent society. As we have seen, the ewes were required to produce one lamb a year, but twins were not expected in medieval hus- bandry.[18] Less obvious today is the early importance of the sheep in terms of milk and its products. After his passage on the milk yield of cows, Walter continues:[19]

> And twenty ewes which are fed in pasture of salt marsh ought to and can yield cheese and butter as the two cows before named. And if your sheep were fed with fresh pasture or fallow, then ought thirty ewes to yield butter and cheese as the three cows before named. Now there are many servants and provosts and dairymaids who will contradict this thing, and that is because they give away and waste and consume the milk!

It is evident that all these products of the living beast must be taken into account when we attempt to reconstruct the husbandry and agrarian economy represented by the animal bones on archaeological sites. But it is equally important to stress that the dead beast provided more than just a supply of table meat. Sometimes the by-products are demonstrated by actual site evidence. The use of horn, for instance, is well shown by the great numbers of horn-cores, interpreted as workshop debris, from a medieval site in Well Street, Coventry.[20] But with more perishable organic substances (sinew, gut, and above all hides) the archaeological evidence may fail us, and we must then depend on the hints provided by literary documents.

Some examples may now be quoted at random from the Welsh Laws.[21] The steward of the Royal court was 'to have the skins of a hart to make vessels to keep the horns of the king and his cups ... The chief groom is to have an ox hide in winter and a cow hide in summer to make halters for the king's horses.' Whereas the king had leather hose, the summoner of the court had 'the legs of the cattle slaughtered in the kitchen to make untanned shoes that are not to be higher than his ankles'. On the uses of horn: the chief huntsman blows his horn when the king goes to foray; and for performing this duty he has 'a hornful of liquor from the king, and another from the queen, and the third from the steward'.

In conclusion, this paper has attempted to indicate how documentary sources can amplify, illuminate, or in some cases cast doubts on the interpretations which we base on the animal bones recovered from archaeological excavations. The documents available

[18] R. Trow-Smith (1957).
[19] E. Lamond and W. Cunningham (1890); D. Oschinsky (1971).
[20] R. E. Chaplin (1971), 138.
[21] M. Richards (1954), 31–43.

are numerous, and have been little quarried even by economic historians. But we might hope for the future that they will not be overlooked by archaeologists and their biological colleagues.

III

Since the Lancaster paper was delivered in 1974, reports have been published on the animal bones from a number of early medieval sites, and there have been many discussions of the principles and methodology of bone-studies: so many, indeed, that any survey must necessarily be both limited and eclectic. Three topics particularly deserve discussion here.

Firstly, in view of the importance attached in Chapters 2 and 4 to the need for written sources to aid the economic interpretation of archaeological material, we should examine the relative importance of ethnographic comparisons and historical documentation in the study of animal bones. It might be thought self-evident that medieval statements about farming practices, and about the husbandman's expectations, are of greater relevance than even the most acutely observed descriptions of the exploitation of animals by hunter-gatherer groups. Given the difference between the hunting of wild animals and the raising of domestic stock, this generalization might be applied to all farming communities: certainly it must be true of medieval farmers. Despite this, an account of the ethno-archaeology of the Nunamiut Eskimos[22] features more prominently in the bibliographies of recent papers in zooarchaeology than do the writings of Walter of Henley. Happily, there are also hints in the literature of a proper appreciation of written sources.

Thus, Noddle[23] quotes literary evidence from eighteenth-century Norfolk 'to suggest that the animal trade was in the hands of tanners, whose main concern was the skin', and who therefore 'slaughtered their stock with care to avoid saturating a small meat market'. Clutton-Brock, having quoted a compelling instance of a discrepancy between the evidence from excavated animal bones and that from written sources, then demonstrates[24] at length the value of Anglo-Saxon documents, especially legal documents, for understanding the animal husbandry of the period. King uses a Roman cookery book, and an imperial price edict, to account for the popularity of pig in late Roman Britain.[25] He concludes that cultural factors of the kind indicated by the documents 'were probably as, if not more, important than environmental constraints to the Romano-British farmer and must be evaluated as such in the interpretation of his refuse'. To complete this brief survey, we should note Lauwerier's use of both Roman and medieval treatises on animal husbandry (including both Walter of Henley and the anonymous *Hosebonderie*) to determine the breeding regime of pigs, and so to establish the season at which they were slaughtered.[26]

Secondly, since Payne's seminal studies in 1972,[27] there have been intensive, and often agonizing, discussions of the interrelated problems of the mode of occurrence of animal bones on ancient sites; of their disposal, and subsequent dispersal and attrition; of their

[22] L. R. Binford (1978); (1983), 144 ff.
[23] B. A. Noddle (1975), 257.
[24] J. Clutton-Brock (1976).
[25] A. King (1978), 225.
[26] R. C. G. M. Lauwerier (1983).
[27] S. Payne (1972a); (1972b).

recovery, especially by refined techniques of flotation and wet-sieving; of statistically-valid sampling of what are often very large quantities of bones; of the calculation of the numbers of animals originally present on the site; and of the relevance of all this information for the interpretation of the stock-raising economy. One such discussion, notable for its diachronic sweep, was Barker's study of animal (and also plant) remains from Classical and medieval sites in Italy.[28] One of his case studies, of Monte Ingino, a medieval garrison post above Gubbio, Perugia, is of particular interest in relation to Dinas Powys. The site was distinguished by a preponderance of young animals: and Barker speculates that these may represent 'selected high quality rations, or perhaps the result of poaching by the soldiery'.[29]

Other recent case studies include those by O'Connor of selected groups of bones from medieval sites in York, which has especially useful introductory and discussion passages;[30] and Hodgson's work on the medieval towns of Aberdeen, Elgin, and Perth, which shows a high awareness of relevant documentary evidence.[31] Of more general interest as an analysis of the possibilities and pitfalls in reconstructing the so-called subsistence economy from faunal assemblages, is a paper by J. Rackham.[32] His conclusion is 'that many of the analytical techniques currently being applied in osteoarchaeological studies are inadequate as a basis for the interpretive consideration of man's husbandry practices, the establishment of the structure of the death assemblage, and the behaviour which generated it ...'

These discussions must leave us feeling very pessimistic about the value of the animal bones from Dinas Powys as evidence for stock-raising in early medieval Wales. For a start, the excavations predate the widespread use of wet-sieving and flotation techniques. Moreover, only about one third of the bones which had been recovered by the crude techniques of the time was then retained: and what was discarded could have provided much evidence for butchery, cooking, and meat-eating habits in general.

There may be a lesson in academic humility to be read here. The selection of bones for retention at Dinas Powys was carried out in accordance with the best advice available at the time, in order to answer the kind of questions about numbers, stature, and age of slaughter, which were then thought relevant. Unfortunately, the theories and presuppositions which guide and illuminate our approaches to the evidence, and the specific questions to which we seek answers, may also blinker us to other approaches, and to other equally important questions which we should be asking.

The third topic to be explored here is the ageing of skeletal material: the establishment of the pattern of ages of death across an animal population, with all its implications for stock-raising practices and agricultural economy. In recent years there has been much discussion of the problems of estimating the killing-age from tooth eruption or wear, or from epiphyseal fusion. To the archaeologist who is not also an archaeozoologist, the conclusions drawn from such discussions must often seem discouraging. For instance, Watson has stated that the method based on fusion of the epiphyses of the long bones contains 'a serious flaw in its logic'.[33] Workshops organized in 1978 and 1979 by the

[28] G. Barker (1978).
[29] Ibid., 44.
[30] T. P. O'Connor (1984).
[31] G. W. I. Hodgson (1983).
[32] J. Rackham (1983).
[33] J. P. N. Watson (1978).

Oxfordshire Archaeological Unit, with the aim of improving the methodology of ageing and sexing bones from archaeological sites, revealed many of the outstanding problems. In the volume which resulted from these workshops[34] and elsewhere,[35] Grant had demonstrated the value of tooth wear among domestic ungulates for revealing relative age at slaughter. She has also emphasized that the ages for epiphyseal fusion, and tooth eruption and wear, that have been derived from modern domesticates are not absolutely applicable to ancient animals, especially because modern animals are bred for early maturity. Significantly, Bourdillon and Coy use the expression 'modern equivalent' when attempting to put an age in months or years on fusion, eruption and wear stages.[36] It may well be that the Dinas Powys animals—and indeed those from other archaeological sites—were in fact rather older than the ages quoted in Table 1, and the accompanying histograms, above.

Despite this, it is of course perfectly reasonable to compare the age-of-slaughter patterns from Dinas Powys with those from other early medieval sites. Particularly interesting are the figures from Pictish, pre-Norse levels at Brough of Birsay,[37] though it should be stressed that the total number of animals is too small to carry great significance. In Phase 1, 80 per cent of the cattle were older than those at Dinas Powys, and in Phase 2 the figure is still 50 per cent for cattle over $3\frac{1}{2}$ years at death. It is suggested that these had been used for breeding, milk, and as draught animals. Overlapping the Dinas Powys age range, 17 per cent were killed between $1\frac{1}{2}$ and $3\frac{1}{2}$ years in Phase 1, and 50 per cent in Phase 2; these had been killed for their meat. At Dinas Powys, no sheep were over 2 years old: at Birsay, 85 per cent were over that age in Phase 1, and 80 per cent in Phase 2. Finally, 56 per cent of the Birsay pigs were over 2 years old, while the remaining 44 per cent were less than 1 year old.

Looking at the Birsay figures, and those from broadly contemporary Saxon sites, it becomes apparent that there is no significant discrepancy between the age of slaughter of pigs at Dinas Powys and elsewhere. Among cattle, there is normally some overlap, but on some sites, there are also many beasts over 3 years old, the maximum age of the Dinas Powys animals. At Saxon Hamwih, for instance, about 45 per cent had been killed before they were 3.[38] At Ramsbury (Middle Saxon) there was a killing peak between 6 and 18 months, but the second peak was of mature animals, 3–4 years or older.[39] Saxon Porchester shows a peak around 2, but thereafter the cattle are 4 years or older.[40] In tenth-century levels at Skeldergate, York, the slaughtered cattle were principally between 18 months and 4–5 years of age, a few younger, a few older:[41] again this overlaps on the Dinas Powys figures.

It is in the case of sheep that the differences become most marked. At Hamwih, it is true, about 38 per cent were slaughtered under the age of 2 years, and in Saxon Porchester, some were killed between 1 and $2\frac{1}{2}$ years. But at Porchester, the majority were between 2–$2\frac{1}{2}$ and 6–7 years old at death; at Ramsbury there was a killing-peak for sheep that were

[34] B. Wilson, C. Grigson and S. Payne (1982), 91–108.
[35] A. Grant (1975), 393–9; 437–50.
[36] J. Bourdillon and J. Coy (1980), Figs. 17.2, 17.4.
[37] T. J. Seller (1982).
[38] J. Bourdillon and J. Coy (1980).
[39] J. Coy (1980).
[40] A. Grant (1976).
[41] T. P. O'Connor (1984), 16–19.

2 years or older; and at Skeldergate, most of the sheep were between 2 and 3 years old. At Dinas Powys, by contrast, it appears that all the sheep had been butchered by the time they were around 2 years old.

Recently, a further set of highly relevant figures has been published from Ireland.[42] At the sites of Moynagh (*c.* AD 800), Knowth II (tenth–twelfth centuries) and Marshes Upper III (eleventh–twelfth centuries), 63 per cent, 53 per cent and 56 per cent of cattle were slaughtered before the age of 2, predominantly in their second year. There is also some evidence, from sexual dimorphism in the bones from Moynagh, and from the royal crannog of Lagore, that the mature animals were predominantly female. This overall age is regarded as characteristic of a dairying economy, in which the production of calves is necessary to initiate lactation; most of the male calves are then slaughtered for meat in their second year, leaving a very few bulls for breeding, rather more steers for draught purposes, and a large number of females for breeding and milk production. This is reflected in a seventh–eighth century law tract, *Crith Gablach*, which quotes the minimum cattle stock of a freeman farmer as comprising 20 cows, 2 bulls and 6 oxen. There is abundant written evidence for the importance of dairy-farming and the consumption of butter and a variety of cheeses in early medieval Ireland, and the available animal bone evidence is thoroughly consistent with this. It should be added that McCormick's paper is an excellent instance of the correlation of historical evidence with that from zoo-archaeology, in order to produce a convincing synoptic account of the farming economy.

To summarize the discussion so far: despite all the problems of ageing animal bones, and especially the need to use modern equivalents as a basis for estimating the absolute killing-age, it is evident that there is a useful measure of agreement between the several methods for establishing relative ages. In any case, it is not suggested that the differences between modern equivalent and actual ages are very great. We can, therefore, validly compare the age-of-slaughter patterns at Dinas Powys with these on other, broadly contemporary sites. It is immediately apparent that the total population of cattle, sheep and pigs at our site had been killed much younger than elsewhere; and that when sites exhibit two peak ages for slaughter, the Dinas Powys figure coincides with the younger of the two, and provides no match at all for the older peak.

On other sites, it is generally considered that the young animals had been killed for meat, whereas the older ones had been retained for breeding, milk, traction, wool and other non-flesh producing purposes. Applying this interpretation to Dinas Powys, the conclusion would be that we are seeing nothing of the breeding stock, except possibly in the case of pig; nothing of the dairy stock, whether of cattle or sheep; and little if anything of the animals which might have produced wool or hides. At the simplest level, the bones from Dinas Powys represent only that element in the overall stock which had been killed for meat.

In the past, I have always resisted this simple explanation by means of a two-pronged argument: (1) the site is a princely one; and (2) the Welsh Laws emphasize the maturity of the animals that had to be delivered to the prince in food gifts. The first of these arguments still stands, but the second must be open to further discussion. Jones's claim that the bondmen were to present the king with young animals, with the implication that only young animals were involved, has been disposed of already (p. 73). A resolution of the problem may, perhaps, be found on the following lines. While the Laws of Hywel Dda, as

---

[42] F. McCormick (1983).

we find them in documents of the late-twelfth and early-thirteenth centuries, certainly have elements which go back to the fifth and sixth centuries; and while the custom of food renders is certainly a primitive one, and may well be one of the early elements in the Laws; this is not to say that the food renders remained unchanged in every detail over some seven centuries. If the texts of the Laws provide irrefutable evidence that mature animals were preferred as royal food-gifts in the central middle ages, then the animal bones from Dinas Powys 4 provide equally irrefutable evidence that in the early medieval period sub-adult animals predominated on the prince's table. This appears quite consistent with the earlier killing peak at other, contemporary sites of varied social status. Our conclusion may be that the written texts of the Laws reflect a definite change in royal tastes, or in the character of stock-raising, between the occupation of Dinas Powys 4 and the writing down of the Laws.

IV

Part III had been written before Roberta Gilchrist's analysis of the remainder of the Dinas Powys animal bones had been completed. It will become apparent that her work now necessitates modifications to some of the comments of Part III; but it has been allowed to stand, essentially as a bridge between my position as set out in 1963 (and elaborated at Lancaster in 1974), and the interpretations which seem most reasonable now that the total collection of bones from Dinas Powys 4 has been studied.

To contrast first the material that was recorded in *Dinas Powys* (1963) and that which has now been analysed: Cornwall examined a total of 1,677 bones, Gilchrist 5,576, more than three times as many.[43] The first sample formed a stratigraphically compact group derived from the northern middens, Cuts VI and VI W. The second came from all the other bone-yielding contexts on the site: rock-cut features in the interior, layers stratified beneath Bank I (especially at the north-east corner), and material which had been thrown on to the back of Bank I in Phase 5, but which, it has been argued (above, p. 12), had originally been derived from contexts of Phase 4. In other words, whereas the first sample had been in some sense functionally determined (that is, as a deliberate refuse deposit), the second, as it was recovered during the excavations, represents totally haphazard dispersal and survival. It is not now possible to get back behind this haphazard mode of deposition to establish the original causes of the occurrence and dispersal of animal bones at Dinas Powys. To that extent, our interpretation of the bones in relation to the function of Dinas Powys, and to the activities of its inhabitants in the fifth to eighth centuries AD, is inevitably defective.

Before Gilchrist's results are considered in detail, it is worth re-examining the problems which arise from the theory and methodology of our collecting policy in 1954–8: problems which have led to various critical comments.[44] If these criticisms are wholly valid, then Gilchrist's analysis, no less than Cornwall's, will have been pointless. In fact, she has been able to calculate the relative frequencies of the various species, and the age of slaughter; and, with less certainty, to estimate stature and sex. Of the various questions which are nowadays asked of bone collections, only one remains largely unanswerable

[43] Further comparisons are developed below, pp. 81–2.

[44] The most searching of these are by C. Gamble (1978). Such criticisms well demonstrate the development of archaeozoology over a span of some 20 years, and in particular, they illustrate the revolutionary increase in the available resources for faunal studies.

from the Dinas Powys material, namely the methods of butchery. This limitation is directly related to Cornwall's original comment that the bones are strikingly from the less edible parts of carcasses. Gilchrist likewise shows that the bones which she studied are mainly those with low to medium meat value.

This may mean that there is a serious under-representation of already butchered meat, brought to Dinas Powys in the form of joints. But there is also a positive side to this. Whether or not butchered joints were brought to the site, the presence of inedible parts of carcasses and especially the large number of bones from the extremities, demonstrate that whole animals had been present within the enclosure. Most probably they came to Dinas Powys on the hoof, and quite certainly they were butchered there. This is absolutely consistent with the food renders of the Welsh Laws, which refer not to joints of meat—with the exception of sides of bacon—but to carcasses or to animals as such.

The fact that jaws were among the bones that had been retained made it possible for Gilchrist to calculate the minimum number of individuals among the various domestic animals on the basis of a count of mandibles. For Phase 4, the figures for the three leading types are: cattle 49, sheep 28 and pig 70. These numbers, of course, give only a doubtful indication of the actual populations involved. They may be expressed as percentages of the domestic stock: cattle 33 per cent, sheep 19 per cent, pig 48 per cent. One conclusion is clear: whatever the living animals might have furnished in the way of milk, offspring, wool, and traction, and whatever the carcass might have yielded as skin, horn, bone and gut, if we assume that the main purpose of the animals at Dinas Powys was as meat, it follows that beef was more important than pork, and mutton was of minor importance. A major factor in this estimate is, of course, that cattle have several times the meat-weight of pigs.

Turning now to the individual species: epiphyseal fusion indicates that most of the cattle were fully adult when they were killed. In more detail, tooth eruption and wear show that about 20 per cent had been killed under 18 months. Of these, 15.5 per cent were between 9 and 18 months old, corresponding on a minor scale to one of the peaks in dairy farming, when newly weaned males are killed off. Some 70 per cent of the cattle were more than 3 years old at death, and of these, 40 per cent were over 4 years old. On the whole, this pattern appears to represent mature animals brought in for their meat as a food render, and for their hides as well.

As for the sex of the cattle, only one horn core has the oval flattened shape characteristic of bulls. The slenderness index of metacarpals shows that 3 out of 14 come from mature males, but these may represent oxen as well as bulls. In size, the cattle are similar to those from contemporary sites in Ireland.

Among the sheep, the evidence from the mandibles and from epiphyseal fusion shows that a few were slaughtered between 6 and 12 months; but at least 80 per cent were more than 2 years old, and indeed 50 per cent of all sheep were more than 3 years old. This may suggest that they had been kept for wool, and also for milk; but it also recalls one of the summer food-gifts of the Welsh Laws: 'a fat wether three years old'. The length:breadth ratio of 9 metacarpals indicates 1 ram, 3 wethers and 5 ewes. In size, the sheep were small to medium, comparable to those from pre-Roman Iron Age sites.

A few pigs survived to maturity at $3\frac{1}{2}$ years or more: these would correspond to the food-gift of 'a sow of three winters three fingers thick' (in her hams). But the majority were immature, many under 6 months old, and 60 per cent less than one year. This demonstrates the intensive breeding of pigs, perhaps, as Gilchrist suggests, for curing, maybe even for export. It is notable, however, that while Gilchrist's figures cannot readily be compared with Cornwall's (Table 1, p. 68) they show a much greater emphasis on the slaughter of juveniles. This is a point to which we must return.

Of other animals, Gilchrist reports that the birds were predominantly domestic fowl, but with about 10 per cent being domestic ducks. Particular interest attaches to the cervical vertebra of a roe deer which had been sawn into quarters. This indicates the presence of a deer carcass on the site, and therefore implies hunting, and not merely the collection of shed antlers for making pins, combs, and knife-handles.

This summary of Gilchrist's results reveals how the fuller study of the Dinas Powys bones has extended and enriched our knowledge of the animal husbandry of the site in Phase 4. Above all, the newly available age-of-slaughter estimates for cattle and sheep make it clear that the stock could readily have been maintained; and also make it possible to accommodate the osteological evidence to the documentary evidence for the food renders to Welsh princes. As a corollary, the validity of Cornwall's age-of-death estimates must, once again, be questioned. Gilchrist raises the possibility that the northern midden represents waste from a restricted area of the site where young animals were slaughtered and butchered. In other words, the midden may represent not a deposit characteristic of the site as a whole, but a highly specialized one.

Before this conclusion is examined further it is necessary to recapitulate why the material from Cuts VI and VI W had been considered representative or characteristic of the site as a whole. Not surprisingly for the late 1950s this view was not based on a statistical analysis of the locations of all finds from Dinas Powys, but on a subjective judgement built up during five years of excavation, that the finds from the northern midden were indeed characteristic of Phase 4. The evidence for such a statistical analysis is not currently accessible to me, but it would indeed be available in the site records and the finds themselves in the National Museum of Wales, Cardiff. None the less, on the basis of the stratigraphical information in *Dinas Powys* (1963), Part II, it is possible to say that the midden yielded a considerable quantity of Class B pottery, a little Class E, and less Class A. There were also sherds of glass, rubbing-stones, an iron knife, and a lignite pinhead, among other objects less certainly attributable to Phase 4. Given such artefacts in the midden, it was not unreasonable to believe that the animal bones were likewise representative of Phase 4 activity.

Gilchrist's work now makes it possible to test this belief not merely in terms of age-of-slaughter patterns, but through the relative frequencies of the three major domestic species. Given the form of Cornwall's analysis, it is not possible to compare the minimum number of animals in the two samples, but since Gilchrist also gives figures for the number of identified fragments, a straight comparison is possible. Expressed as percentages the figures are:

	Cornwall	Gilchrist
CATTLE	21.35%	50.67%
SHEEP	14.06%	24.43%
PIG	64.37%	24.76%

This massive difference between the two samples, especially in relation to pig and cattle, demonstrates that the northern midden derives from an area specializing in pig-butchery. In other words, it is not characteristic of the site as a whole. It is therefore possible to accept that it also reflects some specialization in the slaughter of young animals, cattle and sheep as well as pig.

One wider issues deserves comment here. Given the small area of Dinas Powys 4, the animal bones display a remarkable degree of intra-site variability. It may be that this variability would be even more strongly marked if the bones which Gilchrist examined had been analysed by horizontal distribution. However that may be, we cannot extrapolate from these figures into the unexcavated areas of the site.

For the present, however, it might be possible to obtain a more rounded picture of the animal husbandry of Dinas Powys by adding together the analyses of Cornwall and of Gilchrist. Unfortunately this can only be done on the basis of numbers of fragments, which may have unquantifiable biases in favour of cattle, or indeed of pig.[45] For what they are worth, the summed figures are: cattle 42 per cent, sheep 21 per cent, pig 35 per cent. This reduction in the percentage of pig, and the corresponding increase for cattle, brings the relative frequencies closer to those from contemporary Irish sites.[46] But since the latter have been calculated on the basis of minimum numbers of animals, they should not be compared too finely with the Dinas Powys figures. None the less, the overall picture which now emerges is that the animal husbandry of Dinas Powys 4 is closer to that of other contemporary sites than had at first seemed to be the case. By the same token, it is less at variance with the documentary evidence, whether for the food renders of the Welsh Laws, or the farming practices outlined in the medieval manuals of husbandry. Finally, in its finer detail, (such as the absence of a strong peak for the slaughter of young male cattle), it is consistent with the interpretation of Dinas Powys 4 as a princely stronghold receiving tribute in the form of food renders, rather than as the centre of a working farm.

[45] R. E. Chaplin (1971, 65) has argued that the large bones of cattle may be chopped into a number of pieces, all identifiable. On the other hand, S. Payne (1972b, 68) notes that a pig has 48 phalanges against a cow's 24, a matter of some importance given the bone-collecting policy of Dinas Powys. In the circumstances, M. Maltby's figures (1979, 6), for bias in favour of cattle may not apply.

[46] For recent figures, see Table 1 in F. McCormick (1983).

CHAPTER 4

New Perspectives on Dinas Powys 4

Looking back, after more than twenty years, at my original discussion of the social and economic aspects of Dinas Powys 4, I find that much of it still seems largely valid today. This is especially true in the areas of the basic farming economy, diet, and the technology and organization of craftsmanship. Much of this was laid under tribute for Glanville Jones's major survey of the agrarian economy of post-Roman Wales.[1] As we have seen, both the analysis and the interpretation of the animal bones from the site have demanded further discussion (above pp. 67f.). Moreover, in terms of the actual techniques of excavation, and the consequent recovery of both artefactual and environmental information, it cannot be stressed too strongly that the excavation took place before the introduction of the flotation and sieving techniques which are now customary. This is relevant especially to small animal and fish bones, insects, and small but significant artefacts such as glass beads. In the light of the recent work on the significance of pollen analysis for determining the arable element in the farming economy[2] it must be said that this was not considered at Dinas Powys, on the grounds that a limestone site was unlikely to yield usable quantities of pollen.

One recent investigative technique was hinted at, but not extensively developed: that of site catchment analysis. Thus it was suggested that 'the numbers of pig . . . would imply the existence of widespread forest in the vicinity . . .' and the small numbers of sheep were held to suggest that 'the range of the Dinas Powys stock-raisers did not extend to the open moors, less than 10 miles to the north' (p. 34 above). Likewise, analysis of iron ores made it possible to identify haematites from the Carboniferous Limestone, which might have been found within 2 miles of the site (p. 41 above). From a contemporary perspective, it might be thought that such hints should have been followed up intensively, and the results demonstrated on maps illustrating the availability of those natural resources which demonstrably were utilized in Dinas Powys 4. Such analyses are, admittedly, invaluable in interpreting the economies of hunter-gatherers and primitive agriculturalists; but it may be questioned whether they are relevant to more developed social units, which might acquire resources by trade or other forms of exchange, and above all, by tribute. It cannot be doubted that this applies to developed Celtic societies, such as those of post-Roman Wales. At a site which appears, purely on archaeological grounds, to be high in the social hierarchy, it would be inappropriate to formulate interpretations on the basis of mapping locally-available resources. This is true at the level of general social theory; but at our site it is confirmed empirically by the recovery of pottery from Mediterranean and Gaulish sources, as well as scrap glass and metal from Teutonic or Anglo-Saxon sources, which could not be encompassed within the methods of site catchment analysis.

[1] G. R. J. Jones (1972), 291–2.
[2] D. J. Maguire (1983).

A major area in which new information has led to new interpretations is that of sites comparable with Dinas Powys 4: fortifications built, or at least used, in Celtic Britain in the period 400–800. Even in confining the evidence and discussions to Wales and Dumnonia, and ignoring the forts of the Picts and Scots, this is a very large topic. It is therefore treated separately in Part 3, where some of the supporting evidence is deployed.

Apart from this empirically derived revision, a major theoretical attack has been mounted recently on my use of historical, documentary evidence as a basis for the social and economic interpretation of Dinas Powys 4. The strongest statement of my own position is to be found, not in *Dinas Powys* itself, but in a paper to the Second International Congress of Celtic Studies (Cardiff, July 1963), where I wrote:

> Archaeological evidence may enable us to make inferences about social, military and economic aspects of the fifth to seventh centuries AD; but its interpretation requires the assistance of a variety of literary sources.[3]

One line of attack is mounted from a position of archaeological purism: the belief that, even in a historical period, archaeological evidence must be interpreted wholly within its own terms, without reference to written evidence. It is difficult to take this position seriously: first because, in a period when the evidence is so scattered and fragmentary, it is essential that we should exploit every available fragment if we are to understand human activities. Secondly, and no less important, written sources were generated within the societies whose archaeology we are studying, and constitute an inseparable element in their culture.

The second line of attack is far more serious. Its epistemological basis is the reductionism of some present-day historians of early medieval Britain, who lay overwhelming emphasis on two points: that no document may be quoted, even by a historian, let alone an archaeologist, until it has been edited to modern standards; and that even when this has been done, a document of, say, the thirteenth century is evidence for that century alone, and for no other period.[4] Despite the cautionary note with which I originally prefaced my use of documentary evidence as an aid to archaeological interpretation (above, p. 31), the rigorous application of these narrow standards would implicitly invalidate such a use.

The most emphatic criticism has been that of Burrow in his survey of the use of hill-forts in Roman and post-Roman Somerset. In discussing what he calls the *llys*-model for post-Roman hill-forts, which is derived ultimately from Dinas Powys, he shows, on valid archaeological grounds, that it has only a limited value for wider archaeological generalizations. He then continues: 'a more basic criticism recently argued by Dumville (1977), relates to the documentary material upon which Alcock's model depends'.[5] In general, these comments are symptomatic of the way in which Dumville's 1977 paper has deflected archaeologists from an open-minded approach to written sources. In the particular context of Dinas Powys, they are inappropriate, for two reasons. First, Dumville's paper is concerned solely with the political history of fifth- and sixth-century Britain; it does not concern itself with social and economic matters, or with the kinds of documents which are involved. Secondly, what Burrow has called Alcock's *llys* and *neuadd* model, as

---

[3] L. Alcock (1965b), 5–6.
[4] For examples of this reductionism, D. N. Dumville (1977b); W. Davies (1983). Davies implicitly dismisses a century of Welsh scholarship.
[5] I. C. G. Burrow (1981a), 10–11.

set out on p. 50 above, would have been inferred from the archaeological observations even if they had come from an anahistoric context. The terms *llys* and *neuadd* would not, of course, have been used: instead, one might have written of 'a redistributive centre of a chieftain'.

On the other hand, in an anahistoric context, we would lack all the other insights which literary sources may furnish: insights which are by no means contained within the terms *llys* and *neuadd*. It must be admitted at once that none of the documents cited in *Dinas Powys* exists in a manuscript contemporary with Dinas Powys 4; and many of them do not even represent an oral tradition of that period. It is therefore necessary to discuss each class in turn, in order to assess their possible relevance.

At the greatest remove in time from Dinas Powys 4 are the thirteenth-century manuals of husbandry, and the slightly earlier writings of Giraldus Cambrensis (Gerald de Barri). In the 1960s, it would have been unthinkable not to quote Gerald as evidence for early Welsh diet, farming practice, and other customs. My own purpose was to show that any phrase of his which has been used to support the traditional view of early Welsh pastoralism can be opposed by another, from the same pen, but in a contrary sense. Even today, any discussion of the development of economic historiography in Wales, up to the revolution initiated by Glanville Jones, would need to quote Giraldus in just this way.

Altogether more innovatory and more questionable was my use of manuals of husbandry which were remote not only in time but also in place, and therefore, probably, in farming practice as well. Despite this remoteness, it seemed to me instructive to know what a farmer's expectations might be in relation to stock-breeding, or the production of milk and butter, provided of course, that the source was prior to the post-medieval agricultural revolution. Certainly such information could not be derived from the only hard evidence that was available, namely the bones themselves. In broad terms, I do not think that this idea is seriously weakened by Noddle's demonstration of secular genetic changes in cattle and sheep from Neolithic, Roman and medieval sites.[6] Moreover, it is heartening to see an archaeozoologist quoting both Walter of Henley and the anonymous husbandry as a useful source of information about the breeding and slaughtering of pigs in early times.[7] We cannot escape the conclusion that the thirteenth-century manuals are among the relevant sources of information to be used in interpreting the farming economy of Dinas Powys 4. If there is a clear weakness, it is my failure to use Roman sources as well.

A far more serious problem is presented by my anachronistic use of the Welsh law tracts. Davies has recently reviewed the evidential value of the Laws within the framework of a historical synthesis.[8] She emphasizes their character as 'a late mediaeval corpus of law'—by which she means early thirteenth century—'whose origins are supposed to lie in the distant past'. She admits that there are passages which 'are very difficult to explain in anything other than a pre-twelfth century context'. In this, she echoes the view of Jones Pierce:[9]

> the accent still rests so heavily on the obsolete and primitive as to give the texts in question greater value for retro-active interpretation of pre-Norman customs and institutions than for understanding how the law was being recast ... between 1180 and 1280.

[6] B. A. Noddle (1983), 218–19.
[7] R. C. G. M. Lauwerier (1983).
[8] W. Davies (1982), 203–5.
[9] T. J. Pierce (1963), 48.

Despite this, Davies considers that:

> at present, there is no easily available method of disentangling the later from the earlier, and this
> means that the law texts as such are not useful for the pre-Conquest period.

In adopting this minimalist stance, Davies ignores, or implicitly rejects, the work of other historians. As long ago as 1926, Jolliffe pointed to parallels between the Welsh Laws, and a twelfth-century custumal of the lands of the bishop of Durham, and went on to argue that these parallels are evidence for a stratum in the laws which must predate the Anglian settlement of Bernicia.[10] Jolliffe's arguments were subsequently amplified by Rees; and the whole case has recently been reaffirmed, with some modification of the details, by Kapelle.[11] So far as I am aware, this case has never been refuted in a scholarly argument; and until it has been so refuted, it clearly must stand.

The dues common to the Welsh laws and to the Durham custumal, which may thus be placed as far back as the sixth century, refer to the erection of certain buildings on behalf of the king or bishop by bondmen: *villani regis* in the Latin texts of the Laws. With minor variations between the various redactions of the Laws, nine buildings are specified, including a hall, a private chamber, a kitchen, a stable, a dog-kennel, a granary and a privy. From this list, we can begin to create a picture of a royal court, which is fuller than any derived at present from archaeological evidence.

In both Latin and Welsh texts of the Laws, the clause about the nine buildings is immediately adjacent to one specifying the responsibilities of the bondmen in relation to the king's military expeditions. While proximity is no proof of contemporaneity, it is not unreasonable to believe that this also belongs to an archaic stratum in the Laws, and it is therefore considered further in Part 3 in a discussion of the organization of military activities. Other clauses reveal that the bondmen were settled in nucleated villages, under the supervision of a royal official known as a *maer*, and that these bond settlements were visited by the king and his bodyguard on regular circuits. There is no direct proof that this clause likewise belongs to an early stratum; but this may be inferred from the distribution pattern of *maerdref* place-names, which argues that the institution goes back before the intrusion of normanizing influences. Finally, it needs no arguing that the system of food renders and royal circuits has primitive roots. While it would be impossible to prove the antiquity of any specific item, it cannot be doubted that the Welsh Laws encapsulate a picture of the organization which supported early Welsh kingship from the time of its emergence in the early post-Roman centuries.

I turn now, with considerably more reserve, to the value of creative works, whether in verse or prose, as aids to archaeological interpretation. In the 1960s it was accepted widely, though no doubt uncritically, that the *Gododdin* poem was a useful guide to the dress, equipment and methods of warfare of British warriors in the sixth century. But the poem's emphasis on gold collars, which had vanished from the archaeological record long before that date, caused me to point out the possibility of anachronistic elements in oral poetry (*Dinas Powys*, p. 52; reprinted above, p. 48). This theme is further developed in Part 4 (p. 248) in a discussion of discrepancies between the poetic and archaeological evidence for the culture of the 'Men of the North'. My conclusion is that there is considerable anachronism in the *Gododdin*; and the same comment must be levelled at other supposed poetic sources for the period. In defence of my use of *Culhwch and Olwen*, I would

[10] J. E. A. Jolliffe (1926).
[11] W. Rees (1963); W. E. Kapelle (1979)

say only that the best opinion available to me was that it went back, in part at least, to the middle of the tenth century.[12] More recent opinion would still suggest that it predates the influence of French and Anglo-Norman literature in Wales.[13] Beyond this, it has been claimed that *Culhwch and Olwen* drew on learned traditions of considerable antiquity.[14] This does not imply that the tale takes us back precisely to the fifth or sixth century; but it is a useful reminder that we are dealing with a society in which neither material nor intellectual culture were changing at a rate comparable to that of the later twentieth century.

There is an important general issue here in regard to the relationships between archaeological evidence and written evidence. *Culhwch and Olwen* contains a list of 'the ceremonial possessions of a traditional ruler—sword, knife, whetstone, drinking-horn, cauldron, draughtboard, mantle ...'.[15] There is an obvious challenge to the archaeologist to fit material artefacts to the list; and the scholar of literature can hardly remain indifferent to such an endeavour. Indeed, Gillies, in discussing the role of the craftsman in early Celtic literature, specifically seeks the collaboration of archaeologists in furthering his understanding of the texts.[16] Moreover, Davies, writing as a Celtic historian, wants the archaeologist to answer questions about the environment; about the economy, in terms of subsistence, surplus and exchange; and about settlement forms.[17] In expecting satisfactory answers from the archaeologist, she shows no awareness that, just as answers about the environment come from the collaboration between archaeologists and environmental scientists, so those about the economy and about settlements depend on the collaboration and cross-fertilization of archaeologists and historians.

A case in point here is the nucleated bond settlement, the *maerdref*. The Welsh Laws indicate the existence of such a unit. The *maerdref* place-names indicate broadly where the fieldworker might look for them. When several have been found and excavated, the archaeologist will be able to provide a statement about their physical appearance and material character. But it will then be necessary to return to the law tracts to discover how the *maerdref* functioned within the economy and society of the time.

To round off this discussion of the use of written sources in archaeological interpretation, and to place it on an altogether wider plane than that of the specific case of Dinas Powys, two points may be made. The first concerns the interdict of the reductionist historian, that no documentary sources should be used until a definitive edition is available, and has been worked up into an acceptable historical synthesis. Archaeologists should consider, in the light of their own experience of the discipline of scholarship, whether the concept of a definitive, once for all, piece of research or reportage is a realistic one; or whether it is at once unrealistic and intellectually arrogant, on the grounds that all scholarship is interim and contingent. They should then consider the state of their own data base: incomplete publication of inadequate excavations carried out patchily on a few of the sites which have survived from ancient times. They might then ask themselves whether this is any basis for generalization or synthesis.

[12] G. Jones and T. Jones (1949), ix.
[13] T. M. Charles-Edwards (1970), 288.
[14] D. Edel (1983).
[15] D. Edel (1983), 265.
[16] W. Gillies (1981).
[17] W. Davies (1983), 70–1.

What they can be sure of is that the data base available to the historian of early Celtic Britain is no worse than that of the archaeologist of the period.

Secondly, except in the simplest mode of descriptive cataloguing, archaeological material is not self-explanatory or self-interpreting, especially in terms of the social and economic functions which originally created it. So, the archaeologist must seek insights from observations of functioning societies. He may find these among non-Indo-Germanic societies, separated by thousands of miles, and frequently by major technological and economic stages, from the society whose archaeology he studies. If his field is early prehistory, he may be well content with such insights. But if his research is on the later Celtic archaeology of Britain, he may reflect that even formally anachronistic documents like the Welsh Laws were the products of societies which had their roots in the area and period which he studies, and which are separated by no change of population, language, technology or basic economy. He may then consider that, used with some comprehension of their limitations, such documents provide significant aids to the interpretation of his material. This belief inspired my original analysis of the social and economic aspects of Dinas Powys 4 (above pp. 31 ff.); and it has subsequently inspired the other interpretative papers which are gathered together in the following pages.

We may now turn to some necessary revisions of my 1963 synthesis. The first concerns the Mediterranean and Gaulish pottery from Dinas Powys: in particular, the intensity of its occurrence, and its possible implications for trade (compare p. 50 above).[18] The total number of such vessels recovered from the excavation is not high. The calculated minimum numbers are, for the Class A red-slipped dishes, nine vessels; for the Class B amphorae of various types, ten; for the Class D grey wares, nine, representing four different types of pot; and for the Class E table-wares, a further nine: a minimum figure of thirty-seven vessels in total. Towards the end of the five seasons of excavation, the excavators' impression was that it was as common to recover further sherds from vessels that had already been recognized as to discover new vessels. It seems likely that even the total excavation of the site and of its middens would not have increased the numbers by a factor as high as five.

Compared with the numbers of pots found on Roman sites, and especially on villa-excavations, this must seem a very meagre haul; and at first sight it casts doubt on the attribution of high social status to Dinas Powys. But the discrepancy between social status and quantity of prestige finds is even more acute at Cadbury-Camelot, a fort much larger and more intensively excavated than Dinas Powys, for this yielded only 3 Class A, and 15 Class B vessels, and a single Class D sherd. In my account of Cadbury (below p. 190), these numbers are compared with those derived from other contemporary sites, some of which are undoubtedly of royal or princely status. It then becomes apparent that social and architectural distinction may be associated in the archaeological record with a disproportionate ceramic poverty. A possible reason for this is that, the higher the social status, the greater the possibility that refuse would have been removed and that buildings would have been kept clean internally.

Turning now to the implications of the imported pottery, this has long been regarded as evidence for trade with the lands in which it originated: north Africa, the eastern Mediterranean, and western and northern France. On the other hand, some historians of the

---

[18] The generalizations of this section are based on the major survey by A. C. Thomas (1981), supplemented by evidence from my own excavations.

period have criticized the interpretation of exotic artefacts in terms of commercial trans-actions[19] and have emphasized rather the concept of gift-exchange, with its concomitants of reciprocal obligations and systems of alliances. It is true, of course, that rare and precious artefacts can be readily moved around—to use a carefully neutral term—by non-commercial methods. For instance, the Frankish metalwork recorded in Ireland could have been introduced by noble warriors in exile. In the discussion of Cadbury, I suggest that two Saxon jewels reached that site in the trinket boxes of Saxon brides (below p. 208). Beyond this, historical evidence plainly shows that kings and bishops, popes and emperors, made gifts one to another; but it may be questioned whether this was done with the formality of a Melanesian exchange system, or with the professed intention of creating reciprocal obligations. At the most basic level of analysis, it is not helpful to equate stone-based technologies and those of Iron Age Celtic Europe as 'simple technologies': to do so is to undervalue the complexities of both craft specialization and the search for raw materials in a metal-using society.

At a rather later date there is, of course, abundant evidence for aspects of trade among Germanic societies in England, Scandinavia and on the continent.[20] More immediately relevant to Dinas Powys are two well-known incidents from saints' lives. The first, related by Adomnan to illustrate Columba's gift of prophecy, concerns the 'Gallic sailors coming from the provinces of Gaul', whom Columba met at a *caput regionis*:[21] a provincial centre, perhaps even an emporium under royal control. The interpretation of this as a reference to the importation of the wine necessary for the celebration of the Mass at Iona[22] goes beyond the strict limits of the evidence, but may be nonetheless correct. There is no suggestion that this was a casual visit, or that the Gallic ship had been driven off course by a storm. Very different is the incident of the storm-driven Alexandrian ship which ex-changed a cargo of grain for one of tin, allegedly at some Dumnonian port. This account is so firmly embedded in an elaborate miracle story about St John the Almsgiver that it can only reflect a general memory of the tin-trade between Britain and the Mediterranean, not an actual trade link of the sixth and seventh centuries AD.[23]

Turning from these generalities to the pottery itself, two questions immediately arise: is it evidence for trade at all; and if so, how representative is it of actual ships' cargoes? It is helpful to begin with Class D, the *sigillée paléochrétienne grise* of French archaeologists. The relatively wide range of forms and ornament recovered at Dinas Powys makes it quite certain that this comes from the Bordeaux region. It has been recovered in minute quantities from British sites, and is curiously absent from Ireland. The minimum numbers of vessels are: Dinas Powys, nine; Tintagel, perhaps six; possibly two each from Mote of Mark and Congresbury; and one only from Dunadd and Cadbury. It would be ludicrous to argue for a trade in *sigillée grise* between Bordeaux and western Britain, and no less so to think of gift-exchange. Yet there plainly was some form of contact: a contact which, except for this pitiful handful of grey-ware vessels, was represented by items invisible to the archaeologist.

The most obvious suggestion for the northward movement is that it consisted of wine in wooden casks or barrels. It is worth pointing out that although pottery amphorae provide

---

[19] P. Grierson (1959).

[20] P. H. Sawyer (1977); R. Hodges (1982); R. Hodges and D. Whitehouse (1983).

[21] VC 30b, 31a.

[22] A. O. and M. O. Anderson (1961), 124.

[23] E. Dawes and N. H. Baynes (1948), 216–18.

the preponderant archaeological evidence for wine and its transport, they were, in fact, extremely inefficient. Whereas amphorae take up about 40 per cent of available cargo space, wooden casks may require as little as 10 per cent.[24] As a result, in the early medieval centuries casks gradually took over from amphorae for transport within the Mediterranean. They had, however, long been dominant in Gaul, thanks, it would seem, to superior Celtic craftsmanship in cooperage. Unfortunately for the archaeologist, they have a poor survival value, for even the binding hoops are likely to be of withies, not iron. As a result, it is only when casks were re-used as well-linings, and consequently were preserved by waterlogged conditions, or when they appear on Roman sculptures, that we recognize their importance in north-west Europe.[25] It is very likely, then, that the Class D sherds are the tangible relics of an otherwise invisible and hence unquantifiable trade in Bordeaux wine in cask; and it is probable that this is what the Gallic sailors whom Columba met were bringing.

In the case of the Class B amphorae we need not doubt that they brought wine (and perhaps oil as well) from various parts of the Mediterranean to the shores of western Britain and Ireland, whence they were distributed largely to princely residences. But did they form the main cargo, or even a substantial part of the cargo, of the ships which brought them? In examining these questions, a useful starting-point is provided by the seventh-century Byzantine wreck at Yassi Ada off the Turkish coast.[26] This had its cargo intact, and it demonstrates that the cargo itself consisted of some 850 to 900 amphorae, which could be classified into no more than two regular forms; only in the galley area of the ship was there a wider range of pottery vessels.[27] This is exactly what we might expect of highly organized commerce: the standardized use of mass-produced containers, with a very high ratio of vessels to vessel-forms. But if this is the ratio at source, on a cargo-ship, it is very far from being the pattern at the consumers' end, at least so far as insular sites are concerned.

I have attempted to demonstrate this contrast between the cargo ratio and the site or consumer ratio by means of the histograms in Fig. 4.1. So far as the evidence at the consumers' end is concerned, I have taken the examples of three sites where the pottery is readily available to me: Cadbury-Camelot, Dinas Powys, and Dumbarton Castle Rock (Alt Clut). The minimum number of amphorae of Classes Bi and Bii has then been set against the minimum number of different amphorae forms. For Yassi Ada, I have plotted the massed figure for amphorae of Types 1 and 2, because the published report does not give the separate total for each.[28] As the histograms show, the cargo contains two standard types of amphora; there is also a clear tendency to standardization in Class Bi (though the histogram masks minor variations); but in the case of the Bii amphorae, 18 variants are present among only 25 vessels. Plainly this does not reflect the use of standardized containers.

It would seem, then, that the Class Bii ratio is not compatible with the entry into Britain of a number of cargoes each of which had comprised several hundred amphorae of

[24] R. W. Unger (1980), 52; F. C. Lane (1974), 278–9.
[25] G. C. Boon (1975); D. Ellmers (1978), Figs. 12, 15 and 16.
[26] G. F. Bass and F. H. van Doorninck (1982).
[27] G. F. Bass (1982).
[28] G. Bass (1982), 155–60. It should be noticed that, given complete vessels, minor differences can be seen within each type; but they are not of an order which could be detected among the kind of sherds on which the British figures are based.

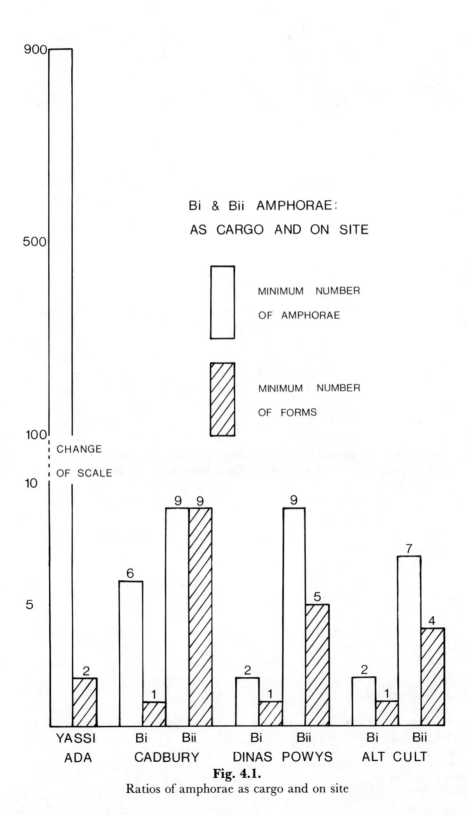

Fig. 4.1.

Ratios of amphorae as cargo and on site

a standardized form. From this it may be concluded that cargoes comparable with that in the Yassi Ada wreck were not reaching these islands; and a further inference would be that Mediterranean amphorae had probably formed only part of the goods in any one-ship-load. We have neither historical nor archaeological evidence as to the remainder of the cargo; but we should at least admit that it would be very unwise to take the story of St John the Almsgiver as evidence that the main cargo was of grain.

A further point is relevant in relation to the mixed cargoes which we must now envisage. Given the very different navigational conditions in Mediterranean and Atlantic waters, and the related differences between ships in the two areas,[29] it is very unlikely that pottery of Classes A and B was ever brought to Britain or Ireland in a vessel which had sailed from north Africa or the eastern Mediterranean. Despite the lack of archaeological evidence, for instance along the Narbonne–Bordeaux route, or the Rhône valley,[30] it seems probable that the amphorae would have been transhipped between the Mediterranean and the Atlantic. If this was so, it would have provided an obvious opportunity for the wine-jars to become mixed with other goods.[31]

Another topic which requires considerable revision in the light of more recent scholarship is that of the supposed Roman influences on the foundation of the early Welsh dynasties, especially those of Gwynedd and Dyfed, which I emphasized in 1963 (above, pp. 64–5). It will be appreciated that this was written before the development of the modern school of historical criticism, represented for instance by Dumville (especially 1977), Hughes (1980), and above all by Miller (1976a, 1978a, 1978b). At that time, appraisals of the dynastic genealogies were still quite naïve: for instance, the simple calculation of 33 years to a generation, such as had been used by Meyer[32] to establish the date of the settlement of the Dési in Dyfed, was still generally accepted. Against this, I argued that the 'genealogy' of a dynasty is as likely to be a king-list as a record of genetic relationships, so that the length of reigns is more relevant than that of biological generations; and that among Dark Age rulers, reigns were likely to be short and to end in violence if not in battle. I then drew attention to a well-documented series of obits for a succession of rulers: between AD 955 and 1154, England had fourteen rulers, even omitting Swegn Forkbeard and Edgar Etheling.[33] This modest contribution to a reappraisal of the chronology of genealogies has now been completely overtaken by the critical studies of Miller and others.

For Gwynedd, Miller stresses two very particular statements in the tradition: first, that the dynasty was founded by the *atavus*, or great-great-great grandfather of Maelgwn Gwynedd; and secondly, that the migration from Manau Guotodin, around the upper Forth estuary, to Gwynedd took place 146 years before Maelgwn was reigning.[34] Part of that reign is fixed to the years 545 × 549 by Gildas's attack on Maelgwn.[35] On this basis, the dynasty appears to have been founded not by Cunedda, but by Maelgwn's *atavus*, according to the genealogy, Padarn Pesruid, Paternus of the red robe. The date to be

[29] R. W. Unger (1980), 55 ff.
[30] D. P. S. Peacock (1978).
[31] For a diachronic examination of relevant aspects of trade, M. Fulford (1978). For trade between Gaul and Ireland, C. Doherty (1980), 77; E. James (1982), 382–3.
[32] K. Meyer (1896), 58.
[33] *Dinas Powys* (1963), 58 n. 4; not reprinted above.
[34] M. Miller (1978b).
[35] M. Miller (1976).

inferred would be within the fourth century, and therefore, as we now know from re-examination of the coins and other finds, very probably within the period of military use of the Segontium fort;[36] or at any rate, and perhaps significantly, at the very end of that period.

The case of the dynasty of the Dési in Dyfed is rather less straightforward. It is common ground that the Irish and Welsh versions of the genealogy agree back to Tryffin, grandfather of Voteporix, who was already white-haired when Gildas attacked him in AD 545 × 549. Before that 'the Irish material is early and reasonably straight-forward'[37] and shows that the Dési were brought from Leinster to Dyfed by Eochaid *allmuir*, great-grandfather of Tryffin. Miller has shown that over the ten generations from Voteporix to Maredudd son of Tewdwr, the dynasty exhibits an average of twenty-five years to a generation. If we may extrapolate this dynastic average back from Voteporix to Eochaid then the settlement should have occurred about AD 400 × 425. This might suggest a date after, rather than before, the British assertion of independence from Rome in AD 410. Certainly it is well after the latest coin from a military site in south Wales, which appears to be one of Gratian (367–83) from Cardiff.[38] Perhaps, therefore we should expect no Roman influence behind the settlement of the Dési.

At this point, however, we should take account of the title on Voteporix's monument, MEMORIA VOTEPORIGIS PROTICTORIS.[39] As Miller shows, the title *protector* had probably already been borne by Cyngar, brother of Tryffin. Behind that again, when the genealogies are hopelessly unhistorical, we find mention of Protec son of Protector, which may enshrine a memory that the title had long been hereditary in the family. The significance of the term itself is difficult to assess, and it does not help at all to translate, as is sometimes done, 'Voteporix the protector'. We are dealing with a somewhat obscure, but nonetheless well-established, Roman rank or commission: one which was obtained by appearing personally before the emperor to 'adore the purple'. Ideally the corps of *protectores* comprised soldiers promoted on the strength of proven ability, but there were other channels of entry as well, and it may be significant here that a case is known of the son of a German noble being promoted directly. Normally, *protectores* could expect promotion to the command of a unit, so the corps acted as training unit or staff college.[40]

All this may seem very remote from Dyfed around AD 400, but it may help to clear away some of the misconceived interpretations which have gathered around Voteporix. It is scarcely appropriate for instance, to write of 'the high Imperial title of *Protector*, to which he could certainly have had no right', and to see this as an attempt, in the sixth century, 'to ape the Romans'.[41] If the head of a dynasty had been looking for a title denoting military rank, it is surely more likely that he would have chosen *comes, dux, magister, praepositus* or *tribunus*, rather than the obscure, and relatively lowly, *protector*. If this line of reasoning is sensible, it might further follow that this title, which by the generation of Cyngar and Tryffin had become an hereditary honorific, had originally been bestowed on an ancestor who had indeed 'adored the purple'. The precise

---

[36] G. C. Boon (1975), 64; (1976); R. B. White (1978); P. J. Casey (1979b).
[37] M. Miller (1978a).
[38] RCAHM(W) (1976), Part 2, 93 n. 8.
[39] ECMW No. 138.
[40] A. H. M. Jones (1964), 636–40.
[41] K. H. Jackson (1950), 208.

circumstances under which this might have happened remain obscure to us; but an imperial authority accessible to an immigrant Irish chieftain is more likely to date before 410, or even 407, than after.[42]

I would no longer press the suggestion that the imperial authority in question was Magnus Maximus, and that a member of the Demetian dynasty—perhaps indeed one of the sons of Eochaid—had served as an officer cadet on Maximus's staff;[43] nor would I see the establishment of the immigrant dynasties of Gwynedd and Dyfed as the acts of Maximus himself. Nonetheless, it is worth recalling briefly the remarkable hold which Magnus Maximus had over Welsh tradition and dynastic ideology. The most celebrated instance of this is in the much later tale, *The dream of Macsen Wledig*, that is, Magnus Maximus, 'the handsomest and wisest of men, and the best fitted to be emperor of all that had gone before him'.[44] But the place of Macsen Wledig in the earlier, unhistorical generations of the Welsh genealogies makes it clear that, just as the Christian English thought it appropriate that their rulers should be descended from a pagan god, so the Welsh, when eventually they began to construct genealogies, considered that their kings should descend from Magnus Maximus. This ideology is, of course, another example of the respect, and even reverence, which the barbarian people as a whole showed for Roman authority.

Finally, we may turn to the wider correlation of archaeological and historical evidence. Jones has well demonstrated how the archaeological material can be readily integrated into a synoptic view of economic history.[45] His synthesis is not seriously affected by my reconsideration of the intensity of the Mediterranean and Gaulish trade represented by the imported pottery (above, pp. 89–92). Altogether more difficult is the correlation with political, administrative and social history. In its more immediate form, the problem was well posed by Richards in his 1970 O'Donnell lecture: 'we have yet to discover what significance, if any, there may be in the connection between a hill-fort like Dinas Powys and the local dynasty'.[46] In a very real sense, it is the shadowy nature of the documentary evidence for that dynasty, rather than the defects of the archaeological evidence, which makes it difficult at present to discern a connection.

A more hopeful line along which to seek archaeological and historical correlations lies with Davies's analysis of the Llandaff charters in terms of the location and administration of early historic estates.[47] Much of her synthesis is concerned with the fundamental social and economic disturbance which she discerns in the eighth century: and it therefore overlaps very little, if at all, with the Phase 4 occupation of Dinas Powys. Altogether more relevant is her attempt to demonstrate continuity between, on the one hand, Romano-British villa estates and other rural settlements in the Vale of Glamorgan and elsewhere, and on the other, the estates documented in the Llandaff charters which were in existence in south-east Wales 'at an early post-Roman period'.[48] Such continuity, if it were indeed convincingly demonstrable, ought to overlap the occupation of Dinas Powys in the period AD 450 × 500–650 × 700.

---

[42] *pace* Miller (1978a), 40–1.
[43] L. Alcock (1971; 1973), 124.
[44] G. Jones and T. Jones (1949), 79–88.
[45] G. R. J. Jones (1972), 291–3.
[46] M. Richards (1971), 334 n. 2.
[47] W. Davies (1978a, 1978b, 1979b).
[48] W. Davies (1979a), 156.

In fact, the limitations of the evidence make it inevitable that the hypothesis of continuity, in terms of the derivation of early historic estates and tenurial arrangements from those of Roman Britain, must remain an article of faith, incapable of proof. For a start, the claim that the existence of estates can be demonstrated at an *early* (my italics) post-Roman period is somewhat misleading. For none of the charters is a date earlier than *c*. AD 555 suggested; there are then seven in the period 555–95, (but the first three of these are corrupt). These are followed by twenty-one in the period 600–50, while Davies's chronological list of early estates gives a further thirty-five post-650.[49] In other words, even the earliest of the charters scarcely comes within two centuries of the final occupation of villas such as that at Llantwit Major. Moreover, Davies herself admits that 'the most striking aspects of a map which records known Roman settlement and known early estates is the lack of any *exact* (her italics) correlation between the incidence of the two ...; and secondly, the occurrence of villas in areas where there are no estates, and vice versa'.[50] Granted all that she says about the possibility of undiscovered Roman sites, and the impossibility of identifying all early estates, the evidence is for discontinuity, rather than the opposite.

So far Davies's arguments have been considered for south-east Wales as a whole. If we return to Dinas Powys itself, the most obvious feature is its isolation. This is best brought out on a colour-coded map of places granted in the charters.[51] From this it is immediately apparent that no land-grants are known in the vicinity of Dinas Powys in the period 500 (sic) to 625, though it is claimed that there were six in the years 650–785. Even these estates stand at some remove from our site. This may be because it is located, to judge from the soil maps in the Glamorgan *Inventory*,[52] in an area of permeable soils largely surrounded by impervious soils, while the early estates lie on more favourable ground beyond those again.

The maps published by Davies,[53] do indeed appear to suggest that Dinas Powys was isolated from both Romano-British settlements and from early estates, but this impression is not susceptible of proof by the methods of locational analysis. But, in another sense its geographical and chronological isolation is very real. Accepting the interpretation that the rare Roman objects discovered during the excavations were brought in during Dinas Powys 4 (above pp. 21–3), there is no Roman precursor on the hill-top itself; nor is any recorded in its vicinity. In so far as the earliest of the Llandaff charters may overlap chronologically with Phase 4, there is no evidence for early estates in the neighbourhood. That an exceptionally rich site should have neither antecessors nor successors would in itself seem to be a strong argument for an unconformity in the power structure of south-east Wales in the fifth century AD.

Finally, any discussion of continuity must take account of the claim that hill-forts in Wales and the Marches continued for some centuries to serve as the centres of large territorial units. This problem, however, must be deferred until we have established in Part 3 which, if any, hill-forts were indeed occupied after AD 400.

---

[49] W. Davies (1979a), 169–71. The late Dr M. Miller commented on a draft of the present paper that 'none of these [charters] should be dated before 690'. P. Sims-Williams thinks it 'equally possible' that the earliest charters 'fall into the seventh century' (1982, 126).

[50] W. Davies (1979a), 160.

[51] W. Davies (1979b), 97.

[52] RCAHM(W) (1976).

[53] W. Davies (1979a).

Part Two:
The Finds from Dinas Powys 4

The purpose of Part Two is to deploy the artefactual evidence which dates Phase 4 at Dinas Powys, and which provides the archaeological basis for the economic and social interpretations advanced in Chapters 2 and 4. In effect, it furnishes an illustrated summary catalogue, condensed from the original expansive account in *Dinas Powys* 1963, of those objects which can be attributed to Phase 4 on typological or stratigraphic grounds.

Something should be said about the lines on which the catalogue has been summarized. Originally the finds were treated by material—metal, pottery, bone, stone and glass— and that arrangement has been retained. One effect of this was to disperse the evidence for jewellery-making, so a new section has been added on this important topic. For each material there was a general introduction. Where, as in the case of the imported pottery, this has been superseded by more recent research, it has been wholly rewritten; elsewhere it has been modified to bring it up to date. The section on glass has been left exactly as it was first published, at the request of its author, Dr D. B. Harden.

I have largely omitted the parallels given for individual objects, and I have also omitted the stratigraphic details for individual objects. All this information can readily be found in *Dinas Powys*, 1963. I have, however, retained the original tables of stratification, because these provide the basic evidence for the chronology both of the site and of the finds. These tables use a system of letters to denote the rampart stratification, as set out on pp. 9–12 above. In addition, the tables include the letters U for unstratified finds; H for objects from the humus layer in the interior of the site (and therefore virtually unstratified) and G1, G2 ... G6 for finds from the rock-cut gullies in the interior, which appear on Fig. 1.8.

From the perspective of the 1980s, one further aspect of the treatment of the finds requires comment: namely, the absence of scientific analyses of the composition of artefacts. Appendix 7 of *Dinas Powys* (1963)[1] did indeed provide technical notes on iron-working at Dinas Powys, but beyond this there has been no analysis, for instance, of the copper alloy objects which are here described as bronze; nor of the slags and metallic residues in the crucibles; nor of the objects here described as made of bone, in order to determine whether or not they are actually of antler. These and other analyses, which are largely regarded as routine today, were not readily available to me in the late 1950s. Since 1962 the finds have been in the care of the National Museum of Wales. It may well be that the information which they might provide is by no means exhausted.

---

[1] L. Alcock (1963a), 216–19: not republished here.

CHAPTER 5

Metalwork and Jewellery-making

BRONZES (Figs. 5.1, 5.2)

In addition to globules of molten copper, copper slag, and scraps of sheet bronze, Dinas Powys produced a varied collection of bronze objects, both whole and fragmentary. In so far as these were stratified, they came predominantly from the C and C/D layers of Bank I. This suggests, of course, that they are to be referred to Phase 4; and this suggestion gains confirmation from the discovery of an important piece—No. 21—in an O layer and Nos. 6, 16, and 19 in A layers. In short, these bronzes are for the most part a feature of the Phase 4 occupation of the site, and they provide a valuable clue to the date of that phase. With the exception of a fragmentary La Tène III brooch, they could all belong to the fifth to seventh centuries AD.

In view of this date, the most remarkable feature of the more determinate bronzes is that only one of them—No. 12—is certainly Celtic in inspiration. Of the remainder, Nos. 1 and 5 are unambiguously Anglo-Saxon (or at the least Teutonic) in style; on the basis of their parallels, the same may be said of Nos. 2 and 15; while punch-decorated belt-ornaments like Nos. 6 and 10 do not appear among the copious bronze-work of the period known from Ireland. The source of a group of bucket-fittings—Nos. 9, 14, and 21—is also probably Teutonic. Wooden buckets were doubtless in use in the Celtic West just as in pagan England, but the evidence from the Irish crannogs suggests that the Celtic buckets lacked ornamental binding strips of the type we have here. Without doubt, the bulk of the bronzes from Dinas Powys show Teutonic and not Celtic influences.

What form did these influences take, and what was the source of these Teutonic objects in south Wales? Three possibilities must be examined:

(a) The objects may be refuse from an actual Anglo-Saxon or Teutonic settlement at Dinas Powys.

(b) They may be the fruits of raids across the Bristol Channel against Pagan Saxon communities established in Somerset from the late sixth century.

(c) They may have been brought by trade, either
(i) as actual objects—buckets, jewellery, and the like—or
(ii) as scrap or waste metal, intended to be melted down and recast for trinkets in the Celtic style.

It should be stressed that, from the way in which these objects occurred on the site, it may clearly be inferred that many of them were indeed scrap about to be melted down. Significant pointers here are the rough gash in the centre of No. 1, the severed rivets of No. 16, the folded strip No. 21, and the bronze ingot No. 18. If a significant proportion of this material was merely scrap metal, this would seem to militate against the suggestion that the bronzes had come in through a trade in Teutonic metalwork. It might also count against the idea that they are the spoils of raiding against the Anglo-Saxons. It could perhaps be suggested that the ornamental disk No. 1 had been ripped off its backing in the

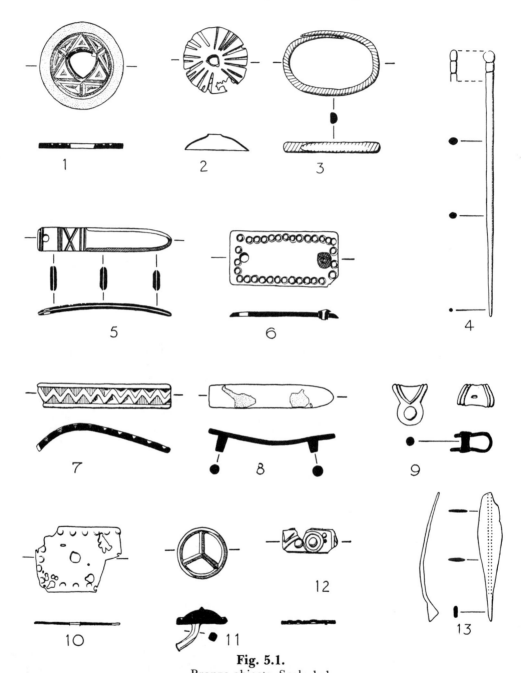

Fig. 5.1.
Bronze objects. Scale 1:1
On nos. 1 and 8 stippling denotes white metal; on no. 7 vertical hatching marks enamel

heat of a raid; but it is impossible to believe that any raider would bother to sever the rivets of a piece like No. 16 in order to gain a mere backing-plate.

The character of the bronze-work can indeed best be accounted for if we take it to be

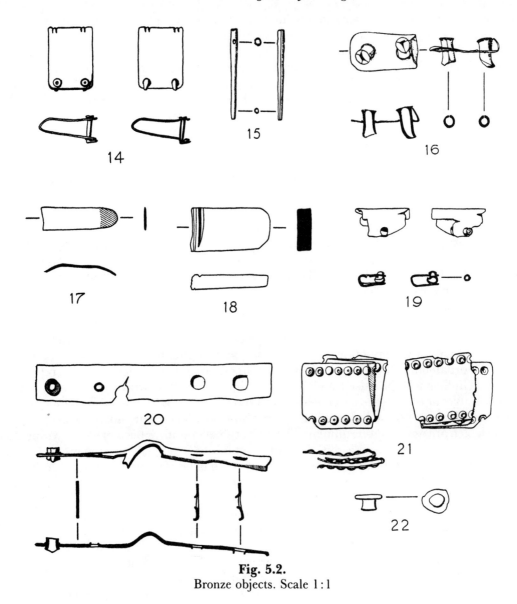

Fig. 5.2.
Bronze objects. Scale 1:1

scrap metal either produced on the site itself by a group of Teutonic bronze-workers or brought in from some external source.

If we accept the first alternative, then we must believe that there was a Teutonic craftsman actually resident on the site, producing trinkets in the Teutonic style, and, when they were old or damaged, melting them down again to provide further raw material. This would account for the occurrence of some pieces in more or less mint condition (like the strap-tag No. 5) along with a preponderance of scrap. At first sight it would also agree well with the abundance of Teutonic glass vessels and beads in this same Phase 4. But the suggestion that there had been any marked Anglo-Saxon or Teutonic penetration of Glamorgan by AD 600 seems so revolutionary that we would require much confirmatory evidence before we could regard it as sound.

We are left, then, with the possibility that most of the bronze-work discovered at Dinas Powys was brought to the site as scrap from Saxon England, to be melted down for use in the manufacture of Celtic trinkets. The absence of actual examples of the latter is not difficult to account for on a living site, where they would be kept on the persons of their owners. But it seems more difficult to believe that scrap metal would have been exported from lowland England, an area deficient in copper ores, to Wales where copper had been mined in Roman times and long before; if anything, the trade should have been in the opposite direction. To this objection there are two answers. Firstly, from the geological point of view, south-east Wales belongs rather with lowland England than with the copper-bearing regions of mid and north Wales. Secondly, the craftsman manufacturing bronze jewellery was doubtless less interested in supplies of copper ore, requiring refining, than in pure copper ready for immediate use. A supply of scrap, from whatever source, made it possible for him to by-pass the extractive and refining stages, for which he may have lacked the technological resources. There is thus a close analogy between the scrap Saxon bronze and the scrap Teutonic glass at Dinas Powys, for in the case of the glass, jewellers who could not manufacture glass from raw materials were nonetheless able to utilize scrap glass in the production of ornaments and enamel.[2]

Finally, we may consider the technological aspects of these bronzes, bearing in mind that these comments apply to Teutonic, not Celtic, metalworking. For a start they exhibit familiarity with a variety of decorative techniques, ranging from cast—including chip-carved—ornament, through simple incised lines, to punched designs and repoussé bosses. Gilding was practised and was sometimes combined with the use of a white metal—silver or tin—in the best pagan Saxon style. But undoubtedly the most interesting technical feature of these bronzes is the common (though certainly not exclusive) use of rivets which are not solid but tubular. These rivets had doubtless been made by wrapping a thin sheet of metal round a rod. Sometimes one edge is lapped over the other, but in other cases the two edges butt. When a tube of metal had been formed in this way, one end was doubtless folded down—perhaps using pincers—as we can see in No. 14. The rivet would then be placed in position and the other end would be beaten out in the usual way. Such rivets were sometimes passed through quite thick objects and beaten out over a washer or backing-strip (No. 16). The advantages of a hollow rivet are that it conserves metal, it is light in itself, and when used on delicate objects it requires less forceful hammering out than a solid rivet. Even a cursory examination of the bronzes from pagan Saxon and continental cemeteries shows that the Teutonic craftsman was well aware of these advantages. It may be said, however, that hollow rivets are more conspicuous on the objects themselves than in the archaeological literature about them.[3]

---

[2] Compare the presence of folded strips of bronze together with crucibles, moulds, and fragments of glass from Mote of Mark (National Museum, Edinburgh).

[3] The technique certainly goes back, in Romano-British and native contexts, to the first century AD. Thus in the National Museum, Edinburgh, the Carlingwark Loch cauldron, and some mess-cans from Newstead have patches held in place with hollow rivets. A cursory examination of Teutonic materials in the British museum has shown that they occur in the Harnham Hill (Hants.), Sleaford (Lincs.), and Herpes (Charente) cemeteries.

Stratification of illustrated bronze objects

Layer	N	O	A	B	C	C/D	D	H	U
Number of objects	—	1	3	—	5	6	—	3	4

1.   Bronze disk, ornamented in 'chip-carving' with an equilateral triangle set within a circle; the segments thus formed are then bisected. The area within the circle is gilt, while the rim of the disk has been plated with silver or some other white metal (shown stippled) which spreads into the groove of the circle. An irregular hole in the centre, partly demarcated by grooves within the triangle, shows that the disk has been ripped off some central fixture. The coarse 'chip-carved' technique, together with the combination of gold and white metal, proclaim this as the product of an Anglo-Saxon (or at least a Teutonic) rather than a Celtic craftsman.

2.   Shallow domed cover, with a central perforation apparently punched out from underneath, and ornamented with irregularly-disposed radial grooves which seem to have been executed by striking the upper side with a chisel.

3.   Large ring of semi-circular section, its outer face decorated with incised diagonal lines. It appears to have been made by bending a short strip of bronze, the ends of which had first been carefully tapered off so as to lie flush; the join may then have been soldered. The large size of the ring suggests that it was intended for wear on the thumb or toe, unless, indeed, it is the ring from a loose-ring pin.

4.   Simple bronze pin, with a crude disk head surmounting a collar moulding, originally silver-washed or plated.

5.   Strap-end, made of two thin strips of metal soldered together. (In the drawing, the two strips are shown separated.) The strap was fixed by means of a single rivet. The attached end of the tag is decorated with parallel grooves and a saltire. The free end is plain and has a marked bevel on its upper surface, and a less marked one underneath.

6.   Rectangular plaque with two rivet-holes on the long axis presumably for fixing to a leather belt. The edge is bevelled and just within the bevel is a slightly irregular line of punched circles. One rivet-hole contains the badly rusted remains of what appears at first sight to be a hollow iron rivet; but a tubular rivet of iron is so unlikely that it is probable that the central hole has been produced by the corrosion of the iron

7.   Fragment of bronze strip ornamented with a running chevron pattern reserved against a background of champlevé enamel (marked by vertical hatching). The present colour of the enamel is green, but this may be the result of decay. While the left-hand end of the strip is clearly fractured, the right-hand end may be original.

8.   Ornamental bronze fitting, with two stubby shanks for fixing to a backing, perhaps of cloth, leather, or wood. Two remaining areas of silver-plating (shown stippled) show that the whole upper surface was originally silvered.

9.   Small clamp for fastening a rim-binding strip to a bucket, drinking-horn or leather cup.

10.   Thin plate or strip of bronze, decorated with punched crescents. While the left-hand edge is certainly original, it is probable that the right-hand one is not, and that the piece we have has been cut from a longer strip.

11.   Gilt bronze stud, with shank for fixing to a backing, perhaps of leather. The rim is defined by a raised ridge, and the field is divided by three similar radial ridges.

12.   Fragment of a silvered bronze strip with repoussé decoration of bosses and scrolls. It is doubtful whether any edge is original, so the former size and shape of the piece cannot be determined. There are traces of an iron rivet (shown cross-hatched) to the right of the central scroll. The Celtic affinities of the ornament are clear, though no good parallels are available.

13.   Fragment probably from the bow and part of the catch-plate of a La Tène III brooch of Nauheim type, decorated with pairs of punch-marks along the bow.

14.   Clamp for attaching the rim-binding of a wooden bucket. At the rim are two pairs of ornamental grooves.

15.   Fine, slightly tapering tube of bronze made by lapping over a thin sheet of metal. Perhaps a shoe-lace tag of the type rarely found by the ankles of skeletons in Anglo-Saxon graves.

16.   Bronze backing-plate, with two large tubular rivets of a sufficient size to determine the method of manufacture. As preserved, one end of each rivet has been hammered out and is clearly original, representing the inner, under, or concealed side of whatever object the rivets passed through; but the other end of each rivet has obviously been sheared through. The implication is clear that the heads of the rivets have been lost and with them, of course, the presumably ornamental fitting which they served to attach. It seems indeed likely that the rivets were cut through in order to free the ornament.

17.   Thin strip of bronze, the one end broken, the other showing an original curve. Though this strip is thinner than the two that make up the strap-end No. 5 above, it is possible that it has broken off a somewhat similar tag.

18.   Thick bronze strip, the one end with an original curve, the other snapped off after two or three attempts to cut it with a cold chisel, most likely a bronze-worker's ingot.

19.   Fragment of rim-binding strip from a bucket or other vessel, with a tubular rivet still in place.

20.   Binding-strip or bracket, originally 'L' shaped, with a pair of rivet-holes in each arm of the 'L'. It is not easy to see how this strip was intended to be fixed. The right-hand arm has its holes punched from above and one edge is bent over, so presumably this ran along the upper edge of a piece of wood or other material; but the left-hand arm is flat in section and has its holes punched from below so that it is most reasonable to think of it as attached to the under-side. It is not inconceivable that this is a strengthening-piece from a wooden box.

21.   Ornamental bronze strip, decorated with a row of repoussé bosses along each edge; wear and corrosion have removed the tops of most of the bosses: found doubled up in an ash layer derived from bronze-working.

22.   Small bronze stud.

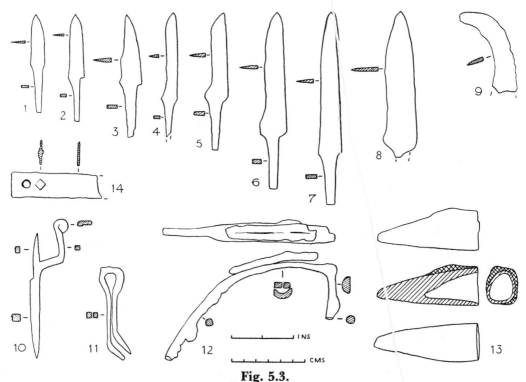

Fig. 5.3.
Iron knives and other objects. Scale 1:3

IRON OBJECTS (Figs. 5.3, 5.4)

Just over one hundred objects and fragments of iron were recovered, the majority of them in a very bad state of corrosion. In many cases the body of an object was penetrated by layers or bands of rust. It was therefore impossible to treat such pieces by normal methods of electrolytic reduction. On the whole, the only cleaning carried out has been by mechanical means, and in many cases, where the rust proved resistant, even these have not been carried far. Nonetheless, it is frequently possible to see the solid original form of a piece under the accretions of rust and dirt; and in such cases an attempt has been made to draw the original rather than the present state of a piece. To that extent the drawings are frankly interpretative.

Many of these iron pieces were unstratified. For the most part stratified pieces occurred in the rubbish layers of the bank, the bulk of them in the C/D layers. A significant pointer to a date in Phase 4 for most of the ironwork is provided by the discovery of two knives, Nos. 4 and 6, respectively in the O and A layers.

Where their function was identifiable, these iron objects appear to be wholly domestic or industrial. Apart from nails, knives form the largest group; the occurrence of comparable knives in both male and female pagan Saxon graves suggests that they would be carried by all adults. Second in importance to the knives are the awls, of which five certain examples were recognized, while others are doubtless represented now by indeterminate iron rods. These awls, together with a group of heavy needles, reinforce the evidence of the polishing stones for leather-working on the site. Another domestic industry, that of

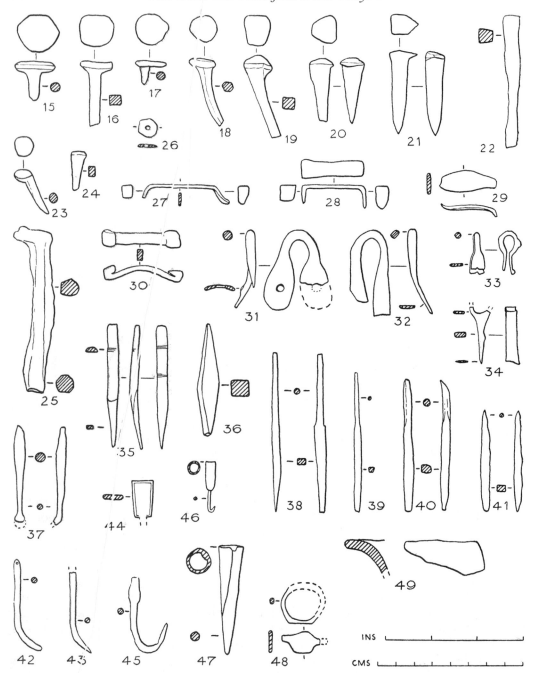

Fig. 5.4.
Miscellaneous iron objects. Scale 1:2

carpentry, appears to be represented by drill-bits and a file. A bill-hook is evidence for farming. Miscellaneous pieces include loops for straps or harness, and possibly a bucket handle and suspension loops. The total absence of weapons—unless the ferrules be taken as coming from spear-butts—is interesting; but it should not be taken as imputing a wholly civilian character to Dinas Powys in Phase 4, for even such purely military sites as Roman auxiliary forts often yield very few weapons to the excavator.

From the typological point of view, the most important group of iron objects is, of course, the knives. The form of these, with their thick-backed, straight or curving blades, shoulders more or less marked, and thick tangs, clearly relates them to those found on early Christian sites in Ireland, as well as in pagan Saxon graves in England and cemeteries of the Migration period on the Continent. But the resemblances are general rather than specific, and few of the knives have any precise analogues. This may suggest that the form of knives was governed rather by the skill and fancy of individual smiths than by any strong typological tradition.

With the remainder of the ironwork, there may appear to be a marked contrast with the bronzes in that parallels appear as readily in Ireland as in Teutonic contexts. This may be because we are not dealing largely with scrap (as with the bronze) but rather with objects used and discarded on the site. On the other hand, it may merely reflect our fuller knowledge of domestic sites in Ireland than in pagan England; for most of these objects are not such as one might expect to find in graves. If the connections of the Dinas Powys ironwork are indeed with Ireland, then the absence of two classes of objects common elsewhere in the Irish Sea Zone may be significant. These are the slotted-and-pointed tools, and the three-pronged socketed tools, which are common in Ireland and occur also at Dunadd. The former class, at least, is known in Glamorgan, at the Lesser Garth Cave, so its absence from Dinas Powys can scarcely be explained as due to a lack of cultural connections with Ireland. The reason is more likely to be chronological. It is possible to

Stratification of illustrated iron objects

Layer	Quantity		Catalogue Numbers
N	—		
O	1		4
A	4		6, 14, 27, 31
B	1		5
C	5		9, 23, 43, 45, 46
C/D	17		1, 2, 3, 7, 8, 11, 16, 17, 19, 29, 32, 35, 36, 38, 41, 42, 47
D	6		3 (2 e.g.), 4, 10, 28, 39
H	—		
U	23		

suggest that slotted-and-pointed objects are characteristic of the eighth to ninth centuries AD rather than of fifth to seventh centuries. If this is so, then their absence from Dinas Powys may indicate a terminal date about AD 700 for Phase 4. It is at least unlikely that their apparent absence is due solely to the chances of discovery, for they are quite common on Irish sites.

1–8. Tanged knives, with thick backs and marked shoulders. In many cases the blade has been much reduced by whetting.

In addition to the illustrated examples, a further 11 fragments of blades or tangs were identified.

9. Tip of a wide curved blade from a billhook or sickle.

10. Pronged object, probably a candlestick.

11. Simple hasp or eye.

12. Probably the central part of a bucket handle, on the assumption that the curve was originally smooth, the right-angled bend being the result of damage.

13. Socket point, probably too small to be interpreted as a plough-tip, and more likely a tip for the tine of a wooden hay-fork.

14. Iron strip, with empty rivet hole, and probably the head of a second rivet rusted on. Representative of other miscellaneous strips, some with rivets.

15–25. Nails and studs, illustrating the range among a total of 14.

26. Small washer.

27–29. Staples or clamps.

30. Strip with recurved ends.

31–2. Hoops or eyes, perhaps suspension hoops for buckets.

33. Strap loop with perforated terminals, now broken.

34. Tanged eye.

35. Tanged file, of plano-convex section, some teeth still visible.

36. Drill bit?

37. Fragmentary spoon-drill?

38–41. Representative awls with quadrangular tangs and points of circular section.

Among a further 14 indeterminate iron rods, some may have been from nails, others from awls.

42–3. Heavy needles, perhaps for stitching leather.

44. Eraser end of a stylus?

45. Heavy fish-hook?

46. Socketed hook, the socket containing traces of a wooden handle.

47. Heavy socketed point or ferrule.

48. Finger-ring with flat bezel.

49. Fragment from lip of bowl or other vessel.

SILVER AND LEAD (Fig. 5.5)

1. Fragmentary strip of base silver or silvered bronze, broken at both ends. The front is ornamented with a double row of roughly triangular punch-marks, not very regularly disposed. The punched ornament suggests a Teutonic rather than a Celtic source, so this probably belongs with the scrap metal imported in Phase 4.

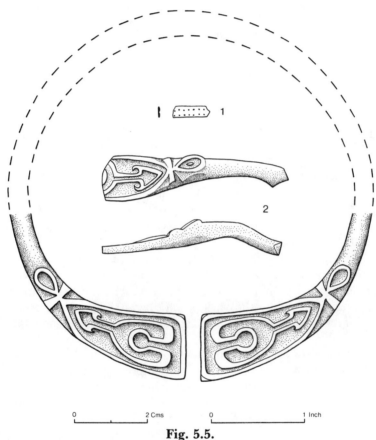

Fig. 5.5.
Silver and lead objects, and reconstruction of penannular brooch

2. Fragment of a lead[4] die for stamping a clay mould to be used in the manufacture of a penannular brooch of Kilbride-Jones Class C_4,[5] with zoomorphic terminals ornamented with a devolved palmette motif, picked out in enamel.[6] In 1963 I was hesitant about defining the function too positively; though, in seeking comparisons, I drew attention to the deeply carved bone motif-pieces from Lagore, suggesting that they were intended as working dies, rather than as preliminary sketches.[7] Lead dies are indeed rare in the

---

[4] I am grateful to Dr D. L. Carpenter, Department of Metallurgy, University College, Cardiff, who informs me that no other metal was detected.

[5] H. E. Kilbride-Jones (1980a), 221; (1980b), 133.

[6] The stylistic affinities were first recognized by the late P. J. Hartnett.

[7] This interpretation was endorsed by J. Raftery in 1967, quoted by U. O'Meadhra (1979), 8.

literature, no doubt because they could readily be melted down for re-use, as had doubtless been intended with the present fragment; but a good parallel comes in the form of a lead die or model for a bird-brooch (*Vogelfibel*) from the Runde Berg (Baden-Württemberg), a hill-fort broadly contemporary with Dinas Powys 4.[8] There is also a fragment of what has been claimed as 'a leaden die ... presumably used by a brooch manufacturer' from a Roman level at Lydney.[9]

Kilbride-Jones is no doubt correct in assigning the brooch which would have been produced from the die to his Group C_4; but the date which he suggests[10] is at least a century too early for the site evidence from Dinas Powys (as well as for other well-established associations for these brooches). The die was found in an A layer of Bank I, immediately overlying an O layer which contained numerous fragments of lidded crucibles. It therefore belongs among the jewellery-making debris characteristic of Dinas Powys 4.

JEWELLERY-MAKING IN DINAS POWYS 4

In *Dinas Powys* (1963), the finds were described and catalogued not by function, but by material, and a similar arrangement has been followed here. As a result, the very varied evidence for jewellery-making has been dispersed through Chapters 5, 6 and 9. Given the importance ascribed to the jeweller's craft in the social and economic interpretation of Dinas Powys 4 (Chapter 2), it seems desirable, in this concluding section of Chapter 5, to bring together the relevant material, and then to make some comparisons with contemporary sites, both in Britain and Ireland, and in Scandinavia.

The major evidence for jewellery-making consists of the raw materials brought to Dinas Powys for this purpose, and the debris from the manufacturing process. In the first category we must place the majority of the bronzes. For the most part these were incomplete in themselves; or like the various binding strips and clamps, had originally formed part of larger objects; or they had been forcibly torn from some larger ornament, like the disk from a disk-on-bow brooch (Fig. 5.1, 1), or the strips with sheared rivets (Fig. 5.2, 16). No. 18 was almost certainly part of a bronze ingot, cut through in order to make a piece of suitable size to fit into one of the contemporary crucibles. The most striking instance of a piece of scrap bronze being utilized as raw material is the repoussé ornamented strip, almost certainly off a bronze-bound wooden bucket of Anglo-Saxon type (Fig. 5.2, 21). Having been ripped off, this had then been tightly folded to a size which, like the ingot-fragment, is ideal for charging one of the Dinas Powys crucibles. Comparable folded strips of bronze are known, along with much other jewellery-making debris, from the contemporary small fort of Mote of Mark.[11]

The second major group of scrap, imported for re-use as raw material, comprises the Teutonic glass (Chapter 9). Altogether, 256 fragments of recognizable Teutonic (that is, Merovingian, Frankish, or Saxon) glass were recovered. Fifteen rims, mostly from various forms of beaker, were capable of being illustrated (Fig. 9.1); there was also a claw from a claw-beaker; and the bulk of the remaining sherds were from the walls of beakers. Only two bases were present: one from a cone beaker, and the other possible, but not certainly, from the butt end of a drinking horn (Fig. 9.1, 93 and 115). Given the fineness,

---

[8] R. Christlein (1971).
[9] R. E. M. and T. V. Wheeler (1932), 15; pl VIA, 1.
[10] H. Kilbride-Jones (1980b), 67.
[11] A. O. Curle (1914), 162, mentions these briefly, but they await adequate publication.

and therefore fragility, of the vessel walls, in contrast to the solidity of bases like 93, or still more those of claw-beakers, this is a remarkable ratio of bases to other fragments. It is, indeed, impossible to reconcile with the idea that complete drinking vessels of glass had ever been present on the site, however much poems like the *Gododdin* may lead us to expect them.[12] The only reasonable explanation is that we are seeing here importation of cullet: broken glass, to be used as raw material in the manufacture of glass objects such as beads and bangles, or vitreous pastes for enamelled inlays on penannular brooches, hanging bowl escutcheons, and other fine metalwork.

In addition to the scrap Teutonic glass, there are other pieces relevant to jewellery-making. These include rare fragments of emerald green and pale green glass which had probably been chipped off blocks of raw glass; and 18 pieces of heavily fused glass, in various colours, with dark blue and amber predominating. More important, however, despite their small numbers, are two slender rods of blue glass, and a third with a chequer pattern of white in a brown matrix. The latter is quite certainly a millefiori rod, admittedly of indifferent quality when compared with much of the millefiori work known from the terminals of penannular brooches,[13] or the actual workshop example from Garranes.[14] The other two rods probably represent the first stage in the construction of a millefiori pattern, which would be made by fusing together a number of coloured rods, and then drawing out the resulting bundle to the desired fineness.

The actual manufacturing process is best represented at Dinas Powys by fragments of crucible. As will be seen in Chapter 6, whenever the form of these can be determined, they belong to a distinctive type of lidded and knobbed crucible, which has parallels in Scotland at Dunadd, and in Ireland at Garryduff. Crucibles embodying the same basic concept of a lid to reduce heat-loss, and a knob to facilitate handling, are also known from Helgö and elsewhere in Scandinavia.[15] More than 150 fragments were recovered at Dinas Powys, coming from at least ten vessels: very probably this figure should be considerably higher, but it represents the best estimate which can be made by counting the most indestructible part of a lidded and knobbed crucible, namely, the knob itself.

The crucibles plainly imply the casting of relatively small objects, principally of bronze. It therefore appears remarkable, at first sight, that Dinas Powys produced no identifiable moulds of the kind long known from Mote of Mark and Dunadd, and more recently recognized at Brough of Birsay, Clatchard Craig and Dunollie. At best, there were five pieces of fine baked clay, possibly from moulds, but with no recognizable patterns; significantly, four of them were associated with crucible sherds. Despite the reasonable expectation that moulds and crucibles should be found together because of their functional interdependence, a survey of leading Celtic sites of our period reveals that Dinas Powys is by no means the only one where crucibles have not been accompanied by moulds. (Very occasionally, a mould is found with no accompanying crucibles, as at Craig Phadraig.) In some instances, the discrepancy may simply reflect the limited scale of excavation or, in the case of older excavations, defective recovery of artefacts. It is also possible that the finishing of the products may have been carried out at a different part of a site from the casting; if the object was left in the mould until then, the distribution of

[12] K. H. Jackson (1969), 35; 102; 142. Compare Chapter 16, p. 248.

[13] H. E. Kilbride-Jones (1980b), passim.

[14] S. P. Ó Ríordáin (1942), Fig. 15. See also the simple glass rods, and blue-and-white chequered millefiori, from Lagore: H. O'N. Hencken (1950), 132.

[15] K. Lamm (1980), Fig. 1.

Table 1[16]
Jewellery-Making on some Insular Sites

Site and Reference	Crucibles	Heating trays	Moulds	Dies, motif-pieces
ALT CLUT, DUMBARTON L. Alcock (1976)	–	–		
BALLINDERRY 2 H. O'N. Hencken (1942)	–	–	–	
BALLYCATTEEN S. P. Ó Ríordáin and P. J. Hartnett (1943)	–			
BALLYVOURNEY M. J. O'Kelly (1952)	–			
BROUGH OF BIRSAY C. L. Curle (1982)	+		+	–
BUISTON R. Munro (1882)	–			
CARRAIG AILLE S. P. Ó Ríordáin (1949)	–			
CLATCHARD CRAIG J. Close-Brooks (forthcoming)		–	+	
CRAIG PHADRAIG R. B. K. Stevenson (1972)				–
DINAS POWYS L. Alcock (1963a)	+			–
DUNADD D. Christison (1905); J. H. Craw (1930)			+	–
DUNDURN L. Alcock (1978a)	–		–	–
DUNOLLIE L. Alcock (1979a)	–		–	
GARRANES S. P. Ó Ríordáin (1942)	+		–	
GARRYDUFF M. J. O'Kelly (1962)	–			–
LAGORE H. O'N. Hencken (1950)	–	–		–
LOUGH FAUGHAN A. E. P. Collins (1955)	–			
MOTE OF MARK A. O. Curle (1914); L. Laing (1975a)	–	–	+	
NENDRUM H. C. Lawlor (1925)	–			–

[16] This table does not aim to be complete, but none the less it provides a summary of the metalworking evidence from representative insular sites. No attempt is made to distinguish between lidded and other forms of crucible, because of the fragmentary character of the remains. It is, however, possible to distinguish as 'heating trays' certain shallow, flat-based bowls, which are thought to have held glowing charcoals, used in conjunction with a blowpipe for fine metalworking. The heading 'moulds' refers only to those used for jewellery-making: ingot moulds, which are quite common, are expressly excluded. The heading 'Dies, motif-pieces' includes the Dinas Powys die, the disk of uncertain purpose from Brough of Birsay, and the motif-pieces catalogued by U. O'Meadhra (1979). The published evidence rarely allows any numerical analysis, but it is at least possible to distinguish abundant examples of a type by a cross +; other occurrences are marked by a single dash —.

discarded moulds might well differ from that of crucibles. Even at a largely excavated site like Dinas Powys, there are unexcavated areas—the north-west corner, or the east side of the interior—which may still conceal a quantity of broken moulds.

In the absence of direct evidence, however, we can turn to other contemporary sites for an indication of the character of the moulds which are likely to have been used at Dinas Powys. In 1963, I suggested 'that penannular brooches were cast in open clay moulds as well as by the waste wax technique' (*sic*: read lost wax). My colleague Dr Elizabeth Slater points out to me, however, that the use of an open mould is unlikely for casting a thin bronze object, even one with a plain back, because of the oxidation which would result. She also considers that there is no definite evidence for the use of the lost wax method. In Britain, the most thoroughly studied and best published moulds are those from Brough of Birsay.[17] It is quite certain that these were predominantly, and perhaps wholly, two-piece moulds. Stevenson had already noted that the abundant—but regrettably unpublished—moulds from Mote of Mark 'are shown by their keyed edges to be two-piece ... so they were evidently formed by impressing a pattern or model made of wood or soft metal'.[18]

Stevenson continues by drawing attention to the lead die or brooch model from Dinas Powys, (Fig. 5.5, 2). This indeed provides the only evidence on our site for the character of the moulds: its very presence demands the existence of two-piece moulds. It also illustrates a major step in the process of brooch-making, namely the carving of a positive pattern out of wood, bone or soft metal. And beyond its technological interest, it furnishes our only certain clue to the types of object which the Dinas Powys bronze-smiths were producing.

Before developing this point, however, it is of interest to look at the spatial and stratigraphical distribution of the evidence for jewellery-making. Overwhelmingly, the metalworking debris occurs, like the imported pottery, in the make-up of Bank I, the C and C/D layers. Crucible sherds occur notably in the O layers, as well as in A layers. Glass is quite plentiful in the A layers, which also yielded three pieces of scrap bronze. Perhaps significantly the folded bronze strip (Fig. 5.2, 21) was found in Cut XII in the O layers, which also yielded substantial fragments of two or three lidded crucibles. The lead die came from the A layer in the same cutting. There is a minor concentration of glass immediately north of Cut XII, in an area which is also characterized by built hearths and layers of ash and charcoal, all suggestive of industrial activity. But the major concentration of glass was around hearths J and K, and to the south and east of them: in fact, in the yard, open to the south-east and backed to the north and west by the stone buildings of Phase 4B. Here, too, was a cluster of crucible fragments. These observations suggest something of the pattern of jewellery-working activities across the site; but lacking the distribution of moulds, our perception of the pattern is necessarily incomplete.

Turning now to the products of the Dinas Powys jewellers, the only certainty is that they were making zoomorphic penannular brooches with enamelled terminals. The best proof of this would, of course, have been provided by the discovery of moulds. Failing these, the lead die is satisfactory evidence, because there can be no reason for its occurrence on the site other than to stamp moulds for just such brooches. Its further importance is that it demonstrates the manufacture in Britain of a class of brooch of which the finished products are known only from Ireland.[19] Two other bronzes may reasonably be con-

[17] C. L. Curle (1982), 26–39.
[18] R. B. K. Stevenson (1974), 19, n. 8.
[19] Maps in H. E. Kilbride-Jones (1980b).

sidered as products of local craftsmanship, rather than as imported scrap: the bronze pin (Fig. 5.1, 4), simply because it is complete; and the ring (Fig. 5.1, 3), on the assumption that it comes from a loose-ring pin. This point is not pressed, but somewhat similar rings are known from such pins, for instance at Lagore and Garryduff.[20] Fanning has recently suggested that what he calls 'spiral-ringed' pins could begin as early as the fifth–sixth centuries AD, a date which would well fit the Dinas Powys example.[21]

The other classes of trinket which might have been expected, given the available raw materials, are glass beads and bangles in a Celtic fashion, such as are so common in Ireland.[22] None were found, however, nor are there any examples of the ornamented glass studs known from Iona, Garryduff and Lagore,[23] either as moulds or as actual studs. Even when all allowance is made for the inevitable removal of finished products from a work-shop, the total absence of glass beads and bangles of Celtic design from Dinas Powys is remarkable. It may suggest that the Teutonic cullet had been imported solely for enamel-ling the terminals of zoomorphic penannular brooches and the escutcheons of hanging bowls.

Finally, we may turn briefly to compare Dinas Powys with other jewellery-making sites of comparable date in Celtic Britain, Ireland and Scandinavia. The most comprehensive and accessible account is that by Kristina Lamm,[24] for though this takes its starting point from the settlement site of Helgö in central Sweden, it ranges widely over Celtic, Germanic and Slavic Europe. At first sight, there is a striking parallel between Dinas Powys and Helgö, for the Swedish site produced a great quantity of 'whole and fragmentary crucibles'; and raw material in the form of ingots and scrap metal, some of the latter 'comprising thin sheet bronze which was folded up and compressed into small "packets",' obviously intended for melting down.[25] An important difference is that at Helgö the *c.* 300 kg of crucibles were accompanied by about 50 kg of moulds, from which Lamm has been able to draw major conclusions about the methods of casting elaborate jewellery in piece-moulds. In the Celtic areas, a similar technological study has as yet only been published from Brough of Birsay, where there was a similar use of piece-moulds, charged from small handled (but not lidded) crucibles.[26]

The major difference between Helgö and other Scandinavian metalworking sites on the one hand, and Dinas Powys and other Celtic sites on the other, lies not in the technology of jewellery-making, but in the social context. Helgö has been described by Lamm as 'an early developed nucleated settlement with pronounced trading and manufacturing func-tions'.[27] As a proto-urban site it begins unusually early, perhaps in the late fifth century. By the eighth century there were other settlements in Scandinavia with a similar combi-nation of trading and industrial activities, such as Haithabu and Ribe; and in England, Hamwih represents a similar development.[28] All of these, in terms of size and range of activities, may be described as proto-urban, if not indeed fully urban.

[20] Lagore: H. O'N. Hencken (1950), Fig. 14; Garryduff: M. J. O'Kelly (1962), Fig. 2.
[21] T. Fanning (1983).
[22] For rare Roman, Coptic and Teutonic beads from Dinas Powys, see pp. 148–9 with Fig. 9.2.
[23] Iona: J. Graham-Campbell (1981); Garryduff: M. J. O'Kelly (1962), 71–4; Lagore: H. O'N. Hencken (1950), 129–32.
[24] K. Lamm (1980).
[25] K. Lamm (1980), 98.
[26] C. L. Curle (1982), 26–42; especially the contribution by N. Robertson, 35–7.
[27] K. Lamm (1980), 97.
[28] R. Hodges (1982), especially Chapter 4; R. Hodges and D. Whitehouse (1983).

In Celtic Britain and Ireland, by contrast, we are dealing with small forts such as Clatchard Craig, Craig Phadraig, Dumbarton, Dunadd, and Mote of Mark in Scotland, Dinas Powys in Wales, and Garranes and Garryduff in Ireland; or with semi-defensible places such as the crannogs of Buiston (Scotland) and Lagore and Ballinderry No. 2 in Ireland, or the tidal island of Brough of Birsay. Some, such as Nendrum, and more doubtfully Brough of Birsay, were monastic rather than secular. Dumbarton was indeed described by a contemporary as both *urbs* and *civitas*:[29] but in modern terms, not one of these sites could be regarded as urban, or even proto-urban, in respect of its size, density of population, and intensity of industrial and trading activities. That many of them had an important political and administrative role is another matter, not relevant here. The major question, which can be posed but not answered at present, is whether the difference in scale of commercial and industrial activity between Dinas Powys and, for instance Helgö, is merely quantitative: or whether a qualitative difference is implied as well.

[29] J. Campbell (1979a).

CHAPTER 6

Pottery

INTRODUCTION

The excavation of Dinas Powys coincided with a revolutionary advance in knowledge of the pottery of post-Roman Celtic Britain.[1] Following on Radford's account of the imported pottery of the fifth and sixth centuries AD from Tintagel, Thomas had set out a wider scheme for Britain as a whole.[2] Despite certain reservations which I advanced, for instance in the original version of *Dinas Powys*, Thomas's scheme has largely stood up to discussion, and it has recently been confirmed and elaborated.[3] As a result only the briefest of generalized comment is needed in the present account: for fuller discussion, the reader is referred to Thomas (1981).

In accordance with Thomas's 1959 scheme, four classes of imported pottery are recognized in Dinas Powys 4:

Class A: fine red bowls and dishes, occasionally with stamped or rouletted ornament
Class B: large amphorae
Class D: grey bowls, including mortaria
Class E: kitchen vessels.

CLASS A (Figs. 6.1, 6.2)

A total of 86 sherds was found, representing a minimum of nine vessels. Thomas, following Hayes, has shown that the red Class A dishes and bowls of insular archaeologists belong to two groups: African Red Slip Ware from north Africa, and Phocaean Red Slip War (PRSW) from the east Mediterranean.[4] At Dinas Powys, he assigns four vessels to PRSW, nos. A 1, 2, 3 and 7. A date in the early sixth century seems to be indicated.

Stratification of sherds of Class A

Layer	N disturbed	O	A/O	A	B	C	C/D	D	H	U	G1	Total
Number of sherds	1	1	3	21*	3	18	7	10	5	16	1	86

* At least 14 sherds from one dish.

1. PRSW bowl with stamped ornament, reconstructed from about 20 sherds. Freestyle stamped ornament of six or more running felines.

[1] The impact of the revolution in Wales is discussed more fully in Chapter 10.
[2] C. A. R. Radford (1956); A. C. Thomas (1959).
[3] A. C. Thomas (1981).
[4] A. C. Thomas (1981); J. W. Hayes (1972), (1980).

2 & 3.   Rims from **PRSW** dishes.

4.   Rim from a flanged bowl.

5.   Rim sherd, apparently from a hemispherical bowl, but too small to establish the angle or diameter.

6.   Flanged-rim bowl.

7.   Base of a PRSW dish.

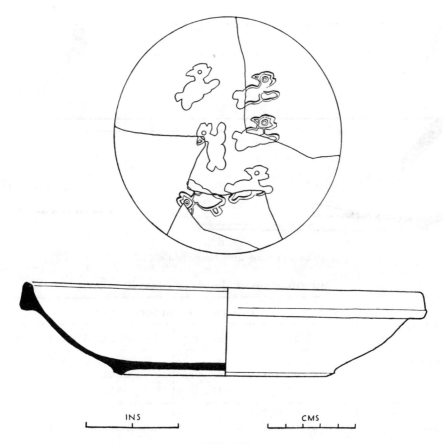

INS

CMS

Fig. 6.1.
Reconstructed Phocaean Red Slip Ware bowl, with stamped design of running felines.
Scale 1:2

CLASS B (Fig. 6.3)

More than 170 sherds come from amphorae of Class B; but given the size of the original vessels, and their ready tendency to fragment, this does not indicate any large number of vessels at Dinas Powys. Indeed, nearly half the sherds came from a single amphora. Nonetheless, at least 10 different vessels are represented.

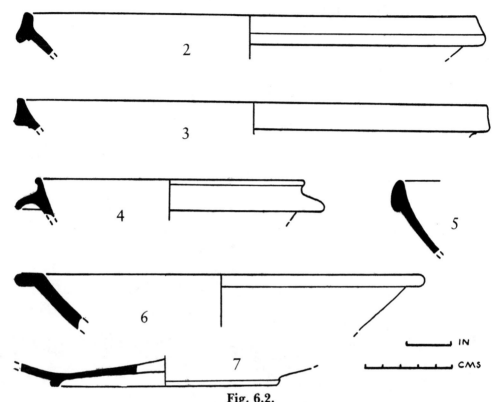

Fig. 6.2.
Class A rims and base. Scale 1:2

Stratification of sherds of Class B

Layer	References to catalogue of class B			
	No. 1: Bi	Nos. 2–4: Bii	Nos. 5–6: B MISC	No. 7
N (disturbed)	—	1	—	—
A	2	1	5	11
B	2	3	—	4
C	1	6	1	—
C/D	22	17	59	1
D	1	2	6	—
H	2	—	1	—
U	4	2	15	—
Phase 6	—	1	—	—

Thomas originally proposed the division of Class B into four sub-classes,[5] and this is followed in the table of stratification presented here. In his new classification, Bi is derived from the Aegean; Bii comes probably from the east Mediterranean in the mid- or late-sixth century; and Biii, of uncertain origin and chronology, is now designated B MISC.[6] Sub-class Biv is not present at Dinas Powys.

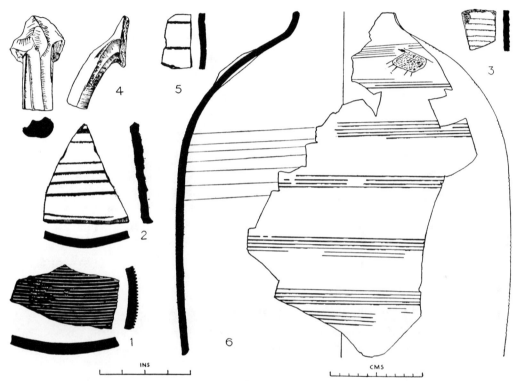

Fig. 6.3.
Characteristic sherds of Class B amphorae. Scale 1:4

1.   Characteristic sherd from a Bi amphora, with deep spiral grooving; there are a further 28 ungrooved sherds in identical fabric, all probably from the same vessel.

2–3.   Ribbed and imbricated sherds characteristic of Bii.

4.   Amphora handle in Bii fabric.

5.   Representative sherd out of 5 in a fabric comparable with no. 6, and therefore attributed to B MISC.

6.   Twenty-six joining sherds from an amphora of the B MISC group: a further 58 fragments from the same vessel could not be joined.

7.   Fourteen other sherds probably belong to Class B amphorae, but are not susceptible to further classification.

[5] A. C. Thomas (1959).
[6] A. C. Thomas (1981).

CLASS D (Fig. 6.4)

Class D bowls, in a distinctive soft grey fabric with a blue black wash, were first recovered from Dunadd in 1929;[7] and subsequently they have been found, in ones and twos, at other sites in western Britain. Only at Dinas Powys has any quantity of sherds been found: a total of 46, representing a minimum of nine vessels, of four different forms. Thomas therefore follows the classification proposed in *Dinas Powys*:

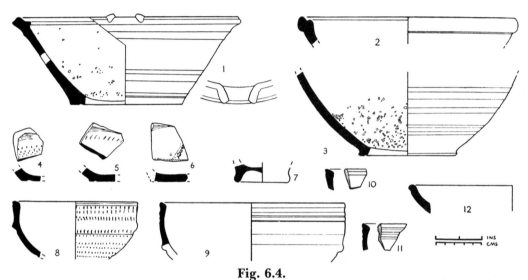

Fig. 6.4.
Reconstructed vessels and sherds of Class D. Scale 1:4

D1:   Mortaria with thick rims, spouts of unusual form, sparse grits, and thin bases, with a groove which gives the effect of a footring. Very rarely the exterior is ornamented with rouletting.
D2:   Bowls with grooved bases comparable to those of D1, which cannot however be mortaria because the interior is not gritted and is frequently decorated with rouletted or stamped ornament. The rim form has not been identified, but it may well be similar to that of the mortaria.
D3:   Fine deep bowls with the shoulder emphasized by a raised cordon. The outside may be ornamented with rouletting or parallel grooves.
D4:   There are also other fine bowls, some of which certainly do not have the shoulder-cordon of Type 3, though others may.
D5: A pedestal foot may belong to a bowl of type 3 or 4.

In 1963, I suggested that the grey fabric and black slip were intended to imitate pewter. The metallic form of the shouldered bowls would support this, as would the rouletted ornament, copying the punched decoration appropriate to metal. I would still hold to this view. On the other hand, my hesitant attempts to trace the ancestry of Class D in Roman Britain have now been wholly superseded by the recognition that Class D has convincing parallels in the 'group atlantique' of the 'sigillées paléochrétiennes grises et orangées' of Gaul.[8] A source in the vicinity of Bordeaux is indicated, and it is very reasonable to suggest that Class D pottery came to western Britain as a minor accompaniment to a trade

---

[7] J. H. Craw (1930), Fig. 10, 12/21.
[8] J. Rigoir (1968). L. Alcock (1971; 1973), 204. J. & Y. Rigoir and J-F. Meffre (1973).

in Gaulish wine in casks. Neither in Gaul nor in Britain is there any clear evidence of date, but the sixth century seems probable.

Stratification of sherds of Class D

Layer	N	O	A/O	A	B	C	C/D	D	H	U	G5	G6	Phase 6	Total
Number of sherds	—	—	2	1	—	—	10	3	3	19	5	2	1	46

1–3. Mortaria of form D1, with characteristic thick rims, crude pouring spouts,, lid-ledges, and interior gritting.

4–6. Bases from bowls of form D2, externally grooved, with rouletted or stamped ornament in the interior: the design hinted at on no. 6 has good parallels in Gaul. The basal diameter of nos. 4 and 5 is around 7 inches.

7. Pedestal base of form D5.

8–11. Certain or probable examples of shouldered bowls, form D3. No. 8 is characteristically rouletted, and nos. 9 and 11 are ornamented with horizontal grooves.

12. Beaded rim from a shallow bowl of form D4.

CLASS E (Fig. 6.5)
In contrast to the rather fine table-wares already described, Class E is a coarse pottery, more fitted to the kitchen, and used accordingly for cooking-pots, jars, bowls, and pitchers. Its most distinctive feature is the lavish use of quartz grits and of grog to temper the paste. Vessels are normally hard-fired—indeed they are sometimes hard enough to class as stoneware; but a few are distinctly softer. The colour of the paste varies from a warm

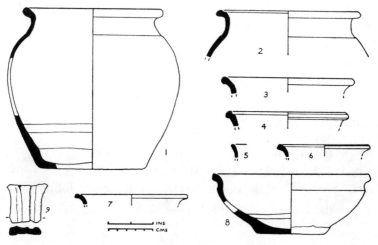

Fig. 6.5.
Reconstructed vessels and sherds of Class E. Scale 1:4

pink through creamy-white to grey or buff. The surface colour is equally variable. Sometimes, especially when the paste is creamy-white, the surface is the same colour; frequently the surface is a grey or blue-grey as a result of firing in a reducing atmosphere; occasionally there are traces of a thin buff slip or wash. Throwing grooves are prominent on the inside of vessels, while the outer surface often has a wiped effect.

Five main forms have been defined by Thomas, and all but one of them are present at Dinas Powys, where eighty-nine sherds represent a minimum of nine vessels: They are:

E1. Cooking-pots or storage jars of medium size, often with a lid rebate or groove on top of the rim: the Garranes jar.
E2. Small thin-walled jars or cooking-pots: the Buiston beaker.
E3. Shouldered bowls: the Dunadd bowl.
E4. Strap-handled pitchers.
E5. Pot lids: not recognized at Dinas Powys.

Pottery of Class E is widespread in Dumnonia, Wales, northern Britain (including British, Pictish and Scottic areas) and Ireland. It is generally agreed that it was imported into Celtic Britain. As yet, however, no wholly convincing continental parallels have been recognized, and there is no agreement as to whether it was manufactured in western or northern France.[9] In consequence, no external dating evidence is available, and the chronology of Class E is dependent on scanty stratigraphic, radiometric and historical dating in insular contexts. At Clogher it is stratified above Class B amphorae.[10] At Dunollie, sherds came from a large hearth, which has produced radiocarbon dates which calibrate, at the 2-sigma level, at AD 640–750.[11] This is consistent with the historical dating at sites such as Dunadd and Castle Rock, Dumbarton;[12] and with the associated artefacts at other sites such as Dinas Powys itself.

Stratification of sherds of Class E

Layer	N	O	A/O	A	B	C	C/D	D	H	U	G1	G3	G6	G7
Number of sherds	—	—	1	6	—	10	23	28	4	11	1	2	2	1

1–4. Medium-sized cooking pots or storage jars of form E1. Nos. 2 and 4 have well marked internal ledges for lids. The lower part of no. 1 exhibits characteristically pronounced throwing grooves.

5–7. Fine, thin-walled vessels, most probably of form E2.

8. Shouldered bowl of form E3.

9. Strap-handle, most probable from a pitcher of form E4.

CRUCIBLES (Figs. 6.6, 6.7)
Dinas Powys yielded about 150 fragments of crucibles. The earliest stratified sherds came from the O layers, especially at the north-east corner of the site, for instance from Section

---

[9] For an early stage in the discussion, see D. P. S. Peacock and A. C. Thomas (1967); for the present state, E. Campbell (1984) with comments by Peacock and R. Hodges.
[10] R. Warner (1979).
[11] L. Alcock (1981b), 234.
[12] L. Alcock (1981a).

4, Layer (7). In general, however, crucible fragments occur in the C and C/D layers: in other words, in refuse derived from Phases 4A and 4B. In the interior they clustered around hearths J and K, in the supposed work yard of Phase 4; and it may be taken that this was a focal point for their original use.

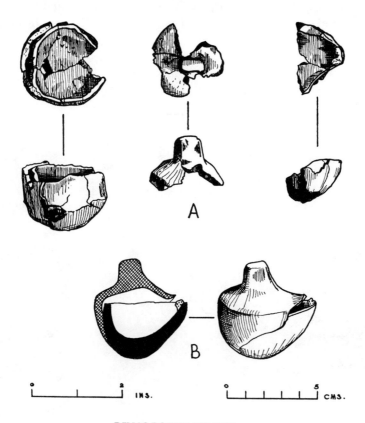

DINAS POWYS [GLAM.]
A: fragments of lidded crucibles
B: suggested reconstruction
Fig. 6.6.
Reconstruction of a lidded crucible. Scale 1:2

Despite the very fragmentary character of the Dinas Powys crucibles, it is clear that they belonged principally to a single type, with a thin-walled hemispherical bowl; a single spout pulled out from the bowl to give a pear-shaped plan; and a knobbed lid, which had been made separately from the bowl, but which was then luted on so that it was not detachable. Somewhat similar lidded crucibles have been reported around the Irish Sea at Garryduff I and Dunadd,[13] though neither is exactly comparable with the pear-shaped bowls of Dinas Powys. Lidded and knobbed crucibles, dating between the Roman and Viking periods, are also known from Scandinavia, and especially from a rich workshop

[13] Garryduff: M. J. O'Kelly (1962), 98, Fig. 21. 374; Dunadd: J. H. Craw (1930), 128, Fig. 8.5.

connected with the settlement site on Helgö, central Sweden. It should be observed, however, that there are marked differences in the form of the lids and knobs between the Helgö and the Dinas Powys crucibles. It is difficult, therefore, to follow Lamm's claim that 'this type of crucible cannot have emerged contemporaneously and independently in two such widely separated areas'.[14]

As Tylecote has pointed out, a major problem with the small crucibles characteristic of our period is the rapid loss of heat when the crucible is removed from the fire. The use of a

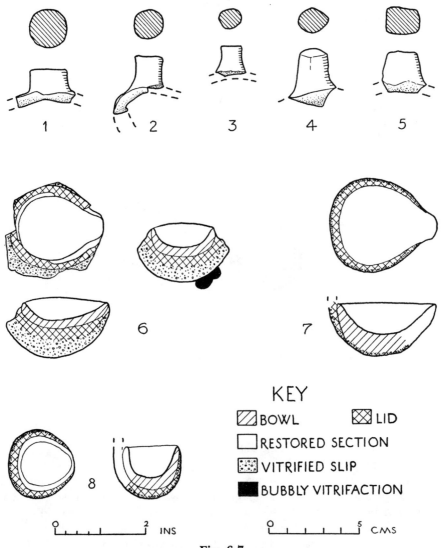

KEY

▨ BOWL   ⊠ LID
▢ RESTORED SECTION
▨ VITRIFIED SLIP
■ BUBBLY VITRIFACTION

Fig. 6.7.
Knobs and bowls from lidded crucibles. Scale 1:2

[14] K. Lamm (1980), 101.

lid helps to delay the cooling process. A further advantage is that the knob, whether it be on top of the lid or to one side, can be grasped with tongs to facilitate handling the crucible for pouring into a mould.[15] Given these technical advantages, and given, moreover, that the period was one of considerable technological experiment both in Scandinavia and around the Irish Sea,[16] it is not surprising that, among a considerable variety of crucible forms, similar types should emerge in both areas. Moreover, this very variety made it premature, in 1963, to attempt to determine the ancestry of the lidded crucible.[17] Even now, it cannot be said that we have enough well-published examples to enable us to establish the typology of crucibles.

Traces of metal and metallic dross, adhering to the inside of the bowl, and especially to the lip of the spout, show that the Dinas Powys crucibles had mostly been used for bronze-working. One, however, had a globule of gold, 0.5 millimetre diameter, in the spout, as well as minute flecks of gold both in the spout and towards the rear of the bowl (Fig. 6.6). There is no evidence that any of these vessels had been used for the preparation of vitreous paste (enamel).

The overall stratification of crucible sherds is tabulated below:

Layer	N	O	O/A	A	B	B/C	C	C/D	D	H	U	Total
Number of sherds	3*	11	2	5	3	6	22	38	12	11	43	156

* Vitrified clay, not certainly from crucible.

Fig. 6.6. Fragments of bowl, lid, and spout of two or three lidded crucibles, found together in an extensive ashy patch under Bank I (Section 4, layer (7), O layer) together with a reconstruction of the type.

Fig. 6.7. 1–5.   Type series of knobs from lidded crucibles.

6.   Complete bowl from a shallow pear-shaped crucible, originally lidded, as is shown by the double thickness of the rear wall.

7–8.   Fragmentary bowls from lidded crucibles.

[15] R. F. Tylecote (1962), 130–41.
[16] K. Lamm (1980); L. Alcock (1963a), 141.
[17] Compare Tylecote's attempt to establish a typology: R. F. Tylecote (1962), 135 with Fig. 31.

CHAPTER 7

Bone Objects[1]

Bone was frequently used at Dinas Powys for objects of utility and ornament; but apart from a group of combs which are considered in detail below (pp. 127–33) no lengthy introduction is needed. Many of these pieces have rather indifferent parallels on those Irish early Christian sites where bone was well preserved.

In addition to the illustrated pieces there was also a number of bones with knife-cuts which may either be relics of the kitchen or bones discarded from manufacturing pins or other ornaments. Several utilized teeth were also noticed. Five pieces of red deer antler were also found, none of them stratified. One is certainly from a shed antler.

The stratification of bone objects was as follows:

Layer	N	O	O/A	A	B	B/C	C	C/D	D	H	U	G1	G6
Bone Objects	—	—	—	2	1	2	6	8	4	3	5	—	1
Combs	—	1	1	1	—	—	3	8	1	1	3	1	—
Utilized bone	—	—	—	1	—	—	4	2	—	—	1	—	—

1.   Complete polished pin with plain head. There is a rather larger pin of the same form from Buiston crannog.[2]

2.   Bone pin with plain head ornamented with finely incised lines making an irregular spiral: the point is missing. For a pin with even feebler spiraliform ornament, cf. Cahercommaun.[3]

3.   Pin with slightly hooked head; or less probably an attempt to make in bone an ear-scoop or toilet-spoon based on Roman examples of bronze.

4.   Elaborately ornamented fragment, perhaps from the head of a pin. One end is preserved, but the other is broken, and only about one-third of the original circumference is intact. The ornament consists of two pairs of mouldings separated by two zones each with three tapering pits. The ornament undoubtedly recalls that of some ornate Roman bone pins.

---

[1] A. G. MacGregor (1985) shows that bone tissue derived from red deer antler was preferred for many purposes to bone tissue derived from the rest of the skeleton. Strictly, therefore, some of the objects catalogued here should be described as of antler, not bone; but since this was not recognized originally, I have continued to use the general term bone.
[2] R. Munro (1882), Fig. 205.
[3] H. O'N. Hencken (1938), Fig. 23, 271.

Nos. 1–4 all have circular cross-sections. There are four other fragments of circular-sectioned pins.

5.   Bone animal-headed pin or 'toilet article', with shaft of flattened section; the point is missing. The head bears a superficial resemblance to Roman bone pins or ligulae with dolphins or dragonesque heads.

6.   Crudely-carved bone peg, representative of a group of nine such pegs. Two appear to have been whittled out of broken pins, but the remainder were probably carved from slivers of bone. They range in length from $1\frac{1}{4}$ inches to $\frac{5}{8}$ inch. They may have been intended for playing a board game like that for which a board was found at Ballinderry No. 1.[4]

7.   Bone needle with a broad flat head with circular perforation. The pointed end snapped off anciently, and the stump was then crudely trimmed to a blunt point, presumably for use as a peg.

8.   Bone cylinder, with socket to take a metal shank, probably of an iron pin. Two examples.

9.   Tubular bone object ornamented with shallow grooves, perhaps a bead.

10.   Fragment of a bone ring. The existing arc suggests a diameter of rather less than 1 inch for the inner curve, which would be suitable for a finger- or toe-ring; but the ring itself seems too thick and clumsy for such a purpose.

11.   Bone plaque, ornamented with dot-and-circle motifs, and perforated for fixing to some larger object, perhaps a wooden box.

12.   Segment from the tusk of a wild boar, perforated and fixed with an iron nail to some larger object as an ornament. Also two other examples, not illustrated.

13.   Bun-shaped spindle-whorl or bead very regularly made, doubtless on a lathe, and ornamented with fine concentric grooves.

14.   Spindle-whorl made from the head of a femur. A second example is not illustrated.

15.   Metacarpal of sheep or goat, with transverse perforation, perhaps a bobbin for winding wool for weaving.

16.   Irregular bone disk, perhaps a gaming-piece.

COMPOSITE ANTLER COMBS[5] (Figs. 7.1, 17 and 7.2, 23)
Fragments of a score of double-edged combs were recovered at Dinas Powys. These had been made as follows. Several thin plates of antler, of the thickness required for the teeth of the comb, were laid side by side, with the grain of the antler lying in the line of the proposed teeth. The plates were then clamped together between two ribs or connecting strips with their grain running the length of the comb; that is, at right angles to the teeth. These ribs had already been shaped, and perhaps even decorated, before they were

---

[4] H. O'N. Hencken (1936), 175–90. Bone pegs were also commonly used in Scottish brochs and wheel-houses for fastening together composite objects of bone.

[5] The original account of these combs (*Dinas Powys* 1963, 154ff) has been modified in the light of A. G. MacGregor and J. D. Currey (1983).

Fig. 7.1.
Objects of worked bone and antler. Scale 1:1

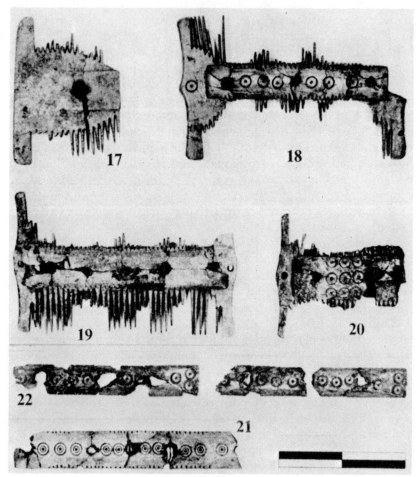

Fig. 7.2.
Composite antler combs. Scale of inches

fastened to the teeth-plates with iron rivets. (There is no evidence for either bone pegs or bronze rivets at Dinas Powys). After the blank comb had been put together in this way, the teeth were sawn; the cuts normally extended on to the fastening ribs. In 1963, attention was drawn to the grooves which occur on the narrow edges of the teeth, and continue only a little way on to the faces. This beading, common though it is on combs of the period, had not previously attracted notice. MacGregor has now suggested that it is the result of abrasion when the comb is dragged through tangled hair.

Composite combs of this form, with varied dot-and-circle decoration, are characteristic of the Roman period, and more especially of the Dark Ages in both Celtic and Teutonic areas. In so far as significant parallels can be drawn among such combs, which were doubtless fabricated locally as well as in large proto-urban craft centres, it is the shape and decoration of the fastening ribs and of the end plates which provide the basis of comparison. On the whole, the combs from Dinas Powys are more closely related to those from Ireland and Scotland than to those found in pagan Saxon graves.

Study of the composite combs found in the Irish Sea area prompts several questions. Firstly, why were the combs made of antler at all, given that the raw material had largely to be obtained from shed antlers, which had to be gathered by following herds of red deer in the spring? Presumably one reason was the relative availability and cheapness of bone tissue, as against more suitable materials such as boxwood and ivory, from which one-piece combs might have been carved. Bone and antler would have provided a tough, somewhat elastic substance, that could readily be cut to shape. Both are considerably stronger along the grain than across it. This in itself determined the need for the composite comb, in which the two elements, the teeth-plates and the fastening ribs, have their grain at right angles. The price that had to be paid was, of course, a thick and heavy article. The reason for the choice of antler was that, as no doubt experience had shown, it is tougher than other bone tissue, and is therefore less likely to snap under the sudden strain of snagging in entangled hair. We may also wonder whether antler was a cheap substitute for ivory: the appearance of the two is sufficiently alike for early antiquaries to have mistakenly classified some antler combs as being of ivory.

The second question one must ask is why such a large number of these combs—and certainly all those found at Dinas Powys—were double-sided. Roman double-sided combs have, as might be expected, a small number of coarse teeth along one side, and a significantly larger number of finer teeth along the other. This difference is maintained on many continental combs of the Migration period. For instance, out of eleven adequately illustrated combs from Köln-Müngersdorf, only one from grave 37 appears to have a more or less even number of teeth on both sides; the remainder are markedly uneven, that from grave 131 having only thirty-five coarse teeth to seventy fine ones. Among the pagan Saxons, however, a marked disparity between the two rows of teeth is less common. Baldwin Brown illustrates a comb from Arreton Down,[6] of which the best-preserved portion has twenty-four coarse teeth to thirty-eight fine teeth; and a comb from Lackford exhibits a ratio of 2:3. But on the preserved part of the comb from Burwell grave 79, there are twenty-three teeth on one side and only three more on the other; and all these teeth are more or less equally coarse. The same is true of the combs from Abingdon. In short, among the pagan Saxons, the two sides of a comb do not always differ in the number and fineness of the teeth. Finally, in the Celtic West we find that it is normal for the two sides to be closely similar, differing at most by six teeth out of some fifty on either side. Thus, two well-preserved combs from Buiston crannog have respectively 46:49 and 34:35 teeth, while combs from Lagore show proportions like 29:31, 34:34, and 40:44. The same is broadly true of combs from Cahercommaun, Carraig Aille, Dunadd, and Bantham, and also of the present series from Dinas Powys. The teeth on these Celtic combs tend to be rather finer than the coarse teeth on the Romano-British combs, but it is doubtful whether they can match the delicacy of the fine teeth. This would suggest that it was indifferent craftsmanship which led to the abandonment of the differentiation between the two rows. But since the main reason for having two rows is surely to have both coarse and fine teeth on one and the same comb, it is difficult to see why the double-edged comb was not abandoned. That it maintained its popularity down to the coming of the Vikings is surely a witness to the control of tradition over craftsmanship.

Thirdly, we may ask whether these more or less ornate combs were meant to be worn about the person, perhaps in the hair. The tale of *Culhwch and Olwen* provides a hint that

[6] G. B. Brown (1903–30), IV, Pl. LXXXV, 3.

this may be so. For when Culhwch and his companions go for the second time to the court of Ysbaddaden Chief Giant, we are told:[7]

On the morrow with pomp and with brave combs set in their hair they came into the hall.

It is naturally tempting to equate the 'brave combs' with the double-edged composite combs of bone found so commonly on Celtic sites, and to interpret these as intended for adorning as well as for dressing the hair. But other considerations suggest that this is unlikely. In the first place, a single-edged comb with relatively long teeth is far more serviceable than a double-edged one with short teeth for holding hair piled on top of the head. Indeed, the composite comb, made heavy and clumsy by its central ribs and rivets, would have been singularly difficult to fix in the hair, even if the grooving of the teeth was intended to give them purchase. Secondly, there appears to be no unambiguous archaeological evidence that the northern and western barbarians of the Migration period wore such combs in their hair. Apart from the stele of a Frankish warrior from Niederdollendorf interpreted by Salin against all probability as showing a comb in the hair,[8] the chief evidence comes from the position of combs in pagan burials. Occasionally, it is true, one is found beneath or against the skull, suggesting that it had been in the hair of the dead person. Salin quotes as an example the burial of a chieftain from Monceau-le-Neuf (Aisne) with a comb beneath the head;[9] and in a rather cursory survey of the literature I have noticed examples from Harnham grave 4, by the right side of the head, and Mitcham grave 45, behind the head. But these examples are clearly exceptional. Where a cemetery is fully illustrated with drawings of individual graves, as is that at Köln-Müngersdorf, it is clear that only very rarely is the comb even in the region of the head (graves 78, 81, 138); the normal positions are by or below the waist, or below the feet. In all these positions the comb may be associated with shears and other hair-dressing instruments, all of which had probably been held in a wallet or box. Even when the comb is under the head, it is doubtful whether this represents anything more than a location governed by association of ideas; for in at least four instances at Köln-Müngersdorf, toilet shears were found hard by or even under the skull (graves 27, 70, 83, 110)—and clearly these cannot have been intended as hair-ornaments. Very occasionally a comb is found on the chest of a skeleton (e.g. Burwell, grave 83) in such a way as to suggest that it had originally been hung around the neck, and this may well have been so with the combs which have perforated ends. But there seems to be no other evidence for the wearing of composite bone combs, either in the hair or about the person, among the Teutonic peoples. Obviously this is not conclusive evidence of Celtic practices; but it suggests the general probability.

Finally, we should notice the importance of hair-dressing and the combs and other instruments associated with it among the northern and western barbarians. Significant here is Pope Boniface's gift of a silver mirror, together with a gold and ivory comb, to Ethelberga, wife of Edwin of Northumbria, at the time when Paulinus was seeking to convert Edwin to Christianity.[10] The frequency with which combs, sometimes accompanied by shears and other toilet articles, occur in Teutonic graves emphasizes the highly personal nature of these objects. The model or token combs and shears found with

[7] G. Jones and T. Jones (1949), 112.
[8] E. Salin (1950–9), I, 105, with Pl. I.
[9] E. Salin (1950–9), II, 243.
[10] HE ii, 11.

cremations at Abingdon may point to a ritual of hair-dressing. The magical significance of hair- and nail-cuttings is well known, and it is possible that this extended in some way to the toilet instruments themselves. In the Celtic world, important clues can be found in the most primitive of the Mabinogion tales, that of *Culhwch and Olwen*. Several of the tasks assigned to Culhwch and his comrades are concerned with providing implements for shaving the beard and dressing the hair of Ysbaddaden Chief Giant on his daughter's wedding day. Indeed the task which is most fully reported in the tale as we have it, and which was most costly for Arthur's followers, was to obtain the comb and shears from between the ears of Twrch Trwyth. And the first boon which Culhwch asked of Arthur, his cousin, after his flamboyant entry into the king's hall was to have his hair trimmed.

Arthur took a golden comb and shears with loops of silver and he combed his hair.[11]

Here we seem to have an echo of some pagan ritual connected with the first dressing of a young man's hair, perhaps on his entry to manhood. A christianization of such rituals may underlie the liturgical use of the comb in the consecration of bishops.[12]

17.   Fragment from a comb with straight ends: one iron rivet preserved in position; even number of teeth either side. From nearby in the same level came part of an undecorated rib of plano-convex section which is probably from the same comb. This piece is important in any discussion of the method of manufacture of the combs. The right-hand edge is not a fracture, but is the original edge of one of the strips from which the comb was built up. The emplacement of the ribs shows as a raised zone along the centre of either face, suggesting that the strips from which the teeth were cut were tapered out to the edge, probably by rubbing down, after the ribs had been fixed; the zone under the ribs would, of course, be protected and would remain as a raised or reserved band. If this marks the full extent of the rib, then it stopped unusually far short of the end of the comb leaving a large number of teeth unsupported.

18.   Comb with flattened ogival ends ornamented with a single dot-and-circle motif. The central ribs are of thin rectangular section with bevelled edges and are held by three iron rivets; they are decorated with two groups of three dot-and-circle motifs. The flattened ogival end is a distinctive local feature, seen again on Nos. 19 and 20.

19.   Comb with flattened ogival ends, each with a small perforation and plain ribs of thin rectangular section with bevelled edges, held by five iron rivets. The perforations found on other combs of this type may have been for attaching a safety loop; but some pagan Anglo-Saxon evidently wore elaborate combs suspended on bead-bedecked loops around their necks, e.g. Burwell, grave 83. There are forty-five teeth on one side, but only thirty-six on the other.

20.   Fragment comprising rather more than half of a comb; flattened ogival end with perforation; ribs of thin rectangular section with bevelled edges held in place with an iron rivet at either end and a closely set pair of rivets in the centre; ribs decorated with two square groups of six dot-and-circle motifs. Teeth apparently even on both sides.

---

[11] G. Jones and T. Jones (1949), 100.
[12] P. Lasko (1956), 343.

21.   Greater part of one rib from a comb of which the other fragments could not be reconstructed. Originally held in place with five iron rivets, and ornamented with dot-and-circle motifs arranged in the order 3–2–2–3. Teeth apparently even on both sides.

22.   Fragments of both ribs of a comb of which the other fragments could not be reconstructed. Truncated wedge section, with a marked splay at either end. The splayed ends are decorated with three dots-and-circles, and the flat top of the ribs has two groups of three such motifs, separated by the holes for three iron rivets.

23.   Fragment from the rib of a comb ornamented with bunches of diagonal grooves; there are four such grooves on this and a second fragment. This seems to be a late motif, for it occurs in Period III, perhaps the tenth century AD, at Lagore, and also at Ballinderry crannog No. 1, dated late tenth century.[13]

[13] Lagore: H. O'N. Hencken (1950), Fig. 97, 1,283; Ballinderry No. 1: H. O'N. Hencken (1936), Fig. 6E.

CHAPTER 8

Utilized Stone

SANDSTONE (Figs. 8.1, 8.2, 8.3)

In terms of bulk, the most conspicuous material at Dinas Powys was sandstone, of which about 170 lbs. weight had been introduced to the site. As the table shows, its stratification is characteristic of Phase 4: that is, it appears first in the O and A layers, but is principally present in the C/D layers. The sandstones used were mostly fine-grained and deep red, though browns and greys also occur. Occasionally lumps measuring up to 7-inches cube were used as pounding-, rubbing-, and whetting-blocks, while thick slabs might be used as hearthstones; but most of the sandstone was imported in hand-sized or smaller pebbles. The ultimate source of these was doubtless the Old Red Sandstone and other sandstone outcrops to the north of Dinas Powys; but the smoothly rounded shape of most of the pebbles shows that they had been derived immediately from drift deposits—whether boulder clays or outwash fans—or less probably from stream beds.

Stratification of sandstone in pounds and ounces

Function	O	A	B	C	D	C/D	H	U	Total
					Layer				
Whetstones	1.10	2.1	—	0.14	0.8	1.5	0.4½	1.4	7.14½
Rubbing-stones	3.4	2.1	0.12¼	0.12¼	11.4	20.6	2.11	15.10½	56.13
Bake-stones	0.15	1.3	—	0.8	0.7	3.11	0.13	0.6	7.15
Rotary quern	—	—	—	—	—	18.0	—	2.15	20.15
Saddle quern	—	—	—	—	9.8	8.8	—	—	18.0
Unclassified	2.8½	1.14	—	1.8	5.8	17.11	3.5¾	26.2	58.9¼
Total	8.5½	7.3	0.12¼	3.10¼	27.3	69.9	7.2¼	46.5½	170.2¾

Although many of the sandstone pieces are too fragmentary or featureless to provide any clue to their original use, a significant number can be classified in functional terms. Thus thin slabs, often with one side fire-blackened, may have come from griddles or bake-stones (though the one restorable example (Fig. 8.3, 13) seems too small for this, and may have been a pot lid). Pebbles with their sides or edges dished or concave and noticeably smoothed had clearly been used as whetstones. By contrast an important series with highly polished or glossy surfaces which are convex, not concave, can certainly not have been whetstones, and are here described as polishing- or rubbing-stones. Small

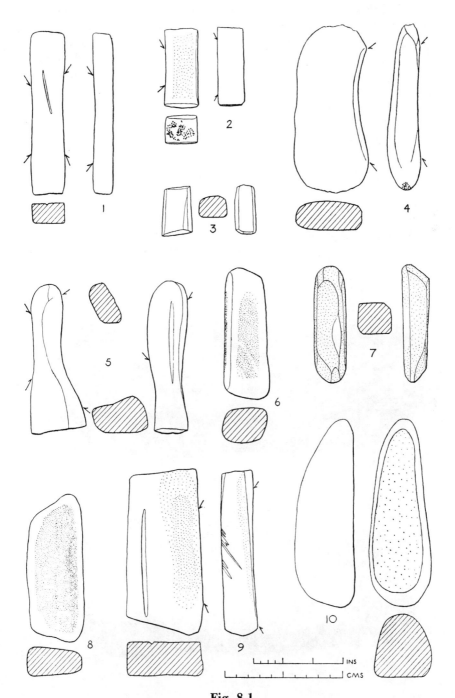

Fig. 8.1.
Whetstones and rubbing-stones. Scale 1:3
Arrows indicate dished (i.e. whetting) surfaces; fine stipple marks polish; coarse stipple
shows battering

globular or ovoid pebbles suggest slingstones. Finally, a very few pieces belong to querns. These various classes must now be given more detailed consideration.

The whetstones fall into two broad classes: those in which the section is noticeably rectangular, with sharp arrises, and those in which it is more irregular. In some cases, the rectangular section may represent the original shape of the pebble, as it seems to in Fig. 8.1, 1; here the rock is markedly laminated, and presumably fractured naturally with joints and bedding planes at right angles. In other cases, like Fig. 8.1, 2, the rectangular section seems to be artificially contrived in order to produce a neat and readily portable hone. Where a long pebble has been picked up and utilized in its natural state, with first one side and then the other in use for whetting, extremely irregular shapes like Fig. 8.1, 5, may result. Again, some rubbing-stones show faces or arrises which have lost their polish and have become dished through secondary use as whetstones. A number of stones bear straight, shallow grooves on one surface; these are usually interpreted as intended for sharpening the points of pins of metal or bone. All these features can be paralleled on sites in the Celtic West, and especially in Ireland. (On the other hand, whetstones perforated for suspension, though common in Ireland, are unknown at Dinas Powys.) Such

INS

Fig. 8.2.
Stone bearing (see also 8.3) and rubbing-stone

comparisons suggest that the whetstones at Dinas Powys are a feature of the early Christian metal industry and especially of the manufacture of the knives which are so plentiful among the iron objects. This suggestion is confirmed by the discovery of two of the most definite whetstones from the site (Fig. 8.1, 1 and 5) in O and A layers in the north-eastern industrial quarter.

The distinction between whetstones and rubbing-stones outlined above deserves further emphasis. There is firstly a clear difference in surface effect, in that the working surfaces of a whetstone are merely smoother than the unused faces of the same stone, whereas the surface of a rubbing-stone is highly polished, often to the extent of acting as a mirror (Fig. 8.2). It is true that some degree of polish may result when a whetstone is used dry; but it is doubtful whether this would produce a mirror-like polish. In any case, the curvature of the polished surface tells against the interpretation of these rubbing-stones as hones. With a whetstone, the pressure of the knife or other blade being sharpened in-evitably wears down the surface of the stone, so that it becomes dished along the axis of use (normally the long axis of the stone). But with the rubbers, there is no dishing along either the long or short axis; on the contrary the working surface, as shown by the distribution of polish, is frequently convex, for the gloss sometimes continues from the main faces of a stone over the sides as well. It may be suggested that just such a polish could only be produced by rubbing or smoothing a slightly resilient substance. The most likely explanation of these rubbing-stones is that they were used for finishing and polish-ing leather, though they may also have been used as linen-smoothers.

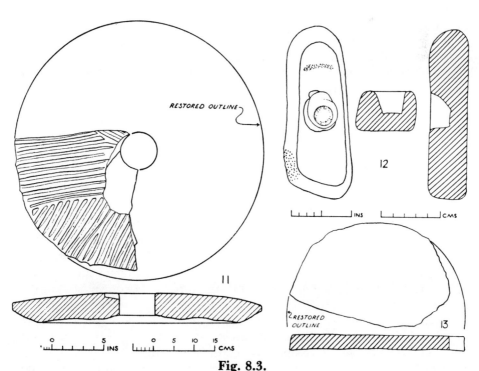

Fig. 8.3.
Fragment of a rotary quern, stone bearing (8.2), and fragment of supposed bake-stone.
Stipple shows polish

The stones used as polishers are invariably natural pebbles of a convenient size for the hand and a suitable shape for the job. There is no evidence that such pebbles were worked or trimmed to shape, and here is a further contrast between the polishers and the whetstones. Three main shapes may be distinguished: the pebble may have a squarish cross-section (Nos. 6 and 7); it may be flattish or slabby (Nos. 8 and 9); or more rarely it may be keeled (No. 10). Now stones of these shapes have frequently been found on Celtic sites of the sixth to eleventh centuries AD, and have usually been interpreted as whetstones. In default of a detailed description of the wear or polish, it is usually impossible to tell whether they should really be thought of as hones or as polishers. Thus, among the stones from Garranes are some which could have served as rubbing-stones; but personal inspection has shown that they lack the characteristic polish, and must therefore be whetstones. Among the very large collection of comparable stones from Garryduff, the majority are clearly whetstones, and only a few show signs of polish suggesting that they may have been used as rubbers. On the other hand, the supposed whetstones from Ballycatteen, to judge from the published drawings, show very little sign of axial dishing, whereas the excavators state expressly that 'both flat surfaces were, in most cases, polished from use'; these, then, may well be rubbing-stones. Clearly there is need for more work on excavated material, as well as for more detailed reporting in future excavation reports, before the incidence and distribution of whetstones and rubbing-stones can be established for the Celtic West.

One further important use of sandstone on the site was for querns. Two large but badly shattered blocks or slabs (one originally more than $10\frac{1}{2}$ by $6\frac{1}{2}$ by $1\frac{3}{4}$ inches; the other more than $7\frac{1}{2}$ by 6 by $2\frac{3}{4}$ inches) have slightly dished upper surfaces, and seem to have been used as saddle querns, or at least as pounding- or grinding-stones. There are two pieces from the rims of upper stones of rotary querns, both so fragmentary that they reveal nothing of the form of the querns themselves; one has its grinding surface roughened by pecking. Finally, there is one-quarter of a lower stone from a table-mounted quern with grooved grinding surface and central perforation to permit the adjustment of the upper stone (Fig. 8.3, 11).

A representative series of whetstones and rubbing-stones is illustrated in Fig. 8.1. Nos. 1–5 are whetstones, ranging from small, neat examples like 2 and 3, to very irregular ones like 5. Nos. 6–10 have all been used, to a greater or lesser extent, as rubbing-stones: No. 5 shows use as a whetstone as well. Nos. 1, 5 and 9 all have pin-grooves. Figure 8.3 illustrates a fragment of rotary quern, a stone bearing which may have come from such a quern, and a fragment from a bake-stone or pot lid.

11.   One-quarter of the lower stone of a rotary quern of sandstone. The upper surface, which is damaged towards the central hole, bears rather irregularly-disposed radial grooves up to 3 millimetres deep; some of the lands between the grooves have been rubbed almost flat near the perimeter of the quern. The underside was left roughly flaked. The object of this is to ensure a good grip when the quern is bedded down, so that the lower stone does not turn with the friction of the upper stone. The presence of a central hole makes it clear that the quern was not bedded in the floor. Moritz suggests[1] three possible reasons for perforated lower stones which must come from querns in which the upper stone is supported on a spindle passing through the lower stone: (1) they make it possible to adjust the distance between the two stones; (2) they make it possible to drive the upper

[1] L. A. Moritz (1958), 122–8.

stone from below by means of man-, animal-, or water-power as with the Vitruvian water-mill or the 'large Saalburg' mill; (3) they also occur on certain tripartite querns known, for instance, from La Tène. The last two reasons certainly cannot apply to the Dinas Powys quern, and it follows that this was an adjustable model.

Our quern, then, may be reconstructed as set in a clay bed on a bench or table, like the Scottish querns of recent times described by Mitchell and photographed by H. B. Curwen.[2] In the central hole would be a wooden block to act as bearing for the spindle on which the upper stone was set. The spindle would pass down through the lower stone and the table to rest on a bearing of wood or stone so arranged that its height could be finely adjusted, thus altering the separation of the two stones. It has usually been supposed that the purpose of this adjustment was to make it possible to produce coarse or fine flour at will, but Moritz's experiments appear to suggest that this was not so.[3] It seems more likely that grain was first ground at a coarse setting in order to remove the bran without pulverizing it; much of the flour produced at this first grinding would already be fine. The grist would then be sifted to separate the bran from the flour proper, which would then be ground again with the quern-stones set closer. Apart from this, however, some means of adjusting the setting of the stones must have been needed to compensate for the wear of the stones, which would have been especially pronounced with grooved stones.

The relative thinness of this lower stone, the low angle of its grinding surface, the grooving, and the central hole all concur in pointing to a date not earlier than the late Roman period.[4] Given the general cultural history of the site, it seems most reasonable to see the quern as part of the sub-Roman legacy at Dinas Powys, and to place it in the fifth to seventh centuries AD as its find spot—a C/D layer at the head of the northern slope— would suggest. If this dating is accepted, then it is interesting to notice that the present quern is distinguished from the contemporary Irish and Scottish series by the rough flaking of the bottom surface and the grooving of the grinding surface.

12.   Old Red Sandstone pebble used as a bearing for some form of rotating spindle (Fig. 8.2). The socket was presumably cylindrical originally, but is very much worn down on the one side through the spindle not running true. The bottom of the socket is highly polished, and there is a fainter band of polish lying concentric with the socket across the upper face of the bearing. The pebble itself is a convenient size to hold in the hand, and would therefore make a suitable butt-bearing for a bow-drill. But such a use would not account for the concentric band of polish, which suggests that the spindle had a wide flange or projection which rubbed on the top of the stone as the spindle rotated. It seems unlikely that this is a lathe-bearing, but it could well be the bottom bearing for an adjustable quern like No. 11.

In addition to its use as a bearing, the pebble shows signs of smoothing, and even a slight polish, on both sides and on the base, so presumably it had also been utilized as a rubbing-stone. Marked battering at the lower left corner suggests that it may occasionally have been used for pounding, too.

13.   Fragment from a disc of Old Red Sandstone. Many other fragments of sandstone slabs of comparable thickness were found on the site and in the numerical analysis these

[2] A. Mitchell (1880), 33; E. C. Curwen (1937), Pl. III.
[3] L. A. Moritz (1958), 156.
[4] E. C. Curwen (1937).

have been treated as bake-stones. This is the only piece which provides any evidence of the size and shape to which these slabs might be worked, and it must be admitted that it seems too small to make a satisfactory bake-stone. Some of the other fragments, however, were considerably larger than this and showed signs of burning, so they may well have come from bake-stones. The present piece may be a pot lid.

FLINT AND CHERT

The original Dinas Powys monograph (pp. 168–75) contained a detailed discussion of 169 pieces of flint and chert, the majority of them bearing traces of human working. This discussion was based on an examination and report by Dr G. J. Wainwright. It was shown that 12 per cent of the flints were either securely stratified in the N layers, where the associated pottery made it possible to assign them to the pre-Roman Iron Age (Dinas Powys 1), or came from the lowest make-up of Rampart I, the B layers, which were immediately derived from the N layers. Of the remaining 88 per cent some might have been rubbish survivals from Dinas Powys 1, or alternatively might have been used and discarded in Phase 4. It seems certain that, in spite of the abundance of iron in Phase 4, flint and chert continued to be utilized as they were on other sites of the Celtic West. But neither typology nor stratification provide any clear grounds for dividing the flint and chert objects into an Iron Age and an early Christian industry. Consequently, it has been thought best to omit Dr Wainwright's discussion and illustrations from the present volume.

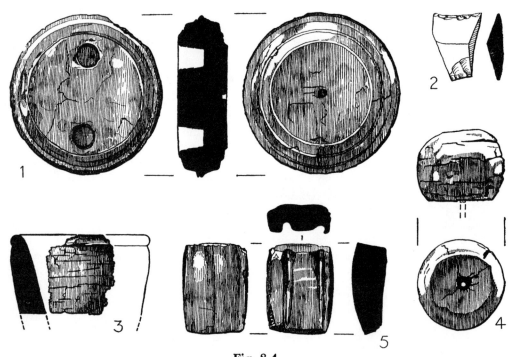

Fig. 8.4.
Objects of shale and lignite, and flint lathe-tool. Scale 1:1

OBJECTS OF SHALE AND LIGNITE (Fig. 8.4)

These were all found in a very fragile condition, and it was therefore necessary to impregnate them immediately with polyvinyl acetate in order to preserve them. Because of this, it has not been easy to establish for certain the material of which some of them are made.

1.   Kimmeridge shale core or waster from the lathe-manufacture of armlets. The core belongs to Calkin's Class C,[5] with two peg-holes to receive the chuck on one face and a slight central depression on the other. Probably Romano-British, but not otherwise closely datable.

2.   With the armlet core is to be associated a flint lathe-tool made on a section of a triangular blade. The slightly hollow working edge is finely-chipped with use. The tool is comparable to Calkin's Fig. 8, No. 25.

The implications of the discovery at Dinas Powys of these by-products of the Isle of Purbeck shale armlet industry are discussed on p. 23.

3.   Fragment of a shale (?) cylinder, perhaps part of a handle. The section tapers from the broken edge towards an original lip or rim which is slightly beaded.

4.   Lignite bobble head for a bronze pin: a fragment of the shank of the pin is preserved. Such pin-heads appear to be a distinctively Scottish type. Examples in cetaceous bone occur in brochs in Orkney and Caithness such as the Broch of Ayre, Orkney; their date is not readily established, but Stevenson would assign them to the late, i.e. post-Roman, Iron Age.[6] Other bone examples, close in size to that from Dinas Powys, were found at Buiston crannog, where a central date in the seventh century seems possible.

5.   Fragment of a jet bead, rectangular in plan, sub-rectangular in section, with two longitudinal perforations.

[5] J. B. Calkin (1955).
[6] R. B. K. Stevenson (1955), 292–3.

CHAPTER 9

Glass

by D. B. Harden

ROMAN (not illustrated; see p. 21)
The only fragments of glass of indubitably Roman date were the following:[1]

1.   Green: fragment of window glass of the matt/glossy variety which occurs in the first and second centuries (later window glass being double-glossy, i.e. not matt on one side).

2.   Purple with opaque white marbling: two joining fragments of side, with part of a rib, of a pillar-moulded bowl. Mid first century. For type and dating, see Harden in *Camulodunum*,[2] p. 301 f., and for marbled glass, see ibid., 292 ff.

3.   Dull green: fragment of side or base of cylindrical or prismatic bottle of early Roman (later first to second centuries) type. This piece shows internal strain-cracks caused by faulty annealing, a rare phenomenon on Roman green glass (in contrast to Roman colourless, which often shows such strains). This Roman green glass was usually well annealed.

4.   Green: fragment of lip of bottle, as last piece. From a rim that has been folded outwards, upwards, and inwards.

5.   Dark cobalt blue: fragment of bowl or beaker of first century showing polishing marks and a faint horizontal rib on exterior. The fragment thickens slightly towards one end, where it appears to be nearing the junction between side and base of vessel. The blue of this fragment is much deeper and more vivid than that of all others in this Dinas Powys group, and resembles that of a number of early Roman examples. I have no doubt that this piece, alone of all the blue ones, is early Roman, especially as it shows polishing marks, another early Roman trait.

TEUTONIC (Fig. 9.1, Scale 1:2)
The vast majority of all the fragments found at Dinas Powys belongs to vessels that fall within the general orbit of Teutonic glass. It is best to use that word, rather than Anglo-Saxon (for there is nothing to show that any one of these pieces was made in Britain), or Frankish or Merovingian, both of which terms might seem to assume too much about the glasses' origin and date. To call it Teutonic begs no questions about it, other than that it comes from north-west Europe, rather than the Mediterranean, and that it is post-Roman and earlier than 1000. We shall see later whether we can tie it down more closely than that in origin and date.

---

[1] For a Roman glass counter, see p. 149, with Fig. 9.2, 9.
[2] C. F. C. Hawkes and M. R. Hull (1947).

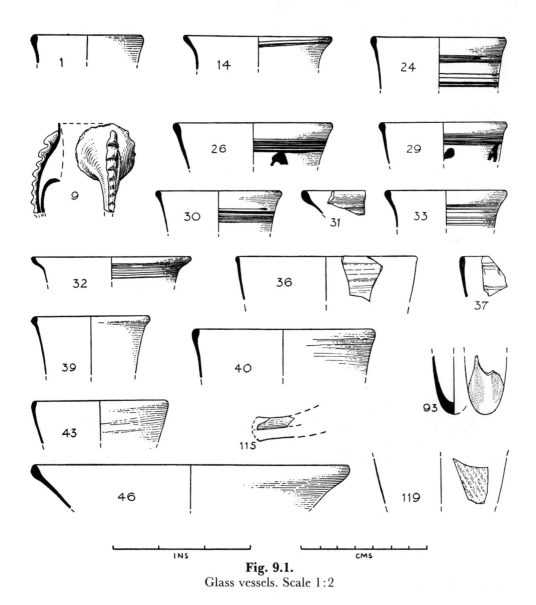

Fig. 9.1.
Glass vessels. Scale 1:2

It will be convenient to describe the glass in groups according to colour. The predominant colour is pale yellow, and many of the fragments of this colour have marvered trail decoration of opaque white as well. It is, indeed, remarkable how many fragments with opaque white trailing occur in this group. The proportion is much greater than it is in glass found in Anglo-Saxon graves, and it may be that these fragments were specially chosen for bringing to the west.[3] In Saxon graves the types which have white trails belong to groups[4] I (stemmed beakers), III (cone-beakers), V (bell-beakers), VI (bag-beakers—

[3] For a discussion of the implications of this, see above, p. 48.
[4] As classified in D. B. Harden (1956b).

the small variety only), and XI (bowls). There are also occasional examples among the pouch-bottles (VII—one only) and the squat jars (VIII—three out of seventy-nine). These types with white trails belong, as has been pointed out, to the fifth and sixth centuries, and do not, it seems, overrun into the seventh. This is certainly true for groups I, III, V, and XI. I was hesitant in Harden (1956) in deciding whether the two small bag-shaped beakers (VI) with opaque white trails could be put as late as the seventh century (the date to which I ascribe the large bag-beakers), and it is also consistent with this dating pattern that only one pouch-bottle and three squat jars should have such trails, for those shapes belong to the seventh century rather than earlier.

This trailing, then, of itself, puts this Dinas Powys group of Teutonic glass in the fifth or sixth centuries. It is interesting to note that the Mote of Mark fragments[5] also contained a fair proportion of pieces with white trails, and indeed proved to be an assemblage very closely allied in shape and decoration with the Dinas Powys group. In discussing them I inclined to date them to the sixth to early eighth century, and said they could come from 'cone-beakers, pouch-bottles, palm-cups, bowls, and squat jars'. I now see that I was wrong to include palm-cups in that list, and should rather have included stemmed beakers and bell-beakers, for it is those two groups and cone-beakers which are the most likely Teutonic glasses to have white trails. Nor should I have spread the date of the group beyond the sixth century or, at the very latest, the early seventh century.

The stratification[6] of the Teutonic glass from Dinas Powys, including both beads and fused glass, was as follows:

Layer	A/O	A	B	C	C/D	D	H	U	G1	G3	G6
Number of sherds	2	26	1	64	73	11	55	66	1	4	2

The great bulk of the stratified Teutonic glass comes, then, from the C and C/D layers of Bank I, that is the middens of Phase 4, which were thrown into the bank in Phase 5. The presence of twenty-six sherds in A layers makes it clear that glass was plentiful in Phase 4 B; but the fact that only two sherds (one of them minute) occurred in a possible O or A/O layer, suggests that glass was not imported in Phase 4 A.

The horizontal distribution of the glass is also of some interest. One hundred and fifty sherds—about one-half of all the glass—came from the restricted area of the north end of Cut IV, the south end of Cut X, the west end of Cut XVII, and Cuts XV and XXX between IV and XVII. No less than seventy sherds came from Cut XV alone. This would suggest that the middens in which the glass had lain before it was incorporated in Bank I had accumulated around the southern and eastern edges of the work-yard outside Houses I and II (p. 31). By contrast, the north-east corner of the site (Cuts XXII–XXIX), so rich in evidence of metalworking, produced only seventeen sherds of glass. The fused glass, on the other hand, showed a remarkable concentration in Cut XVIII, which produced ten out of the eighteen lumps of fused glass from the site. It should be added that the distribution of crucible sherds was somewhat similar: a marked concentration in Cuts

[5] D. B. Harden (1956b), 150, with Fig. 27 and Pl. XVII B.
[6] This and the following paragraph are by L.A.

IV, XV, and XVII, but very few at the north-east corner, except for fourteen sherds from Cut XII, ten of which came from the O layer.

The following is a catalogue of the listable pieces, by colour. The catalogue is numbered serially, illustrated sherds being distinguished by an asterisk*. Dimensions are given for unillustrated sherds: D = diameter, L = length, W = width.

Dark blue
*1. Fragment of rim of cone-beaker (?) or bag-beaker (?): rim folded solid, and rounded in flame; much weathered on exterior.

2. Fragment of body of cone-beaker (?) or squat jar (?), misshapen: on body part of a trail of similar glass. L. 3.5 centimetres.

3. Fragment of side, very thinly blown: three horizontal lines of opaque white trails. L. 1.3 centimetres.

4. Fragment as last, with two horizontal lines of opaque white. L. 1 centimetre.

5. Fragment of side of vessel, misshapen: two tooled knobs on what was formerly the exterior of the vessel, but now looks like the interior. L. 3 centimetres.

6–8. Three featureless fragments of side of vessels.

Yellow to dark brown
*9. Claw, dark brown, from a claw-beaker (Group II): on exterior, vertically, a nicked trail. A well-made claw from a claw-beaker of Class C (so-called 'degenerate' type) of the sixth century. It closely resembles the claws on the Fairford and Howletts examples (Harden (1956), Fig. 25 and Pl. XVII, A).

10. Fragment of body of cone-beaker (?), amber, with two thin vertical trails of opaque white, 5 millimetres apart. L. 1.1 centimetres.

Emerald green
11. Fragment, perhaps chipped off unworked block. This is almost certainly an ancient piece, yet no other example of this colour exists in this assemblage.

Dark olive-green
12. Two contiguous fragments of side of cone-beaker (?), featureless. L. 2.7 centimetres.

Green
13. Fragment of rim of bowl: thickened rim, rounded in flame; straight tapering sides. D. doubtful, but at least 12 centimetres, i.e. too big for a cone-beaker.

Pale green
*14–15. Two fragments, not contiguous, of cone-beaker (?) or bowl (?): rim folded solid and rounded in flame. Opaque white trail just below rim. Bubbly glass, much weathered, and showing a few strain-cracks.

16–17.   Two fragments of sides (near rim) of stemmed, bell, or cone-beakers showing horizontal spiral marvered trails of opaque white. Too small to give dimensions of vessels.

18–19.   Two fragments of sides of beakers showing horizontal unmarvered trails in similar glass. Too small to give dimensions of vessels.

20–22.   Three fragments of sides of vessels, featureless; exact shapes uncertain.

23.   Fragment, perhaps chipped off an unworked block: almost certainly ancient.

Pale yellow
This group outnumbers all the other glass from the site put together, and this is somewhat surprising since normally, at all periods, it is green glass, not yellow, that is the most frequent. More than half the fragments listed show portions of opaque white trailed decoration, and seeing that such decoration is never used as an all-over pattern, but only as a partial one at the rim or at the middle of the body, or on the base (especially of shallow bowls), we may assume that these fragments, as a group, represent a greater number of trailed than of plain glasses, if, in fact, the pale yellow glasses represented here were not *all* trailed on some part or other of their surface.

Rims with opaque white trails: all thickened and rounded in flame
*24.   Three contiguous fragments of cone-beaker; rim not bent outwards: horizontally-laid spiral trail, starting 1 centimetre from rim and with a broad gap in it a little lower down body.

25.   Small fragment as 24, but trail begins nearer rim. D. uncertain.

*26.   Two contiguous fragments of cone-beaker; rim not bent outwards: horizontally-laid spiral trail, starting 8 millimetres from rim; below trail is the tip of a merrythought chevron.

27.   As 26, but trail begins 1.5 centimetres from rim. D. 10 centimetres.

28.   As 26, D. uncertain.

*29.   Three contiguous fragments of cone-beaker; rim not bent outwards: horizontally-laid spiral trail starting 6 millimetres from rim; below trail the tips of two merrythought chevrons, one joining with horizontal trail, thus showing that the trail and the chevron band were drawn from the same gathering of glass.

*30.   Another fragment as last, but trail different in pattern, so not from the same vessel.

*31.   Fragment of shallow bowl; rim not bent outward: horizontally-laid spiral trail (faint now, through weathering), starting 5 millimetres from rim. D. *c.* 13 centimetres.

*32.   Fragment of cone-beaker; rim strongly outbent: horizontally-laid spiral trail, starting 4 millimetres from rim.

*33.   Two contiguous fragments of cone-beaker; rim slightly outbent: horizontally-laid spiral trail starting 8 millimetres from rim.

34.   Fragment of cone-beaker, rim bent outward: horizontally-laid spiral trail starting 4 millimetres from rim; fragment shows the broadened end of trail, where it was dropped on to the vessel. D. 9 centimetres.

35. Fragment resembling 32, and probably from same vessel.

Rims, plain: all thickened and rounded in flame
*36. Fragment of cone-beaker; dulled.

*37. Fragment of cone-beaker; some strain-cracking.

38. Fragment of shallow bowl. D. uncertain.

*39. Three fragments of cone-beakers (only one illustrated), all from different vessels. D. 9 centimetres, 7.5 centimetres, and 6.5 centimetres, respectively.

*40. Fragment of cone-beaker: dulled and rough surface.

41. Tiny fragment as 40: strain-cracks of feathered type.

42. Fragment of shallow bowl. D. uncertain.

*43. Fragment of cone-beaker.

44–45. As 43. D. 8.5 centimetres and 8 centimetres, respectively.

*46. Fragment of shallow bowl: thicker and heavier than others at rim.

Fragments of sides of cone-beakers, bell-beakers, or stemmed beakers with opaque white marvered trails
47–61. Vertical loop or merrythought trails.

62–69. Swags.

70–92. Horizontal trails, single or in spirals.

Fragment of base of cone-beaker with opaque white marvered trail
*93. Base of cone-beaker, rounded end, no pontil-mark, but a jagged line 15 millimetres up the side on one side only which might be the mark of a cylindrical post-attachment. Three vertical loops coming almost to the bottom.

Fragments of sides of cone-beakers, plain
94–103. Thin walls.

104–108. Thick walls.

Fragments of sides of stemmed (?) beakers, plain
109–110. Thin walls.

111. Thick walls.

Fragments of sides of shallow bowls, plain

112–114. All with thin walls.

Fragments of end of a drinking-horn, plain
*115. Two contiguous (?) fragments of vessel of small diameter (*c.* 1.2 centimetres) which tapers a bit towards the end, where it bends inwards. It could therefore come from the butt end of a drinking-horn, and I can find no other shape that it resembles at all. But

these drinking-horns are, I think, usually of thicker glass, for they are all large pieces. I am not, therefore, confident of this identification.

Fragment with unmarvered trails of opaque white glass
116.   Fragment of body of stemmed beaker with horizontal trails.

Fragments with unmarvered trails of similar glass

117.   Fragment from near base of a claw-beaker with horizontal spiral trail. For its position on a claw-beaker cp. the Finglesham claw,[7] or the Howletts claw.[8] D. *c.* 2.2 centimetres.

118.   Fragment of side of cone-beaker (?) with single trail.

Fragment of cone-beaker with pre-moulded ribbing
*119.   Fragment of side, thin glass, with faint, closely-set, and slightly wrythen ribbing. From a cone such as Harden (1956), Pl. XVII, A b.

BEADS (Fig. 9.2, Scale 1:1)
Eight beads in all were found, and they seem to be of mixed origin—some Teutonic, some Coptic, and some perhaps Roman survivals. Illustrated beads are marked with an asterisk*.

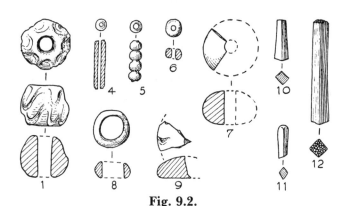

Fig. 9.2.
Glass beads (1–7), counter (9), and rods (10–11), and stone bead (8). Scale 1:1

*1.   Opaque, white, spherical: formerly with wavy overlapping marvered trails of one, or perhaps two, other colours, but these have disintegrated through weathering. Teutonic type.

2.   Opaque red with white marvered spot: tiny fragment of a spherical bead. Teutonic type. D. of fragment 4 millimetres.

3.   Colourless; tiny fragment, perhaps from a tubular bead of hexagonal section, for parts of two adjoining surfaces seem to be discernible. If so, probably a Coptic and not a Teutonic type. L. 1 centimetre.

[7] S. E. Chadwick (1958), Pl. IV C.
[8] D. B. Harden (1956b), Pl. XVII A a.

*4.   Clear blue, cylindrical; wire-wound, with bevelled ends showing where bead was knocked off from the next ones on the wired string. Perhaps Mediterranean or Coptic, certainly not Teutonic.

*5.   Gilded colourless, segmented: wire-wound, with knocked-off ends; four spherical segments. Coptic.

*6.   Brown, flattened spherical, 'ring'-type, much weathered, with pitted surface. This kind of plain bead occurs at all periods and is difficult to date, especially when in a weathered state. Probably Teutonic or Roman.

*7.   Pale yellow, spheroid: fragment only, with little weathering. Probably Teutonic or Roman.

*8.   Short cylindrical bead of stone. The Department of Geology of University College, Cardiff, reports that the stone is possibly a fine-grained igneous rock with some felspar crystals visible.[9]

SEGMENTAL COUNTER (Fig. 9.2, 9)
*9.   Opaque light blue, plano-convex, fragment only. Roman. The type is ubiquitous during the first to fourth centuries AD.

RODS (Fig. 9.2, 10–12)
*10.   Dark blue, square-sectioned, tapering slightly; broken off at each end.

*11.   Blue, square-sectioned, no taper; broken off at one end, the other rounded.

*12.   Brown (?) and opaque white, square-sectioned, slight taper, weathered. The cross-section shows pin-points of white set in a brown (?) background: i.e. this is a millefiori rod, cf. a more elaborate example from Garranes.[10]

INLAY
13.   Fragment of inlay, yellowish, 1 millimetre thick, and very slightly thicker at one end than the other. The fragment retains at least one original edge smoothed by grinding, and perhaps parts of two others. Original shape of fragment not ascertainable. L. 1.3 centimetres.

FUSED GLASS
Apart from only slightly deformed fragments of vessels that have been in contact with heat, a number of fragments of heavily fused glass with no recognizable shape occurred. The following colours exist:

   Dark blue—seven fragments.
   Amber—five fragments.
   Pale green—two fragments.
   Olive green—three fragments.
   Olive green and dark blue fused together—one fragment.

[9] Natural stone rings (i.e. fossil crinoids with a central hole) were fairly frequent on the site. They may have been deliberately collected from the limestone bedrock, in which they certainly occur, for use as beads; but it is equally possible that they had merely weathered out of the rock by natural processes.
[10] S. P. Ó Ríordáin (1942), Fig. 15.

These pieces are not, however, molten droppings from crucibles at a normal glass furnace site, but resemble rather glass that has been heavily burnt in an open hearth. I would suppose that their very quantity suggests glass-working of some sort, though I must admit that fragments of a glass vessel that had been heavily burnt in a cremation-fire could look just like these bits, and such fragments (of beads as well as vessels) have been found often enough in Saxon urns (though not often recorded in print). On glasses from cremation urns see my summary of the evidence in Harden (1956b), p. 134f.

It is perhaps surprising that dark blue examples are the most frequent. But I do not think the total quantity recorded is sufficient to permit us to draw statistical evidence from it.

Numerical analysis of the glass from Dinas Powys

	Listed	Not listed	Total
Roman vessels, etc.	5	—	5
Teutonic vessels:			
Dark blue, plain	6	8	14
do. opaque white trails	2	—	2
Yellow/brown, plain	1	—	1
do. opaque white trails	1	—	1
Emerald green, plain	1	—	1
Olive green, plain	1	—	1
Green, plain	1	—	1
Pale green, plain	5	10	15
do. opaque white trails	2	2	4
do. other decorations	2	—	2
Pale yellow, plain	34	99	133
do. opaque white trails	59	26	85
do. other decorations	4	—	4
Beads	8	—	8
Counter	1	—	1
Rods	3	—	3
Inlay	1	—	1
Fused glass	17	—	17
	154	145	299

Teutonic vessels:

plain	158
opaque white trails	92
other decorations	6
	256

Part Three:
Forts in Wales and Dumnonia AD 450–750

The attempt, in *Dinas Powys* 1963, to set the Phase 4 defences against a wider background led me to considerable research in the field and in the literature, both ancient and modern. These researches have continued up to the present. Since 1973, the fieldwork has been largely carried out in Scotland, and much of the work on the written sources has likewise centred on northern Britain. These northern researches have obviously influenced my interpretations, but the actual field results are deliberately excluded from the present volume, which concentrates on Wales and southern, especially south-western, England.

Part Three begins, then, with a review of the fortified sites of Wales and Dumnonia which appear to be contemporary with Dinas Powys 4. The interpretations of Chapter 10 are supported by a catalogue of sites in Chapter 11. The major excavated site of the area and period is undoubtedly Cadbury–Camelot, which engaged me over the field seasons 1966–70, and which has never been far from my thinking since then. Chapter 12 provides an early summary of the results, which sets the fifth- and sixth-century Cadbury (Cadbury 11) against a background of four millennia of development. My mature reflections on Cadbury 11, influenced to some extent by my northern work, appear as Chapter 13. The final chapter of Part Three turns to historical evidence—Welsh, English, and Scottish—in an attempt to see how military expeditions and the building of forts were organized in our period.

CHAPTER 10

New Perspectives on Post-Roman Forts

In no aspect of this study is the contingent nature of archaeological generalization better seen than in my attempt to establish, for Wales and the Marches, a list of sites contemporary with, and comparable to, Dinas Powys 4 (above, pp. 58 ff.). It is not necessary to trace here the various modifications of the original list: suffice it to say that the first one appeared within months of the publication of *Dinas Powys*.[1] The catalogue offered here in Chapter 11 represents the views of Elizabeth Alcock and myself on the current state of the art, but we would not expect it to be totally acceptable to other competent workers in the field. In the present chapter, my first purpose is to discuss how such a catalogue may be established. Then, on the assumption that our list of 19 sites is acceptable within a tolerance of ± 10 per cent, I explore some of the generalizations which arise from it.[2]

In attempting to identify the fortified sites of a historical or near-historical period, our first tool is obviously that provided by the evidence of historical and traditional sources. These range from contemporary notices by writers of the status of Bede, through supposedly contemporary annals, to later (i.e. ninth to eleventh century) notices of events attributed to the fifth and sixth centuries, and ultimately to sixteenth-century records of traditions of uncertain age and reliability. In northern Britain, confident identifications can indeed be made, and confirmed by excavation, on the basis of information derived from monasteries at Iona and in Northumbria.[3] For Wales and Dumnonia, unfortunately, we have no such wealth of historical evidence. Indeed, the only contemporary notice is the reference by Gildas to the 'Bear's Stronghold', *receptaculum ursi*, of King Cuneglasus, possibly to be identified with the fort of Bryneuryn, Dinarth.[4]

We are therefore forced back on traditional associations: of Castell Degannwy with Maelgwn Gwynedd; of Dinas Emrys with Ambrosius Aurelianus and Vortigern; of Cadbury–Camelot and Tintagel with Arthur; and of Castle Dore with King Mark of the Tristan and Iseult story. Few, if any, of these associations would be taken seriously by historians; yet the excavations which they have helped to inspire have yielded archaeologically-acceptable evidence of occupation in the fifth and sixth centuries AD in all these cases. In terms of archaeological prediction, this must be reckoned a high success rate; and it seems reasonable therefore to speculate on the possibility that there may have been some genuine folk memory or tradition going back to those centuries which later crystallized around major figures of legend and romance such as Vortigern and Arthur. Such thoughts underlie Padel's analysis of the place of Tintagel in both the Arthurian and

---

[1] L. Alcock (1963b).
[2] An alternative approach, by the doyen of hill-fort studies in Wales, gives broadly similar results: H. N. Savory (1976), 286–91. For a parallel, but more intensive survey of part of Dumnonia: I. C. G. Burrow (1981a); for Cornwall, N. Johnson & P. Rose (1982).
[3] L. Alcock (1981a; 1981b).
[4] K. H. Jackson (1982), 32–4.

Tristan romances in terms of a possible twelfth-century folk tradition that the early fortification had protected a dwelling of the rulers of Cornwall.[5]

These proven correlations, however, can hardly justify the claim that 'in identifying sites of this period, tradition is as good a criterion as many'.[6] This was put forward with specific reference to Clegyr Boia, Dyfed, on the grounds that Boia was an Irish chieftain whose fort is mentioned in the eleventh-century (and later) Lives of St David. The fort is pre-eminently in an area open to the importation of Mediterranean and Gaulish pottery, yet none was found in excavations there.[7] In the absence of pottery or other artefacts characteristic of forts of the period (below, p. 168), it seems an unlikely claim that a radiocarbon date of 1 ± 116 ad from gate timbers 'could represent heart wood used within a late or post-Roman context'. Another traditional site is Garn Boduan, where 'Boduan' may indicate the 'residence of Buan', grandson of Llywarch Hen. Here a large, characteristically Iron Age hill-fort had a small work inserted on the very summit of the hill.[8] This is indeed likely to be later than the main work, but in the absence of either imported pottery or durable metalwork it is not reasonable to argue with conviction for a post-Roman date.

Our next analytical tool in identifying forts of our period is that of site morphology: the location of forts, their plans, and the structural character of their defences. Here the foundations were laid as long ago as 1920 by Morgan.[9] He identified a group of forts, situated not on the summits but on the slopes of hills, as a response to Danish bowmanship. The idea that such hill-slope forts exhibited the decay of Iron Age traditions of fortification, and must therefore be attributed to the sixth and later centuries AD, was subsequently argued with much circumstantial detail.[10] Ultimately, however, it was seen, on the basis essentially of the finds from excavated examples in Dumnonia, that hill-slope forts were actually a regular Iron Age type.[11] There is a warning hint here that what appears to one generation as anomalous in an Iron Age context is not therefore necessarily attributable to the post-Roman period.

By 1963, taking account of the evidence deployed in *Dinas Powys* (above, pp. 58 ff.) and elsewhere,[12] I could see no basis for predicting, from surface indications, which forts might be attributed to the fifth and later centuries AD. This view was implicitly endorsed by the Royal Commission in commenting on Dinas Powys itself:

> its character was entirely unknown until its excavation, and the original defences would have been superficially indistinguishable from a weak pre-Roman promontory fort[13]

Such comments are certainly true in Wales and the Marches, and no less so in Dumnonia, where the forts of our period are frequently founded on those of the pre-Roman Iron Age. An attempt to distinguish later use and occupation on the basis of surface indications alone[14] has given quite inconclusive results. To conclude this dismissive

---

[5] O. J. Padel (1981).
[6] H. James and G. Williams (1982), 304.
[7] A. Williams (1952).
[8] A. H. A. Hogg (1960).
[9] W. Ll. Morgan (1920), 220–3.
[10] C. & A. Fox (1934).
[11] A. Fox (1952).
[12] L. Alcock (1963b).
[13] RCAHM(W) (1976, Part 3), 12.
[14] I. C. G. Burrow (1981b).

survey of site morphology as a predictive tool, it should be added that the nuclear fort, distinguished by Stevenson as a characteristic Dark Age capital in Scotland,[15] is absent from the archaeological record in Wales and Dumnonia.

It follows that excavation alone can tell us which sites were occupied in our period. In particular, it is only through excavation that we can determine whether a fort was erected *de novo* in the fifth or later centuries AD; or whether it was founded, with or without structural modification, upon an earlier work, of the pre-Roman Iron Age or of the Roman centuries. More important still, it is only through the most refined stratigraphic analysis that we can tell whether there was continuity of occupation from earlier centuries, or whether the later occupation was separated by a definite hiatus. On such analyses depend important issues concerning the continuity of economic and social organization from the prehistoric to the medieval period.[16]

In dating the structural phases of his sites the student of post-Roman fortifications in Britain has the standard resources of scientific dating and of artefact typology. As it happens, neither radiocarbon nor tree-ring dating has been used in our period on sites listed in Chapter 11. Out of nineteen examples, three only have yielded datable jewellery; and overwhelmingly, it is the evidence of pottery which has established their post-Roman occupation. The greatest single change between my 1963 list for Wales and the Marches and the present list is the result of new interpretations of some of the pottery. To understand and evaluate these changes, it is necessary to consider, albeit briefly, the history of the subject over the past forty years.

In the first systematic presentation of settlement sites in Dark Age Wales, Fox[17] had identified a class of very coarse pottery which was not acceptable as belonging to the pre-Roman Iron Age. Moreover, at Pant-y-saer it occurred in a settlement which, on morphological grounds, belonged at earliest to the third or fourth century AD, and it was associated with a base-silver penannular brooch of the fifth to seventh centuries.[18] A similar date could then be extended to forts such as the Breiddin, Old Oswestry and Castell Odo, which had yielded similar pottery. The scheme was somewhat weakened when further excavation at Castell Odo showed that there, at least, the pottery belonged to an early phase of the pre-Roman Iron Age, perhaps in the fourth or third century BC.[19]

Meanwhile, the whole study of post-Roman settlements in western Britain and Ireland had been revolutionized by Radford's initial publication of imported pottery which was firmly dated, on evidence outside these islands, to the later fifth and subsequent centuries AD.[20] On some of the relevant sites Harden had also identified fragments of glass of the same date.[21] It thus became possible to bring together long-known excavations in Scotland and Ireland, and to correlate them with excavations currently in progress at Dinas Powys and Dinas Emrys[22] in Wales, and at Gwithian in Cornwall.[23] It seemed reasonable initially to accommodate both Fox's coarse pottery and the imported wares in a new,

[15] R. B. K. Stevenson (1949).
[16] G. R. J. Jones (1960), (1961).
[17] A. Fox (1946).
[18] C. W. Phillips (1934).
[19] L. Alcock (1960a).
[20] C. A. R. Radford (1956).
[21] D. B. Harden (1956b).
[22] H. N. Savory (1960).
[23] A. C. Thomas (1958).

more elaborate and sounder synthesis. This was the genesis of my scheme for pottery in Wales and the Marches, following the breakdown of the Romano-British pottery industry (above, pp. 45 ff.). I suggested that Group I represented local attempts to manufacture pottery, leading to the production of coarse wares; while Group II, the imported pottery, replaced these from about AD 450. This implied a probable or possible fifth-century date for several hill-forts in north Wales and the northern Marches (above, fig. 2.4).

The concept of 'alleged Dark Age coarse wares' was, however, immediately rejected by Savory in his review of *Dinas Powys*,[24] especially in its application to the forts of the Breiddin and Eddisbury. Shortly afterwards, in an altogether more radical reappraisal of pottery allied to my Group I it was argued that the very coarse pottery of north Wales and the Marches (conveniently abbreviated VCP) was of pre-Roman date, and represented salt containers or ovens rather than normal pottery vessels.[25] This revolutionary interpretation was firmly based on the analysis of pottery from hill-forts and other enclosures in the southern Marches and adjacent areas. Its blanket application to include the northern Marches and north Wales may, however, be too simple, and it is worth stressing that the characteristic Droitwich salt containers have not been recognized in these northern areas.[26]

Beyond this general comment, a pre-Roman date for VCP may be queried at two sites relevant to this study. At Garn Boduan, sherds of VCP were found within the small summit fort which, on both structural and artefactual grounds, has been thought to be late Roman or later.[27] No pottery at all was recovered in the excavation of buildings in the main fort, so it is impossible to follow Gelling and Stanford in regarding the VCP as residual from the pre-Roman occupation of the large fort. At Pant-y-saer, an Iron Age date would involve placing the settlement two or more centuries earlier than similar enclosed hut-groups; dismissing the relevance of the penannular brooch; and disregarding the occurrence of VCP as occupation material in a secondary building. The purpose of these comments is to encourage a critical approach to the hitherto monolithic dating of VCP. They should not be construed, however, as establishing a firm post-Roman date for either Pant-y-saer or Garn Boduan.

In general, we should recognize that so-called VCP is just very crude pottery, with no built-in functional, cultural or chronological indicators. So far as the material itself is concerned, we need to see many more petrographic and other analyses published and subjected to peer review before we categorize VCP as either homogeneous or heterogeneous. And in relation to the sites on which it occurs, it is necessary to read their excavators' reports with sympathy as well as with critical awareness before we essay radical reinterpretations. Finally, we might recognize that it is inherently likely that there should have been local coarse wares in Wales and the Marches as there were in parts of Dumnonia in the post-Roman period.[28] Two sites in our catalogue (Chapter 11), Goldherring and Maen Castle, are indeed credited with post-Roman occupations on the basis of such evidence.

Nonetheless, it is the imported pottery which must, at present, form the best criterion

[24] H. N. Savory (1964).
[25] P. S. Gelling and S. C. Stanford (1967).
[26] Map in E. L. Morris (1981), Fig. 5.5.
[27] A. H. A. Hogg (1960).
[28] P. A. Rahtz & P. Fowler (1972); A. C. Thomas (1968).

for identifying structures and occupation levels of the period AD 450–750. Out of the nineteen forts in the catalogue, ten can be firmly dated on this basis, and there are another three probables. Imported glass also provides a sound criterion: on five of our sites, it provides confirmatory evidence, but at New Pieces it is the sole reason for extending the occupation into the fifth century and beyond.

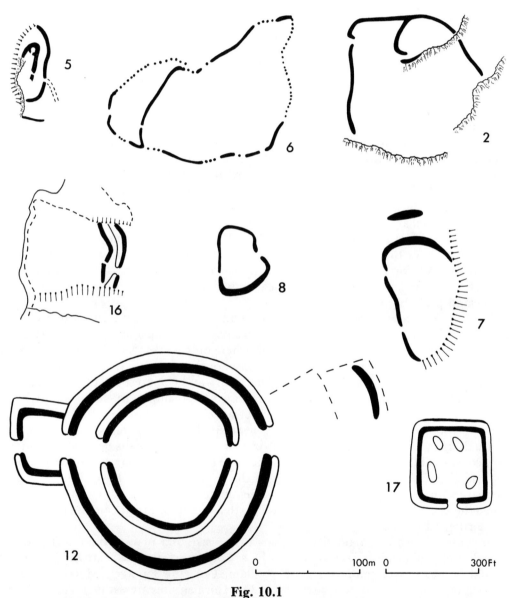

Fig. 10.1

A sample of Welsh and Dumnonian forts. 2 Dinarth; 5 Carreg-y-llam; 6 Dinas Emrys; 7 Coygan; 8 Dinas Powys; 12 Killibury; 16 Maen Castle; 17 Grambla. For locations, see the index map, Fig. 11.1. For other sites, see Fig. 13.11.

On the basis of the catalogue it is possible to generalize about the characteristics of our sites, and to compare them with contemporary forts in northern Britain. It is at once apparent that there is a very considerable variety in their size and in the form and structural history of their defences.[29] The range in size of the internal area is especially marked: from 8.0 ha at Cadbury 11 and 3.5 ha at Congresbury to the lower extremes of 0.08 ha at Golderring and 0.03 ha at Carreg-y-llam. There are two small clusters, one around 0.5 ha (Coygan, Castle Dore, New Pieces and Bryneuryn) and the other around 0.19 ha (Trethurgy, Chûn and Dinas Powys).[30] It is noteworthy that the minor enclosure at Carreg-y-llam falls just below the figure of 0.0375 ha which the Royal Commission on Ancient Monuments, Scotland, has chosen at the upper limit for defining the small, strongly defended homesteads which it classifies as duns.[31] In Scotland, it would be appropriate to add those duns which have evidence of occupation in the sixth and later centuries AD to our list. Other relevant Scottish sites would be the largest known Pictish fort, Burghead, at 2.8 ha, and the small but exceptionally rich Mote of Mark at 0.14 ha.

In Dumnonia, forts of our period are frequently based on long abandoned hill-top, hill-slope, or promontory forts of the pre-Roman Iron Age, or represent a continuous occupation, from the Roman period, of the small oval enclosures known as rounds. In both cases, therefore, the plan is determined by the earlier earthwork. In the case of the rounds, no refurbishing or other alteration of the original defence was necessary, and in the case of Iron Age forts, with the exception of Cadbury 11, no significant new work was carried out. Even at the latter site, where an elaborate timber-laced rampart was raised on top of the innermost Iron Age bank (below, pp. 191–5), there were no surface indications of this. It follows that the re-used sites are indistinguishable, before excavation, from normal Iron Age forts, characteristically with two or more earthen banks or rubble walls. In Wales, too, earlier defences were re-used, with no visible modification, at Coygan, New Pieces and probably Dinas Emrys as well.

The forts which were newly founded in the fifth and later centuries normally used a single line of wall or of bank and ditch, often in a position of considerable natural strength. The most economical was that at Tintagel, where only a short length of earthwork was needed to secure a large headland. At Dinas Powys, a simple bank and ditch made excellent use of a steep-sided spur. Both Degannwy and Congresbury utilize steep-sided hills: at Degannwy this was probably surrounded by a simple dry-stone wall, whereas Congresbury has the uncommon features of an elaborate gateway, and a cross wall dividing the enclosure into two more or less equal parts. Carreg-y-llam is the most unusual, in other ways besides its small size: two concentric walls occupy a position of very considerable natural strength, the inner one having a circular cell, 6.0 m diameter, embedded in it. It is notable that none of the new foundations have timber-lacing to compare with Cadbury 11, whereas timber-reinforcements, sometimes using iron nails to fasten the beams, were very common in the sixth and later centuries among the Picts and the northern Britons.

In contrast with the marked variations in the size and plan of these forts, there is considerable uniformity about their locations. For a start, there is a strong tendency to coastal siting: thus Degannwy, Carreg-y-llam, Coygan, Tintagel, Maen Castle and Trevelgue are actually on the coast; all the other Cornish sites are within a short distance,

[29] This is well brought out in a study with comparative plans of Cornish sites: N. Johnson & P. Rose (1982).
[30] The figures are largely derived from A. H. A. Hogg (1979).
[31] RCAHM(S) (1971), 18.

as also are Bryneuryn, Aberffraw and Dinas Powys. In fact, only Cadbury and New Pieces are more than twenty miles from the sea. Of course, given that our principal criterion for assigning forts to the late fifth and later centuries is the occurrence of imported, and therefore sea-borne pottery, it might be thought that we are merely seeing here an index of the limited inland penetration of such imports. That it should have reached Cadbury does, however, argue against this inference.

Another characteristic of the forts in Wales and the Marches is that they are restricted to the lower end of the altitudinal range of Iron Age forts. In north Wales and the Marches a dozen pre-Roman forts rise to heights between 1300 ft. and 1800 ft. OD.[32] In contrast, the highest of the post-Roman forts in Wales, Carreg-y-llam, is no more than 460 ft. above sea level. Degannwy attains 354 ft.; Dinas Powys only 200 ft. In case it should be thought that this is simply a reflection of nearness to the coast, it should be noticed that one of the group of high forts, Tre'r Ceiri, is itself only two miles inland. On the other hand, given the very large number of forts in Wales and the Marches, our sample of eight is too small to carry any weight. In Dumnonia, given the frequency with which pre-Roman forts were re-used, there is no significant difference in altitudinal range: the two highest forts, Cadbury–Camelot and Cadbury–Congresbury both enclose the 500 ft. OD contour line.

Inside some of the forts, traces of buildings have been revealed by excavation, but the interpretation of most of them is far from satisfactory. At Castle Dore it was claimed that two large rectangular halls were raised on earth-set posts. Rahtz's reappraisal of their plans was intended to cast doubts on their reality. Nevertheless, it is clear that there were large rectangular buildings at Dore, even if their full plans elude us.[33] A more complete plan of a rectangular hall appears at Cadbury 11 (below, pp. 202–4), but even here it is necessary to restore ploughed-out wall slots and lost post-holes in order to produce a plausible reconstruction. At Congresbury, both rectangular and circular buildings of timber await full publication.[34] Circular and rectangular buildings of dry-stone may occur in our period at Pant-y-saer. Carreg-y-llam, with its circular house embedded in a thick wall, represents a more massively defended version of the same type of enclosed homestead. Dinas Powys provides a hint of a rectangular timber building in Phase 4A, which was replaced by dry-stone sub-rectangular buildings in Phase 4B. Finally, the date, function—secular or religious?—and social status of the buildings at Tintagel are currently a matter of unresolved debate. All in all, these examples do not lend themselves to fruitful synthesis. But both circular and rectangular buildings are found widely in Celtic Britain and Ireland in the first millennium AD; and the supposed hall of Cadbury 11 conforms closely to our expectations about noble halls, as does Doon Hill A among the northern Britons.[35]

In addition to their siting and structural features, excavated forts provide evidence about the activities of their occupants. Apart from fort-building itself, with its implications for the organization of building services, the only activity that is revealed on a majority of the sites is the acquisition of imported pottery. This in itself has wide implications: for the drinking of wine; for some kind of international exchange system which fell short of systematic, commercially-organized trade (above, pp. 89–92); for the accumulation of wealth, presumably in raw materials and animal products, to exchange for the

---

[32] J. Forde-Johnston (1976), 54–5.
[33] C. A. R. Radford (1951); P. A. Rahtz (1971).
[34] I. C. G. Burrow (1981a).
[35] N. Reynolds (1980), 52–4; B. Hope-Taylor (1980).

imports; and, perhaps, for the concentration of wealth and imports in major centres such as Tintagel and Cadbury–Camelot, and their distribution to lesser centres such as Dinas Powys itself. In their wider extensions, these inferences are inspired by theories of Celtic social and economic organization and have little empirical basis or control in either archaeology or history.[36]

From some sites, indeed, we have only a handful of sherds of imported pottery or glass as evidence for our period. In part this is the result of the very limited scale of excavation at sites such as Chûn, Degannwy and Killibury, but it can hardly explain the absence of evidence for craft activities at Cadbury, Castle Dore, Tintagel or Trethurgy. Although the scrap glass at Cadbury, New Pieces and Tintagel hints at jewel-making, only Congresbury, Dinas Emrys and Dinas Powys have produced more extensive evidence for metalworking, such as crucibles. This is in striking contrast with contemporary defensive sites, including crannogs, in Scotland and Ireland, for there such evidence is commonly found (list of sites, above p. 112).

The apparent dearth of crucibles, moulds, slag, ores and scrap metal from the overwhelming majority of post-Roman forts in Wales and Dumnonia must lead us to question how far the range and wealth of craft activities at Dinas Powys are truly representative. Partial explanations for the richness of the record there lie in the preservation of bone, which is normally absent from Cornish sites on granite bedrocks; the relatively large scale of excavation; and the completeness of publication. These factors may all lead us to predict that fuller excavation and publication will reveal that post-Roman forts in southern Britain were normally centres for craft activities, and especially for jewelsmiths, as they certainly were in the north.

It must be admitted that such evidence is needed before my model of craft activities as an integral feature of princely forts can be justified. It becomes necessary to ask whether Dinas Powys 4B was an enclosed court—a *llys*—with craftsmen, especially metalworkers, in attendance, or whether it was really a strongly-defended industrial site. I suggest below (p. 239) that Mote of Mark, a key site of the northern Britons, 'was a purely industrial site, rather than a princely stronghold with a resident jewel-smith'; and I follow Gillies[37] in drawing attention to Caulann, smith to King Conchobar, who, according to the *Táin Bó Cuailnge* possessed his own *liss* or defended homestead. If we were to accept the alternative structural hypothesis which places Bank I in phase 4B, then the small, densely-packed enclosure which results is comparable in size to the habitable area within the rampart of Mote of Mark.

One activity which seems implicit in the very term 'fortification' is, of course, warfare. In northern Britain, among both the Britons and the Picts, there is archaeological evidence, in the form of fire-destroyed ramparts, which can readily be interpreted in terms of military action. No such evidence has been reported from post-Roman forts in Wales and Dumnonia. There is an interesting parallel in the documentary evidence. In the later seventh and early eighth centuries, contemporary annals record sieges, burnings and destructions at a number of identifiable forts in Scotland.[38] In Wales, prior to the notices of Viking attacks from 866 on, the only annalistic reference is to the destruction of the citadel of Degannwy by the Saxons in 822. A wider consideration of the warfare between the Saxons and the southern Britons (below, Chapter 15) shows that it took place in the

---

[36] C. Doherty (1980) discusses the Irish evidence.
[37] W. Gillies (1981), 76.
[38] L. Alcock (1981a).

open, often at river crossings; and that, although hill-forts and walled towns are some-times mentioned in the records, they appear as reference points rather than as scenes of action.

This would agree with the view that I advanced in 1963, that 'defended strongholds played no great part in the military activities of the Dark Ages' (above, p. 62). But two modifications are necessary. First, as we have just seen (and as, indeed, I had hinted in 1963 p. 61 above), this is not at all true in the north of Britain: there is a quite striking contrast between the two regions of Celtic Britain. Secondly, however justified I was to correlate this lack of military activity with the 'puny nature of the defences of settlements' in Wales, this would not be wholly true of Dumnonia. There, the two major sites were massively defended, Tintagel by nature, and Cadbury by art. So far as the latter site is concerned, I have no doubt over-emphasized its military role in the past.[39] Nonetheless, its strategic position, its natural strength, and the formidable refortification of Cadbury 11, all make its military potential undeniable.

Despite this, as will appear in Chapter 13 (pp. 185 ff.), I would now wish to emphasize its administrative, rather than its military role. Such a reappraisal has two roots: Burrow's intensive survey of hill-forts in Somerset in the first to eighth centuries AD, which included an examination of socio-political and economic models for their post-Roman re-use; and my own work on the forts of northern Britain, where contemporary documents provide evidence for their status and function.[40] The results of this reappraisal are set out below (pp. 211–13) where such expressions as 'the defended homesteads of Celtic warlords or warrior chiefs' are specifically questioned, and are then replaced by an interpretation in terms of administrative centres in the hands of the king or of some royal official.

The statements in Chapter 13 were directed to a better understanding of Cadbury 11, and they deserve some amplification here. First, it should be emphasized how far Cadbury 11, Congresbury and Tintagel stand out among contemporary forts because of their size. Even the smallest of them, Congresbury, is larger than Bamburgh, the one northern *civitas* for which we can reasonably calculate an area. On these grounds alone, all three may be thought to deserve to be called *civitas*, whatever the word may mean when it is used by Bede or Eddius.[41] In the case of Cadbury 11, it is very reasonable to believe that this represents the transfer of the administrative role of Ilchester, *civitas Durotrigum Lindiniensis*, from a vulnerable low-lying site to one massively defended by both nature and art, in the later fifth century. What we cannot see is what, if any, features of romanized urban life were also transferred, or what the actual political institution might have been: romanized *ordo* or post-Roman *tyrannus*? In the case of Tintagel, there was no such Roman precursor, and we can therefore see it as the novel foundation of a British king, as Padel has tentatively hinted.[42]

Secondly, it is worth considering Burrow's economic models in relation to Dinas Powys. He distinguishes, presumably for purely analytical purposes, four separate models. The first is for a subsistence basis, in which 'the identified sites carried on their own subsistence activities'. In the second model, the site is used 'for exchange of goods, and perhaps services, on a local basis', defined in terms of a journey of one day or less. In the third model, the site is a centre for long-distance trade, of the kind implied by the

[39] Contrast pp. 183–4 and pp. 208–12 below.
[40] I. C. G. Burrow (1981a), 152–71; L. Alcock (1981a), 179 for a preliminary statement.
[41] J. Campbell (1979a).
[42] O. J. Padel (1981).

imported pottery (though Burrow is very sceptical about such implications). Fourthly, the site may have been an enclosure 'within which essentially industrial activities were carried out'. Now however useful it may be to construct these four models for the purpose of analytical discussion, it is plain that they are in no way mutually exclusive or incompatible: indeed the possibility of long-range trade must depend on a surplus in the subsistence economy, which may also feed a local market. Moreover, craft specialization depends on long-range trade for its raw materials, and probably also supplies a local market. These interlocking relationships can be readily multiplied in a theoretical analysis: their empirical proof is provided by Dinas Powys itself, where all four models are represented (above Chapter 2, especially pp. 49–50).

Moreover, the individual site should not be regarded in isolation, or as set within its own definable catchment area.[43] I have hinted (above, p. 83) at my considerable reservations on the use of site-catchment analysis in a developed Celtic society. The Welsh Laws provide evidence which is no doubt formally anachronistic, but which, as we have seen (pp. 85–6) has elements derived from the period of our study. These might include building and military services, food renders from both free and bondmen, and circuits by the king, his bodyguard and his officials. All these would break down the isolation of any individual site, and would tie it into a network of other sites. For such inferences we are not, however, dependent solely on the Welsh Laws. Bede, writing a century later, tells us of King Edwin of Northumbria (slain in 632) 'riding around his cities, townships and sub-kingdoms, with his thanes'. Eddius, in the early eighth century, reports of King Ecgfrith (slain in 685):

> the king with his queen, was making a progress through chief towns, forts and townships (*civitates et castella vicosque*), with worldly display and daily rejoicing and feasting.[44]

Here we see a progress, or circuit, through royal centres, in which the feasting represents the consumption or redistribution of food renders, which had been accumulated at the centre in anticipation. In view of this, it would be quite wrong to think of any of our forts in self-sufficient isolation, however much the character of archaeological research demands that initially we investigate each site as an independent unit.

Eddius, in the form of words which he uses, appears to present a hierarchy of sites, in which undoubtedly the *civitas* stands at the top. If this is so, then some of the comments of my 1982 paper need modification: in particular, my suggestion that the royal township, the *villa regalis* or *vicus regis* of the Northumbrian documents, stood high in the ranking of royal centres, and that Cadbury 11 might be regarded as such a site. There are indications, however, that royal townships were more common than the places designated *civitas*; and an anonymous *villa regia* might be located with reference to the *civitas* or *urbs regis* of Bamburgh, implying an inferior status.

At the top of the hierarchy we should see places like Bamburgh and Dumbarton which Bede calls both *civitas* and *urbs*. Campbell has very reasonably suggested that in these cases Bede 'is using *civitas* here for a particularly important kind of *urbs*, the main royal fortress'.[45] Below this, we may believe, comes the *urbs* which was not a *civitas*. As the case of Dunbar shows, this might still be a royal town or fort, and might be in charge of a royal official: at Dunbar, a *praefectus* or thane. An *urbs* of this status might be equated with the

[43] Contrast Burrow (1981a) fig. 31.
[44] HE, ii. 16; VW cap. 39.
[45] J. Campbell (1979a), 37.

castellum of Eddius's triad. The royal township, *villa* or *vicus*, might then form a third level.[46] It must be stressed here that this suggested ranking is based not merely on the word order of Eddius's phrase *civitates et castella vicosque* but on other occurrences of *villa regis* and comparable terms. On the other hand, it does not seem conformable with the size and architectural magnificence of the only *villa regis* known from excavation, namely, Yeavering.[47] It was, indeed this which led me, in 1982 (below, p. 212) to imply high status for the royal township.

It now seems more likely to me that the royal *villa* or *vicus* should be equated with the *maerdref* of the Welsh Laws: literally the reeve's township, a demesne vill of the king, inhabited by the king's bondmen.[48] Unfortunately, our archaeological knowledge about places known as *maerdref* (or derivatives such as Faerdre or Vardre) is even more limited than that about Northumbrian *villae regales*. Our best evidence is the place-name Vardre attached to the environs of Degannwy Castle. Essentially, the site consists of a level saddle between two rocky hillocks, of which the larger, surrounded by a dry-stone wall, has produced fragments of Class B amphorae. This is the *arx* or citadel destroyed by the Saxons in 822; evidently a place of major politico-military significance, because its destruction was followed, according to the Welsh Annals, by the Saxon seizure of the sub-kingdom (*regio*) of Powys. Given this importance, it is likely that the *arx* might also have been described as *civitas*, or at least *urbs*. In any case, there was evidently a royal bond vill in the immediate vicinity of a principal royal fortress, most probably on the saddle between the hills. These conclusions are in no way dependent on the later tradition that Degannwy was the *llys* of Maelgwn Gwynedd; but they may suggest that the tradition was not without foundation.[49]

To conclude this part of the discussion: it is clear that considerably more research is needed, by both historians and archaeologists, and preferably by both in collaboration, before we can write convincingly about the character of the places known to contemporaries as *arx*, *castellum*, *civitas*, *villa*, *vicus*, *urbs* or *maerdref*. In particular, we need to free our minds from the thought that the excavation of Yeavering has presented us, once and for all, with the type specimen of a *villa regia*. We need to identify on the ground all examples of the places to which these various terms have been applied; and we need a systematic programme of excavation to reveal their physical details. Meanwhile, we can accept that Cadbury 11 and Dumbarton give us two fragmentary pictures of a British *civitas*. As for Dinas Powys, we must remain uncertain whether to think of it as a *villa regis*, or more probably an *urbs* like Dunbar.

The final major topic for discussion here is the evidence which the forts provide for continuity from the pre-Roman Iron Age, or at least from the Roman period, into the fifth century and beyond. This evidence has significance, at a theoretical level, for ideas on the long-term continuity of Celtic administrative arrangements,[50] but I propose to confine my discussion to the wholly empirical evidence of excavation.

I begin with the observation that in 1961, my map of enclosed and defended places in Wales and the Marches, which might be dated AD 400–700 (above, fig. 2.4), had on it eleven positive symbols (and also one cave); my present map of fortified sites (fig. 11.1)

[46] J. Campbell (1979a), 43–51.
[47] B. Hope-Taylor (1977).
[48] G. R. J. Jones (1972); Ordnance Survey (1973).
[49] L. Alcock (1967c); J. E. Lloyd (1911; 1939), 129, n.17; W. Davies (1982), 22.
[50] G. R. J. Jones (1960).

has only eight. Moreover, the earlier map bore some twenty-three negative symbols, for excavated forts which had produced no evidence for occupation in that period. Over the past score of years, the number of excavated forts in the area has approximately doubled; but with the exception of Coygan, and the more debatable one of Aberffraw, no further positive symbols have been added to the map. From this it is clear that the absolute number, and therefore the relative proportion of negative symbols have increased. It can be stated as a firm rule for Wales and the Marches that a fort is unlikely to have been re-used after AD 450, even if it had been in occupation as late as the third or fourth century AD.

In Dumnonia, the statistics are different: excavations since 1961 have added Cadbury, Congresbury, Grambla, Killibury and Trethurgy to the list of forts with evidence for occupation both before and after AD 400. This general observation must be seen, however, in the light of Burrow's intensive study of the evidence from Somerset.[51] He has recognised there 89 hill-forts and hill-top settlements of which 26 have been sampled by excavation. Of these, a score has produced Romano-British material, indicating, for the most part, either domestic occupation or religious use. But not more than three hill-forts have yielded imported pottery as evidence for occupation after AD 450; and among these, the status of Ham Hill is so doubtful that it is excluded from our map. In Cornwall, the figures are: out of a total of 630 sites, 31 have been excavated, and 9 of these have yielded evidence, often very slight, of post-Roman occupation. Three of these, Goldherring, Grambla and Trethurgy were established in the Roman period, whereas the others are foundations of the pre-Roman Iron Age. Slight though these figures are, they exhibit a firmer tendency to post-Roman continuity or re-use in Dumnonia than in Wales and the Marches; and within Dumnonia, the tendency becomes more marked in Cornwall, the area least subjected to romanizing influences.

These generalizations now need to be filled out with some detailed case studies, beginning with the reasons for rejecting no fewer than six of the sites which had appeared on the 1961 map. Even at that time, five of them were accorded a status no higher than 'possible/doubtful'. In a paper in 1963,[52] I had argued that the coarse pottery from Castle Ditch, Eddisbury, probably belonged to the pre-Roman Iron Age, and so, by implication did that from Old Oswestry. This view was reinforced by Savory's comments.[53] Doubts were cast on the attribution of the pottery from Garn Boduan to a post-Roman, rather than pre-Roman date by Gelling and Stanford;[54] and though I have suggested above (p. 156) that their case is weak, we have preferred to leave Boduan out of the present catalogue. Excavations at the Breiddin from 1963 onwards led the excavator, Musson, to reaffirm the concept of a late Roman reoccupation, while dismissing the belief that the fort continued to be occupied into the fifth and later centuries: again, this reinterpretation was strongly supported by Savory.[55] At Moel Fenlli, the occurrence of fourth-century coin hoards and a sherd of Argonne ware can no longer be taken as implying the possibility of a date after AD 400. The most difficult case is Dinorben, where a glass bead and a fragment of Germanic metalwork[56] had long hinted at activity after AD 400. This hint is reinforced

[51] I. C. G. Burrow (1981a).
[52] L. Alcock (1963b).
[53] H. N. Savory (1964).
[54] P. S. Gelling and S. C. Stanford (1967).
[55] C. R. Musson (1976), 302; H. N. Savory (1976), 289–91.
[56] W. Gardner & H. N. Savory (1964).

by radiocarbon dates of 350 ± 65, 400 ± 50 and 475 ± 55 ad from animal bones high in the outermost ditch.[57] There is, however, no convincing evidence for any refurbishment of the defences, and the whole character of this late activity remains very shadowy. To sum up, it can now be affirmed that in Wales and the Marches, out of a large number of excavated Iron Age forts, some of them with Romano-British occupation as well, none is certainly refortified after AD 400, and only Dinorben, Coygan and doubtfully Garn Boduan, have slight traces of occupation after that date.

Two further sites, Cadbury and Congresbury, deserve further study because of the contrasting evidence which they offer on the relationships between late Roman and post-Roman occupations. In my 1982 paper on Cadbury (below, p. 189), I emphasized the physical separation of the late fifth- and sixth-century imported pottery from any traces of third- or fourth-century activity. A concentration of late Roman pottery in the innermost rampart had no causal link with the building of the rampart, except as discarded material which happened to be lying around when the post-Roman bank of Cadbury 11 was constructed. In brief, at Cadbury the evidence is for a clear hiatus between the late Roman use of the hill-top, most probably in connection with a pagan Celtic shrine, and its refortification, some time after AD 450, as a military, political and administrative centre.

At Congresbury, Romano-British pottery, some of it typologically datable to the third century, is present in some quantity.[58] Stratigraphic and distributional analysis shows that it had appeared before the first occurrence of imported wares. Unlike Cadbury, however, Congresbury shows no signs of a hiatus, and the Roman pottery continued in use alongside the imports. Burrow has produced a series of ingenious models of pottery manufacture, use, discard and survival, to show how this might have come about. A simple interpretation is, however, made difficult because some Roman pottery and other third- and fourth-century rubbish and building material were admittedly brought to the site, in an already broken condition, in the later fifth century. Other Roman pots, on the other hand, had certainly been used and broken on the site.

In Burrow's interpretation, the point most difficult to accept is that the pottery of the pre-import phase, which elsewhere would be dated as early as the third century, is here attributed to the fifth. It would seem more reasonable to allow the occupation to be dated by the pottery typology, and to see it as beginning before AD 300, and continuing without break until after AD 500. We could envisage a long-retarded use of a small quantity of Roman pottery during an aceramic phase in the early fifth century, until the range of material culture was extended by the importation of Mediterranean wine in pottery amphorae. Whether this interpretation is correct or not, two points about Congresbury are clear: it is, on present evidence, the only major fortification in Wales and Dumnonia to have produced acceptable evidence for continuous occupation from the third through into the sixth century AD; and the chronological position of the defences and internal buildings within this time-span will only become clear when the full report on the excavation is published.

It is appropriate to round off this examination of the post-Roman use of fortifications of native type with a cursory glance at enclosed places, whether civil or military, of purely Roman character. Northern Britain provides obvious examples of the longevity of some Roman structures. At York, the headquarters building of the legionary fortress preserved

---

[57] G. Guilbert (1979); (1980); and *in litt.*
[58] I. C. G. Burrow (1979); (1981a).

its roof until the ninth century; at Carlisle, as Bede reports, Cuthbert was taken to see the city walls and a Roman fountain. Bede also refers to a *villa regia* at Campodonum, which may retain the name of a Roman fort near Leeds. Another *vicus*, probably also a royal one (below, p. 250) succeeded the Roman town, and subsequently fort, at Catterick. Further afield, the Scottish Regnal Lists tell us of the death of Donald, son of Alpin, in 862, and the slaying of Kenneth, son of Malcolm, in 995, both in *Rathinveramon*, a place very reasonably identified with the former Roman auxiliary fort of Bertha at the confluence of the Almond with the Tay.[59]

In Wales, the place of Segontium in tradition and romance is well revealed in the *Dream of Macsen Wledig*, 'Emperor of Rome'. Numismatic evidence may carry the date of the latest military occupation of the fort beyond 395, and two penannular brooches may indicate a British presence into the fifth century,[60] but there is no evidence of building activity or prolonged occupation. The Brecon Gaer was refortified with a dry-stone wall so substantial that it appears to the excavator 'as something more than a merely temporary expedient'; but apart from the non-Roman character of the work, there is no evidence for its date or historical context.[61] The most striking evidence comes, however, from the town of Wroxeter, where a magnificent building, classical in style though built not of stone or brick, but of timber, was erected over the demolished baths basilica. This two-storeyed, porticoed hall, 'more probably the private desmesne of a great man' than a public or religious edifice, appears to be a work of the fifth century. For all its grandeur, and the wealth, organization, and romanized sensibility which it implies, it is unlikely that it outlasted the fifth century.[62]

One further example has been claimed in Wales of a Roman auxiliary fort which had been refurbished in the post-Roman period: that at Aberffraw.[63] It is not to be doubted that there is a bank-and-ditch defence on the site; but two considerations make it necessary to question whether the primary phase was a Roman military work. The first is the striking scarcity of Roman material, especially pottery, both from the defences and from excavations in the interior of the enclosure. The second is the character of the make-up of the supposed Roman bank: a stoneless sandy loam, with no tip lines, which lies on the natural boulder clay with no intervening fossil soil. It seems more reasonable to interpret this sandy loam, not as a rampart, but as a natural weathering product of the boulder clay, as it appears to be in the interior of the site. The occurrence in it of two minute pot-sherds would not contradict this interpretation. If these arguments are accepted, then the excavator's Phase 1 rampart vanishes, and with it, the Roman fort. We are left, then, with a very definite defensive work (the excavator's 'Phase 3 Rampart'), comprising a ditch, and a bank of rubble and clay with a dry-stone revetment to the rear, and probably timberwork at the lip of the ditch. The character of this is completely un-Roman. It can, however, very reasonably be regarded as a fortification of the royal house of Gwynedd in the fifth and later centuries.

The ultimate conclusions to be drawn from this survey of post-Roman fortifications in Wales and Dumnonia are that much new evidence has been gathered since 1963. Most of it comes, however, from very small-scale excavations, which allow us to say something of

[59] L. Alcock (1981a), 177.
[60] P. J. Casey (1979b), 76–7; H. E. Kilbride-Jones (1980b), fig. 52.
[61] P. J. Casey (1971), 94–6.
[62] P. Barker (1981).
[63] R. B. White (1980).

the character and structural history of the defences, but little about the other activities of those who had built and occupied them. We are still a long way from being able to write a broad-based synthesis of the material culture of Wales and Dumnonia in the period AD 400–800, even in terms of those agricultural, industrial and economic spheres where archaeological evidence has the greatest potential.

From this examination of new perspectives on post-Roman forts in Wales and Dumonia, Part Three continues with a catalogue of those fortifications which can reasonably be dated to our period. There follow two studies of the major excavated fort in the area, Cadbury–Camelot. Chapter 12 looks at the post-Roman refortification against the background of developments over four millennia, and especially in the Celtic Iron Age. Chapter 13 concentrates on the structures and finds of phase 11 at Cadbury, and reviews them in terms of both archaeological and documentary evidence from contemporary sites throughout Britain. Finally, Chapter 14 examines the scanty documentary evidence for the building of forts and the raising of military expeditions.

CHAPTER 11

Catalogue of Fortified Sites in Wales and Dumnonia, c. AD 400–800[1]

This catalogue provides the basic documentation for the generalizations of Chapter 10. Formally, it comprises a map with a numerical index, and an alphabetical gazetteer of the relevant sites. Each entry in the gazetteer begins with the map index number, modern name (and ancient name where this is relevant) and grid reference. This is followed by (a) a brief statement of the character, dating and area of the fortifications; (b) a digest of the evidence for a date in the fifth and later centuries; and (c) a non-comprehensive list of key references. The principal reference is normally to the excavator's own account of the site—in all too many cases, no more than a brief interim note. Where appropriate, this is supplemented with references to important commentaries.

The major reason for including a fortification in this catalogue is the occurrence of imported pottery of classes A, B, D and E: in such cases, the identification derives almost entirely from Thomas's major survey.[2] A few sites also produce trinkets or metalworking debris of the period; or glass dated to the fifth to seventh centuries by Harden.[3] In one case only, Bryneuryn (No. 2), is the chronological attribution based on a supposed identification with a fort noticed in a contemporary document. Arguments for dating the rampart and ditch at Aberffraw (No. 4) to the post-Roman period are set out above (p. 166).

The provisional nature of lists such as this has already been stressed sufficiently (above p. 153). Several miscellaneous points should be noticed here. First, the area given for each site is often difficult to calculate, given the irregular plan of many forts; and, where the interior is rocky, it may have little relevance to the extent of the habitable area within the defences. Where available, the area (along with other details) has been derived from Hogg's classic gazetteer of Iron Age forts.[4] In outlining the chronological range of sites, the abbreviations PRIA and RB have been used respectively for the pre-Roman Iron Age (i.e. before c. AD 50) and the Roman period (c. AD 50–400): all sites are considered to have been occupied, for an uncertain length of time, after AD 450 (or, allowing for a more precise dating of the imported pottery, after AD 460–70). Finally, in addition to the specific site references of the gazetteer, mention must be made of the magisterial surveys of Cornwall by Johnson and Rose,[5] and of Somerset by Burrow:[6] these have greatly facilitated our own work of analysis and comparison.

[1] Based on a schedule originally compiled by Elizabeth A. Alcock.
[2] A. C. Thomas (1981).
[3] D. B. Harden (1956b), 148–9.
[4] A. H. A. Hogg (1979).
[5] N. Johnson and P. Rose (1982).
[6] I. C. G. Burrow (1981a).

Key to map and gazetteer

1. New Pieces, Breiddin, Montgomeryshire.
2. Bryneuryn, Dinarth, Denbighshire.
3. Degannwy Castle, Caernarvonshire.
4. Aberffraw, Anglesey.
5. Carreg-y-llam, Caernarvonshire.
6. Dinas Emrys, Caernarvonshire.
7. Coygan Camp, Carmarthenshire.
8. Dinas Powys, Glamorgan.
9. Cadbury-Congresbury, Somerset.
10. Cadbury-Camelot, Somerset.

11. Tintagel, Cornwall.
12. Killibury, Cornwall.
13. Trevelgue, Cornwall.
14. Chûn Castle, Cornwall.
15. Goldherring, Cornwall.
16. Maen Castle, Cornwall.
17. Grambla, Cornwall.
18. Trethurgy, Cornwall.
19. Castle Dore, Cornwall.

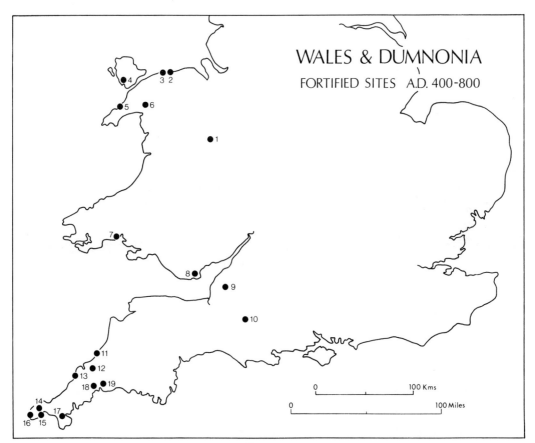

Fig. 11.1.
Map: fortified sites in Wales and Dumnonia, AD 400–800

Gazetteer of Forts

4. ABERFFRAW   SH 3568
    (a) Ditch and bank enclosure of unknown size and plan.
    (b) Character and stratification of rampart.
    (c) White 1980.

2. BRYNEURYN, Dinarth (Din Eirth = *receptaculum ursi*)   SH 8379
    (a) Stone walled citadel and enclosure: 0.4 ha.
    (b) Documentary reference: DEB 32.1.
    (c) Sims-Williams 1983a: 8.

10. CADBURY 11   ST 6225
    (a) Timber-laced wall on top of multivallate PRIA fort (with some RB activity), with timber hall: 8.0 ha.
    (b) Imported pottery (A, B, D), jewellery, glass.
    (c) Chapters 12 and 13 below.

9. CADBURY-CONGRESBURY   ST 4465
    (a) Stone-walled double enclosure with elaborate entrance, circular and rectangular buildings, uncertain RB activity: 3.5 ha.
    (b) Imported pottery (A, B, D), trinkets, metalworking, glass.
    (c) Fowler, Gardner and Rahtz 1970. Burrow 1981a.

5. CARREG-Y-LLAM   SH 3343
    (a) Double stone wall on cliff edge, incorporating round house: 0.03 ha.
    (b) Possible wheel-thrown pottery.
    (c) Hogg 1957.

19. CASTLE DORE   SX 1054
    (a) Possible refortification of PRIA bivallate fort, possible timber buildings: 0.5 ha.
    (b) Post-Iron Age structures, ? imported pottery.
    (c) Radford 1951. Rahtz 1971.

14. CHÛN   SW 4033
    (a) Re-used PRIA fort with 2 concentric stone walls, some alteration of entrance: 0.19 ha.
    (b) Imported pottery (B).
    (c) Leeds 1927, 1931. Thomas 1956.

7. COYGAN CAMP   SN 2809
    (a) Re-used PRIA/RB promontory fort: 0.53 ha.
    (b) Imported pottery (A, B).
    (c) Wainwright 1967.

3. DEGANNWY CASTLE   SH 7879
    (a) Possible single stone wall around craggy hill-top, with uncertain RB activity: 0.3 ha for citadel only.
    (b) Documentary references: *Annales Cambriae* s.a. 812, 822. Imported pottery (B).
    (c) Alcock 1967c.

6. DINAS EMRYS   SH 6049
    (a) Single stone wall around craggy hill-top, with entrance outworks; uncertain RB activity: 1.0 ha for main enclosure.
    (b) Imported pottery (B, E), metalworking, glass.
    (c) Savory 1960.

8. DINAS POWYS   ST 1671
    (a) Bank and ditch enclosure of spur tip, with two subrectangular drystone build-
        ings: 0.18 ha.
    (b) Imported pottery (A, B, D, E), bonework, trinkets, metalworking, glass.
    (c) Parts One and Two above.

15. GOLDHERRING   SW 4128
    (a) Oval walled and ditched 'round', founded in PRIA, occupied in RB and post-
        Roman periods: 0.08 ha.
    (b) Platters comparable with post-Roman examples from Gwithian.
    (c) Guthrie 1969.

17. GRAMBLA   SW 6928
    (a) Rectangular ditch and bank enclosure, founded in RB period, continuing into
        fifth century: 0.36 ha.
    (b) Imported pottery (A?, B).
    (c) Saunders 1972.

12. KILLIBURY   SX 0173
    (a) Re-used PRIA double-banked concentric fort with additional enclosures:
        1.2 ha.
    (b) Imported pottery (B).
    (c) Miles et al. 1977.

16. MAEN CASTLE   SW 3425
    (a) Re-used PRIA promontory fort: 0.9 ha.
    (b) Grass-marked pot base.
    (c) Crofts 1955.

1. NEW PIECES, BREIDDIN   SJ 2913
    (a) RB foundation, double-banked around much of perimeter: 0.5 ha.
    (b) Glass (identified by J. R. Hunter, ex. inf. C. R. Musson).
    (c) O'Neil 1937: 107–12. Mytum 1982.

11. TINTAGEL   SX 0489
    (a) Large peninsula cut off by short bank and ditch across narrow neck, with prob-
        ably contemporary rectangular buildings: c. 6.0 ha for headland.
    (b) Imported pottery (A, B, D), glass.
    (c) Radford 1935. Burrow 1973. Thomas 1982.

18. TRETHURGY   SX 0355
    (a) Oval walled and ditched 'round', founded in RB period, continuing into fifth
        century and later: 0.2 ha.
    (b) Imported pottery (A, B, E?).
    (c) Miles and Miles 1973.

13. TREVELGUE   SW 8263
    (a) Re-used PRIA promontory fort, some RB activity: 3.2 ha.
    (b) Imported pottery ? (B?).
    (c) Andrew 1949.

CHAPTER 12

Excavations at Cadbury–Camelot, 1966–70[1]

'Cadbury Castle or Camelot' is the name given by the Ordnance Survey to the 18-acre (*c.* 7-ha) multi-ramparted hill-fort which stands above the villages of Sutton Montis and South Cadbury in the county of Somerset (NGR ST 6225) (Fig. 12.1). Abbreviated to Cadbury–Camelot,[2] it serves conveniently to distinguish this fort—the scene of intensive excavations in 1966–70—from Cadbury Castle by Cadbury, Devon (NGR SS 9105), Cadbury Camp by Congresbury (NGR ST 4464), or various other Cadbury Camps and Castles. The 'Camelot' element is enshrined in antiquarian and topographical writings from the sixteenth century on, and for this reason alone Cadbury–Camelot is to be preferred to the unwarranted neologism South Cadbury Castle. Before we survey the results of the excavations, it would be as well to ask what may be implied when we attach the name Camelot to this hill-fort.

In 1965, when I was appointed by the Society for Medieval Archaeology as one of its representatives on the Camelot Research Committee, I certainly believed that the historical Arthur might have had a fortified court called Camelot. I now know that Camelot is a place that never was; an invention, in fact, of French poets of the late twelfth and thirteenth centuries, which first appears in the variant manuscripts of Chrétien's *Lancelot*.[3] Having assimilated Arthur to a medieval king, the poets had to provide him with a suitable court. They ignored the Welsh traditions of Celliwic in Cornwall, and Geoffrey of Monmouth's references to Caerleon, and invented Camelot.

When this name came back to Britain, it provided both romancers and topographers with a problem of identification. Malory always identified Camelot with Winchester; but when Caxton printed the *Morte d' Arthur*, he referred to 'the toune of Camelot ... which dyvers now lyvyng hath seen ... in Wales'. The identification with Cadbury Castle was first made by John Leland, explicitly in his *Itinerary*, and by implication in his *Assertio inclytissimi Arturii Regis Britanniae* (1544, fol. 10). What was the basis of this new identification? Did Leland on his travels see the magnificent defences towering above his route; and knowing of the neighbouring villages of Queen Camel and West Camel (which he corrupted to Quene Camallat), did he leap to the conclusion that this was indeed the Camelot 'much resorted to' by Arthur? If so, the whole Arthurian connection of the site may be an invention of the 1540s. Or did he, in response to open-minded questioning, receive the reply that the fort had been the resort of Arthur? And was the Arthurian connection already as firmly embedded in local folk-traditions as it became later?

Stukeley's comments are a powerful blow to this theory of folk tradition: 'the country people are ignorant of this name (sc. Camelot) which has generally obtained among the

---

[1] The Marett Memorial Lecture for 1970–1, reprinted by permission of the Governing Body of Exeter College, Oxford, and of the Editor of *Antiquity*. First published in *Antiquity*, 46 (1972), 29–38.
[2] I owe this felicitous short-hand expression to Professor Charles Thomas.
[3] C. E. Pickford (1969), 158.

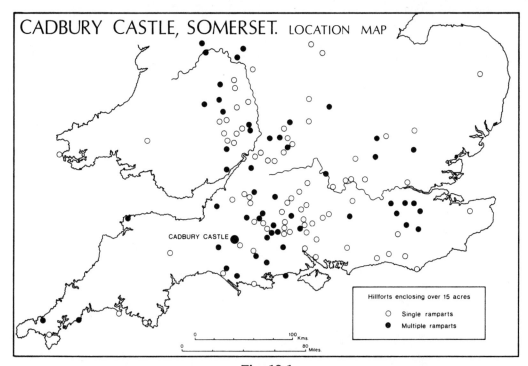

Fig. 12.1.
Cadbury–Camelot: location map

learned'.[4] Camden's witness, on the other hand, provides equally powerful support: *incolae Arthuri Palatium dicunt*, 'the locals call it Arthur's Palace'.[5] And there is other evidence that Arthurian traditions were attached to Cadbury Castle by, or even before, Leland's visit. The Welsh chronicler Elis Gruffydd refers to a cave under a hill near Glastonbury where Arthur lay sleeping.[6] He does not name the hill, but Glastonbury Tor has no sleeping-king associations, and Cadbury is the most likely candidate. So we have here the possibility that, although Leland was responsible for the identification with Camelot, he was inspired by deep-rooted folk traditions which connected Cadbury Castle with Arthur.

EXCAVATION STRATEGY, 1966–70

Whatever weight there might be in these folk traditions, nothing of Arthurian date was found in St George Gray's excavations in 1913.[7] The first recognition of relevant material came in the 1950s, with the discovery of Mediterranean pottery which had been turned up by ploughing.[8] The belief that the pottery provided 'an interesting confirmation of the

[4] W. Stukeley (1776), 150.
[5] W. Camden (1586), 153.
[6] T. Jones (1966), 175.
[7] H. St. G. Gray (1913).
[8] C. A. R. Radford and J. S. Cox (1955); M. Harfield (1962).

traditional identification of the site as the Camelot of Arthurian legend' was a major motive in the formation of the Camelot Research Committee; but it was not the sole reason for the decision to promote large-scale excavations. For a start, Cadbury–Camelot did not fit the model for sixth-century strongholds which I had proposed in 1963;[9] indeed, it challenged the validity of my interpretation. Secondly, granted that it was high time an Iron Age hill-fort was examined in the light of modern ideas and techniques, the known sequence[10] at Cadbury made it pre-eminently worthy of attention. Finally, there was the opportunity to examine a late Saxon *burh*[11] which was not encumbered by medieval and modern buildings.

It was the need to excavate a hill-fort in the light of modern hypotheses that governed the strategy of excavation. Much was already known about the chronology and structure of the defences of hill-forts,[12] and there had been all too much emphasis on their military

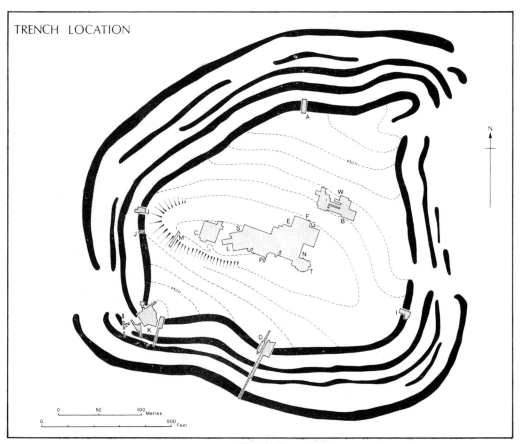

Fig. 12.2.
Cadbury–Camelot: plan of defences and location of trenches

[9] L. Alcock (1963a), 66–8.
[10] C. A. R. Radford and J. S. Cox (1955).
[11] R. H. M. Dolley (1957).
[12] R. E. M. Wheeler (1952).

functions. By contrast, very little was known about what happened inside the defences: whether the inhabitants were soldiers or civilians, permanent residents or occasional refugees, few or many, rich or poor. I had posed some of these questions in 1964,[13] largely on the basis of Welsh evidence. Now I had the opportunity to test my ideas against the richer evidence of a southern English fort, one which stood in hill-fort country *par excellence*. The defences and gates of Cadbury–Camelot were not to be ignored, but the main effort was to be concentrated on the interior of the site (Fig. 12.2).

The implementation of this strategy was assisted by developments in geophysical prospecting and, above all, by the invention of an easily portable instrument of simple but reliable design, which made it possible to survey the whole interior.[14] For mechanical reasons, the geophysical survey began on the central summit plateau, and significant buildings were immediately located.[15] These were cleared in 1967,[16] and thereafter the excavations were largely, but not exclusively, concentrated on the plateau.[17] This policy was strongly criticized by those who maintained that the ancient inhabitants would have avoided the 'windswept' summit and would have confined their dwellings to the north-eastern lee slopes or even to a narrow zone immediately behind the ramparts. In fact, the profile of the hill is such that the plateau is relatively windless, and so it is not surprising that we found there temples, workshops and timber buildings of various dates. At Cadbury, the geographical centre of the fort was certainly the focus for important activities.

EARLY PHASES OF OCCUPATION

Human occupation of the Cadbury–Camelot hill-top began in the mid-fourth millennium BC, on the evidence of two radiocarbon dates of 4460 ± 120 bp and 4705 ± 115 bp (I. 5970 and I. 5972).[18] These dates may be calibrated to about 3300 and 3500 BC respectively. Pottery, flints, and both human and animal bones came from pits in the interior, and beneath the innermost rampart on the southern slopes of the hill. But our knowledge of this, and of the succeeding late Neolithic activity[19] is too scrappy to merit further discussion here.

The main history of the site begins in the late Bronze Age about the eighth century BC, when a farming community established houses and ovens on the plateau. Pottery and bronzes suggest that these settlers were natives rather than invaders. There is no evidence that defence was the motive which brought them to the hill-top, and it is more likely that it was the post-glacial Climatic Revertence which had driven them to seek well-drained upland soils to farm. This does not necessarily imply arable cultivation, and the presence of a well-marked, stone-free humus beneath the earliest Iron Age defence implies that the hill-top had been under pasture for some considerable time before the rampart was built. The discovery of a gold bracelet of Covesea type shows that there was a wealthy element in the population of this settlement, but it would be idle to speculate whether some late

[13] L. Alcock (1965a).
[14] M. Howell (1966).
[15] C. R. Musson (1968).
[16] L. Alcock (1968a; 1968b).
[17] L. Alcock (1969a; 1969b; 1970a; 1970b; 1971).
[18] For a fuller discussion of the radiocarbon dates from Cadbury–Camelot, L. Alcock (1980b), especially 708–9.
[19] L. Alcock (1970b), pl. VII a.

Bronze Age noble was acquiring tenurial rights which were to survive in his family for centuries.

What is certain is that in the seventh and sixth centuries, exotic elements appear on the hill. In addition to Hallstatt C razors and Hallstatt D pins,[20] there is also pottery which owes nothing to insular Bronze Age ceramics, but which may be paralleled among the coarser pottery of the Urnfield and Hallstatt cultures. This suggests that the pottery is as exotic as the bronzes, and makes it likely that all these objects were brought in by folk-movement rather than by trade. I see no reason to doubt that the men and women who introduced both the new bronzes and the new pottery were Celtic invaders. So, not only did they initiate our insular Iron Age ceramics; they were to set the tone of life, the character of society over these islands for the next millennium or more.

HEROIC SOCIETY AND HILL-FORTS

That tone of life was heroic; and though it would be anachronistic to talk of the Celtic Heroic Age as early as the seventh or sixth centuries BC, none the less the foundations of heroic society were being laid. On the continent, abundant Hallstatt graves make it clear that a warrior nobility constituted the most important element in society. In this country the graves are virtually lacking, but the weapons, horse-gear and ornaments of the nobility are well known. We may be sure that warfare, within well-defined conventions, was the only fitting pursuit for a gentleman.

It may be thought that this emphasis on warfare created the social need for hill-forts. But there is no reason to think that the capture or defence of fortified positions was a major objective or a principal tactic of Celtic warfare. The swift, incisive cattle-raid, the sudden ambush in pursuit of a blood-feud, the clash of champions in front of the armed hosts, are the patterns of Celtic warfare, not the protracted siege or the costly assault. Nevertheless, in my 1964 article,[21] I probably underestimated the role of hill-forts in protecting wealth—cattle, grain, women, slaves—against raiders. The thought that there may be evidence for Celtic attacks on hill-forts lurking in unexcavated sites is prompted by the recent recognition of vitrifaction in the entrance passage of Castle Bank, Llansanffraid-yn-Elfael (NGR SO 0856). And the known history of Maori *pa*, similar in many ways to our own hill-forts, shows that people at a tribal level of society can sustain sieges against the fortified settlements of their neighbours.[22]

There is, in fact, no evidence that Cadbury was assaulted before the Roman military machine rolled in, practised as it was in attacks on fortified places. Nevertheless, between the first construction of defences in the sixth or fifth century BC and the Roman conquest, the main rampart was remodelled at least three times, while the south-west gate was probably re-designed five times. Two points of particular interest may deserve comment here. First, immediately before the final re-building of the Iron Age gate, the passageway was nothing more than a grassy depression through the ramparts. This implies a long period of dereliction in the defences, and raises the question whether the whole fortified town had been abandoned. This might perhaps account for a typological hiatus between the early and mature aspects of Durotrigian culture at Cadbury.

Secondly, the construction of each successive defensive work demanded large resources of organized labour. The earliest rampart, for instance, required a 30,000-metre run

[20] L. Alcock (1970a), pl. VIII.
[21] L. Alcock (1965a).
[22] R. Firth (1927), 77–8.

(100,000 ft) of dressed timber. When it was refurbished, massive blocks of Jurassic lime-stone were quarried on the site, and were then faced with Lias slabs which had to be carted in from some distance away.[23] What were the social arrangements which made it possible to exact and to organize labour services on the required scale? This question is inevitably posed by the archaeological evidence. To answer it, we must attempt to extrapolate from historical documents. In the Welsh Laws, we find that bond townships were responsible for providing men with axes to build the king's strongholds.[24] This may represent the last feeble survival, into an age when fortifications have almost vanished from the archaeological record, of the kind of customary labour services which built the hill-forts of the Iron Age. In early Welsh society it is the king who commands these services. When the Celtic tribes of Britain first came on the scene of history, they were ruled by kings. Here the witness of Caesar is supported by that of the inscribed coins, which bear not only the names of rulers, but also, occasionally, the word REX or its Celtic equivalent RICON.

CELTIC SOCIETY AT CADBURY–CAMELOT

Inscribed coins are unknown, however, in the territory of the Durotriges, in which Cadbury–Camelot lies. This is curious, because the tribe was by no means backward in other aspects of its culture, and its immediate neighbours, the Dobunni and the Atrebates, certainly struck inscribed coins. Was it that the Durotriges were ruled by a tribal aristoc-racy rather than by a single king? However that may be, we can reasonably infer that the actual exaction of labour services for building hill-forts was in the hands of the nobility. Now in my 1965 article I had refuted the view that the forts were the seats of chieftains. 'We might hesitate to speak of the social level of their inhabitants; but the absence of prestige finds and activities must incline us to believe that it was lowly.' In particular, the fine metalwork of the warrior nobility had scarcely ever been found in a fort. There was a marked contrast here between the pre- and post-Roman periods, for forts of the later period, which can be shown on historical grounds to have been the strongholds of princes, have yielded costly imports, fine metalwork, and aristocratic buildings.

The Cadbury excavations now make it necessary to modify drastically statements about the absence of prestige finds and activities from Iron Age forts. In addition to minor pieces of weaponry[25] the excavation has yielded three important pieces of La Tène art: a cast bronze pendant with opposed duck's heads embellished with coral or paste studs;[26] a shield boss with repoussé scroll-work in the high Celtic style;[27] and a bronze disc with a repoussé horse, which had been cut from some larger object.[28] Sociological implications apart, these are noteworthy additions to the repertory of insular Celtic art.

As for prestige activities, we have the evidence that in early Welsh and Irish society the patronage of skilled craftsmen was the prerogative of the aristocracy, with the archaeological implication that where we find relics of craft-working, we can infer a chieftain in the vicinity. Similar arrangements may be projected back into pre-Roman Celtic society, as a reasonable inference from the character of the fine metalwork, but actual evidence for craft-working has not normally been noticed. At Cadbury, however, it

[23] L. Alcock (1969a), Figs. 1 and 2.
[24] M. Richards (1954). See also Chapter 14, below.
[25] L. Alcock (1970b), pl. VIII.
[26] L. Alcock (1969b), pl. XIX b
[27] M. G. Spratling (1970b).
[28] L. Alcock (1971a), pl. II b.

takes two forms. First, a group of ovens which are too elaborate to suggest domestic use are likely to mark a bronze-smith's workshop. The shield boss was found nearby, along with other scrap-bronze intended for the melting-pot. Secondly, scattered more widely were examples of the iron and bronze tools used to produce repoussé and traced patterns.[29] For all their technological significance, these tools are very simple-looking objects,[30] and it is very probable that similar objects lie unrecognized and unpublished among the collections from other forts. The implication that some hill-forts were centres of fine metal-working under aristocratic patronage is obviously far-reaching.

The Cadbury excavations have also provided evidence to confirm the hypothesis that hill-forts were centres of religious activity. It is common knowledge that temples to Celtic deities were built within hill-forts during the later Roman centuries. One possible reason for founding pagan temples in places remote from urban centres may have been to escape official attention in an Empire which was nominally Christian. We may recall here that the *pagani* were originally merely the 'country-folk'. But there has also been speculation that the late Roman temples had been built on the sites of pre-Roman shrines, whose sanctity had been maintained spiritually, even if not materially, over the intervening centuries.[31] From this it was a short step to the inference that the forts themselves had been religious or ritual centres, comparable perhaps with the later sacred enclosures of Ireland such as Tara or Emain Macha. But attractive though the hypothesis was, it lacked the material proof of archaeology.

At Cadbury, however, the evidence is clear. For a start, there are rock-cut pits in which the skulls of cattle or horses had been carefully buried.[32] There is no evidence that originally the pits were anything other than normal grain storage pits. Usually after these pits became sour they served as dumps for the disposal of rubbish, including both broken crocks and food-refuse, especially animal bones. But when animal skulls have been placed right way up, sometimes on a bed of stones, it is difficult to believe that they are merely rubbish, and an explanation in terms of ritual seems far more probable. There was a notable concentration of these pits with skulls on the highest part of the plateau, suggesting that this was a focus for the cult.

Farther east along the summit ridge was the rock-cut foundation trench for a timber shrine (Fig. 12.3).[33] Its main element was an almost square *cella*, internally about 2.7 m wide, and opening off this was a porch about 1.2 m deep. This shrine apparently replaced a simpler structure, immediately in front of which a cow had been buried. Beyond this again, within quite a narrow zone, were numerous other animal burials. Newly-born calves predominated, but sheep and pigs were also present. To the north of the zone of animal burials were numerous iron objects, especially daggers and scabbards. Some of these had been disturbed by ploughing, but others lay in groups in shallow pits. It seems likely that the weapons found in pits were, like the animals, sacrifices. Perhaps we have here the ritual offerings of both the peasant and the noble warrior.

HOUSES AND POPULATION

The domestic life of the pre-Roman Iron Age was also well represented on the summit plateau. Post-holes and wall trenches for both rectangular and circular buildings were

[29] M. G. Spratling (1970a).
[30] L. Alcock (1970a), pl. VIII: 4–8.
[31] A. Ross (1967), 43–8.
[32] L. Alcock (1969b) pl. XIX c.
[33] L. Alcock (1970a), Fig. 3; (1970b), Fig. 2.

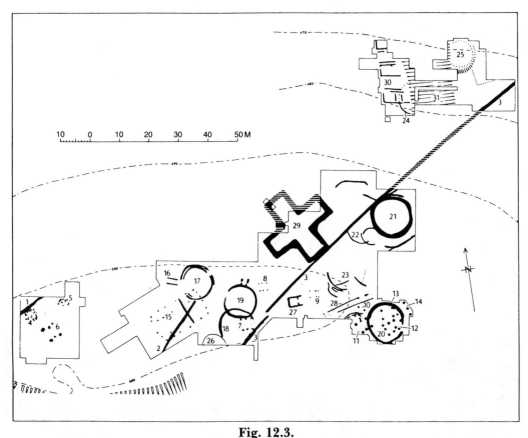

Fig. 12.3.
Principal structures in the interior. 1–3 field ditches; 4, 5 post-hole clusters, perhaps house-sites; 6–14 six- (and four-) post buildings; 6 and 9 are possibly shrines; 15 Arthurian-period hall; 16 ancillary building; 17–21 ring ditches of Iron Age houses; 22, 23 palisades and post-trenches, not certainly for houses; 24, 25 stake-built houses; 26 possible house-site; 27 porched shrine; 28 fence bounding zone of animal burials; 29 foundation trench of Ethelredan church; 30 probable Roman military building; 31 hollow-way

uncovered. The rectangular buildings were quite small six-post structures, up to 4.0 m by 6.0 m. There is slight evidence that they are early in the Iron Age, but the fact that several of them overlapped makes it evident that they spanned several phases of re-building. The medium-sized circular house is, however, the predominant Iron Age house-type uncovered at Cadbury. Six of these were cleared completely, and parts of others were examined. In some cases the main structure was a drum of wicker-work, with no substantial posts, but in the majority the walls were made of split timbers set upright in a rock-cut trench. Several of them had evidently been rebuilt on more or less the same site, with only a slight shift of centre. This suggests continuity of occupation or ownership on a building plot.

The larger houses are usually about 10.5 m in diameter, giving a floor area of almost

90 sq m (Fig. 12.4: 2, 3). This is much the same as that of a small three-bedroomed bungalow today (Fig. 12.4: 1), and by Iron Age standards could no doubt have housed quite a large group in relative comfort. We know nothing of family-structure among the prehistoric Celts, but we may suppose that each house held a three-generation family group, perhap 20 in all. If we were to make such an assumption, could we then calculate the size of the Iron Age population during the period when round houses were in use? Early in our campaign we believed that this would be possible, because the rock-cut wall-trenches registered strongly in our geophysical survey of the plateau. It therefore seemed reasonable to expect that if we surveyed the whole interior, we would locate all the houses. But as the excavation proceeded, it became evident that geophysical prospecting had located not more than half the houses on the plateau, while on the slopes of the hill it had given no reliable indications at all. It is a chastening thought that a combination of total geophysical survey and very extensive excavation should still fail to determine the size of population of a hill-fort.

Comparison with the houses which have been excavated at other forts such as Maiden Castle or Hod Hill shows that they have floor areas less than half those of the Cadbury

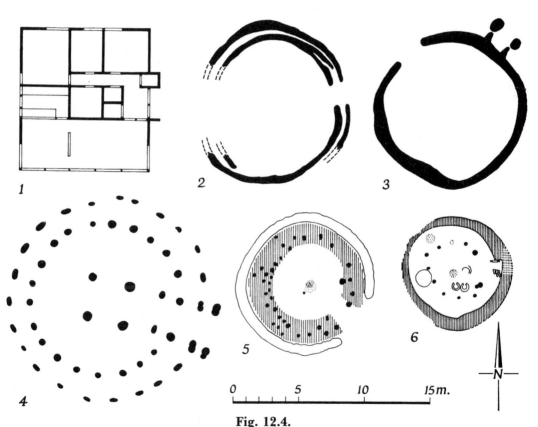

Fig. 12.4.
Comparative house-plans. 1 three-bedroomed bungalow with floor area of 96 sq m; 2, 3 houses on Site P at Cadbury–Camelot; 4 Little Woodbury (after Bersu 1940, Fig. 25); 5 Hod Hill (after Richmond 1968, Fig. 14); 6 Maiden Castle (after Wheeler 1943, Fig. 18)

dwellings—30 to 40 sq m as against 90 sq m (Fig. 12.4: 5, 6). As it happens, the larger houses at Cadbury lie within the main area of excavation at the ritual centre of the fort and have a bronze-smith's workshop close at hand, whereas the excavated examples at Maiden Castle are mainly peripheral. Those at Hod Hill are not in a dominant position though the surface plan suggests that similar houses may have occupied much of the interior. (One of the Hod houses has indeed been claimed as that of a tribal chief, but there is nothing in its position, size, or associated finds to substantiate the hypothesis.) Can it be that the differences in size and in location are inter-related, and that they reflect differences in the status of the householder? And if this is so, are the small peripheral houses those of bondmen, and the larger central houses those of the warrior nobility? And where do yet larger houses, typified by Little Woodbury with a floor area of some 180 sq m (Fig. 12.4: 4), fit into this scheme?

CADBURY–CAMELOT IN THE ARTHURIAN PERIOD

Space does not permit any further description of the Iron Age culture of the Durotriges, or of its destruction at the hands of the Romans. I turn instead to the early post-Roman or Arthurian period. I am aware of course that 'Arthurian' has been criticized as a chronological term on the grounds that it lacks the precision of 'Flavian' or 'Trajanic'. But I would ask the critics to reflect on the common usage of terms like 'Elizabethan', or 'Georgian' or 'Regency'; and in particular I would ask Romanists to reflect on 'Antonine II', which needs re-defining every three or four years. I am here taking it for granted that Arthur was a historical person.[34] Recent advances in source-criticism have shown, to any reasonable standard of historical proof, that the so-called *Annales Cambriae* are based on Easter Annals written down contemporaneously from the mid-fifth century.[35] Two of these contemporary annals record Arthur's victory over the Saxons at Badon and his death at Camlann. For technical reasons, and in particular, confusion either between the Incarnation and the Passion of Our Lord, or between lunar cycles, there may be a 28- or 19-year margin of error. So, Badon may be 490, 499 or 518. This multiple chronology casts no doubt on Arthur's historicity: Patrick of Ireland and Hammurabi of Babylon are examples of historical figures for whom two chronological schemes are possible.

Beyond these two entries in the Welsh Easter Annals, any account of the historical Arthur becomes increasingly conjectural. Fortunately such speculation is outside the scope of this article, and we can turn instead to an account of Cadbury–Camelot in the Arthurian period. The crucial dating evidence is provided by imported pottery: fine red bowls (Class A) from some unlocated Mediterranean source; amphorae (Class B) from the Mediterranean; and grey bowls and mortaria from the Bordeaux region.[36] At Cadbury–Camelot, the occurrence of early amphorae (Class B iv) and the absence of coarse-gritted kitchen wares (Class E) argue for a date centred on AD 500. Mr Hayes's dating of individual red-ware dishes from the site conforms with this, so we can say that the fort was occupied within the Arthurian period in the narrowest sense of the term.[37]

On the summit of the hill we found the post-holes and wall-trench of a rectangular timber building which could be securely dated to this period on the evidence of both sealed and scattered pottery. This building was about 19 m long by 10 m wide (Fig. 12.5:

[34] L. Alcock (1971; 1973), 45–88; 1972a.
[35] These claims would be rejected by D. N. Dumville (1977b).
[36] J. Rigoir (1968).
[37] For fuller comments on the imported pottery in general, see pp. 88–92 and Chapter 6 above.

1): about three-quarters the floor area of the largest royal hall of Yeavering, half as large
again as the earliest hall at Cheddar (Fig. 12.5: 2), and slightly larger than the seven-
teenth-century hall of Exeter College (Fig. 12.5: 3) (where this paper was first read).
Given both its size and its central position, this was the principal building of the Arthurian fort: the feasting hall of whatever noble warrior lived at Cadbury with his war-band.
Although such halls feature in the poetry of the Dark Ages, few have been satisfactorily
excavated and published (Laing gives an unsatisfactory account of the few)[38] so this is a
noteworthy addition to knowledge.

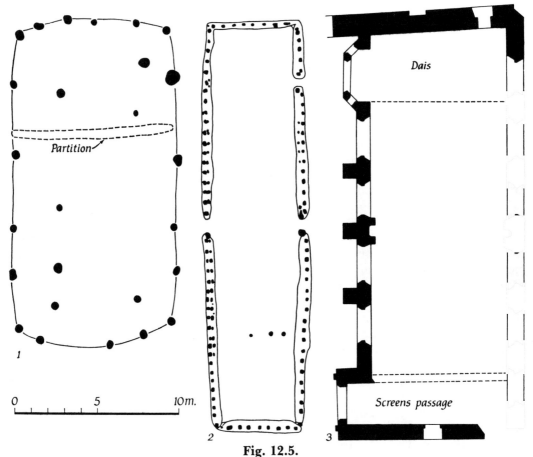

Fig. 12.5.
Comparative hall plans. 1 Arthurian-period hall at Cadbury–Camelot; 2 The Long
Hall at Cheddar (after Rahtz 1963, Fig. 20); 3 Exeter College, Oxford (after RCHM
Oxford, 55)

Even more noteworthy was the information about the defences and the south-west gate.
The hill-top had been re-fortified with a timber fighting platform, faced with dressed
stone and anchored down with rubble.[39] The dressed stone had been quarried from

[38] Ll. R. Laing (1969); but now see B. Hope-Taylor (1977); N. Reynolds (1980).
[39] L. Alcock (1970a), Fig. 1.

derelict Roman buildings, but it was used in an un-Roman manner, without mortar. On the other hand, the timber gate-tower had a clearly Roman ancestry, for it was derived from the simplest type of auxiliary fort gate. It is interesting here to see how much of Roman military technology had been preserved, and how much more had been lost, by AD 500.

THE MILITARY ROLE OF CADBURY–CAMELOT

But the major interest of the Arthurian defences is their sheer extent: nearly eleven hundred metres, the same as the Iron Age perimeter. The shape of the Cadbury hill is such that it would have been easy to construct a well-defended stronghold with only a half or a quarter the area of the Iron Age fort. The decision to build a large fort must be considered in relation to the size of contemporary strongholds, the size of contemporary armies, and the possible strategic purpose of Cadbury–Camelot. Imported pottery of Classes A, B and D has been found to date on twenty-eight sites in these islands. At least eleven, and possibly as many as thirteen, of these were forts, some of them known to be the strongholds of historical princes. With the exception of Cadbury–Congresbury, none is more than one-fifth the area of Camelot, and some are considerably smaller. Congresbury is half the size, but it is more likely to be a derelict Iron Age fort re-used as a monastic enclosure than a secular stronghold.[40]

As for the armies which used these strongholds, the British evidence comes from the *Gododdin* poem, with its poetically-rounded force of three hundred mounted warriors. It has recently been argued that this figure is too low by a factor of ten.[41] But this suggestion cannot be reconciled with other evidence for the size of Dark Age armies, or with the probable social structure of the Britons.[42] It can be affirmed that the *Gododdin* figure is about right for an army raised principally, but not exclusively, from a single kingdom. The war-band of an individual prince or chief might have run from thirty to a hundred, and these figures would be quite consistent with the archaeological evidence for small strongholds. But the length of the Cadbury–Camelot perimeter makes no sense for such an army. Can we find an appropriate strategic situation for a fort of this size?

We know that the gate-tower was put into a state of repair in the later sixth century. It is reasonable to see this as a reaction by the Britons of the south-west, from Gloucester to Cornwall, to the Wessex aggression which culminated in 577 in the victory of Dyrham and the capture of Gloucester, Cirencester and Bath. The earlier phase of activity, dated by imported pottery to around 500, is contemporary, within the limits of archaeological evidence, with the campaigns which had their climax in the British victory at Badon. There is general agreement that this battle was fought in southern England, and clearly Cadbury would have made an excellent base for campaigns against the Saxons in either the upper Thames or the Hampshire Avon valleys. And if Arthur was the victor of Badon, and if, as early traditions suggest, he fought on behalf of the kings of the Britons, his combined force might have numbered around a thousand men, appropriate therefore to the size of the Cadbury defences.

If this last sentence is dismissed as conjecture, it is none the less beyond dispute that on the present evidence Cadbury–Camelot stands on its own as a fortification of the

---

[40] L. Alcock (1971; 1973), 218–9; but see now I. C. G. Burrow (1981a) on Congresbury.
[41] K. H. Jackson (1969), 13–18.
[42] L. Alcock (1971; 1973), 335–6.

Arthurian period. Presumably therefore it served some outstanding strategic role. Beyond this, if we allow the unhistorical Camelot any value as a symbol for the principal stronghold of the greatest warrior of his day, Cadbury provides just what we need to turn symbol into reality.

CADANBURH AND AFTER

With the continued expansion of Wessex, Cadbury was abandoned for some four centuries. Its role as a *burh* in the last years of Æthelred and the first of Cnut—roughly 1010–20—has been inferred from coins minted at *Cadanburh*.[43] Excavation showed that the *burh* had been defended by an excellent masonry wall and bank,[44] with monumental gateways dressed with Ham stone. Its life was too short for any substantial urban development, but Æthelred had intended that a church should be the central feature.[45] Under Cnut, however, the *burh* was promptly abandoned, and its wall and gates were almost totally slighted.

Some time later, the gateway was rebuilt in the crudest imaginable manner, but the historical context of this is unknown. After that, the history of Cadbury–Camelot is one of peaceful agriculture and antiquarian speculation. The antiquaries' notices are full of Roman coins dug up daily, and 'remnants of arches, door-jambs, bolts, hand-grindstones, and great quantities of round pebble-stones' all found in the course of ploughing and subsequently lost or destroyed. Indeed, reading these accounts, one might well speculate whether there was anything left for a twentieth-century excavator to discover. Happily, this speculation, at least, proved unfounded.

[43] R. H. M. Dolley (1957).
[44] L. Alcock (1967b), pl. XV a.
[45] L. Alcock (1968a), Fig. 2.

CHAPTER 13

Cadbury–Camelot: a Fifteen-year Perspective[1]

I

It is very fitting that a series of lectures established in honour of Sir Mortimer Wheeler should include one on the Cadbury–Camelot excavations, and I am personally most grateful for the opportunity to record his large contribution to the success of that work. I had served an important part of my own archaeological apprenticeship under him at Mohenjo-daro and Stanwick. Consequently, when it was suggested to me, as Director of Excavations for the Camelot Research Committee, that he should be invited to serve as President of the Committee, I warmly welcomed the proposal, though I had no illusions that he would be a mere figurehead. In the event, he only once intervened in the day-to-day running of the excavations when, at the end of the 1966 season, he urged me to begin a cutting across the innermost rampart which I had intended leaving until the following year. On two memorable occasions, he brought his heavy guns to bear on the Committee; each time, I am glad to say, in support of the Director's own strategy and budget. Above all, by his energetic quest for funds, and by his personal influence with grant-giving institutions, he ensured that there were fully adequate resources to carry that strategy through to a successful conclusion. Finally, as editor of the 'New Aspects of Antiquity' series, he made it possible for me to present a very lavishly illustrated summary of our results within two years of the end of the excavations.[2]

Given the fullness of that summary, it might seem that I can add little in the course of an hour's lecture, even if I confine myself to the 'Arthurian' aspects of Cadbury. Some of my statements will indeed seem familiar to anyone who has read the 1972 summary. This is a tribute to the way in which my field colleagues kept both observation and interpretation fully up to date during the four digging seasons. In writing this paper, however, I have re-examined all the relevant evidence, and so I can now present some major reinterpretations. Even more important, our whole picture of the archaeology and history of post-Roman Britain has been revolutionized over the last dozen years, as a result of the publication of major new syntheses, critical studies, and excavation reports. I myself have investigated four royal centres of the sixth to eighth centuries AD in northern Britain; and indeed, in personal terms, the sub-title of this paper could as well be 'the four-hundred mile perspective'.

I must begin, albeit briefly, with Camelot and Arthur. In the 1972 summary I explained how my views on these two topics had developed since my appointment as Director of Excavations in 1965. About Camelot, as an invention of French poets in the

[1] Mortimer Wheeler Archaeological Lecture, read at the British Academy 13 October 1982. Reproduced from Volume LXVIII (1982) of the Proceedings of the British Academy, published by the Oxford University of Press (1983), and reprinted here with the permission of the Academy.
[2] L. Alcock (1972a).

later twelfth century, I have nothing new to say. As the first recorded name for Cadbury Castle by South Cadbury, it remains a valuable term for distinguishing that particular Cadbury from those by Congresbury or Tickenham or above Exeter. As such, I shall continue to make use of it.

The Arthur of history is another matter. Whatever value my essay in source-criticism may have had in 1971, it has been largely swept away by the studies of Drs Dumville, Miller, and the late Kathleen Hughes. Largely, but not, I think, entirely; and certainly the debate is too large to enter into here. But I must first observe that an open discussion is not helped when the words of deceased scholars are misrepresented, or when Latin texts are shrouded in arcane mystery by being described as 'Celtic sources'. To this I would add three positive comments. Gildas's *De excidio* demonstrates that the western Britons had an interest in history, however defective it may have been in technical terms. Secondly, the *Annales Cambriae* date for the battle of Badon is independent of any chronology which might reasonably have been deduced from Gildas. Thirdly, until we can explain why the *Annales* were set out in the form of a Great Cycle, we remain ignorant of the basic purpose of the document. It must therefore be unwise to dismiss absolutely any of its entries as unhistorical.

At present, however, my position on the historicity of Arthur is one of agnosticism, and for the present I shall discuss Cadbury–Camelot without Arthur. If anyone wishes to protest that this is the equivalent of discussing the archaeology of Troy without Priam or without Homer, I can only recommend them to read the Mortimer Wheeler lecture given by one of my distinguished precursors, Professor Moses Finley.

But if I am not to write of 'Arthurian' Cadbury, how should I identify the relevant period? 'Cadbury in the middle first millennium AD' is reasonably accurate, but altogether too cumbersome. Taking a further hint from Troy, to which Cadbury has often been compared, not least by Wheeler himself, I shall categorize it by a structural and cultural phase number: Cadbury 11. This is precise in itself, and it serves as a reminder that at Cadbury we uncovered one of the longest stratified sequences in Britain, or for that matter in western Europe. Out of a span of four millennia, we shall be looking here at little more than a single century. This is the moment to recall, however, that one thrust of our excavation strategy was that we should deal fairly and impartially with all phases of the site, with no bias towards the fifth and sixth centuries AD. The other major thrust, of course, was to redress the balance between the excavation of the defences and that of the interior. In this respect Cadbury has now been spectacularly surpassed by Professor Cunliffe's excavations at Danebury, but in the late sixties this was a pioneering policy that was frequently misunderstood by visiting excavators. Strategy is necessarily influenced by the weapons available, and our exploration of the interior was certainly guided by our possession of a new instrument for geophysical survey which was both sensitive and unusually rapid in its operation.

II

To the eye, Cadbury Castle is a normal, albeit spectacular, multiple-ramparted hill-fort of the southern British pre-Roman Iron Age (Figs 13.1, 13.2). A brief excavation in 1913 had yielded appropriate pottery, as well as other pottery and metalwork which demonstrated further occupation in both the early and late Roman periods.[3] The first hint that the fort had also been used in the mid first millennium AD—the phase ultimately designated

[3] H. St. G. Gray (1913).

Fig. 13.1
Cadbury–Camelot from the air, showing the three inner ramparts

Cadbury 11—came when Dr Ralegh Radford recognized pottery of that date among surface collections made when the fort interior was ploughed in the 1950s.[4] This pottery, along with sherds from both the early Neolithic and the first millennium BC, had survived considerable ploughing and soil erosion. Subsequently, during the excavations of 1966–70, pottery of three major classes, all imported into Britain, was recognized: Class A, bowls of Phocaean and African Red Slip Wares; Classes Bi, Bii, and Biv, amphorae of Mediterranean origin; and Class D, grey-ware goblets and bowls from the Bordeaux region. Altogether, about a score of imported vessels can be distinguished.

The first significance of this pottery is, of course, that it provides a broad chronology for Cadbury 11.[5] The earlier pieces, of Phocaean Red Slip Ware (formerly late Roman C), were dated on site by Dr John Hayes to *c*. AD 460–70. He has recently reaffirmed his dating for the relevant form of Phocaean Red Slip Ware, so we can take 460–70 as the actual date of manufacture, however much later the date of deposition on site may be. The Bi vessels appear to belong to an early type, with straight, not wavy grooving, and they should therefore be dated before AD 520 or 530. The Bii amphorae occur in both an earlier form with closely-spaced ridging, and a later group with notably stepped ridging: again a late fifth- and early sixth-century date is indicated. The external dates for the imported

[4] C. A. R. Radford (1956).
[5] J. M. Hayes (1972); (1980).

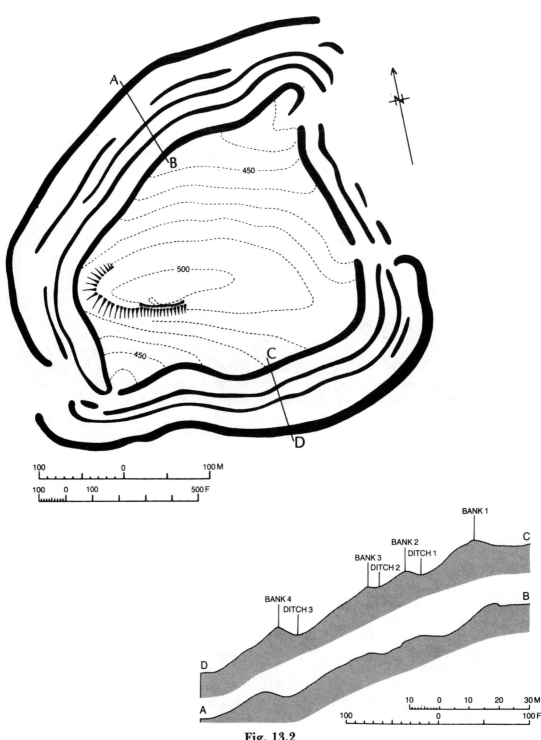

Fig. 13.2
Simplified plan of the defences, with profiles across them.

pottery show therefore that Cadbury 11 could begin as early as *c.* AD 460–70, and that it certainly continues through much of the sixth century. As we shall see, a secondary phase, Cadbury 11B, can be dated to the later sixth century by a Saxon silver ornament. A date for the end of Cadbury 11 is suggested by the absence of pottery of Class E, which belongs to the seventh and eighth centuries. Since Class E imports occur in western Dumnonia and the south Welsh coastlands, but are absent from central and eastern Dumnonia, it appears that the latter area had undergone an adjustment of its trading contacts; and it is tempting to attribute this to the advance of Saxon colonization.

Few of the imported sherds came from significant layers. The majority of stratified pieces, thirteen in all, were in dereliction layers separating the Cadbury 11 defence (Rampart E) from the late Saxon mortared wall and bank (Rampart F) of Cadbury 12. In the fort-interior, sherds from one or two freshly broken Bi amphorae had been tamped into a wall slot of a large timber hall (Building L/1), and there was a weathered Bi sherd in a wall-trench of the minor building S/1. The make-up of the Cadbury 11 roadway in the south-west gate yielded a Bii fragment, and a Bi sherd may come from Rampart E itself, but in a disturbed area. This may not appear an impressive list, but it certainly represents a ceramic chronology which is wholly consistent with that established on structural grounds.

It is necessary here to emphasize the physical separation of the imported pottery from any traces of late Roman—that is, third- or fourth-century—activity. A major concentration of late Roman pottery was found in the make-up of Rampart E in a single trench (Cutting J on the west side of the hill); but this is without parallel elsewhere in the circuit of the defences, and it has no causal connection with the building of the rampart. It represents the incorporation into the rampart-body of material which happened to be lying around in the vicinity, just as pottery of Cadbury 9 was incorporated even in the Cadbury 12 rampart, or, at Dinas Powys, pottery and metalwork of the sixth to eighth centuries were scooped up into the eleventh-century ramparts. There is not a single piece of Cadbury 11 pottery along with the late Roman material.

This is in marked contrast with Congresbury, where the mingling of Roman and imported pottery is considered to demonstrate a large overlap in the chronology and use of the two.[6] At Camelot, the physically separate distributions argue for a hiatus between phases 10 and 11. The latter must be regarded as a separate entity, owing nothing to the former. This incidentally is a powerful argument against the peculiarly Dumnonian heresy that the occurrence of late Roman pottery and coins in a hill-fort entails an occupation in the period 400–700 AD.

To anyone accustomed to the quantities of pottery from later Iron Age or Romano-British occupations, the score of vessels from Cadbury 11 must seem meagre indeed, especially since there was no local pottery to swell the total of imports. To put the Cadbury figures in perspective, they can be compared with those from several broadly contemporary sites, on the basis of the extensive lists compiled by Professor Charles Thomas.[7] Of the sites quoted in Table 1, Alt Clut (Castle Rock Dumbarton) is described by Bede as *civitas munitissima*; it lies at the northern limit of the Class B distribution. Dinas Powys is interpreted as a princely stronghold. Cadbury–Congresbury was probably a secular enclosure, but included also a shrine. Tintagel, formerly regarded as the out-

---

[6] I. C. G. Burrow (1979).
[7] A. C. Thomas (1981).

standing example of an early Celtic monastery, has recently been reinterpreted as a secular site with impressive natural defences,[8] whereas Glastonbury Tor has good claims to be a monastery. Finally, I have included the Anglian *villa regia* at Yeavering to demonstrate how historical and architectural distinction may be associated with striking ceramic poverty.

Table 1
Incidence of Pottery on Selected Sites

	A	Bi + Bii	Other
Alt Clut	—	9	—
Cadbury–Camelot	3	15	—
Cadbury–Congresbury	7	21	—
Dinas Powys	9	8	—
Ecclesiastical: Iona	1	—	—
all other	1	2	—
Glastonbury Tor	—	5	—
Tintagel	36	24	—
Yeavering (Anglian)	—	—	4

The table gives the best available figures for the minimum number of vessels of Class A (Phocaean Red Slip Ware and African Red Slip Ware) and amphorae of Classes Bi and Bii. At Yeavering the figure is for vessels not in 'native' fabrics. Sources: Alt Clut, Cadbury–Camelot, personal observation; Dinas Powys, Alcock 1963, 125–33; Yeavering, Hope-Taylor 1977, 170–81; all others, Thomas 1981.

Dr Burrow has rightly emphasized that the figures from Congresbury and Camelot are not strictly comparable, because of the different intensity of excavation, and especially the different strategies of the two excavations. In particular, at Cadbury, 'the selection of areas of excavation was not made on a basis of a sampling procedure for assessing the extent of the post-Roman phase, but in order to examine areas in which important structural and chronological sequences relating to the whole history of the site might be anticipated'.[9] Given this, a twofold difference in Class A between Cadbury and Congresbury, or a threefold difference in Class B between Cadbury and Tintagel, does not appear significant. The major observable discrepancy is with the Class A at Tintagel, and this must be explained in terms of the special character of that site.

A further general issue concerns the role of the Church. It has sometimes been suggested that the Church was the main beneficiary, and therefore probably the organizer, of the importation of wine in Class B amphorae. The participation of secular authority was seen as secondary. The reassessment of Tintagel has shifted the balance quite decisively away from the Church; but even before this, it was sufficiently clear that the imported pottery had been found far more frequently in forts and on other secular settlements than at churches and monasteries. Indeed the only historically known monastery which yields imported pottery is Iona, with a single fragment of African Red Slip Ware.

It has also been customary to treat this pottery, originating in the Mediterranean or in Western Gaul, as evidence for trade; principally in wine, but also perhaps in oil or even dry goods. Here we should remind ourselves that some historians of the period have cast

[8] I. C. G. Burrow (1973); A. C. Thomas (1982).
[9] I. C. G. Burrow (1981a), 108.

doubts on the concept of trade or commerce, and have looked rather to patterns of gift-exchange. Without following them so far as to seek our models among stone-based economies in the Pacific Islands, we must recognize that the implications of the imported pottery do demand critical scrutiny. In particular, the diversity of the Bii vessels from any one Insular site is in striking contrast with the uniformity, extending over some hundreds of vessels, that characterizes the actual wine cargoes found on Byzantine wrecks. Such uniformity in containers is exactly what we should expect from an organized commerce. The variety of forms on British sites implies that, whatever we are seeing here, it is certainly not the relics of normal cargoes.

Another curious feature of the British site collections is that Class D is normally represented by one or at most two vessels on any one site; only at Dinas Powys are there as many as nine. This is sufficient to prove some form of contact with the Bordeaux region, but in itself it can hardly represent commerce. The Class D vessels must have been incidental to a trade in totally perishable goods. The most likely candidate for this is wine in wooden casks, bound not with iron hoops but withies.

III

With the date of Cadbury 11 broadly established, we can now turn to the structures of that phase, beginning with the refortification of the hill-top. This was one incident in the long structural history of the innermost rampart, Bank 1.[10] It must be remembered that this did not stand alone: outside it were three, and in places four, other banks, products of the massive fort-building activities of the pre-Roman Iron Age. Even today, these banks and the intervening ditches form a major obstacle course for a would-be attacker (Fig. 13.3). The natural steepness of the hill makes its own defensive contribution and helps to explain Leland's comment: 'truly me seemeth it is a mirackle both in Arte and nature'.

Unfortunately, the very steepness of the slope has accelerated the erosion of the rampart face, and this, in turn, has caused problems for the observation and interpretation of the defensive structures. For instance, the earliest Iron Age bank was originally over two metres wide, but in most of our sections only its rear toe is preserved. Moreover, the long structural sequence in Bank 1 has not helped preservation, because successive ramparts have been cut into their precursors, often mutilating front revetments of stone or timber.

Rampart E, the defensive work of Cadbury 11, was built in part on the unstable base of a deep plough soil which had accumulated over the ruined Iron Age rampart during the Roman centuries. In its turn, it was partly preserved by the overlying late Saxon bank, but its front had been much disturbed by the building of the associated mortared stone wall. This was especially true at the south-west gate. As a result of these forces of natural erosion and destructive development, no single section across Bank 1 gave a complete picture of the succession of ramparts, or of the structure of any one phase. The evidence throughout was piecemeal, and it is necessary to patch it together from all the available sections and plans in order to create a schematic or idealized version of each rampart. With these qualifications in mind, we can examine the evidence for Rampart E, which was best preserved in Cutting D on the south and Cutting I on the east of the perimeter (Fig. 13.4).

[10] L. Alcock (1980b).

Fig. 13.3
The south-eastern defences from the air

Evidence that Cadbury had been refortified after the Iron Age, but before the building of a late Saxon *burh* wall, was obtained in the first few days of the 1967 season in a mechanically cut trench on Site D. The construction of the mortared wall of Æthelred's *burh* had left a spread of mortar on the eleventh-century ground surface. Beneath this, the humus which had accumulated during a long abandonment overlay the rubble core of a rampart, which in turn lay upon an earlier dereliction layer containing pottery and brooches of the mid first century AD. Apart from its stratigraphical position, no dating evidence was at first available for the rubble rampart core, but it seemed reasonable to assign it to the intermediate cultural phase which was represented by the imported pottery. Further work in 1967 and subsequent seasons elucidated the structural details of this rampart and confirmed its chronology. It was Rampart E, of Cadbury 11, a work of the late fifth and sixth centuries AD (Fig. 13.5).

This rampart was between 4 and 5 m wide. In Cutting D there were traces of a ragged front revetment, and better evidence for a rear face which had been repaired in quite good dry masonry. This repair marks phase 11B. The best evidence for a front revetment was on Site I, where an eight-metre length, four courses high, was uncovered. This was a somewhat ramshackle dry-stone construction, the work of builders who had long lost the skills of their Iron Age ancestors. Vertical gaps showed where upright timbers had stood, at distances ranging from 1.0 to 1.70 m apart. Not all these gaps went down to the bottom

Fig. 13.4
Cutting D: the defences of Cadbury 11 and 12 as revealed in 1967. The mortared wall of
the Ethelredan *burh* (Cadbury 12) is seen on the right overlying the rear of Rampart E
(Cadbury 11)

of the wall, so the uprights were evidently not earthfast, as they had been in Iron Age
Ramparts A and B. At the south-west gate, however, where the stonework of Rampart E
was better laid, the uprights were indeed earthfast (Fig. 13.6).

Behind the face in Cuttings D and I it was observed that lines of squared stones, and
even coursed walling, ran both parallel to the face and at right angles to it. At the
intersection of these transverse and longitudinal lines on Site D was a setting for an
upright post about 25 cm square. This post-setting and the stone lines show that the main
structure of Rampart E was a timber framework, probably consisting of three or more
triple ranks of longitudinal beams, joined to short uprights, and fixed to the front revetment by transverse members at about 3 m centres. This jointed framework explains why
the uprights did not need to be earthfast. Squarish stones were set against the timbers and
as a front face, and the whole frame was then infilled with rubble. No nails were found, so
the frame must have been secured by wooden pegged joints. We should not be surprised at
the implied skill in carpentry, but it is useful to have this established before we have to
consider the interior buildings of Cadbury 11. This timber-framed rampart may be seen
as an interesting reminiscence of the Iron Age timbered ramparts of a thousand years
earlier, or as stark contrast with late Roman methods of fort-building in mortared stone
and brick. But considered in itself, it is a most remarkable work on two counts: the
building effort involved, and the technique of timber-framing.

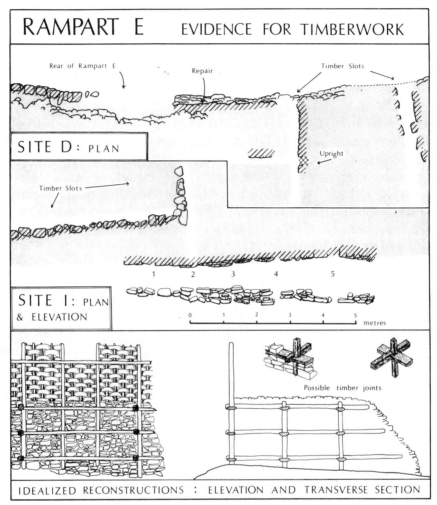

Fig. 13.5
The timber-laced rampart of Cadbury 11

To appreciate the effort, it must first be recognized that the Cadbury 11 refortification encompasses the whole perimeter of the Iron Age fort, nearly 1,200 m. It is the size of its defensive circuit which makes Cadbury–Camelot outstanding among contemporary British forts. The configuration of the Cadbury hill-top is such that it would have been easy to build a fort only a tenth this size, utilizing the internal scarp of the summit ridge as a natural defence on the west. This would have been quite in keeping with the norm for the period. It follows that the large size of Cadbury–Camelot must reflect the deliberate decision of its builders, and we must therefore take its size fully into account when we attempt to establish its purpose.

It was not, however, the length of the circuit alone which demonstrated a massive work-effort. Indeed, if the 14.5 km length of West Wansdyke was built by the Britons about the time of Cadbury 11, then a rampart less than one tenth as long would have

Fig. 13.6
The front face of Rampart E at the south-west gate, showing re-used Roman masonry,
and vertical timber slots.

presented no great task.[11] The timber framework is quite another matter. The nine longitudinal rows which have been suggested would have required over 10,000 m of stout planks or beams. For the transverse and upright beams a further 10,000 m would have been needed, probably in the form of dressed timbers about 20 cm square. Finally, light planks or wickerwork would have formed a breastwork. Without attempting to estimate the manhours required, it is certain that the hewing, carrying, dressing, and fixing of all this timber was a formidable task. It must be admitted, however, that it does not match the extravagant use of wood on many stone-and-timber fortifications in Central and Eastern Europe.[12]

The second remarkable feature of the Cadbury 11 rampart is that it is at present without parallel in post-Roman southern Britain, despite the popularity of various forms of timber-lacing in the pre-Roman Iron Age. Indeed, the importance of wood as a component in fort-building was still recognized in western Britain as late as the ninth century AD. The *Historia Brittonum* tells how Vortigern arrived 'in a mountainous place in which it was fitting to build a citadel'—itself an interesting reference to the significance of hill-top locations for fort-building. Having chosen his site, Vortigern then brought in

[11] For Wansdyke, J. N. L. Myres (1964); I. C. G. Burrow (1981a), 154.
[12] See, for instance, W. Hensel (1969).

craftsmen, specifically stonemasons; and then *ligna et lapides congregavit*, 'he gathered together timber and stones'.[13] Despite this, no timber-framed fortification is known in the post-Roman period in either south-west England, or Wales and the Marches, with the exception of Cadbury–Camelot.

In northern Britain, by contrast, at least five timbered ramparts have been dated between the fifth and ninth centuries AD. The most magnificent is the great Pictish fort of Burghead, where the inner ramparts of the upper and lower forts, a circuit of about 830 m, were about 7 m wide and up to 6 m high.[14] The arrangement of the timbers varied around the perimeter, but in the lower fort there were transverse oak beams, 15–20 cm square, fastened to stout longitudinal planks measuring about 8 by 30 cm. Some of these planks were set along the rear face of the rampart. In both horizontal and vertical planes the beams and planks were about 90 cm apart. It will be obvious how far my Cadbury reconstruction is based on these Burghead observations. There is, however, one striking difference, for at Burghead the timbers were fastened, not by wooden pegged joints, but by large spikes of iron.

Given the popularity of nailed timbered ramparts—the *murus gallicus*—in western Europe around the first century BC, it is remarkable that Burghead was the only Insular example known before 1976. Radiocarbon dates show that, far from being a work of the first century BC, it was not built before the fourth century AD at the earliest. A second example of a Pictish nailed rampart is now known at Dundurn.[15] This had been destroyed by fire, and the debris had then been dragged downhill, so that nothing is known of the details of the timber structure. The iron nails, the charred oak beams which they had fastened, and traces of wattle infilling, serve nevertheless to show its general character. A seventh- or eighth-century date is indicated by radiocarbon assay from the oak beams.

There is a comparable radiocarbon date for a third excavated Pictish fort at Green Castle, Portknockie.[16] This had a framework of vertical, transverse, and longitudinal squared beams which had been mortised together but not nailed. Stones were then packed against the timber frame, which had been set up before the construction of the stone wall faces: another echo of Cadbury. Among the northern Britons there is evidence for timber work in the rampart face, tied back by transverse beams, at Mote of Mark and at Alt Clut, Dumbarton, both sites with radiocarbon dates in the fifth to seventh centuries AD. In each case, unfortunately, destruction by fire has removed any chance of establishing the details of the framework, but at Mote of Mark (and also at Burghead) there are hints that a range of wooden buildings backed on to the rampart.[17]

Does this contrast between the fort-building techniques of the southern Britons and those observed among the Picts and northern Britons mark a cultural difference, or does it merely reflect the haphazard nature of archaeological discovery? In fact, no simple generalizations cover either the reasons why forts of this period have been chosen for excavation, or the results of those excavations. For instance: among the northern forts, Mote of Mark was originally excavated in order to examine reported vitrifaction, and so the excavation was necessarily biased towards the discovery of timber-framing. Alt Clut and Dundurn were explored because of their documented history. Other forts, however,

[13] J. Morris (1980), 70.
[14] H. W. Young (1891); (1893).
[15] L. Alcock (1981a), 168–71.
[16] I. B. M. Ralston (1980) and supplementary information.
[17] Mote of Mark: D. Longley (1982) and references. Alt Clut: L. Alcock (1981a), 157–9.

in both north and south, have been excavated because of their historical, or even legendary, associations with this period, but have yielded no evidence for timbered defences: examples are Castell Degannwy, Castle Dore, Dinas Emrys, Dunadd, and Dunollie. Some timbered forts, it can be shown, were founded on virgin sites, in or after the fifth century AD. Cadbury–Camelot, by contrast, was a pre-Roman foundation which was elaborately refortified after its defences had lain derelict for some four centuries. These observations reveal a problem: its solution will require evidence from many more post-Roman forts.

A further peculiarity of Rampart E is its use of Roman building materials: tufa blocks and tiles for core filling, and dressed masonry to provide a fair face against the transverse timber beams. Dressed Roman masonry is known to have been used in the dry-stone ramparts of the hill-forts on Ruberslaw and Clatchard Craig.[18] In the latter case the masonry had been robbed from the vexillation fortress at Carpow, two miles distant, and then carried up to a height of 250 ft. At Ruberslaw, a stone-built signal station has been invented to provide a quarry for the stone, while at Cadbury the tufa, tiles, and masonry form part of the evidence for a Romano-Celtic temple, of which no architectural remains have ever been observed. At Congresbury there is much Pennant sandstone roofing tile, and some Roman brick, scattered over the site and incorporated in the ramparts. A probable source is the nearby temple in Henley Wood.[19]

This re-use of Roman building material, in an architecturally inappropriate manner, is part of the widespread occurrence of Roman bits and pieces on post-Roman sites, both British and Anglo-Saxon. A very remarkable instance is the discovery, at Dinas Powys in south-east Wales, of a shale core and a flint lathe-chisel from the manufacture of shale bangles at Kimmeridge in Dorset.[20] These objects can have had no utilitarian purpose at Dinas Powys. They seem rather to indicate a lingering respect for, or attachment to, things Roman in the imperial twilight of the fifth century. This concept may also explain the re-use of Roman building material. Where considerable effort was required to transport this to a hillfort, then some correspondingly strong motive must be invoked: perhaps to partake symbolically of the famed military prowess of the Empire. This is surely the case at Clatchard Craig, and it may also be true at Ruberslaw and Cadbury.

The south-west gateway was the other structural element of the defences which we examined (Fig. 13.7). Here nothing has emerged to modify the picture which I presented in 1972, so I can be brief (Fig. 13.8). The main structure of the gate comprised four posts at the corners of a 10 ft. (3 m) square. The posts were about 15 by 20 cm, and were set in pits that were deep enough to penetrate the loose infilling of the Iron Age hollow way down to the solid rock. Heavy threshold beams linked the posts at the front and rear of the gate, while the rampart ends were shored up by planks. At ground-level we can infer two double-leaved doors, pivoting in sockets in the threshold beams and the lintels. The solidity of the corner posts suggests that the rampart walk had been carried across the slight hollow of the gate passage on a bridge, and a light tower is quite possible. Through the gate ran a metalled road, which had been repaired after a late sixth-century silver ring had been lost. This repair, like the refurbishing of the rear face of Rampart E, marks phase 11B. The historical implications of this will be considered later.

Because of the limited extent of excavation on post-Roman forts in Britain and Ireland,

[18] Ruberslaw: A. O. Curle (1905). Clatchard Craig: L. Alcock (1980c), 80; J. Close-Brooks forthcoming.
[19] P. J. Fowler, K. S. Gardner & P. A. Rahtz (1970).
[20] L. Alcock (1963a), 23–5.

Fig. 13.7
The south-west gate in period 11. The road surface is that of Cadbury 11B, with front
and rear timber slots clearly visible. The walling in the right foreground is that seen in
Fig. 13.6.

there are no good contemporary parallels for the Cadbury gate. Some Irish ringforts, such
as Garranes, Ballycatteen, and Garryduff I, have quite elaborate entrance arrangements,
but they cannot be construed as gate-towers. None the less, literary evidence from Ireland
shows that, in the latter part of the first millennium, it was expected that a fort would have
some kind of chamber above the gate. The only archaeological example that I know is at
the curious promontory crannog of Cuilmore Lough II, where there was a 2 m square
setting of four massive posts at the centre of the defensive line.[21]

   Four-post gates, carried up as towers, are, however, well known in Roman auxiliary
forts.[22] Since they are mostly of the first century AD, with only a few Antonine examples, it
is difficult to believe that they could have provided a model for Cadbury 11. Indeed, the

[21] E. Rynne & G. MacEoin (1978).
[22] W. H. Manning & I. R. Scott (1979).

Fig. 13.8
Reconstruction of the gate-tower of Cadbury 11.

most continuous lineage for single-portal timber gate-towers is represented not by four-posters, but by gates with six posts. This runs from early Roman through Carolingian and Ottonian on the Continent, and reappears in a Norman context in south Wales.[23] At present, the Cadbury 11 gate-tower stands alone, as a locally devised and thoroughly satisfactory means of controlling entry to the fort.

IV

In turning now to the excavations within the defences, I would recall our proposed strategy of redressing the balance between the examination of the defences and that of the

[23] R. v. Uslar (1964); L. Alcock (1966).

interior of a hill-fort. As it happened, the extreme complexity of the defence sequence demanded a larger share of effort than had been intended. In compensation, our comprehensive geophysical survey guided us to the location of major buildings which could then be examined very economically. It also led us to concentrate on the central plateau where—contrary to the received doctrine that occupation would be confined to the lee of the rampart—some fifteen hundred years of human activity had been focused.

From our first season of geophysical survey at Easter 1967, we were able to predict the whereabouts of major buildings, attributable both to the pre-Roman Iron Age and to the post-Roman occupations, whether British or Saxon. What criteria had we in 1967 for sorting the geophysical indications into one period or the other? Essentially we worked on the simple formula: round buildings are pre-Roman, rectangular ones are post-Roman. It was already recognized that there were some rectangular buildings in Iron Age Britain, and Cadbury had its quota of them. None the less, the first half of the formula is broadly true. The second half is more questionable, and indeed a recent survey of the Irish evidence reveals that the transition from round to rectangular buildings was taking place over the very centuries with which we are concerned.[24]

In the case of Saxon buildings, all the evidence available in 1967 showed that, both on the continent and in England, from the pagan period through to the late Saxon, these would be rectangular.[25] From British sites, however, the evidence was less clear-cut. At Pant-y-saer there were circular stone houses with rectangular annexes. At Buiston crannog there was a round or oval wooden house, and at Gwithian little oval rooms of dry stone. Drainage gullies at Dinas Powys suggested a round-ended hall with thick dry-stone walls, which may have been preceded by a rectangular post-built structure. Rectangular post-built halls, each with its own special features, had been reported from Castle Dore and Doon Hill.[26] The overall picture appeared to be that in backward areas, or at a lowly social level, roundness prevailed; but for a large fortified site like Cadbury, with the wealth implied by the imported pottery, a rectangular hall would be correct.

This generalization sadly underestimated the social status of the Buiston house, which has a floor area absolutely comparable with that of accepted British and Anglo-Saxon halls. Size in the abstract, of course, is not a sufficient criterion of status; but within a given social framework it is certainly one indicator. At Buiston there are further pointers to wealth and noble status.[27] For a start, there is the cost of the skilled carpentry required to build a large house of dressed and jointed woodwork. The occurrence of weapons argues for a noble military presence, and wealth is demonstrated by gold and bronze jewellery, imported pottery, and the patronage of metalworkers. All this shows that, in fifth- to eight-century Britain, a noble household might live as well in a circular as in a rectangular hall.

It follows that, in terms of plan alone, some at least of the Cadbury round houses may belong to Cadbury 11 rather than to the Iron Age. A building erected in the latter phase might have its wall-trench cut through a litter of pottery and other rubbish of Cadbury 7 to 9, and some of this might then be incorporated in the packing of the trench. Only if

[24] C. J. Lynn (1978).
[25] C. A. R. Radford (1957). To this can now be added P. V. Addyman (1972); P. A. Rahtz (1976).
[26] Summary with references in L. Alcock (1971, 1973), 212–29.
[27] R. Munro (1882), 190–239. The comparative floor areas are: Buiston, *c.* 235 m² (Munro (1882), pl. iv); Doon Hill A, 216 m² (Reynolds (1980), fig. 9); Cadbury-Camelot, 182 m²; Yeavering A2, 273 m² (Hope-Taylor (1977), fig. 60).

imported pottery of Cadbury 11, extremely rare on the site, was also included, would the later date be recognized. The implication is that some of the round houses which have hitherto been attributed to the Iron Age may belong instead to Cadbury 11. This possibility is reinforced by recent evidence from Congresbury, where both sub-rectangular post-hole buildings and sub-circular wall-slot structures appear to be contemporary with imported pottery of the late fifth and sixth centuries.[28]

This, of course, is part of my fifteen-year perspective, but in 1967 and 1968 we were scrutinizing the geophysical indications for rectangular buildings assignable to Cadbury phases 11 and 12. I have told elsewhere how we failed to find them, but were led by chance to the discovery of a sixth-century timber hall,[29] an example of the principle, so marked in Wheeler's own career, that serendipity is the prime attribute of the successful excavator. In brief: in 1968 we found a wall-slot with two unweathered sherds of Bi amphorae in its filling. Between then and the 1969 season we speculated on the likely plan of the building to which the wall-slot belonged. We began the 1969 season by testing these speculations, and found them all wanting. We therefore opened up a wide trench at right angles to the northern end of the wall-slot, uncovering an area of about 540 square metres, which contained over two hundred and fifty rock-cut features (Fig. 13.9).

We were then faced with a problem of recognition, assuming, of course, that the wall-slot proved that there was indeed a building to be recognized. At one level, this was

Fig. 13.9
The hall of Cadbury 11. The white stakes mark the most definite post-holes.

[28] I. C. G. Burrow (1981a), fig. 11.
[29] L. Alcock (1972a), 74–5, 79.

an exercise comparable to a child's spot-the-hidden-faces puzzle; but at another, it posed deep philosophical problems of archaeological perception—problems all too often overlooked by archaeological theoreticians. In many cases, of course, it is possible to recognize the plan of a building, amid a confusion of post-holes, because of the clustering of pit depths and diameters. Elsewhere at Cadbury, for instance, four-post and six-post structures of the Iron Age were indicated in just this way. But in this area, there was no clustering, so the exercise was one of pure pattern recognition. Certain rules can be laid down for this, but they would not provide a program for asking a computer to select a likely pattern. This is an exercise in which the human eye and brain, refined over two million or more years, are still the best available instruments.

Any search for a building plan begins at a two-dimensional level. The essential criteria are overall symmetry and overall unity. In early buildings, as we can see in cases where the structure stood in isolation, there may be no absolute straightness of line or regularity of spacing between posts, or of post depth and diameter. Nevertheless, a reasonable degree of regularity may be expected. An important rule is that, if structural features required for symmetry or regularity are missing, there must be an explanation for their absence. For instance, later features may have obliterated them; or at Cadbury, where most rock-cut features had an undifferentiated black filling, it could sometimes be demonstrated that a later feature had cut an earlier one without leaving any trace of disturbance. Applying these rules a rationally justified building plan may be proposed. It then becomes possible to ask questions in three-dimensional terms: could such a building have been roofed and would it then have stood?

This is essentially an inductive approach from observations on the ground, but one which is guided by principles of unity, symmetry, and regularity. It is no doubt also guided, consciously or not, by an awareness of possible parallels; but the deliberate search for parallels must be the final stage, not the starting-point, of our thinking. Indeed, certain negative rules may be laid down here. In a British context, Anglo-Saxon and Germanic halls and farmsteads must be deliberately excluded. This is particularly true of the developed Yeavering style, which was plainly an exercise in the ostentatious consumption of timber.[30] Again we can dismiss the idea that British buildings would have been crudely wrought in undressed timbers. All that we know of Celtic skills in carpentry argues against this. Finally, even the very earliest standing timberwork is too far removed in time to provide a valid guide as to what might, or might not, have been built around AD 500.

Applying these rules, we can reasonably distinguish the following pattern (Fig. 13.10). At right angles to both ends of the wall-slot are straight lines respectively of five and four posts. Beyond these, at either end, the line angles inwards; and then the two parallels are linked by shallow curves. Within this outer line are two further parallel lines, respectively of four and two posts. In all four lines, evidence for other posts may have been lost in non-contemporary features. This pattern has several interesting attributes. At 19 m long by 10 m wide, it approximates to a double square. The separation of the inner and outer parallels is in the ratio 1:2:1. The wall-slot divides the area in the proportions 2:1. None of these characteristics was consciously in mind when we recognized or created the pattern, but all of them can be paralleled in known building plans. Finally, there is a very curious parallel at the near contemporary British hall at Doon Hill, of which a plan was first

[30] B. Hope-Taylor (1977).

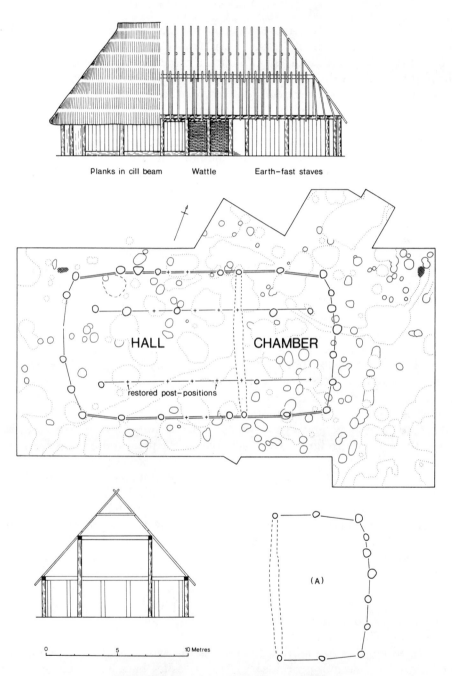

Planks in cill beam   Wattle   Earth–fast staves

HALL   CHAMBER

restored post–positions

(A)

0   5   10 Metres

CADBURY 11 THE HALL

PLAN OF POST-PITS & RECONSTRUCTED SECTION & ELEVATION

showing possible methods of walling & roofing, & alternative building plan (A)

Fig. 13.10

Plan and reconstruction of the Cadbury 11 feasting hall.

published in 1980.[31] There, as at Cadbury, the end bays of the hall taper slightly. It is difficult to accept that this is the result of an error in the original laying out.

Having thus established the skeleton plan of a building, we must immediately recognize the inadequacies of the evidence, and the consequent limitations on any interpretation. We were able to recover evidence only for those structural features which had penetrated the bedrock to a depth of five centimetres or more. Ploughing and erosion have destroyed floors, whether they had been of puddled and beaten clay, or of planks raised on joists. With them have gone any indications of hearths, which might have guided our interpretation of the compartments within the building. Even more serious for a structural interpretation, we may have lost all trace of shallow-bedded wall-staves, or sill beams to hold wattle or vertical planks for the outer walls, as well as evidence for threshold beams and light internal partitions.

It is with this in mind that, in essaying a reconstruction of this building, I have restored a sill beam, holding either wattle or planks, to give solidity to the outer wall. A major reservation has been expressed about previously published restorations, which must cast doubt on the very existence of the building; namely, that the posts implied by the rock-cut features are too slight, and too shallow-bedded, to support a roof. Certainly they would not have supported the monstrous 10 m tie-beams of my 1972 reconstruction. The smallest of the uprights may have been as little as 25 cm square, but most of them were larger. They were bedded in pits which ranged from 7 to 48 cm in the solid rock. To this may be added perhaps 30 to 50 cm of overburden. This may not have been sufficient to ensure lateral stability, but there can have been no problem of subsidence. Solid outer walls and a hipped roof would have taken care of lateral shifting. As for the roof itself, Mr F. W. B. Charles has suggested the use of ring beams on both the arcade and the wall posts, supporting a roof structure of uniform scantling A-frames. He believes that such a building could have stood, and so does the Cadbury Deputy Director, Mr C. R. Musson, who is himself a former architect. Even so, I regard the present drawings as essentially a programme for discussion rather than a definitive statement.

We have, then, evidence for a large structure which, from its location, may be labelled Building L/1. Before its function is discussed, its attribution to Cadbury 11 must be established more firmly. The main evidence is the two completely unweathered amphora sherds from the filling of the transverse wall-trench. Given the softness of the fabric, and the abraded condition of most Bi sherds from Cadbury, I do not believe that these fragments had lain exposed until the next building phase in the eleventh century. They must therefore fix the infilling of the wall-slot in Cadbury 11. The overall distribution of imported pottery reinforces the case, for as Table 2 shows, it is sporadic except for two clusters. One of these, at the south-west gate, implies a midden on the back of the rampart; the other, containing 37 per cent of all the imported pottery from Cadbury, lies around, and especially within, Building L/1.

Before we accept this as confirmation both of the existence of the building and of its Cadbury 11 date, a caution is necessary. At least as far back as the Early Bronze Age, there is evidence that dwellings were kept tidy.[32] Concentrations of finds are therefore appropriate to middens or to slums, not to noble houses. Paucity of finds associated with architectural magnificence is strikingly illustrated by Yeavering. If this doctrine is

---

[31] N. Reynolds (1980), fig. 9; B. Hope-Taylor (1980).
[32] R. Bradley (1971).

Table 2
Incidence of Imported Pot Sherds at Cadbury

Class	Area of site								
	B	C	D	EFG	K	L	N	P	S
A	1	1	1	1	1	4			
Bi	4	9	1	7	33	24	2	2	5
Bii			1	5	2	18	1	3	
Biv					7				
D					1				
Total	5	10	3	13	44	46	3	5	5

For the location of these areas, see Fig. 12.2. The south-western gateway is K; the hall is in area L and the ancillary building in S.

applied rigorously to the area of Building L/1, it follows that in Cadbury 11 this was a slum or a midden. But two other points are relevant. Two or three amphorae had already been broken before L/1 and the associated Building S/1 were erected, because both have sherds in their wall-trenches. Secondly, given that amphorae are large vessels, a total of forty-four fragments is not a large number to have escaped the notice of maidservants amid the straw and bracken on a clay floor or fallen through the cracks of a plank one. So the principle itself is not violated, while the finds allow us to recognize a building where wine had been drunk.

Before the implications of this are explored, it is worth considering the problems raised for sampling strategies by the overall distribution of the imported pottery, with its two tight concentrations on Sites K and L. A well-designed sampling programme would no doubt have established that Cadbury was occupied in phase 11; but, unless the sample had been very large, it would probably have failed to locate one of its major features: Building L/1. This is because, on a large and complex site, human activity is not randomly distributed but purposefully concentrated. The areas of concentration can rarely be predicted; instead, they are to be inferred from the empirically established distribution of artefacts and structures. The Anglo-Saxon village of Chalton has clearly demonstrated the incomplete, and even misleading, conclusions which might be drawn from a carefully devised sampling procedure.[33]

Having examined the arguments in favour of Building L/1 as a large structure 19 m long by 10 m wide, we must now consider an alternative plan which is preferred by some students of early medieval timber buildings. This takes the wall-slot and nearer parallel row of posts as the western and eastern long walls of a slightly bowed or boat-shaped building. At 10 m long by 6.5 m wide, this would be only a third of the area of the building already suggested, and would clearly be of significantly lower social status. The unweathered amphora sherds from the wall-slot would still date it to Cadbury 11. My own objections to this plan are threefold: it maximizes the irregularity of line and spacing of the rock-cut features; it does not answer the supposed difficulty that the post-pits are too small and too shallow for a substantial building; and it does not account for the scatter of

[33] T. Champion (1978).

amphora sherds both sides of the wall-slot, in good conformity with the outline of a 19 m building.

Returning, then, to the plan originally suggested for Building L/1, we see that this was a large structure, costly to build, and set, moreover, in a dominant position on the Cadbury hilltop (Fig. 12.3: 15): the social centre of Cadbury 11. We may legitimately see it as a royal or noble hall: the kind of place in which St Columba visited Brude, king of the Picts,[34] or Mynyddog Mwynfawr feasted the noble warriors of Gododdin.[35] In that feast, indeed, mead and wine were conspicious. These Celtic examples can, of course, be readily matched in Anglo-Saxon history and literature.

One of the most interesting features of the hall plan is the partition which divides it into units of one-third and two-thirds. This obviously has implications for social ritual and convention. In Anglo-Saxon literature there are references to a *bur*, which may gloss *camera*, as an element in the layout of a royal centre. It may be interpreted as a private apartment, sometimes specifically for a royal lady, or the women of the household; the king and queen may retire thither for the night.[36] I know of no comparable references in early British literature except for the formalized statements of the Welsh Laws. None the less, it seems reasonable to regard the smaller space in Building L/1 as a bower or chamber, and the larger one as the hall proper.

An interesting comparison arises here with the British hall at Doon Hill. This had three tranverse divisions, but these must represent two sub-periods. In one of these, the hall is divided in 2:1 proportions in the Cadbury manner. In the other, there is a small chamber at either end, each demarcating about one-sixth of the interior. Since this arrangement also occurs at Yeavering, it may be called the Yeavering type. There the arrangement of the doors suggests that the end compartments are antechambers rather than bowers. It was the Cadbury type which held promise for the future, since hall-and-chamber layouts, sometimes in 2:1 proportions, occur in medieval stone castles.

Only one other group of early British buildings can be compared with Building L/1: the two halls excavated by Dr Radford within the lightly redefended fort of Castle Dore. Professor Rahtz's analysis has stressed that only about half of the total area of these buildings was uncovered, and their plans are uncertain in detail. The irregularity in spacing and line of the observed post-holes is an impediment to our understanding of the Castle Dore buildings.[37] This in turn emphasizes the special position of Cadbury, with the only completely excavated plan of a southern British hall, as Doon Hill is our only complete northern example.

What can be said of the ancestry of the Cadbury 11 hall? Clearly this must be sought not in Germanic sources, but in fourth-century Roman Britain. Despite a general tendency to rebuild in stone, the timber buildings of the third and fourth centuries present a confusing array of building plans and constructional techniques, including the use of separate post-pits, continuous wall-trenches, and even cruck construction. The best antecedents for Cadbury L/1 are to be found among the aisled houses of villa complexes. These commonly have the aisle and nave in a 1:2:1 relationship, within an overall double square plan, just as at Cadbury.[38] An apposite example is that at Wakerley, which is

[34] A. O. & M. O. Anderson (1961), 402.
[35] K. H. Jackson (1969), 33–7.
[36] R. J. Cramp (1957), 71–2.
[37] C. A. R. Radford (1951); P. A. Rahtz (1971). See also p. 159 above.
[38] J. T. Smith (1963).

about the same length as Building L/1 and slightly wider. Despite the size of the post-pits, the arcade posts were only 20 to 35 cm in diameter. The evidence for the outer wall consisted of a number of post-holes linked by a continuous wall-slot which was only 15 cm deep. A trench of these dimensions would certainly have been obliterated by ploughing at Cadbury.

Despite such comparisons, there are difficulties in the way of tracing the ancestry of the Cadbury hall to the Romano-British aisled house. Firstly, both internal details, and their position within villa complexes, show that these frequently had a lowly status, as accommodation for slaves and farm labourers, or places for corn-drying and general storage. But some of them also had hypocausts and mosaics, so their lowly rank should not be overstressed. The second difficulty is more decisive, because it is chronological. Most of the aisled houses which had been raised on earthfast posts in the second and early third centuries were replaced by stone buildings, or at least by stone sleeper-walls, in the third and fourth centuries.[39] The chronological gap which this presents is not unlike that which we encounter when seeking the ancestry of the Cadbury 11 gate.

V

Only one other excavated structure can be shown to belong to Cadbury 11 on the evidence of an amphora sherd incorporated in one of its wall-trenches. This, Building S/1, is a rectangular structure, 4 m × 2 m, which lies about 4 m from the northern door of the hall (Fig. 12.3:16). It may have been a kitchen, but the plough destruction of its floor and any associated hearth makes it impossible to determine this. The point has also been made that some of the Cadbury round houses may also belong to phase 11. This is a limited architectural yield from the excavation of a substantial fortress, which may have been a royal or noble centre; but it is consistent with the meagre harvest of contemporary finds. A partial explanation is that only about 6 per cent of the interior of Cadbury was excavated; and further, through the hazards of discovery, no major midden deposit or industrial complex was located.

It is worth asking what else might have been found, given our knowledge of the period and of contemporary sites. A British kingdom would have been Christian, so there must have been a church, possibly of wood like that at West Hill, Uley.[40] Weapons, well known from poems such as the *Gododdin*, are rare on British sites. None were found at Dinas Powys, but Buiston yielded a fine spearhead, as well as iron bolt-heads and the trigger-nut from a crossbow. The major activity missing from Cadbury 11 is undoubtedly metal-working, including iron-smelting and smithing, and the making of jewellery in gold, silver, and bronze with enamel and millefiore inlays. Evidence for such activities is strong at Dinas Powys; jewellery moulds were very common at Mote of Mark; and Buiston, Congresbury, and Dinas Emrys had all yielded traces of metalworking. The activities of both jeweller and blacksmith are, however, both mysterious and physically noxious, so it is likely that they would be kept well away from the hall, as they certainly were at Dinas Powys. This is one more warning of the biased character of the evidence recovered from the partial excavation of a large settlement, in which particular activities would have been markedly segregated.

[39] D. A. Jackson & T. M. Ambrose (1978).

[40] A. Ellison (1980). There are possible traces of a wooden church, largely destroyed by ploughing, within the Late Saxon church at Cadbury: L. Alcock (1972a), fig. 8B.

A further curiosity of the repertoire of artefacts from Cadbury 11 is that two Anglo-Saxon trinkets were found, but none of British workmanship. The first was a gilt bronze button brooch, decorated with a helmeted head, which belongs to a group of over a hundred such brooches, found characteristically in pagan Saxon women's graves. A closely similar brooch comes from Mucking, but Professor Evison and Mr Avent believe that the Cadbury example was made in southern central England in the later fifth or early sixth century. This is consistent with Cadbury 11A.

The second Saxon jewel is a silver ring, crudely altered to make a brooch or buckle, which was found beneath the phase 11B road through the south-west gate. The actual form has no known parallels, but the decoration consists of zoomorphic motifs, especially hind limbs, in Salin's Style I. Allowing for its re-use and subsequent loss, a date in the late sixth century is appropriate for its deposition in Cadbury 11B.

How did these two Saxon trinkets come to be lost in a British fort? At Dinas Powys, there were many fragments of gilded, silvered, or plain bronze from Anglo-Saxon objects, including brooches and bucket bindings. These were interpreted as scrap metal, imported from Anglo-Saxon or Germanic sources along with scrap glass or cullet, to be melted down for re-use in the making of British-style pins and brooches. If a jeweller's workshop had been discovered at Cadbury it would have been easier to assess such an explanation for one or both of the Saxon pieces. Another possibility is that they came on the dresses of Saxon women, captured in war or coming to a British royal centre as brides, a counterpart of the British brides who may have given Celtic names to some of the sons of the Wessex dynasty.

VI

Our archaeological survey has disclosed, in Cadbury 11, a very substantial fortification, built originally a decade or two either side of AD 500, and repaired in the late sixth century. Within it was a major building, interpreted as a feasting hall and bower. What were the political and military contexts, the social status and the economic function of these structures? In 1972 I suggested that the role of the refortified Cadbury was a military one, in a Dumnonian kingdom that was under attack from an expanding Wessex. Its large size, pre-eminent among known forts of the period, fitted it to serve as the base for an army larger than the normal war-band of a British dynasty. A historical context for an augmented army, drawn from several kingdoms, was suggested by the *Historia Brittonum* statement that 'Arthur fought together with the kings of the Britons, but he was the leader of battles'.[41] The founding of Cadbury 11A could be related to the campaigns of Ambrosius and his unnamed successors, culminating in the British victory at Mount Badon. The repairs of phase 11B were then a response to the late sixth-century campaigns which resulted in the Wessex victory at Dyrham in AD 577.

This politico-military interpretation of Cadbury 11 was endorsed by several reviewers, but I now regard it as quite inadequate. It is true that we do know of armies gathered together from several kingdoms: examples include Penda's army at Winwaed, or the Gododdin expedition to Catraeth. It is also probable that the phase 11B repairs were indeed inspired by renewed Anglo-Saxon expansion. But the relationship between Cadbury 11A and the Badon campaign is less clear-cut. Firstly, the date of the battle itself

[41] J. Morris (1980), 76.

cannot be fixed more closely than the bracket 491 × 506, or even 491 × 516.[42] Secondly, the beginning of Cadbury 11A cannot be dated precisely. Some of the imported pottery was manufactured 460–70, but its deposition on the site is not necessarily so early. A bracket from 470 to 530 is as close as we can get for the building of the defences and the hall. So Cadbury 11A may be a work of Ambrosius Aurelianus or his immediate successor, at the time of swaying fortunes between Britons and Saxons; it may indeed have played a part in the Badon campaign; or it may belong to the years of civil strife in Gildas's own lifetime. Neither the historical nor the archaeological chronology is sufficiently precise to decide between these options.

A further objection to the interpretation of Cadbury 11A as the military base for a specific campaign, with its implications of temporary or occasional use, follows from our new understanding of the rampart structure. Now that we appreciate the effort involved in the work of refortification, and especially in the hewing, carting, and building of the timber framework, this all seems more appropriate for a permanent establishment than for a campaign base. What might such an establishment have been? How might it have fitted into British political and social organization? To examine such questions from an archaeological point of view, we must look at other fortifications of the period, and at unfortified political centres as well. Our enquiry must range beyond Dumnonia into the northern British kingdoms and even Northumbria.

Here I follow the views of a long line of historians that the political and social organization of medieval Northumbria encapsulated that of the British kingdoms which the Anglian dynasties had taken over. Consequently there is much to be learned about early British society from Northumbria, as well as from Wales and Dumnonia. This is not to say that British society was a monolithic body, regardless of place and time; but simply that, in the perspective in which we see it, it is easier to discern the broad outlines—like the bulk of a mountain seen distantly through shifting mists—than to detect the details varying from part to part.

We must first establish which Dumnonian forts were defended or at least occupied at the period of Cadbury 11 (Fig. 13.11). Somerset is the most intensively studied area. Here Dr Burrow has published a gazetteer of eighty-nine hill-forts and defended enclosures.[43] In twenty-seven cases there are references, of varied detail and reliability, to the discovery of Romano-British material, especially pottery and coins. Two forts only, Cadbury–Camelot and Cadbury–Congresbury, have also yielded imported pottery of the late fifth and sixth centuries, though Ham Hill may add a doubtful third. Despite intensive study of the area, this number has not increased since 1959. The conclusion is that, in Somerset, it is unusual for a pre-Roman hill-fort to be reoccupied or refortified around AD 500, even if it had been used in the Roman centuries. Elsewhere in Dumnonia, imported pottery may have occurred at the Roman town of Lindinis/Ilchester; and is certainly known from seven Iron Age or Romano-British forts or enclosures where the defences may or may not have been refurbished, namely Castle Dore, Chûn, Grambla, High Peak, Killibury, Trethurgy, and Trevelgue; and in abundance from Tintagel, which has recently been reinterpreted as a secular stronghold rather than a monastery.[44]

The habitable area at Tintagel approaches that of Cadbury, but the work involved in building its defensive bank and ditch is far less. Cadbury–Congresbury has about half the

[42] M. Miller (1976).
[43] I. C. G. Burrow (1981a).
[44] A. C. Thomas (1981) and references.

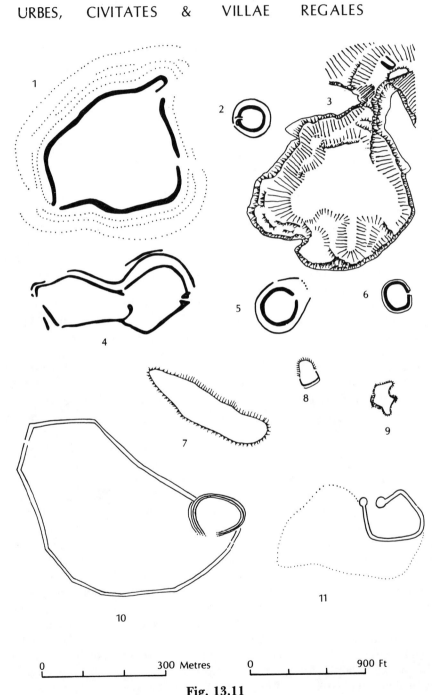

Fig. 13.11
Comparative plans of royal centres. 1 Cadbury-Camelot; 2 Chûn; 3 Tintagel;
4 Congresbury; 5 Castle Dore; 6 Trethurgy; 7 Bamburgh; 8 Dinas Powys; 9 Dunbar;
10 Milfield; 11 Yeavering

area of Cadbury–Camelot, but its defences, apart from the remarkable bastion-like entrance arrangements, are comparatively feeble. Both these sites are none the less exceptional in the size of the enclosed area, and they will require some special explanation in the fullness of time, perhaps as royal centres. Chûn, Castle Dore, Killibury, and Trethurgy are more normal in terms of size; they compare well with small forts such as Dinas Emrys, Dinas Powys, and Castell Degannwy in Wales; Mote of Mark among the northern Britons; Dunadd and Dunollie among the Scots of Argyll; and Dundurn among the Picts. In the past these have been regarded as the defended homesteads of Celtic warlords or warrior chiefs, or at best British princes, though Dunadd, which was certainly a royal inauguration site, has commonly been called the capital of Dalriada. Are these the appropriate terms to use?[45]

Another fort of the northern Britons was Dunbar. The first recorded form of the name, Dynbaer, from Primitive Cumbric *din barr*, ridge (or summit) fort, shows that it was a British foundation. To judge from the coastal stack on which it was built, it was about the size of Dinas Powys or Chûn. It first appeared in history as an Anglian royal town or stronghold, where King Ecgfrith of Northumbria had Bishop Wilfrid imprisoned in *urbem suam Dynbaer*. It may have been one of the *civitates et castella* which Ecgfrith and his queen visited, on another occasion, with pomp and feasting.[46] At the time of Wilfrid's imprisonment it was in the charge of a *praefectus*, an earl or thane. He may have had responsibility for a wide tract of north-eastern Northumbria: the kind of area centred on an *urbs*, in which historians have seen the administrative forerunner of the shires and thanages of medieval Northumbria.[47] This is an altogether more advanced concept than that of the defended homestead of a Celtic warrior-chief.

It follows that a literate seventh-century Englishman would have called one of the smaller British forts *urbs*. *Arx* and *munitio* would be other possible terms. A literate Briton would have used similar words, whereas in his own tongue he would have said *din* or *caer*. *Urbs* would be appropriate for Cadbury as well, but might it also have ranked as a *civitas*? Bede normally uses *civitas* of places which he does not otherwise call *urbs* and which were distinguished by a significant Roman past.[48] But this generalization has two interesting exceptions in northern Britain. Bebbanburh/Bamburgh, originally the British fort of Din Guoaroy, is described as *regia civitas* or as *urbs regia*. It had indeed been occupied throughout the Roman centuries, but presumably as a native promontory fort. The only Roman, as opposed to native, aspect is a hint of a late Roman signal beacon. Alt Clut, identified with Castle Rock Dumbarton, was twice called *urbs* by Bede, but it was also *civitas Brettonum munitissima*. Excavation has yielded no evidence for a Roman presence, and in this case *civitas* presumably indicates a major political centre.

The craggy nature of Alt Clut makes it impossible to calculate the usable area, but the curtain of the medieval castle encloses about half the area of Cadbury. Bamburgh is even smaller. These comparisons suggest that, in terms of size, Cadbury might qualify as a *civitas*. An immediate difficulty arises over its relationship with the known Roman *civitas Durotrigum Lindiniensis*, modern Ilchester, some seven miles to the west. Little is known in detail about the history of Lindinis in the late Roman period, but a few sherds of Class B amphorae are reputed to come from the town. If, as this suggests, Lindinis was still

---

[45] For the northern British sites, L. Alcock (1981a).
[46] B. Colgrave (1927), chaps. 38–9.
[47] P. Hunter Blair (1954), 169–70; G. W. S. Barrow (1973), 66–7.
[48] J. Campbell (1979a), 34–42.

occupied around AD 500, then why was it necessary to refortify Cadbury? A clue may be found in the unsettled second decade of the eleventh century, when Ethelred II transferred moneyers from the mint at Ilchester to the newly built hill-top *burh* of Caddanburh. Had Cadbury 11 likewise replaced Lindinis in the troubled decades of the late fifth or early sixth century?

One other unit of early medieval government should be considered in an attempt to understand Cadbury 11: the *villa regia, villa regalis,* or *vicus regis,* which figure prominently in Bede's Northumbria.[49] Bede never applies these terms to places which he calls *urbs* or *civitas,* though it is difficult to believe that Alt Clut, Bamburgh, or Dunbar did not fulfil the role of administrative centre appropriate to a *villa regalis.* Thanks to air photography, fieldwork, and excavation we now have plans of two of Bede's *villae regales*: Adgefrin/Yeavering and Maelmin/Milfield.[50] To these we may reasonably add Sprouston, on the evidence of rectangular halls with end-annexes in the Yeavering manner.[51] At both Milfield and Sprouston there are traces of perimeter palisades which enclose areas absolutely comparable with the built-up zone at Yeavering and with the interior of Cadbury 11. This correspondence in size suggests at least a convergence of function between Cadbury 11 and the Northumbrian royal vills.

It is commonly agreed that the royal vills were centres for the organized administration and systematic exploitation of the surrounding area. This was no doubt equally true of the royal *urbs* or *civitas,* or the *civitates et castella* among which Ecgfrith made his progress with pomp and, very significantly, with feasting. In other terms, they were the centres of multiple or discrete estates, and this is how we should interpret Cadbury 11.[52] If we do, then its geographical location gains in significance. Not only was it set on a steep-sided hill, immensely strong by nature. Its position, near the scarp of the Jurassic uplands and overlooking the main Somerset basin, fitted it to exploit a variety of environments.

If this interpretation of Cadbury 11 proves acceptable, then it implies that my original explanation in politico-military terms is inadequate. This must be equally true of the other Dumnonian forts, and those of Wales and northern Britain, that were also occupied in the sixth century AD. This is not to say, however, that a military role has no place in our understanding of such forts. The fuller historical evidence from northern Britain reveals that among the Picts, the Scots, the Angles, and the Britons, places like Alt Clut, Bamburgh, Dunadd, Dunbar, Dundurn, or Dunollie were frequently besieged, burned, or otherwise destroyed. Some of these events may have been mere incidents in a personal feud, others mark the kind of civil strife which Gildas records, while some settled the fate of nations, or at least of dynasties. The possibility remains that a war-band set out from Cadbury to take part in the battle of Badon; and the probability is high that a well-defended royal centre, close to the Fosse Way, was involved in the Saxons' advance after their victory at Dyrham.

A final caution is necessary here. It is possible to see the fortified places of the sixth and seventh centuries as the centres of the shires and thanages, the multiple or discrete estates, which later emerged into documented history. But this interpretation cannot be extended to those hill-forts in Somerset or in Wales and the Marches where there is no evidence for post-Roman use, however elastic we make the term post-Roman. At such places we must

[49] J. Campbell (1979a), 43–6.
[50] B. Hope-Taylor (1977).
[51] N. Reynolds (1980).
[52] G. W. S. Barrow (1973); G. R. J. Jones (1976).

infer total abandonment by AD 500. Indeed, an important aspect of the variety, in detail, of early British society is the quite varied histories of individual hill-forts in different parts of Britain, from the pre-Roman Iron Age, through the Roman period, and into the post-Roman centuries. These individual histories can only be established empirically by the excavation of individual sites, not by the extension of ill-founded generalizations to the unexcavated examples.[53]

VII

In the last section I indulged in exploratory forays on the troubled frontier between history and archaeology: a frontier which I, for one, do not propose to treat as no-man's-land. It is for historians to judge the validity of my interpretation of the archaeological monuments in terms of the political, administrative and economic units with which they deal, whether *urbs*, *civitas*, *villa regis* or some other. In particular, the archaeologist is entitled to ask the historian how the great communal effort demonstrated by the building of Cadbury 11 can be interpreted in terms of the history of the decades around AD 500. Who could have organized this massive public work, how was it paid for, why was it built?

For archaeological colleagues, the main problem posed by Cadbury 11 is the validity of its claim to pre-eminence among contemporary fortifications. This claim is based not so much on the size of the area enclosed—for here Tintagel is comparable—but rather on the great effort involved in the construction of the timber-framed rampart. The special position of Cadbury can only be challenged on the basis of evidence from numerous other hill-fort excavations; and these excavations must be at a more intensive level than that of an occasional 10 ft square. I shall no doubt be told that the funds for such a campaign of excavation do not exist, especially because no 'rescue' element would be involved.

I accept that it would not be easy to gather the resources, but I do not accept that it would be impossible. Despite the large shift to State-funded rescue archaeology since 1970, a director who is willing to make the effort can still raise adequate funds from learned institutions and private sources. My own experience is that it is possible to carry out informative research excavations on a hill-fort for a third of the cost of a comparable State-financed excavation. Moreover, a well-conceived research programme can still inspire the devoted labours of skilled amateurs. One such programme would be the selective sampling of hill-forts which had already yielded evidence of late Roman activity. Here, the sense of intellectual adventure, which is so essential an element of research, would be inspired by one of the great themes of British archaeology: how, and by what stages, did Celtic Britain become England, Wales, and Scotland? This is certainly a research strategy that Mortimer Wheeler himself would have commended.

Note. I am most grateful to colleagues who have assisted in the preparation of this paper, by reading the text, by commenting on the finds and structures, and by providing information in advance of publication; notably J. R. Avent, J. C. Barrett, G. T. M. Beresford, I. C. G. Burrow, F. W. B. Charles, H. B. Duncan, V. I. Evison, M. Miller, C. R. Musson, D. Longley, C. A. R. Radford, P. A. Rahtz, and I. Ralston. I must accept full responsibility, however, for the use which I have made of their advice. The copyright of all photographs lies with the Camelot Research Commitee.

[53] I have deliberately confined this discussion to Britain. For the continental re-use of hill-forts in this period, a starting-point is R. v. Uslar (1964), under *Fliehburg, Fluchtburg*.

CHAPTER 14

The Organization of Military Expeditions and of Fort-Building

The later prehistory and early history of western Europe are much concerned with military activities. Weapons, warrior-graves, and fortifications figure largely in the archaeology. Description and classification of the artefacts are relatively simple; but to infer their mode of functioning is another problem. The prehistorian gains little aid from ethnographic parallels, because anthropologists have in general devoted little attention to warfare as a human activity, and their treatment of it is distinctly superficial.[1] With the coming of literacy, of course, we can begin to see something of what men thought about war, including its ethical aspects.[2] We may also hope to catch glimpses of how military expeditions and the building of fortifications were organized. Case studies may be presented from the Welsh Laws of Hywel Dda, from Anglo-Saxon England, and from the military assessment of Scottic Dalriada.

The earliest known version of the Laws of Hywel Dda, Redaction A of the Latin texts (NLW Peniarth MS 28), written down towards the end of the twelfth century, refers to the bondsmen's duty of building forts for the king's hostings:

> Rex debet habere a villanis summarios in expedicione sua, et de qualibet villa rusticana hominem cum securi et cum equo, qui castra regis edificient; sed interim erunt ad expensam regis.[3]

> The king ought to have packhorses from the villeins on his expedition; and from each villein township a man with a felling-axe and with a horse, to build the king's forts; but they are at the king's expense.

A fuller version in Redaction D, of the late thirteenth–early fourteenth century, adds:

> Rex nisi semel in anno de patria sua ad alienam patriam exercitum ducere non poterit; verum in patria sua, quandocumque opus fuerit, ei succurrendum est.[4]

> The king may not lead an army from his own land to another land except once a year; however, in his own land, whenever there may be need, it (i.e. the army) is to come to his aid.

The Welsh version in the *Book of Blegywryd* (Peniarth 36A: after AD 1282) corresponds closely in the translation by Richards.[5]

---

[1] e.g. B. Orme (1981), 194–209. There are, of course, numerous studies of the practice of war among particular peoples, an especially notable example being A. P. Vayda's study of Maori warfare (1970). But even a collection of readings with the title *Law and Warfare: studies in the anthropology of conflict* (P. Bohannan, 1967) devotes only a quarter of its contents to warfare, and provides no general synthesis. For protohistoric warfare in barbarian Europe, with special reference to fortifications, a starting-point is A. L. F. Rivet (1971). There are more sceptical comments in L. Alcock (1965a).

[2] J. E. Cross (1971).

[3] H. D. Emanuel (1967), 137.

[4] H. D. Emanuel (1967), 377.

[5] M. Richards (1954), 57.

Once every year the king is to have a hosting along with him from his country to a border country; always however when it may be necessary a host is to attend him in his own country. From the bondmen the king is to have packhorses in his hosting, and from every bond township he has a man and a horse with axes for constructing his strongholds, and they are to be at the king's expense.

It is accepted that 'none of the extant MSS, either Welsh or Latin, of the Laws represents the original code',[6] which presumably dates before the death of Hywel Dda *c.* 950. Moreover, Richards continues, 'the date of the MSS is no reliable guide to the antiquity of the matter contained in them. Some of the Latin texts may be based on older Welsh texts than those which are extant'. As things stand, there can be no certainty that the clause which restricts the king to a single raiding party in a year is an interpolation into the original code; still less that it reflects a late thirteenth-century modification of existing practice.

As for the building of *castra*, presumably temporary forts of timber, during the course of an expedition, it might be thought that this marks the attenuation of an earlier right to claim labour services for building more permanent works on the home territory: in short, hill-forts. But no evidence is available to demonstrate that this was the direction of development. In Anglo-Saxon England, indeed, it appears that the trend is one of increasing imposition of services by the king throughout the eighth and later centuries.

Brooks has examined the developing evidence for military obligations in England.[7] Already in the Laws of Ine of Wessex (AD 688–94) fines are listed for the neglect of military service: 120 shillings from a noble (*gesith-born*) landowner together with the forfeit of his land; 60 shillings from a landless noble, and 30 shillings from a ceorl.[8] It is tempting here to suggest that the relationship between the last two fines reflects the difference in wealth between swordsmen and spearmen in the pagan graves of Wessex.[9] A half century later, in 749, as Brooks shows, Æthelbald of Mercia is found imposing bridge-work and fortress-defence upon all his people, whether lay or ecclesiastical. It may be that the threat of incursions from Wales was the inspiration for Æthelbald's edict; certainly considerable organization would have been needed to make possible the building of the great dykes of the Welsh Marches. Æthelbald's successor Offa was, it seems, responsible for imposing the construction of bridges and fortresses in Kent in 792, specifically to counter Viking attacks. These led, in turn, to the exaction of fortress-work in Wessex in the mid ninth century.

Brooks considers that the roots of these eighth and ninth century exactions lay in the long-standing right to labour services for the construction of royal buildings and vills. (Elements of this in the Welsh Laws are explored in Chapter 4). He believes, moreover, that the residences of kings and nobles were themselves fortified. This he bases in part on Ine's tariff of fines for *burhbryce*, breaking and entering the residences of the various ranks of king, bishop, and nobility. He also refers to the well-known story of the fight at the royal *burh* of *Merantune*, recorded in the *Anglo-Saxon Chronicle* under the year 755. From the building of such private fortifications, the English kings moved, in the mid-eighth and later centuries, to the imposition of labour services for the construction of defences for both church and people, in much the same way as did their continental contemporaries.

[6] M. Richards (1954), 9.
[7] N. P. Brooks (1971).
[8] D. Whitelock (1979), 404.
[9] See Chapter 17 below; N. P. Brooks (1978) develops a comparable theme about arms and status.

And just as the earliest charters referring to fortress-work are from Mercia, so it was in Mercia that the earliest known Saxon earthworks were built, at Tamworth and Hereford.

Brooks' thesis, elegant though it is, raises certain problems, both archaeological and historical. For a start, at Yeavering, the one Anglo-Saxon *villa regalis* for which archaeology provides a complete plan, the royal halls themselves were at no time defended or enclosed. It is true that, alongside them, was a double-palisaded enclosure which may be regarded as a fort; though the considered view of its excavator is that it should be interpreted as a place of assembly rather than as a defensive work.[10] In any case, its ancestry is certainly British, not Anglian. Moreover, Doon Hill, Bamburgh and Dunbar all present examples of a British defensive foundation—respectively a palisaded enclosure, a promontory fort and a stack fort—which was taken over by the Anglian invaders.[11] There is indeed no archaeological evidence that, among the early Anglo-Saxons, royal and noble residences were necessarily defended.

Moreover, Brooks is not helped by the case of *Merantune*, where the A, D and E versions of the *Chronicle* all read *bur* — bower or chamber, clearly an appropriate place for visiting a mistress. Whitelock points out that the B and C versions 'have wrongly altered *bur* to *burh*, "fortress"'.[12] It is notable also that Whitelock translates *burhbryce* as 'forcible entry into the residence of the king . .', with no mention of 'fortress'.[13] Finally, however early the documentary references to fortress-building may begin in Mercia, there is no archaeological evidence for a pre-Alfredan *burh*, whether at Hereford, Tamworth or elsewhere.[14]

By itself, our information from excavation would suggest that the Anglo-Saxon kings were not organizing the construction of substantial military works before the very late ninth century, always excepting the linear defences of the Marcher dykes. There would seem to be an unconformity of about a century between the historical and archaeological evidence; but at least both would agree that the building of defence works was an increasing exaction on the part of the Saxon kings.

Another region which provides evidence for the assessment of military services is Scottic Dalriada. The *Senchus Fer n Alban* (History of the Men of Scotland), in addition to its genealogical statements, lists the expeditionary strength of hostings from the several kindred groups who held Dalriada, and mentions especially the levy for sea expeditions.[15] There is general agreement that, while extant versions of the *Senchus* derive from a tenth-century compilation, this itself was based on a seventh-century original. Various discrepancies in the figures of hostings suggest that the tenth-century version was a new, and partly revised, edition, rather than a simple transcript. Despite this, it is possible to discern something of seventh-century military arrangements, provided that the detailed figures are not pressed.

The *Senchus* was originally compiled, then, at a time when simple dry-stone forts (so-called duns), such as Kildonan, Dun Fhinn, Kildalloig and Dun an Fheurain were certainly being inhabited in Dalriada.[16] Some larger ones, notably Dunollie and Dunadd,

[10] B. Hope-Taylor (1977).
[11] Doon Hill: B. Hope-Taylor (1980); Bamburgh and Dunbar, Chapter 13, above with Fig. 13.11.
[12] D. Whitelock (1979), 176 n. 1.
[13] D. Whitelock (1979), 404.
[14] C. A. R. Radford (1978).
[15] M. O. Anderson (1973, 1980), 158–60; J. Bannerman (1974), 26–156 for text; D. Ó Corráin (1980).
[16] Kildonan: H. Fairhurst (1939); Dun Fhinn: RCAHM(S) (1971), 83–4; Kildalloig: RCAHM(S) (1971), 87–8; Dun an Fheurain: J. N. G. Ritchie (1971). For general comments on these sites, M. R. Nieke (1983), 302–3.

were demonstrably built or enlarged in the late seventh or early eighth century.[17] Moreover, military actions at fortified places—sieges, burnings and destructions—feature largely in the contemporary Iona Annals.[18] There is, however, no mention of either the building or the garrisoning of forts in the *Senchus*, so we can say nothing about how fort-building or fort-ward was organized. In view of the clear importance of forts in the Annals, this is a curious, not to say disturbing, lacuna in the evidence which the *Senchus* provides towards a comprehensive account of social organization.

One possible enquiry which might be pursued would be the correlation, if any, between the size of the muster in each part of Dalriada, and the number of forts in the same areas. Both might then be related to the extent of cultivable land. The enquiry is rendered difficult from the historical point of view by the arithmetical confusion of the *Senchus*, and from the archaeological side by uncertainty about how many forts there were in seventh-century Dalriada. It can, at least, be said that even when some allowance is made for lost forts, the total is far less than the assessed number of households. This might imply a relatively high social status for fort-owners.[19]

Another element in the *Senchus* where the archaeologist has something to contribute is on the sea-muster. The regular rule of the *Senchus* is 'two seven-benchers from every twenty houses is a sea expedition'. From the final clauses of the *Senchus*, it appears that Cenél n Gabrán, in Kintyre and Cowal, could muster 56 ships; Cenél n-Oengusa in Islay 43; and Cenél Loairn, in northern mainland Dalriada and Mull, a total of 42 ships.

Developments in nautical archaeology make it possible to speculate on the character of the seven-benched boats of the *Senchus*. In strict chronological terms, they lie half-way between the Broighter boat-model (Fig. 14.1) of the first century BC, and the fully-developed West Highland galleys of the fourteenth and later centuries. The Broighter model is of a nine-benched, and therefore eighteen-oared, vessel. It also had a mast, and thereby provides some of the earliest evidence for the sail in northern and western waters. Steering was by a larger oar, fixed to the port side of the model, but perhaps with evidence for a starboard fixing as well. There is an unresolved dispute as to whether the original of the model was a 50 ft long skin boat, or rather a wooden one; and if the latter, whether it was plank built, or an extended dug-out.[20]

If the original of the Broighter boat-model was indeed plank built, then it could lie among the ancestors of the West Highland galley, a type well known from both literary and pictorial sources.[21] In this case, the seven-benchers of the *Senchus* could lie on the direct line of descent, whatever contribution the ships of the Vikings[22] may also have made to the West Highland galley. Certainly, there is evidence from Adomnan that sails as well as oars were in use in the waterways of sixth and seventh century Argyll.[23] It is reasonable to believe that the boat of the *Senchus* was a slightly smaller version of the Broighter boat, with seven rather than nine pairs of rowing oars, a steering oar, and a mast and sail. In medieval Scottish terms it would have been classed as a birlinn, a vessel with up to sixteen oars.[24]

[17] Dunollie: L. Alcock (1979a); Dunadd: A. Lane (1984).

[18] J. Bannerman (1974), 15–16; L. Alcock (1981a).

[19] Preliminary statement in M. R. Nieke (1983).

[20] A. W. Farrell, S. Penny and E. M. Jope (1975); S. McGrail (1976).

[21] I. F. Grant (1961), 252–5; K. A. Steer and J. W. M. Bannerman (1977), 180–4.

[22] S. McGrail (1980).

[23] For contemporary references, see VC 6b, 24a, 25a, 82a, 91a, 101a.

[24] I. F. Grant (1961), 253.

Fig. 14.1.
Broighter, Co. Derry: gold model of boat with mast and oars. Length 183 mm.
Photo: National Museum of Ireland

What was the complement of the seven-bencher? Bannerman assumes that there were two oarsmen to a bench, so that 'twenty houses were expected to provide twenty-eight oarsmen'.[25] But it must be recognized that this is a minimum figure, which makes no allowance either for relief oarsmen, or for more than one rower to each oar. Charles Green long ago pointed out the need for relief oarsmen on the North Sea crossings of Saxon raiders and settlers.[26] McGrail has said of Viking longships that, 'where there was room, two or more men could man each oar, and for long passages it would have been necessary to change crews at intervals'.[27]

Certainly the width of the Broighter model, if it is at all realistic in scale, implies four oarsmen to each pair of oars.[28] It might be argued that in West Highland waters, relief

[25] J. Bannerman (1974), 153–4.
[26] C. Green (1963), 103–13.
[27] S. McGrail (1980), 492.
[28] A. W. Farrell, S. Penny and E. M. Jope (1975), pl. 1b.

watches were not needed, because sea passages would be short. But at a rowing speed of three knots,[29] and making no allowance for favourable or adverse wind, tide and current, the journey from, say, Dunollie to Iona, would have taken some twelve hours. A sea expedition presumably needed to be fighting fit at the end of its voyage. It is certainly significant that the galleys of the seventeenth century carried three men to each oar in wartime.[30]

On this calculation, a seven-bencher might have carried a crew of $7 \times 2 \times 3$ oarsmen, plus 2 steersmen, plus captain: a minimum complement of 45. In this connection it may be significant that, according to the *Senchus*, the ship expedition which brought the sons of Erc, the dynasty of Dalriada, to Scotland comprised one hundred and fifty men; perhaps, therefore, three boatloads. But the other point to stress is the great burden which a sea expedition involved: not, as Bannerman would have it, 28 men from 20 'houses', but 84; a notional 4.2 men from each 'house'.

Now there seems to be agreement that the 'house' (*tech*) of the *Senchus* is the same unit of assessment as the hide of English law, and the *terra unius familiae* of Bede:[31] that is, the holding of a self-sufficient freeman.[32] Brooks has shown that, in England as on the Continent, the single peasant family holding—hide, *mansus, casa*— was used as a basis for assessing rents, taxes and services at least by the later seventh century.[33] In the Carolingian realm, one man from every four *mansi* was required to serve in the host, whereas in tenth and eleventh century England, the rate was one man from every five hides. It is immediately apparent that, if our analysis of the complement of a seven-bencher is correct, the burden on the *tech* of Dalriada was twenty times as great as that on the hide of late Saxon England, at least in terms of furnishing men for a sea expedition. What the *Senchus* does not tell us is where responsibility lay for providing the boat itself.

For a brief tailpiece to this discussion of military obligations in Celtic and Anglo-Saxon societies, we may turn to Ireland. Gerriets,[34] in a discussion of the services owed by a client to his lord, as revealed in Irish legal texts, has shown that these included 'a military expedition, [building] a fort, ... revenge, attack, defence'. In one text, she considers that the general term for service, *manchuine*, 'probably included labour services such as ... building the ramparts around the noble's house'. In the second text, however, 'building a fort—or more likely the earthen embankment around the house of a noble—[is] mentioned specifically, not subsumed by the general term for service'. These are most valuable indications of the social organization which created the ring-forts—30,000 or more of them—which are so conspicuous a feature of Ireland in the first millennium AD. They also hint at the possibility of similar client services in relation to fort-building among the Scots of Dalriada, as well as among the Britons and the Picts. But despite such hints, we remain substantially ignorant about how public works (to use a modern term), such as the construction of royal forts, were organized and paid for.

[29] C. Green (1963), 108.
[30] I. F. Grant (1961), 253, quoting Register of the Privy Council of Scotland, 1st series, X (1613–16), 347.
[31] HE ii 9; iii 4 etc.
[32] T. M. Charles-Edwards (1972); D. Ó Corráin (1980).
[33] N. P. Brooks (1971), 70–1.
[34] M. Gerriets (1983), 53–6.

Part Four:
Contact and Conflict between Britons and Anglo-Saxons

As I have explained in the Introduction, my interest in fortified places led me also to examine the nature of the warfare which had called them into being. In the fifth to eighth centuries AD, this largely implied the historically-documented conflicts between the native Britons or Welsh and the invading Anglo-Saxons or English. My first essay in this field, Chapter 15, used the evidence of the *Anglo-Saxon Chronicle* to locate the battle-sites of these conflicts in southern Britain.[1] Its deeper purpose was to examine, obliquely, the hypotheses that the hill-forts of southern Britain were commonly reoccupied in the post-Roman centuries, and that they featured as defensive centres for the British resistance. So far as the first proposition is concerned, this has been discussed from the archaeological, rather than the historical point of view, in Chapters 10 and 11 above. For the second proposition, Cadbury-Camelot remains the only site with a substantial claim: that claim is stated in Chapter 12 and re-assessed in Chapter 13.

Warfare is also recorded between the northern Britons and the Angles, both in prose and, more especially, in heroic poetry. It seemed appropriate to use the occasion of a Presidential Address to the Cambrian Archaeological Association, delivered on the southern fringe of Cumbria, to discuss the poetry in relation to the archaeological evidence. This forms Chapter 16. Participation in warfare is a mark of status in heroic society, and may be reflected, archaeologically, by the weapons in pagan graves. This theme is therefore explored, again from the evidence of northern Britain, in Chapter 17.

But the relations of English and Welsh were not wholly those of warfare and extermination. In Bernicia, it seems that the Angles took over much of the social and political organization of the Britons: this concept is also explored in Chapter 17. Such relations are, of course, the central theme of the O'Donnell lectures, and significantly, that chapter was largely based on my Edinburgh (1978) O'Donnell lecture. My wider treatment of the theme had been delivered in the University of Wales in 1966, and that fittingly rounds off Part Four.

---

[1] I might have put less weight on the Chronicle evidence had the discussion in P. Sims-Williams (1983b) been available to me.

CHAPTER 15

The Warfare of Saxons and Britons[1]

The relationships of the Britons and the Saxons have been viewed in many different lights in recent years. One thing at least is clear: they involved an element of military conflict. Curiously, however, little attempt has been made to study this military relationship critically and systematically. This is not for lack of evidence, because there are numerous references to battles between individual English leaders and the *Wealas* in the *Anglo-Saxon Chronicle*. The present paper examines these, and the more scanty British sources, in order to establish the character of the warfare which accompanied the establishment of the kingdoms of Kent, Sussex, and Wessex, and the westward expansion of the latter realm. A similar study could be made of the military encounters of the Britons with Mercia and Northumbria; but this would involve the assessment of difficult source material: the northern entries in the *Historia Brittonum*,[2] and poems such as the *Gododdin* and the Cynddylan cycle.[3] The chronological range is from the earliest recorded battles to that fateful year when the King's reeve rode out to compel three ship-loads of strangers to go to the royal manor, and was slain on the spot (ASC, s.a. 787, for 789),[4] the first mention of Viking incursions in Britain. It is not necessary here to demonstrate that the coming of the Vikings brought fundamental changes to weapons and warfare.[5]

Something should first be said of the methods of my inquiry. I have used place-name identifications with caution and, in particular, where Professor Whitelock rejects an identification either implicitly or explicitly, I normally follow her.[6] I do not use hypotheses about the strategy of Saxon penetration and advance as a basis for identifying obscure place-names. Where we can establish with confidence the particular place at which a battle was fought, we can reasonably speculate about the general strategic issues which provoked it and about the political consequences which flowed from it. But we cannot, in simple logic, proceed from the general conjecture to the particular fact. In thinking about strategy, I am sceptical of attempts to use battle-sites to infer where the frontier, or the spearhead of an expansion, lay at any one time. There is evidence that battles were likely to occur in the heart of an enemy kingdom as well as on the frontier.[7] When the battle-sites are plotted on a map they show little more than the general

---

[1] First published, under the title '*Her . . . gefeaht wip Walas*: Aspects of the Warfare of Saxons and Britons', in *Bulletin of the Board of Celtic Studies*, 27 (1976–8), 413–24. The paper has received much helpful criticism and advice from P. Crew, P. J. Fowler, M. Gelling, A. Gordon, C. Lavell and H. Loyn.

[2] L. Alcock (1971; 1973), 29–41; K. H. Jackson (1963); D. N. Dumville (1977a).

[3] K. H. Jackson (1969); M. Richards (1973), 140–4.

[4] J. Earle and C. Plummer (1892; 1899). For simplicity, all relevant placenames are quoted from the A version of the Chronicle (abbreviated ASC).

[5] E. Rynne (1966).

[6] D. Whitelock *et al* (1961), s.a. 455, 456, 571, etc.

[7] L. Alcock (1971; 1973), 338–40.

westward advance of the southern English. Even this, it may be suspected, is more a reflection of the interests of Wessex historiographers than of the strategic realities of invasion and settlement.

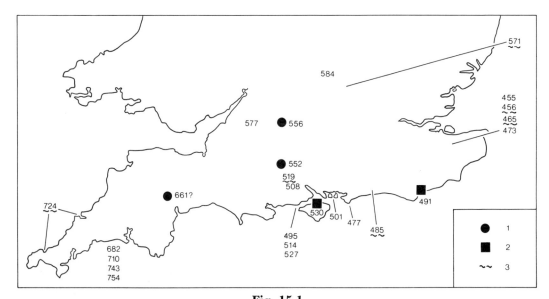

Fig. 15.1.
Map: battles of the Saxons and Britons.
Key: 1 battles *on* or *æt* hill-forts; 2 battles at Saxon Shore forts; 3 battles at rivers or fords. Dates without symbols provide no evidence of the character of the battle; dates around the margin are only vaguely locatable

The earliest conflict between Saxons and Britons of which we have a record is that in which St Germanus of Auxerre led the Britons to the 'Alleluia victory'. It is difficult, whatever one's interpretation of early fifth-century history, to comprehend a politico-military situation in which the Picts and Saxons could combine to attack the southern Britons in AD 429. A recent commentator has indeed suggested that Constantius's account, in his *Life of Germanus*, is 'no more than a tale conceived by someone who had misunderstood the whole situation and supposed that Germanus' victory had been won in a military battle rather than a theological argument'.[8] Without going as far as this, we might nonetheless echo the words of Levison in editing the *vita Germani*: *narrationem de victoria quae dicitur Alleluiatica fabulis immunem non esse apparet*.[9] Certainly there is nothing in Constantius's account to assist us in analysing the location or tactics of the battle.

There are two or three notices of battles between Saxons and Britons in British sources, but the largest collection is to be gleaned from the *Anglo-Saxon Chronicle*. This is obviously a biased source, in that it mostly records the victories of the English, not their defeats. It seems, nonetheless, a reasonable assumption that it presents a fair sample of the character of the warfare of the time. The dates of the *Chronicle* are used here as a convenient reference system, without any commitment to their chronological accuracy in the fifth and sixth

[8] P. Hunter Blair (1963), 161.
[9] W. Levison (1920). Borius would seem to be of the same mind, R. Borius (1965), 86. See also E. A. Thompson (1977), 318, n. 50.

centuries. I reject, however, as baseless several recent attempts to manipulate those dates.[10]

Altogether the *Chronicle* records some twenty-six battles between the southern English and the Britons in the pre-Viking centuries. From the sixth century on there were also many battles between rival English kingdoms or between claimants to the same kingdom. There are also two or three cases where it is unclear whether the defeated party was English or Welsh. The normal formula of the *Chronicle* is: *Her ... gefeaht wiþ Walas*, 'in this year X fought the Britons'. Occasionally we are told that a British noble or other person was slain. In 530 Cerdic and Cynric of Wessex took the Isle of Wight and slew a few men at *Wihtgaræsbyrg*. It might be expected that the defenders would have been Britons as they certainly were at *Anderida* fort, but we shall see that this is not certain.[11] In 652 Cenwalh of Wessex fought at Bradford-on-Avon against an unspecified enemy. Æthelweard, in his Latin version of the *Chronicle*, says that *Cenwalh bellum gessit civile*,[12] but we cannot know whether he had a source for this, or was merely making an inference from the silence of the *Chronicle*.

The recorded battles fall into four small but well-defined categories, and a larger amorphous group. The first set comprises the initial landings of forces which had come either from the Continent or from adjacent parts of England. The *Chronicle* does not tell us where these forces had originated, but Æthelweard adds to the *Chronicle* entry for the landing of Ælle of Sussex and his three sons that they came from Germany. Here again we cannot know whether this is his inference, or is based on superior knowledge.

No initial landing is recorded for Kent, where the *Chronicle* account is of Vortigern's invitation to Hengist and Horsa. In 477 Ælle and his three sons came with three ships to *Cymenes ora*, the Owers south of Selsey Bill, and killed many Britons, and put others to flight into the Weald. In 495 Cerdic and Cynric came with five ships to *Cerdices ora*, and fought against the Britons on the same day. *Cerdices ora* is unidentified,[13] but from Cerdic's subsequent campaigns we can deduce that it was on the Hampshire coast. We have here, then, two records of opposed landings, apparently on the open coast. In 514, there is a further mention of a landing at *Cerdices ora* by Stuf and Wihtgar, but it is usually considered that this is merely a doublet of the landing by Cerdic and Cynric rather than a record of an independent landing.[14]

A genuinely independent invasion of Wessex is recorded, however, in 501, when Port and his sons Bieda and Mægla landed from two ships at *Portes muþa*, Portsmouth, and according to the Laud (E) version of the *Chronicle* 'at once took the land'. They also slew a young British nobleman. The historicity of this annal has been assailed on the grounds that Port is an invention, an eponymous back-formation from Portsmouth, which should derive from a Romano-British place-name *Portus*. Stenton, however, cogently defends the entry, especially on the grounds that the names Bieda and Mægla cannot be explained away thus, and that Port too is a genuine Old English personal name.[15]

It is not clear whether the *Chronicle* phrase *on þære stowe þe is gecueden Portes muþa*, 'at the

---

[10] For a recent critical survey of the *Chronicle*, which does not, however, vitiate my use of it to establish the character of warfare: P. Sims-Williams (1983b).

[11] Below, p. 226.

[12] A. Campbell (1962).

[13] *Pace* O. G. S. Crawford (1952), 193–200; see also A. H. A. Hogg (1972), 222–3.

[14] F. M. Stenton (1943), 22.

[15] F. M. Stenton (1943), 20, n. 1.

place that is called Portsmouth', implies the open coast or Portsmouth harbour itself. In either case, we must consider the possible relationship between the landing and the Saxon Shore fort of Portchester on the north shore of that harbour. Recent excavations at Portchester have produced structures, pottery, and metalwork indicating that the fort was continuously occupied from *c.* 400 to AD 700.[16] What is not revealed, within the limited area of the excavations, is whether the neutral term 'occupied' may be replaced by the militarily more positive term 'garrisoned'. It is at least certain that the diagnostic finds and structures are all characteristically Germanic, and there is no hint of Celtic or Romano-British influence. It would be perverse, therefore, to describe the continued occupation as sub-Roman. If there was a garrison at Portchester at the time of Port's landing, it was already English, not British. However that may be, there is no hint in the *Chronicle* that Portchester played any part in opposing the landing.

The second clear category of battles to be distinguished is that which involved Roman defences. In 491 Ælle and Cissa of Sussex beset *Andredes cester*, that is, the Saxon Shore fort of *Anderida*, medieval and modern Pevensey, and 'slew all who were in it, so that not one Briton was left alive'. We have no means of knowing whether this action resulted from a coast-wise movement from an initial Saxon settlement which had been confined, according to the cemetery evidence, to a block of land between the Ouse and Cuckmere rivers;[17] or whether it was intended to wipe out a British enclave centred on the Saxon Shore fort itself. From the Saxon point of view two matters are worthy of comment. The first is the military achievement involved in capturing a defended place whose walls stand even today to a height of 25 feet. Medieval military history demonstrates that, provided the walls and gates were intact, even the feeblest of forces could hold such a strongpoint unless the attackers were equipped with scaling ladders and other siege apparatus. Secondly, it has been suggested that the slaughter of all those within the fort may reflect a dedication of the war-dead to Woden, and the consequent sacrifice of the Britons to fulfil the vow.[18]

The original version of this paper discussed a second possible instance of an attack on the British garrison of a Saxon Shore fort. This was indicated by the *Chronicle* account of the events of 530, when Cerdic and Cynric seized the Isle of Wight and slew a few men in *Wihtgaræsbyrg*. This name has traditionally been associated with Carisbrooke Castle; and in 1969 Rigold drew attention to the apparent defences of a Saxon Shore fort on the site of the medieval castle. Subsequently, M. Gelling kindly pointed out to me the impossibility of the linguistic equation; and more recently, Young has argued forcefully that the pre-medieval enclosure at Carisbrooke is a late Saxon *burh* rather than a Roman work. This leaves us completely ignorant of the whereabouts and character of the *byrg* captured by Cerdic and Cynric: the more so, because the Isle of Wight contains only one hill-fort, and that, apparently, unfinished.[19]

Our third category is that of battles fought in or near identifiable hill-forts of pre-Roman construction. There are two certain and one probable instances of this, and two other alleged examples which can be shown to be spurious or at least dubious. Before these are examined in detail, two general points must be made. The first is that the cryptic entries of the *Chronicle* provide no basis for discussing whether it was the Britons or the

---

[16] B. W. Cunliffe (1976), 177–84, 190–1, 301–2.
[17] M. G. Welch (1971), (1983) 232–7.
[18] W. A. Chaney (1970), 39.
[19] S. Rigold (1969); C. J. Young (1983).

Saxons who were inside the fort. Indeed, it is not certain that either side was actually in possession of the defences, and it may be that the fort was no more than a rallying place, or even a geographical reference point for a battle fought on a natural line of communication. A brief discussion of the battle of Chester, fought about 616 between Æthelfrith of Northumbria and the Britons of mid Wales, is instructive here. The *Chronicle* (under 607, a date to be corrected from the Welsh Annals)[20] tells us that Æthelfrith led his army to *Lega ceastre* and there slew countless Welsh. This might suggest that the victims, like the hapless Britons of *Andredes cester*, were within the walls of the legionary fortress. There are, however, indications that the battle occurred in the open outside Chester.

Firstly, the Welsh Annals in their brief mention of *gueith cair legion*, 'the strife at the fort of the legion', add: *et ibi cecidit selim filii* (sic) *cinan*. This was Selyf or Solomon, son of Cynan Garwyn of Powys, no doubt a natural defender of the Dee valley, but one whose power-base lay well to the south of Chester. It therefore seems probable that Selyf, like Æthelfrith, had led his army to the encounter at Chester, rather than that it was in garrison there. Secondly, we have Bede's well-known account[21] of how Æthelfrith saw the British monks, allegedly twelve hundred in number, stationed separately in a safer place. This certainly suggests that the battle took place in the open, not in the confines of a walled place.

The second general point is this. Even if the hill-forts mentioned in the *Chronicle* were used as defended strongpoints, whether by the Britons or the Saxons, this does not imply that they were refortified for the purpose. At present, the only compelling evidence for the extensive refortification of a southern British hill-fort in these centuries comes from Cadbury–Camelot, Somerset.[22] A brief excavation at Liddington Castle, Wilts., in 1976, demonstrated that this had indeed been refortified at some post-Iron Age date, but it would be premature to assign this work to the fifth–sixth centuries, rather than to some earlier or later period.[23] Other forts are known to have been occupied in the late fifth and sixth centuries, but without any large-scale rebuilding of their defences.[24] Nevertheless, the grassed-over Iron Age ramparts would still have afforded a useful advantage even without refurbishing. This is illustrated by the final incident in the history of Castle Dore, Cornwall. On 31 August 1644 a Parliamentary force involved in a running battle with Royalists made a stand in Castle Dore from 11 in the morning until dusk, when the Royalists succeeded in storming the original entrance of the fort.[25] It is not fanciful to think that the sixth-century battles at hill-forts might have had a similar character.

To turn from generalities to details. The first of the two battle entries in which a hill-fort is definitely named is that for 552, when Cynric of Wessex fought the Britons *in pære stowe pe is genemned æt Searo byrg*: 'in' (or 'at') 'the place that is called Salisbury'. This is normally taken to refer not to the modern site of Salisbury, but to Old Sarum, a bi-vallate fort of some twenty-seven acres. Desultory excavation there has yielded a late Roman buckle of the decades around AD 400.[26] No evidence has been found of refortification or of reoccupation at the time of the Saxon conquest of central Wessex. The OE preposition *in* is

---

[20] E. Phillimore (1888), 141–93.
[21] Bede, HE ii, 2.
[22] See Chapters 12 and 13 above.
[23] S. Hirst and P. Rahtz (1976).
[24] See Chapters 10 and 11 above.
[25] C. A. R. Radford (1951).
[26] S. C. Hawkes and G. C. Dunning (1961), 54–5.

ambiguous, and consequently, while Garmonsway translates 'at the place', Whitelock has 'in the place'.[27] It should also be noticed that Smith[28] stresses that the precise meaning of *stow* was 'a place where people assembled'. This is no doubt true of the word as an element in place-names. But it is also noteworthy that *in pære stowe pe is genemned*, or some similar expression, is very commonly used of battle-sites in the *Chronicle* between 455 and 577, after which it drops out of use. Since it is used of river-fords[29] and the sea-shore[30] as well as a hill-fort, it would be rash to read much into its use in relation to Old Sarum.

Our second certain entry is that for 556, when Cynric and Ceawlin fought the Britons *æt Beran byrg*. This is the eleven-and-a-half acre hill-fort of Barbury Castle in Wiltshire. This is particularly interesting in the present connection because it has produced an iron battle-knife (*seax*) of the sixth or seventh century AD, as well as other pagan Saxon knives and spears.[31] It might be tempting to think that these mark the burial of Saxon battle casualties, but the circumstances in which the finds were made do not allow us to affirm this.

At present, then, there is no archaeological evidence for a reoccupation of either *Searo byrg* or *Beran byrg*, whether by Britons or Saxons. In the absence of such evidence, we may find significance in the observation that both forts lie close to routes which could well have been used by armies on campaign. Thus, Old Sarum is at 'the focal point of a number of (Roman) roads', and Barbury is in 'a commanding position in relation to the ancient and important Ridgeway'.[32] When we consider the very limited role that the castles of better-documented periods were able to play in controlling routes,[33] we might well be sceptical of the further suggestion that these forts were 'strongpoints related to and, perhaps, temporarily used to control major routes'. This last suggestion is further weakened by reference to two other battles which occurred on the Ridgeway: those of 592 and 715 at *Woddes beorge*, the Neolithic long barrow now known as Adam's Grave. In neither case was a hill-fort involved, though these would not have been hard to find in the vicinity. Clearly the common tactical element in all four battles is proximity to a major traffic line. But it should also be observed that in the two battles at *Woddes beorge* both armies were English, whereas hill-forts are mentioned in both instances where the Saxons had a British opponent.

Another hill-fort identification has been argued for the battle which Cenwalh of Wessex fought at Easter 661 *on Posentes byrg*. The *Chronicle* does not state whom Cenwalh was fighting, which is unusual if the enemy were indeed British. It follows that we cannot use hypotheses about Cenwalh's foe, and about the strategy underlying the action, in order to settle doubts about the location of *Posentes byrg*. Plummer[34] identified the place as Pontesbury in Shropshire, and if this were correct it would be likely that the Wessex king was fighting the Mercians rather than the Welsh. But the early place-name forms—*Pantesberie* (Domesday Book), *Pontesbiri* (1236), and *Pantebur'* (1242)[35]—do not support this attribu-

---

[27] G. N. Garmonsway (1953), s.a. 552; D. Whitelock *et al* (1961), s.a. 552.
[28] A. H. Smith (1956), s.v. *stow*.
[29] ASC, s.a. 457.
[30] Ibid., s.a. 477; 514.
[31] A. Meaney (1964), 265.
[32] D. J. Bonney (1973), 469.
[33] R. C. Smail (1956).
[34] J. Earle and C. Plummer (1899), 28
[35] E. Ekwall (1936).

tion. Hoskins[36] follows the lead of Stevenson in preferring Posbury in Devon, of which the early forms are *Postbir'* (1270), *Possebury* (1276), and *Posbyr'* (1281).[37] If we were to assume the loss of an unstressed internal syllable, such a derivation might seem plausible. The 'bury' of *Posentesbyrg* might then be identifiable with the hill-fort of Posbury Camp.[38] This is in a very ruined condition, with only its southern defences preserved, but it appears to have been a multivallate fort of medium size.[39] No further tactical inferences seem possible.

We turn now to the battles for which a hill-fort location has been claimed on dubious grounds. The earliest of these is the battle of Mount Badon, a decisive victory for the Britons against some part of the invading Saxons, which occurred around AD 500; the date cannot be fixed more precisely.[40] The arguments for locating the battle at a hill-fort may usefully be summarized before they are discussed in detail. It is suggested that the original British name for the battle site was *Din Badon*, 'Badon Fort'; that this was translated by the defeated English into *Baddanburg*, 'Badda's Fort'; and that this name can be recognized in modern Badbury, with several alternative candidates to choose from.[41]

Our primary source here is Gildas who, writing apparently about forty-four years after the battle, refers to the year *obsessionis badonici montis*, 'of the besetting of the Badonic mount'.[42] Although the earliest manuscripts that we now possess are of the eleventh century, we can be reasonably sure that this was what Gildas wrote, because Bede, copying a manuscript at least as early as the beginning of the eighth century, uses the identical phrase.[43] Another early source is presented by the Welsh Easter Annals. The entry for year 72 of the annals begins *Bellu(m) badonis*. The remainder of the entry concerns Arthur's connection with the battle, and ends *brittones victores fuer(unt)* 'the Britons were victors'. It has been suggested that the whole reference to Arthur in the annal is spurious;[44] but even if this is accepted there can be no serious doubt that the original source for the record of the British victory at Badon was an entry in an Easter Table which may well have been written in the actual year of the battle.[45] The manuscript which we possess of the Welsh Annals, British Museum Harley 3859, is a miscellany of documents relating to early British history. It also includes a ninth-century account of Arthur's battles by Nennius in which the action appears as *bellu(m) in monte badonis*.

Gildas and Nennius are in agreement that the battle occurred in or around a hill-top. Gildas's designation of the action as *obsessio* implies a protracted engagement in which one force was blockaded, beset, or encompassed by the other. The possibly spurious Arthurian element in the Welsh Annals refers to an action lasting 'three days and three nights', but there is nothing of this in Nennius. In fact this is probably a conventional expression in heroic literature for a prolonged battle. This suggestion is reinforced by the action recorded in B. M. Harley 3859, folio 188B, when Urien of Rheged blockaded Theoderic of Bernicia and his sons on the island of Lindisfarne for three days and three nights. Gildas's

[36] W. G. Hoskins (1960), 14.
[37] EPNS ix, 406.
[38] National Grid Reference SX 8097.
[39] J. C. Wall (1906), 582.
[40] L. Alcock (1972a), 215–16.
[41] K. H. Jackson (1945), 44–57; (1958), 152–5.
[42] Gildas, DEB, cap. 26.
[43] HE, i, 16.
[44] T. Jones (1964), 5; (1972).
[45] L. Alcock (1971; 1973), 45–55.

designation of the battle of the Badonic mount as *obsessio* is sometimes held to imply that it took place at a hill-fort or other prepared position, but this is not necessarily so. The word is rare in British sources: its only occurrence in the Welsh Annals, for instance, is under year 185: *obsessio catguollaun regis in insula glannauc*, 'blockade of king Cadwallon (by Edwin of Northumbria) on Priestholm', an island which bears no trace of fortifications.[46]

In fact, the main reason for suggesting that Badon took place at a hill-fort is the belief that the original British name was translated into English as *Baddanburg*, where the 'fort' element is clear; so, it is inferred, the British name was very likely **Din Badon*. The difficulties are admitted. No such fort is mentioned in the British sources, Gildas, the Welsh Annals, and Nennius. Nor is it easy to explain how the English, defeated and, to judge from Gildas, heavily slaughtered, nonetheless learned the name **Din Badon*, translated this into Old English *Baddanburg*, and then went on to apply the name of a signal English defeat to three or more decayed pre-Roman hill-forts. Badon must therefore be judged non-proven as a battle at a hill-fort. It follows that attempts to identify the supposed hill-fort in question are fruitless.

Our next battle is an interesting example of the elevation of a conjecture to the status of received doctrine. In 577 Cuthwine and Ceawlin of Wessex fought the Britons at *Deorham*, slaying three named kings, and capturing Gloucester, Cirencester, and Bath. The written record tells us nothing about the condition of the three towns. The archaeological evidence shows that by this time the Roman public buildings in Bath were derelict except for the reservoir enclosure and associated structure of the hot baths.[47] At Cirencester, although commercial life may have continued to the 430s, the main area of the town was subsequently abandoned; but the possibility has been canvassed that the amphitheatre may have been refurbished as a strongpoint, as happened not infrequently in Gaul.[48] At Gloucester, again town life continued into the fifth century, but thereafter the forum became a marsh with alders growing in it, and the medieval street layout came to diverge strikingly from that of Roman times.[49] Such as it is, the evidence suggests that these three towns—forts as they appeared to the Saxon— were mere shells by the time of *Deorham*.

The victory itself is generally regarded as an important strategic breakthrough for Wessex, driving a wedge between the Britons of Wales and those of Dumnonia. This interpretation is certainly supported by the mention—unusual in the *Chronicle*—of the capture of places other than the battle-site itself.

There is no serious doubt about the general location of the battle; it was fought at the place now known as Dyrham, seven miles north of Bath. Indeed a more precise location has been suggested, in a hill-fort above the village. This appears as 'Dyrham Camp' in the Ordnance Survey *Map of Southern Britain in the Iron Age*. Earlier it was illustrated by Hodgkin[50] as 'Dyrham Camp, probable site of the battle of Deorham'. This seems a very convincing attribution, and if it were acceptable it would give us another battle in or near an Iron Age hill-fort to set beside Old Sarum and Barbury. Unfortunately the name 'Dyrham Camp' does not appear in print before 1877, and there is reason to

[46] RCAMW (1937), 141–4.
[47] B. W. Cunliffe (1969; 1983), T. J. O'Leary (1981).
[48] J. Wacher (1974), 312–15.
[49] Ibid., 154
[50] R. H. Hodgkin (1935), 31

believe that it is an invention of about that date. It is true that topographical writers beginning with Camden[51] had remarked on the traces of *amplissima valla castrorum munimenta* in the area, and had conjectured that these had to do with the battle. But the earliest recorded names of the fort are Burrill (1695) and Barhill (1777), perhaps to be derived from Bury Hill.[52] By the early nineteenth century it was being referred to as a 'camp near Dyrham', but the form 'Dyrham Camp' as such cannot be traced back before Playne's account of the Cotswold hill-forts published in 1877.[53] The clear implication is that the attribution of the battle of *Deorham* to this hill-fort is no more than a conjecture; it is as likely that it was fought at the crossing of the river Boyd below the scarp on which the fort stands.

Indeed it is perhaps more likely; for our fourth category of battles, those fought at river-crossings, is marginally our largest. The five instances may be summarized chronologically:

457 Hengest and Æsc against the Britons at *Crecgan ford* (unlikely to be Crayford).
465 Hengest and Æsc against the Britons near *Wippedes fleote* (*fleot*, Old English 'stream, creek').
485 Ælle versus the Britons near the bank of *Mearc rædes burna* (*burna*, OE 'stream').
519 Cerdic and Cynric versus the Britons at *Cerdices ford*, Charford, on the Hampshire Avon.
571 Cuthwulf of Wessex against the Britons at *Bedcan forda* (unlikely to be Bedford).

No further details of these battles are available to enable us to discern the tactics of river-engagements more clearly, but some generalizations are possible. The first is that British sources no less than English demonstrate that battles at river-crossings were a major class of action at this time. For instance, out of the twelve battles which Nennius attributes to Arthur, no fewer than seven were fought at rivers, while two occurred at fortified places, two on hill-tops, and one in a wood. It has been suggested that at river-crossings the mounted Britons would have had a tactical advantage over Saxon foot-soldiers. This may well be suggested by the British sources; but the English victories recorded in the *Chronicle* make it clear that the matter was not at all one-sided. We should be cautious about attributing any tactical superiority here to British cavalry—if, indeed, the southern Britons fought from horseback at all.

There is shadowy evidence for another river-crossing battle, or at least one in a river valley, between Wessex and the Britons. The Welsh Annals for year 278 (*an' cclxxviii*), probably AD 724, record *bellum hehil apud cornuenses*. The most obvious interpretation of 'Hehil among the Cornish' is the river Hayle in west Cornwall; but Ekwall points out that this is also the old name for the Camel estuary, preserved, for instance, in Egloshayle.[54] The more easterly attribution may be preferable for an eighth-century battle.

We come now to the mass of battles which are either impossible to locate or featureless or both at once. These will be surveyed chronologically, with such discussion as seems necessary. In 455 Hengest and Horsa fought Vortigern at *Agæles prep*, which is unlikely to be Aylesford. In 473 Hengest and Æsc fought the Britons at an unnamed site. In 508 Cerdic and Cynric slew a British prince called Natanleod, near the eponymous Netley Marsh in Hampshire, and in 527 they fought the Britons at the unidentified *Cerdices leaga*,

---

[51] W. Camden (1586), 193.
[52] EPNS xl, 50.
[53] G. F. Playne (1876), 219–20.
[54] E. Ekwall (1936), s.v.

which was presumably also in Hampshire. In 584 Ceawlin and Cutha fought the Britons at *Fepan leag*, usually identified with Fetley, near Stoke Lyne in Oxfordshire.

In 614 'Cynegils and Cwichelm (of Wessex) fought *on Bean dune* and killed 2,045 Britons'—or '2,046', '2,065', or '2,040 and more', according to the different manuscrips of the *Chronicle*. *Beandun*, 'the hill where beans grow', has been identified with Bindon near Axmouth in Devon, or with Bindon Hill in Dorset, but neither attribution is compelling. Of the battle-casualties it has been said that 'such an exact figure, even allowing for the minor variations in the count, rings true'. From this an attempt has been made to calculate the size of the British force. On the basis that it was unusual, in those early battles about which we have adequate information, for casualties to exceed 10 per cent, it is argued that 'we have therefore to envisage a British army of some ten to twenty thousand men and a Saxon army hardly less in numbers'.[55]

These figures are hard to accept. The largest British force of the sixth and seventh centuries for which we have a figure is that of the Gododdin, a host supposedly gathered together from several kingdoms, but principally from south-east Scotland, in an attempt to crush the nascent Anglian settlement of Northumbria. Our poetic source gives a figure of 300 (or perhaps 363). It has been suggested that this is the number of the mounted officers, and that each may have been accompanied by a bodyguard of foot-soldiers, giving a total force of up to 3,000.[56] Even this seems too high when we consider the alleged size of the invading armies of the period, both Anglo-Saxon and Scottic: usually two to five ships' companies only, perhaps 100 to 250 men. In the Laws of Ine of Wessex a raiding party of three dozen or more was reckoned an army. Finally, the best estimate for the size of the late Roman field army in Britain is no more than 6,000 men.[57] In the light of all the available evidence, it is incredible that a single successor kingdom—however wealthy Dumnonia may have been—could have raised an army of 10,000, let alone 20,000 men.

Continuing our chronological survey, we next find that in 658 Cenwalh fought the Britons *æt Peonnum* and caused them to flee as far as the river Parrett. This battle has frequently been placed at Penselwood in Somerset, but all that the *Chronicle* really tells us is that the site was one with the Welsh name *pen*, meaning 'head', 'end', or 'hill'. We may infer, from our general ideas about the expansion of Wessex and from the reference to the Parrrett, that the Pen in question was in Somerset, Devon, or Dorset, but there are many candidates, even without allowing for the possibility that the original Welsh name may have been lost.[58] It is best to regard the battle as unlocated, though the probability that it was fought on a hill-top is strong.

The four remaining actions between Wessex and the southern Britons are all recorded so briefly that not one can be located. In 682 Centwine caused the Britons to flee as far as the sea. In 710 Ine and Nun fought the Welsh king Geraint, probably ruler of Dumnonia. In 743 Æthelbald of Mercia combined with Cuthred of Wessex to fight the Britons. In 753 Cuthred again fought the Britons. This brings us to the limits of the present survey.

We can now attempt to summarize the characteristics of the twenty-eight battles recorded between the armies of Kent, Sussex, and Wessex, on the one hand, and the Britons or Welsh, on the other. About the majority of them nothing useful can be said: the notices in the *Chronicle* or in our other sources are so brief that the battles are either

---

[55] W. G. Hoskins (1960), 7, 10.
[56] K. H. Jackson (1969), 13–18.
[57] L. Alcock (1971; 1973), 335–6.
[58] W. G. Hoskins (1960), 15; D. Whitelock *et al* (1961), 21, n. 1.

featureless, or impossible to locate, or both. Nevertheless some significant groups do emerge. For a start, there are three references to the initial landings of the Saxons, all in cases where the landing was opposed. There is no evidence that the forts of the Saxon Shore, however garrisoned, played any part in opposing the initial landings. There was indeed an action at the fort at *Anderida*, but this appears to be part of a second phase of penetration. Other engagements at or near fortified places involved the pre-Roman hill-forts of Old Sarum, Barbury Castle, and probably Posbury Camp. We found no evidence that the hill-fort defences had been refurbished, whether by the Britons or the Saxons, or that the forts were actually occupied at the time. It may well be that the forts figure in our sources merely as topographical markers, for the important thing about both Old Sarum and Barbury is that they lie adjacent to important routes. (This cannot possibly be claimed for Posbury, however.)

One battle was certainly fought on a hill-top, the *obsession badonici montis*, and another, that *æt Peonnum*, may well have been. Finally, five or six engagements took place at river-crossings. We saw that this was the commonest location for military actions in both British and Saxon accounts; and we also noticed that there is no support for the view that river battles favoured mounted Britons against Saxon foot soldiery.

If the overall result of this inquiry seems small, the plea may be made that, in a field and a period where conjecture is rampant, to establish the limitations of the evidence is the greatest service that one can at present perform.

CHAPTER 16

Warfare and Poetry among the Northern Britons[1]

Fellow Cambrians! All those scholars who are invited to fill the Presidency of our Association are much honoured by that office. In my case, I must add that I am very deeply moved, as well as honoured, that you should have chosen me, despite my desertion of the Principality of Wales in favour of the Kingdom of the Scots. As to that migration, perhaps I might excuse it as a kind of exchange for the fifth-century movement of Cunedda and his war-band from the Forth valley to Gwynedd. Moreover, my first hosting in what is now Scotland was directed to the fortified capital known to the Scottic usurpers of northern Britain as Dun Breatann, Fort of the Britons.

It is thoughts such as these which have determined the topic of my presidential offering to you this evening. I propose looking at those of the northern Cymry or Welsh or Britons, who inhabited the territories which lie within the modern boundaries of Scotland: 'Gwŷr y Gogledd', the 'Men of the North'. I shall impose certain limitations on my treatment of the topic. For a start, the history of the northern Britons has been much discussed, notably in Professor Sir Idris Foster's Presidential Address to our Association;[2] so I shall deal primarily with the archaeological evidence. I shall omit any reference to Cumbria, because of, rather than despite, the important researches being carried out by N. Higham, M. McCarthy and D. O'Sullivan. And just as our historical and literary sources confine themselves to the doings of princes and nobles, so I shall deal only with the archaeology of the warrior aristocracy. Again, I am well aware of the major researches, in progress or completed, on rural settlements, especially in the east of my area. But the inclusion of these peasant settlements, and of Cumbria, could only be at the expense of the details which will, I hope, give sharpness and colour to my picture of the noble Men of the North.

My starting-point must be the account, in *Historia Brittonum*, of the defence of the north against Anglian invaders.[3] 'Four kings fought against them: Urien, and Rhydderch Hen, and Gwallawg and Morgant'. The naming of four kings suggests that the northern Cymry were divided into at least four kingdoms; but, in fact, only two out of the four kings can be located in our area (Fig. 16.1). Urien is celebrated in the Taliesin poems as Urien of Rheged, and as Lord of Catraeth, a place to which we must return. Roderc son of Tothal is described in the *Life of Columba* as reigning *in petra Cloithe*, 'on the rock of Clyde'. This is Bede's Alcluith (correctly Alt Clut) 'which in their language'—that of the Britons—'means Clyde Rock'. This is readily identifiable with Castle Rock, Dumbarton, a twin-summitted volcanic plug with conspicuous remains of a medieval and eighteenth-

---

[1] Presidential Address to the One Hundred and Twenty-ninth Annual Summer Meeting of the Cambrian Archaeological Association, Lancaster 1982; printed in *Archaeologia Cambrensis*, *132* (1983), 1–18, as 'Gwŷr y Gogledd: an archaeological appraisal'.

[2] I. L. Foster (1969).

[3] K. H. Jackson (1955); (1963).

century castle (Fig. 16.2). This forms the starting-point of my account of the archaeology of the Men of the North.

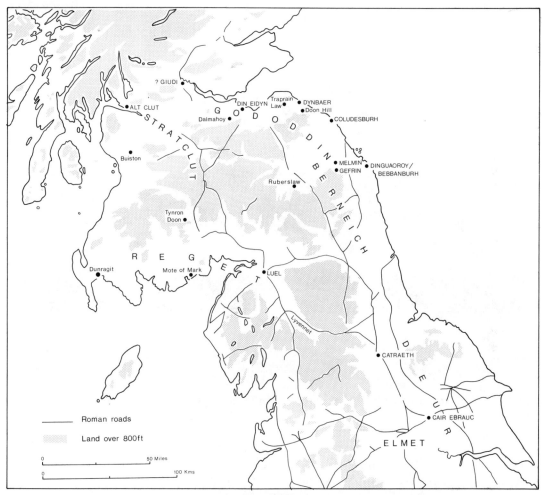

Fig. 16.1.

Map: Northern Britain AD 500–700. No attempt has been made to standardize place- and personal-names, either here or in the text.

At first sight, the recent remains at Castle Rock, Dumbarton, seem to inhibit any search for the Clyde Rock of Rhydderch or of Bede. Encouraged, however, by an earlier success in finding relics of the period of Maelgwn Gwynedd beneath Henry III's castle at Degannwy, the Department of Archaeology, University of Glasgow, excavated at Alt Clut in 1974 and 1975. No coherent defence plan was uncovered; but astride the eastern spur which links the Rock to the mainland was clear evidence for a dry-stone terrace or fighting platform, laced and revetted with timber beams. This had been destroyed by fire, most probably at the successful conclusion of an Irish Viking siege in AD 870. The destruction of Alt Clut exposed the peoples of northern Britain to a massive slave-raid; a striking

Fig. 16.2.
Alt Clut, Castle Rock, Dumbarton, from the north. The fighting platform lies on the
left-hand skyline.

testimony to the strategic importance of the fort. Radiocarbon dates from the oak timbers
of the terrace suggest either that it had been built in the sixth century AD, and repaired in
the seventh, or that it was a unitary work of the later date.[4]

If the second interpretation is preferred, then the known defences were not yet in
existence in the time of Rhydderch. On the other hand, the Rock was certainly occupied in
the sixth century by a family wealthy enough to acquire wine from the east Mediterranean, as characteristic amphorae sherds demonstrate (Fig. 16.3). Probably they had a
resident jeweller as well. This points clearly to Alt Clut as one of the dynastic centres of
Strathclyde by the time of Rhydderch if not earlier. But it is difficult to see here anything of
what Bede calls *civitas Brettonum munitissima*. At Alt Clut at least we must think of *civitas*
not in a physical sense, of city walls and civic buildings, but in an organizational sense, as
an administrative and social centre.

While there can be no doubts about the location of Alt Clut, or of the heartland of
Strathclyde, it is far more difficult to be certain about the Rheged of Urien and Owain. If
we leave Urien's Lordship of Catraeth aside for the moment, we find that Dunragit, in
Galloway, may be the 'Fort of Rheged'; that Carlisle may have been the centre of the
kingdom in both political and religious terms; that Urien's land of Llwyfenyd may lie in
the valley of the river Lyvennet in Cumbria; and that Rochdale in Lancashire may

[4] L. Alcock (1976).

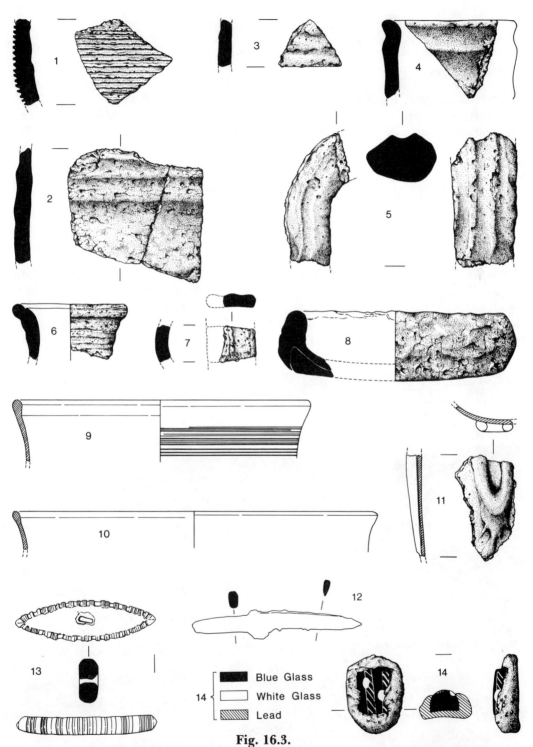

Fig. 16.3.
Representative finds from Alt Clut. 1–5 sherds from Mediterranean wine-jars; 6, 7 rim
and handle of Gaulish pottery; 8 jeweller's heating-tray; 9–11, rims and body sherd of
Merovingian glass; 12 iron knife-blade; 13 iron pommel bar from Viking sword;
14 Hiberno-Viking lead weight with glass inlay. Scales: all 1:2, except 9–11 and 14 at
1:1. After *Proc. Soc. Antiq. Scot.*, 107 (1975–6).

Blue Glass

White Glass

Lead

preserve the name Rheged in its first element. As I have said, for the lack of firsthand knowledge I do not propose to comment on Cumbria, save just to say that, if any of the towns of Roman Britain continued both its corporate and its physical existence into first the British and then the Anglian periods, it must surely be Carlisle.

Dunragit is, however, in my territory. It is a low, steep-sided hillock, which may have a suggestion of an utterly ruined dry-stone bank around its summit, and a second bank at a lower level. But its appearance to the archaeological eye does nothing to dispel that extreme scepticism about the 'Fort of Rheged' and about the territory of Rheged which Professor MacQueen has expressed most forcefully.[5]

Even MacQueen allows, however, that Rheged probably includes south-west Scotland; and if from that area we exclude the territory likely to belong to Strathclyde, then two seats of high status remain to be noticed in the south-west. The one, Tynron Doon, is a veritable high place: a conical hill which is strikingly visible for many miles around (Fig. 16.4). The summit is surrounded by sizeable earthworks of uncertain date, but not necessarily of the pre-Roman Iron Age. What matters in the present context is that small-scale excavation of an extra-mural midden has yielded an iron knife and bone pins, which can all be paralleled on sites of the sixth to eighth centuries AD; and most strikingly, fragments of a gold pendant decorated with filigree scrolls: Anglo-Saxon work of the mid-seventh century or later (Fig. 16.5).[6]

Fig. 16.4.
Tynron Doon. Earthwork defences can be seen on the left skyline.

[5] J. MacQueen (1955).
[6] J. E. C. Williams (1971).

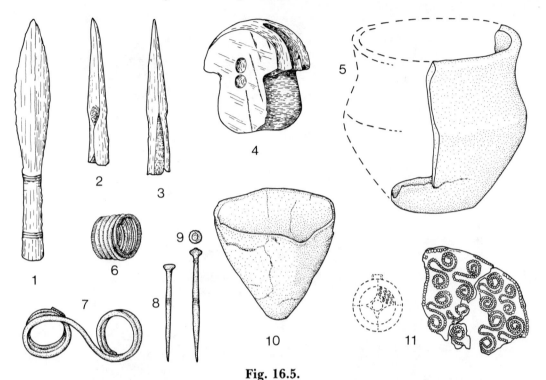

Fig. 16.5.
Finds from Buiston Crannog (Nos. 1–10) and Tynron Doon (No. 11).
1 iron spearhead; 2–3 iron arrowheads or crossbow bolts; 4 antler trigger for crossbow;
5 pottery beaker from Gaul; 6–7 gold finger-rings; 8–9 bronze pins; 10 jeweller's
crucible; 11 fragment (restored) of gold pendant, with enlargement of filigree ornament.
Scale: all 1:2, except 1 at 1:4. Redrawn from Munro 1882 and Williams 1971.

If Tynron Doon has not yet attracted excavations commensurate with its potential, our second site in Rheged has been excavated almost to the point of extinction. This is the minute fort of Mote of Mark, set on a craggy hillock which is tucked away up a side estuary of the Solway Firth.[7] The summit is defended by a timber-reinforced stone wall, which was destroyed by fire at some point in the fort's history. The area enclosed is no more than 75 m at its longest and 35 m at its widest, but much of this is rendered uninhabitable by outcropping rock. Between the outcrops, the raw materials and debris of jewellery-making were found in profusion. Indeed, the quantity was so great as to suggest that Mote of Mark was a purely industrial site, rather than a princely stronghold with a resident jeweller, such as I have suggested at Dinas Powys. Now Professor Gillies, in examining the literary evidence for the role of craftsmen in Celtic society, has drawn attention to the 'respect, not unmixed with awe', if not actual superstitious dread, with which smiths might be regarded. This in itself seems a powerful reason for segregating the craftsman and his magic powers. Beyond this, in the *Táin Bó Cuailnge*, we find that King Conchobor's smith Caulann possessed his own *liss* (Welsh *llys*) or defended homestead.[8] This would seem very apposite to Mote of Mark.

[7] A. O. Curle (1914).
[8] W. Gillies (1981).

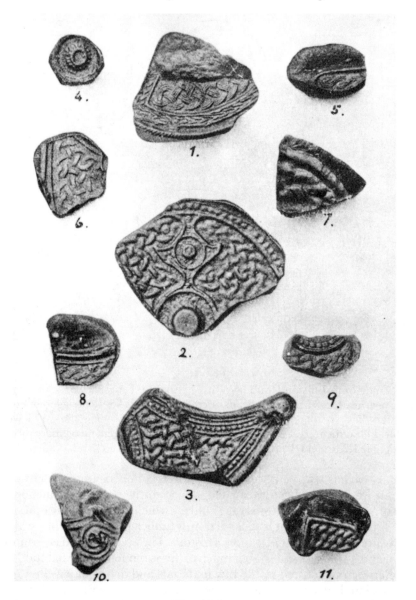

Fig. 16.6.
Mote of Mark: casts from clay moulds. No. 2 is clearly zoomorphic. After *Proc. Soc. Antiq. Scot.*, 48 (1913–14).

The abundant mould fragments (Fig. 16.6) provide good evidence for the jewellery actually produced at Mote of Mark, but this in turn has led to a vigorous debate about the relative role of British and Anglian artistic elements, and even about the dating of the construction and occupation of the fort.[9] There can, however, be no serious doubt that it

[9] Ll. R. Laing (1975a); J. Graham-Campbell *et al* (1976); D. Longley (1982).

was originally a British foundation, if only because such fort-building was quite unknown in the main Northumbrian territory of the Angles. Purely British moulds are rare, so perhaps originally the fort was a princely *llys* with an attendant jeweller. Attempts to estimate the foundation date have not been helped by radiocarbon estimates from the rampart timbers, because this is a period when the Belfast oak calibration curve has considerable detail: there are indeed four possible 'real time' calibrations for one of the C-14 dates. But the stratified occurrence of continental kitchen ware of Class E shows that the rampart cannot have been built much, if at all, before AD 600. Probably within fifty years, south-west Scotland was overrun and partly settled by the Angles. They took over the industrial activities of the Mote, and no doubt its British craftsmen as well, and exploited them vigorously for the production of elaborate jewellery in an early Anglo-Celtic style.

From this brief survey of Strathclyde and Rheged, I turn to the major interface between the archaeology and the written evidence for the Men of the North. According to *Historia Brittonum* 'Neirin and Taliesin and Bluchbard and Cian all at one time were illustrious in British poetry'. Thus we are introduced to Aneirin as a poet of the later sixth century, and so in turn to his heroic verse: 'This is the *Gododdin*; Aneirin sang it'. I am, of course, in no way qualified to comment on the linguistic or other technical aspects of the *Gododdin*, though these are much discussed among contemporary scholars. My only purpose is to show how archaeology can illustrate some at least of the places and objects mentioned in the poem. In attempting this, I am greatly helped by the existence of an excellent printed text and an equally excellent English translation of the *Gododdin*.[10]

It is scarcely necessary to remind an audience of Cambrians that the *Gododdin* consists of a series of elegiac stanzas lamenting the death in battle of the warrior heroes of King Mynyddog Mwynfawr, who was ruler of Gododdin in the sense both of the people and of the land. Mynyddog had gathered together a war-band of three hundred men, and had feasted them for a year in the hall at Din Eidyn. Then they were sent forth to attack the Angles of Northumbria at Catraeth. There, all save one perished. This heroic, even tragic, story is not told as a continuous narrative; rather it has to be inferred, and then pieced together, from passing references. How plausible it is in historical terms is a matter which must be deferred until we have considered the archaeological correlations.

The action begins, then, at Eidyn, or Din Eidyn, or *Eidyn ysgor*, 'Eidyn the fortified town'. Where, and what, was Din Eidyn? There is complete agreement that it is the place known to us as Edinburgh: a place which also appears in historical records in AD 638, when it was besieged, most probably by the Angles in the course of their final overthrow of the nation of the Gododdin and consequent seizure of the Lothians. To be more precise, it was very probably the crag-and-tail hill now occupied by Edinburgh castle, rather than the shadowy earthworks on Arthur's Seat. If it does indeed underlie Edinburgh castle, then there is nothing of it to be seen today. But we may speculate as to what it may have been like, on the basis of a survey of other strongholds which have been explored in the territory of Gododdin.

These fall into two broad classes: stone-walled forts on craggy, and sometimes lofty, hills; and palisaded enclosures on rather lower ground. The classic example of a palisaded—indeed a double-palisaded—enclosure is at Yeavering, in the southern part of

[10] K. H. Jackson (1969).

Gododdin.[11] Here, Dr Hope-Taylor's excavations showed that the Great Enclosure, which was such a major architectural feature of the royal township (*villa regia*) of Edwin of Northumbria in the third decade of the seventh century, had a structural history which goes back to the pre-Anglian period. This suggests that, already in the earlier sixth century, Yeavering was a royal centre, with a palisaded enclosure for public gatherings. In looking for the structural antecedents of the Yeavering enclosure, Hope-Taylor was able to point to a double-palisaded site with comparable entrance arrangements at Harehope in Peeblesshire. Some scholars have considered this to be a poor parallel, because Harehope has been attributed to the pre-Roman Iron Age. It was considered that there was too long a gap between this and the earliest possible date for the Yeavering enclosure. In fact, there is no conclusive evidence for the date of Harehope, which could as well be post-Roman as pre-Roman. More recently, a double-palisade has been recognized as the first phase of the cliff fort of Kirk Hill, St Abb's Head, which later became the Northumbrian monastery of *Coludesburh* or *urbs Coludi*. There the palisade seems to have been built of oak beams with a wicker infilling of hazel, willow and birch. From this comes a radiocarbon date of 1275 ± 85bp (2-sigma level). Whatever problems there may be in calibrating radiocarbon dates in this period, this must represent a calendar date centred on the seventh century AD. The Kirk Hill palisaded enclosure was probably built under Anglian patronage but in the Gododdin tradition.[12]

Our second class of stronghold, the stone-walled fort on a craggy hill, is better known outside the land of Gododdin, among the Picts and Scots as well as the Britons. Among the Gododdin, the partly explored fort of Ruberslaw in Roxburghshire is known to be post-Roman, or at least very late Roman, because its dry-stone walling includes blocks dressed in the Roman manner (some with mortar still adhering to them), which must have been robbed from some Roman fort, signal station or rural temple. An unexcavated example at Dalmahoy, south-west of Edinburgh, was used by Stevenson to define a group of 'Dark Age capitals' which he classed as nuclear forts. Apart from the plan, which contrasts sharply with the multi-ramparted Iron Age fort on the neighbouring Kaimes Hill, the only evidence for Dark Age occupation at Dalmahoy is a tiny gold disc which may be of this period. None the less, two other forts of nuclear plan, Dunadd among the Scots, and Dundurn among the Picts, are shown by both historical and archaeological evidence to belong to the seventh and eighth centuries AD.[13]

With these thoughts in mind, it was possible for Mr Iain MacIvor and myself to examine in detail the shape of the rock which underlies Edinburgh Castle, and to speculate how this might have determined, or at least influenced, the plan of Din Eidyn (Fig. 16.7). We suggested, in the full knowledge that the hypothesis can never be tested, a rather large citadel, with two lower enclosures looping out to the west. On plan, this looks broadly similar to Dundurn, but the level, usable ground is more extensive. This might appear appropriate for one of the principal centres of Gododdin, as compared with a border stronghold of the Picts. But before this plan gains acceptance, it is very necessary to stress that the citadel fort, whether or not of truly nuclear form, is certainly not the only plan to be found among the Britons, the Picts or the Scots.

Contrary to earlier speculation, excavation has failed to uncover nuclear forts at Alt Clut or at Dun Ollaigh. Among the Picts, indeed, both multivallate (Burghead;

[11] B. Hope-Taylor (1977).
[12] L. Alcock (1981b).
[13] Discussion of these and related sites in L. Alcock (1979b); (1981a).

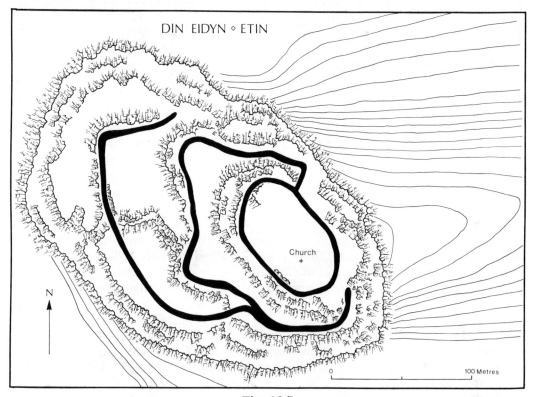

Fig. 16.7.
Din Eidyn, Castle Rock, Edinburgh: hypothetical plan of sixth-century fortifications,
by I. MacIvor and L. Alcock.

Clatchard Craig) and bivallate (Craig Phadraig) forts of essentially Iron Age appearance
were built or strengthened in the fifth or later centuries AD. Such plans have still to be
demonstrated in Gododdin; but again it should be stressed that the whole study of post-
Roman fortifications is still in its infancy.

Within Din Eidyn, it is plain from very numerous references that Mynyddog's feasting
hall was the centre of activity for the king and his war-band. From the *Gododdin* itself, and
from other heroic verse such as the Old English poem *Beowulf*, we have a vivid picture of
these activities. A royal hall (*aula regis*) is also mentioned in Adomnan's *Life of Columba*, on
the occasion of the saint's visit to Brude, king of the northern Picts. Our present concern is to
ask what, in a British context, we can discern of the architectural character of such halls.

Large timber halls, datable to the late-fifth and sixth centuries, have been claimed
among the Britons of Dumnonia at Castle Dore in Cornwall and at Cadbury–Camelot in
Somerset (Figs. 12.5; 13.10). In the north, we might expect to find a comparable hall at
pre-Anglian Yeavering, in view of its apparent role as a royal centre and public meeting
place. In fact, the earliest buildings that are worthy of the title of hall, Buildings A2 and A4,
appear already to be Anglian, and the known British buildings are no more than 29 ft. (9 m)
in length by 19 ft. (6 m) wide, built either of close-set posts or of beams with a wattle
infilling.

The only clear example of a British hall among the Gododdin is at Doon Hill, East Lothian. Here, within a polygonal palisaded enclosure, is a remarkable timber building, Hall A, built of massive squared uprights, presumably with an infilling of thinner planks or wattling. The plan is a rectangle with slightly tapering end bays, and end walls which have been aptly described as being of 'open-book' plan: a plan without any exact parallel. The overall internal dimensions are about 70 ft. (20 m) by 32 ft. (10 m) giving an area of about 2250 sq ft. (216 m²). Further details are the central doors in each of the long walls, and the lateral division into a large central hall, presumably for public functions, with a small private apartment at each end. There is no direct evidence for the date of Doon Hill A but it was superseded by a second hall, built to a different plan. Hall B in turn parallels a building of about AD 640 at Yeavering, so that Hall A is earlier than this, and takes us back to the pre-Anglian period in the Lothians: that is, before the Anglian siege of Din Eidyn/Etin in AD 638. Doon Hill A was certainly an impressive building, and taking account of the surrounding palisade, we should see it, in British terms, as a princely *neuadd* set within the appropriate *llys*.[14]

Doon Hill A is intermediate in size between the Cadbury–Camelot hall (1900 sq ft., 182 m²) and Hall A2 at Yeavering (2850 sq ft., 273 m²). If we might believe that, within a given social structure, the size of a building is a guide to its social status, then we should look at another large building in northern Britain which has not hitherto been regarded as a princely hall. This is the circular house 56 ft. (17 m) in diameter, and 2450 sq ft. (235 m²) in area, which was built on a crannog or artificial island at Buiston in modern Ayrshire (and therefore probably in Strathclyde rather than Rheged) around the seventh–eighth centuries AD. It may be its circular plan which has excluded Buiston from consideration as a princely centre, in a period when it has been assumed that the halls of the great were rectangular. But in addition to its size, we may list the features which indicate its status. These include both the sheer cost of building both the crannog foundations and the building raised upon it, which made use of high-quality carpentry; the presence of weapons, symbolic of a warrior aristocracy; evidence for metalworking, including crucibles, and moulds for silver ingots; and the importation of pottery from the continent (Fig. 16.5). Apart from the carpentry, which is of course only preserved at Buiston because of the waterlogged nature of the crannog site, these are all features of the royal hill-top strongholds of the Britons, the Picts and the Scots.[15]

If we now return to the hall of Eidyn, we have, of course, no means of knowing whether we should be looking for a circular or a rectangular building. On balance the model of Doon Hill A is probably more appropriate than that of Buiston. On the other hand, in seeking the hall of Urien in the land of Llwyfenyd, we should keep in mind that it may have been circular rather than rectangular. In that case, a possible candidate might be the exceptionally large round house which dominates the settlement at Ewe Close, Crosby Ravensworth, above the Lyvennet Beck.[16]

At this point, it is helpful to examine more fully the relations between the power centres of the Britons and the Angles, which have already been mentioned in passing. At Doon Hill we have seen that a princely hall, built in the Anglian style, replaced one in the British mode about the time of the Anglian conquest of the Lothians. There can be no doubt that this represents, in archaeological terms, the replacement of a British prince of

[14] B. Hope-Taylor (1980).
[15] R. Munro (1882). Further commentary in Chapter 13 above.
[16] W. G. Collingwood (1908).

the Gododdin by an Anglian lord of Bernicia. At Yeavering/Gefrin we have a site known to historians as a royal township of the Northumbrian kings: *villa regia*, as Bede calls it. Excavation has now shown that the double-palisaded Great Enclosure, which was a conspicuous feature of the early Anglian township, is the final phase of a structure built originally to a British design; and that in a host of other ways, Northumbrian Gefrin demonstrates the adoption and adaptation of a British centre which itself must surely have been royal.

This takeover of Gododdin seats of power is hinted at elsewhere as well. We first hear of Dunbar as an Anglian royal town (*urbs regis*), in the charge of a *praefectus*, where the great but unruly bishop Wilfrid might be imprisoned. But the name, *Dynbaer*, comes from the British *din-bar*, meaning 'top, or summit, fort'; and there can be no doubt that the origin of the Bernician *urbs regis* was a stronghold of the Gododdin. An even more interesting case is that of Bamburgh, another Bernician *urbs regia* on a massive coastal promontory (Fig. 13.11). Bede and the *Historia Brittonum* agree that it took its name, *Bebbanburh*, from Queen Bebba, wife of King Æthelfrith. The Anglo-Saxon Chronicle claims that it was built by Ida, who is said to have founded the Bernician dynasty in AD 547. But the *Historia Brittonum* also gives it a British name, Din Guoaroy, which plainly implies that it was originally a British stronghold. Small-scale excavations have suggested that, during the late Roman period, the headland may have been garrisoned by men of Gododdin as a lookout and beacon station to pass news of Pictish naval raids to the Roman army on and around Hadrian's wall. More hesitantly, it has been suggested that, in the sixth century, this role of coastal defence was handed over to Anglo-Saxon mercenaries—perhaps even to the Octha and Ebissa of the *Historia Brittonum*—and that from this there sprang the Bernician dynasty.[17]

Other peculiarities of Bernician archaeology have been adduced to suggest that the Angles took over, perhaps peacefully and by invitation, the British political and social organization of the Gododdin, at first south of the Tweed, and then, a century later, up to the Forth. For instance, the few Anglian graves that are known in Bernicia appear to be those of a wealthy warrior class, which can only have formed a small minority of the population.[18] Moreover, in so far as social structure may be inferred from grave goods, there is a marked contrast between Bernicia and, say, Wessex, where in addition to the minority of rich graves, there is a large number of poorer, but still weapon-bearing, graves: the burials of a warrior peasantry. This class was absent from the Bernician graves, and in this respect, the implied social structure seems close to that of the Britons, among whom the bearing of arms was an upper-class privilege and responsibility. It seems probable that the intrusive Anglian dynasty had taken over not only the power centres of Gododdin, and the associated political structure as well, but also the social structure. It should be added that these deductions from the archaeological evidence accord well with conclusions reached long ago by historians.

If the Anglian takeover was facilitated, even in part, by the invitation, or at least the acquiescence of the rulers of the Gododdin, this would be in sharp contrast with the picture we find in British literary sources. Taliesin's poems in praise of Urien of Rheged; the *Historia Brittonum* account of Outigern fighting bravely against the English nation, and of the warfare leading up to Urien's siege of Lindisfarne; and not least the *Gododdin*

---

[17] Dunbar: L. Alcock (1981a). Bamburgh: B. Hope-Taylor (1966).
[18] See Chapter 17 for details.

poem itself: all these bespeak relentless hostility and vigorous warfare. And on the English side, too, Bede's eulogy of Æthelfrith makes it plain that the end of the sixth and beginning of the seventh century was a period of exceptionally vigorous military expansion by the Northumbrians.

Deliberately leaving these wider issues unresolved, I propose now to return to the *Gododdin* poem to see what archaeology has to tell us about the material possessions of Mynyddog's court and war-band. Necessarily I must begin with weapons, since the *Gododdin* is full of blades—sharp blades, blades of steel, blades that are described as blue or red—as well as the more specific mentions of swords or spears. But my treatment of this aspect of the *Gododdin* is deliberately brief and superficial, principally because I hope that we shall soon benefit from the publication of David Morgan Evans's researches in this major field. At present, it must be admitted, the study of weapons in Britain lags behind that in Ireland, where we have recently seen both a classificatory study of pre-Viking iron swords and also, and even more relevant to the swords of the *Gododdin*, a lengthy discussion of the swords of the Ulster Cycle of heroic tales. At present, the only sword known from northern Britain comes from the Scottic, or Picto-Scottic, fort at Dunadd: a fragment of a very simple blade, which looks distinctly pre-Roman. We know neither the overall length of the weapon, nor any details of its hilt.

Spears, which may have had shafts of ash or of holly, are mentioned considerably more frequently than swords in the *Gododdin*. Used as lances, they would be particularly appropriate to a mounted force such as Mynyddog's war-band. It seems, however, more likely that they were used as throwing weapons, a conclusion based on phrases such as: 'he showered shafts in the front rank of the fray, in the javelin fight'. A particularly fine iron spearhead is known from Buiston. Eight-and-a-half inches long, and with a pronounced medial thickening, it is markedly more massive than most of the spears known from Scottic or Irish sites. It looks more suitable as a hand-held lance than as a javelin. Its socketed shaft has two bands of triple grooves, which may once have held silver or copper-alloy wire inlays (Fig. 16.5).

Other military gear is unknown in the British archaeological record, despite its frequent mention in the *Gododdin*. For instance, no shields have been found. Irish and Anglo-Saxon examples suggest that they would have been of wood, possibly leather-covered, and with an iron boss to protect the handgrip (Fig. 19.4). Body armour is also mentioned, and the word used, *lluric*, is frequently translated as 'mail-coat'. It is agreed that *lluric* derives from the Latin *lorica*, which, it must be stressed, means only a cuirass or breast-plate. Unless qualified as *lorica squamata*, scale-armour, or *hamata*, ring-mail, it may mean no more than a protective leather jerkin. Consequently we cannot know for certain that *lluric* in the *Gododdin* implies mail- (or even scale-) armour. Certainly both would have been known to the ancestors of the Gododdin war-band on the bodies of Roman soldiery, alive or dead, and so the epithet 'mail-coat stripping' would have at least a traditional significance. Finally, there is no reference to helmets in the *Gododdin*. This is not at all surprising, since only three of this period are known from the whole of the British Isles. On the other hand, helmets do appear on the eighth-century Pictish cross-slab from Aberlemno in Angus, which may have as a model an Anglian helmet like that recently discovered in York.

Finally, there is one important weapon which finds no mention in the poetry, though its occurrence is well attested in the material remains. This is the crossbow, firing heavy iron-shod bolts. Two such bolt-heads are known from Buiston, and there are other probable examples from the Scottic forts of Dunadd and Dunollie. In the case of Buiston, it has sometimes been suggested that the bolts had been fired by medieval fowlers, pursuing their sport in a swamp long after the abandonment and decay of the crannog. But Buiston also yields an antler nut for the trigger mechanism of a crossbow, and this, it can be shown, is of a more primitive form than those known from medieval sites (Fig. 16.5). There is little doubt, therefore, that the crossbow was in use during the seventh and eighth centuries AD. Since it was a Roman invention, this need cause no surprise. Moreover, pictures of a bow, almost certainly a crossbow, have now been recognized on several Pictish slabs.[19] Unless its use was confined to hunting, it is difficult to understand the silence of the literary sources.

From the poetry and archaeology of weapons, it is natural to turn to the refreshment of the warrior. Bragget, wine and above all mead, figure largely in the *Gododdin*; it was through the mead-feast that Mynyddog bound his war-band to him, and 'paying for one's mead' was a euphemism for death in battle. It might be thought that this is one area in which we can expect no archaeological evidence. But recently, Dr James Dickson has discovered evidence for honey, most probably used for brewing mead, associated with a Beaker in an Early Bronze Age burial. We must recognize the possibility, therefore, of finding honey or mead residues on the inside of a pottery goblet, perhaps on a beaker of the type known from Buiston. As for wine, the evidence for the importation of large wine-jars or amphorae from the eastern Mediterranean to princely sites in the Celtic West is now well known. Ten years ago, the most northerly reach of such imports was Maelgwn's Degannwy; but now that distinction has shifted to Alt Clut (Fig. 16.3). At present, no other stronghold of the Men of the North is known to have imported east Mediterranean amphorae.

But that is not the end of the story. Pottery vessels are, in fact, a very uneconomical way to transport wine, and in Gaul amphorae had never supplanted wooden casks or barrels: at cooperage, as at chariot-building, the Celts were master-craftsmen. Unfortunately, French wines in cask—say claret from Bordeaux—would normally leave no archaeological trace, because the casks were bound with withies, not with iron hoops. But there is some slight, but no less definite, evidence for contact between the Bordeaux region and fortified centres like Dunadd, Mote of Mark, Dinas Powys, Tintagel and Cadbury–Camelot. This takes the form of distinctive mixing bowls and drinking vessels, which were undoubtedly manufactured around Bordeaux in the fifth and sixth centuries. But these vessels occur mostly as singletons: one only at Dunadd, one at Mote of Mark, one at Cadbury. It is impossible to imagine trade at this level, and more reasonable, therefore, to believe that the pottery is merely an imperishable by-product of the importation of perishable commodities from Bordeaux. For these, the most likely candidate is certainly wine in cask.[20]

Archaeology reveals pottery drinking vessels, like those from Bordeaux, or the beaker from Buiston which had probably come from northern Gaul by way of a regular pottery trade in the seventh and eighth centuries. But at all times, pottery was scarce, even on the richest sites, and normal tableware must have been of horn, leather and treen. All these may be found on waterlogged sites where preservation conditions are good for organic substances. But, with the exception of drinking horns, the bards knew nothing of these

[19] J. M. Gilbert (1976).
[20] See Chapters 4 and 6 for a fuller discussion of the pottery.

mundane substances: the heroes they celebrate drank from goblets of gold or silver or from vessels of glass. Fragments of glass from fine beakers or horns, which were ultimately of Rhineland manufacture, do indeed occur on British strongholds. But detailed analysis of a large quantity of such glass from Dinas Powys suggested that actual vessels had never been present on the site: there simply were not enough base sherds in proportion to the rims. It is generally agreed that the glass came to the west and north as cullet (scrap glass) to be used in the manufacture of beads, bangles and inlays for jewellery. As for goblets of gold or silver: very rich burials or treasure hoards may indeed contain silver bowls, sometimes gilt, or silver cups. But even at Sutton Hoo, the richest treasure of the period in Britain, the majority of drinking vessels were of horn or wood with silver-gilt mounts. Evidently Aneirin inhabited an inflated world when compared with real-life kings and heroes.

The mention of precious metals leads to a consideration of jewellery, jewel-making, and the craft of the smith. One stanza specifically refers to a goldsmith, and there are other allusions to gold objects, in addition to the gold goblets which have already been discussed. In particular, we may note 'the gold filigreed shield of the battlefield'. This merits two comments from the archaeologist. Firstly, a gold-ornamented shield would more properly be regarded as a parade or ceremonial piece, rather than for use on the battlefield. Secondly, in the late sixth-century context that is generally accepted both for the Gododdin expedition and for the poet Aneirin, filigree is plainly anachronistic. The earliest evidence for the use of filigree among the northern Britons or the Picts is provided by the Hunterston brooch, which is a clear century later. The allusion to filigree would seem to be an interpolation during the oral transmission of the *Gododdin*. The brooches worn by several heroes would no doubt have been of penannular form; and the archaeological evidence shows that they would have been fashioned from silver, not gold, with plain terminals, like those from Norries Law and Tummel Bridge.

In fact, the commonest ornament attributed to Mynyddog's war-band was the torque or neck-ring of gold. Here again we are faced by an anachronism, but in the opposite time-sense from that represented by the gold-filigreed shield. Neck-rings of bronze or gold are well known among the Celts of the pre-Roman Iron Age, both on the continent and in Britain and Ireland. But there is no evidence that they were made and worn after the second century AD at the latest. It should be noted that their absence from the later archaeological record is not the result of a change in burial rites, for torques are normally found stray or in votive hoards, not in burials. Torques, it would seem, are present in the poetry, but absent from the archaeology; but the opposite is true of the most conspicuous emblem of wealth among the Gododdin: their heavy silver chains (Fig. 16.8). These are sometimes classed as Pictish, because two of them bear Pictish symbols, but their overall distribution proclaims them as characteristic of Gododdin. They are too short to wear round the neck, but they may have been hung on the chest, perhaps as rewards for military prowess, in the same manner as Roman soldiers wore torques not round the neck, but on their chest, as decorations for valour. If we allow for Aneirin's inflated use of gold where the archaeology discloses only silver, it might be suggested that the gold torques of the Gododdin were in reality heavy silver chains. But if this emendation is rejected, then we have here a double discrepancy between the poetry and the archaeology: gold torques in the former, silver chains in the latter.

It is generally accepted that the Gododdin warriors were Christians, who might take communion, lay gold on the altar, or go to church to do penance. I do not propose to

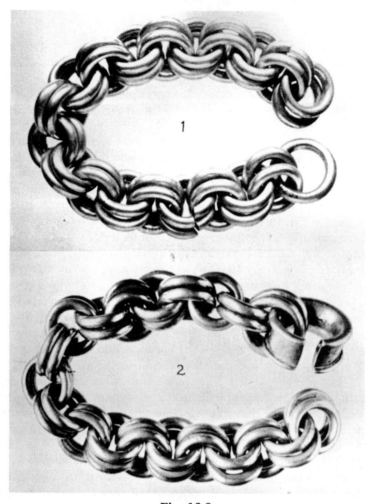

Fig. 16.8.
Silver chains from the territory of Gododdin. 1 Traprain Law, East Lothian; 2
Greenlaw, Berwickshire. Scale 1:2 After *Proc. Soc. Antiq. Scot.*, 73 (1938–9)

explore here the archaeological evidence for Christianity among the northern Britons, for
this is the field which Dr Ralegh Radford and Professor Charles Thomas have made so
much their own.[21] But to a Welsh audience, some comments must be made on the
Latin-inscribed monuments, akin to those of Nash-Williams' Group I, or the Royal
Commission's Class A. For a start, they are relatively rare. Ogham inscriptions and
bilinguals are completely absent. One of the stones, the Catstane, is very firmly associated
with a cemetery.[22] Very broadly, we can discern two groups: one in the south-west, closely
related to the monastic centre at Whithorn, and predominantly of a religious character;
and an eastern group, predominantly with secular or even dynastic inscriptions. These

[21] C. A. R. Radford (1967); A. C. Thomas (1971).
[22] T. G. Cowie (1978).

are in the territory of Gododdin, and they bear witness to a Christian nobility and ruling family.

Finally, I turn to Catraeth. 'Men went to Catraeth': in so far as the *Gododdin* has a story-line, that is it. Where, then, and what was Catraeth? And how far does archaeological evidence harmonize with the witness of history, and with the theme of the poem?

Firstly, there is general agreement that Catraeth, as a Welsh place-name, derives from a Latin form *cataracta*, a waterfall or rapids. This was applied to the falls of the river Swale (near Richmond in Yorkshire) and thence to the nearby Roman fort, and later town, of *Cataractonium*: the modern Catterick Bridge. In the poems of Taliesin, Urien of Rheged appears as lord of Catraeth, and to the men of Catraeth he is their victorious prince. In the *Gododdin* by contrast, the implication is that Catraeth is in the hands of the men of Lloegr, the heathen Angles of Deira and Bernicia. If the line 'he glutted black ravens on the ramparts of the stronghold' refers to Catraeth rather than to some unspecific military action, it was thought of as surrounded by a defensive wall or bank.

By the 620s, under Edwin of Northumbria, Catterick was most probably a royal township. Bede does not in fact call it *villa regia*, but he tells us that, in Deira, where the missionary Paulinus was wont to stay very frequently with the king, he baptized in the river Swale which flows past *vicum Cataractam*. The word *vicus* may mean no more than village, but the specific mention of the king suggests strongly that Catterick was a royal centre. Professor Kenneth Jackson, looking at the historical background to the Gododdin expedition, sees the English settlement of Northumbria spreading from early centres in the Yorkshire Wolds and around York itself. 'By the end of the sixth century' he concludes 'it is likely that all Yorkshire east of and including the Vale of York was in the hands of the English—it is hardly probable . . . that Catterick would have been a royal *villa* . . . in 627, if it was acquired much later than this' (i.e. the late sixth century). It may have been the relatively recent Anglian occupation of Catraeth, coupled with the weakness of Æthelfrith, who had only recently ascended the throne of Bernicia, which inspired Mynyddog to launch his attack, down a strategic Roman road, against a weak point at the junction of the two kingdoms of Deira and Bernicia.[23]

What can archaeology tell us about the relations of Britons, Romans and Angles around Catterick between the fourth and seventh centuries? On the basis of excavations in 1959, John Wacher has argued that the town underwent a very radical reorganization, in or shortly after AD 370, when part of it was turned into a fortified barracks. This was probably an element in the reorganization of British defences under Count Theodosius, in response to the devastation caused by the great Barbarian Conspiracy of 367. Two military buckles and a buckle-plate, together with weapons from late levels at Catterick, may have belonged to the detachment which was then posted to the town (Fig. 16.9). It may be that the garrison was of Germanic origin, though present thinking would play down the Germanic connotations of these late Roman buckles, and would repudiate altogether the idea that we can attribute some specific military or political status, as *gentiles* or *laeti* or *foederati*, to those who wore them. In any case, we should not see in these buckles the beginnings of Germanic—that is to say, Anglo-Saxon—settlement at the northern end of the Vale of York. The military detachment was soon evacuated, and civilian settlement slowly took its place.[24]

The next part of the history of Catterick has to be pieced together from scattered

[23] K. H. Jackson (1969).
[24] J. S. Wacher (1971).

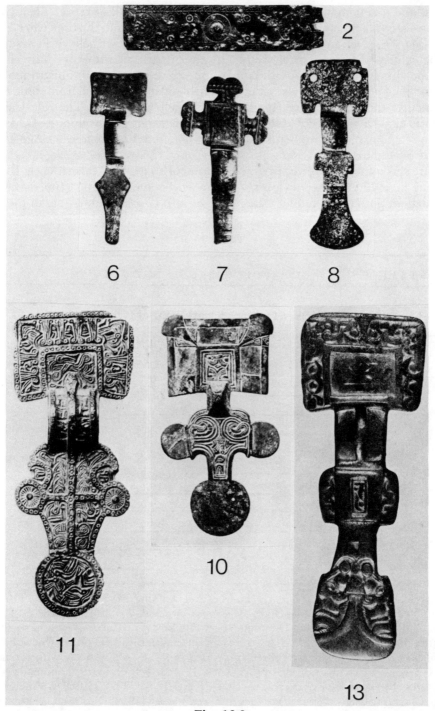

Fig. 16.9.
Catterick; Late Roman buckle-plate and Anglian brooches. See Table 1 for details.
Various scales.

references, and it is therefore difficult to know how far, if at all, it represents a coherent story. Was Catterick deserted between the early fifth century and the time when we see it as a *villa regia* of the Deiran king; or that earlier period when, if we believe Taliesin, it was one of the centres of Urien's princedom? Or, after its use as a military base close to a strategic road junction, in the 370s, did it become a centre for civil administration, first in British, and then in Anglian hands? If so, its control must have passed from some Roman-style council to the rule of Dark Age kings, of whichever nation. The role which late Roman forts may have played in determining the geography of power in the Dark Ages is one of the great unexplored problems of the transition from Roman to Dark Age England, Wales and Scotland.

These are speculations: but we also have a scatter of archaeological evidence. In further excavations in 1972, Wacher uncovered a sunken-floored building (*Grubenhaus*), containing Anglian pottery, including a large bossed urn (*Buckelurne*): a date in the fifth or

Table 1

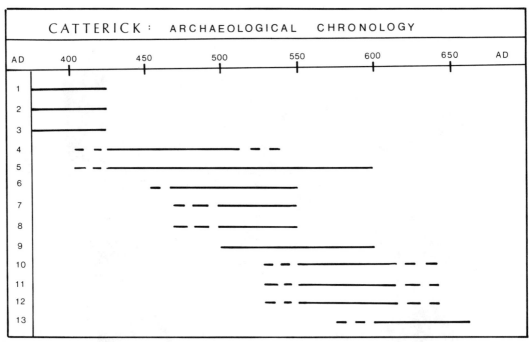

Notes and references. (1) buckle, Class IA (Hawkes and Dunning, *Medieval Archaeol.*, 5 (1961), Fig. 13d); (2) buckle-plate, Class IA/B (Pocock, *Yorks. Archaeol. J.*, 43 (1971), 187–8, Pl. I); (3) buckle, Class IVB (Hawkes and Dunning, 1961, Fig. 22); (4) *Grubenhaus* with large *Buckelurne* (Webster, *Medieval Archaeol.*, 17 (1973), 150-1; (5) iron spearhead, Type H2 (Swanton, *British Archaeol. Rep.* 7 (1974), 40); (6-8) three small-long brooches, respectively with lozenge foot, trefoil type and cross-potent derivative, (Pocock, 1971, 187-8, Pl. I); (9) handmade biconical urn (Myres, *Corpus of Anglo-Saxon pottery* (1977), Fig. 113, No. 337); (10) great square-headed brooch, Class A4 (Leeds, *Corpus of great square-headed brooches* (1949), No. 33); (11) great square-headed brooch, Class B (Leeds, *Corpus,* No. 122); (12) florid cruciform brooch, Group V (a iv) (Leeds and Pocock, *Medieval Archaeol.*, 15 (1971), 13–36, Fig. 4c); (13) great square-headed brooch, Class C2 (Pocock, *Yorks. Archaeol. J.*, 42 (1970), 407–9, Pl. 1).

early sixth century may be indicated. Another item of the fifth or sixth centuries is an iron spearhead, found in a small cemetery in 1959. The late fifth or earlier sixth century is represented by two bronze brooches of the small-long type, while a third belongs to the middle decades of that century. Less precisely datable, but also of the sixth century, is a hand-made biconical urn of Alamannic derivation. A group of large and ornate brooches of the great square-headed and florid cruciform classes comes from the mid and later sixth century (Fig. 16.9), and one of them may even date after the turn of the century. (For details, see Table 1.)

These Anglian pieces may seem few in number, but they are gleanings from a site with an unhappy history of sporadic exploration and desultory publication. And however few they are, this at least can be said: if Urien was slain about 590, or even twenty years earlier, and if he was the British lord of Catraeth, then the *Grubenhaus* with its *Buckelurne*, the three small-long brooches, and probably two of the great square-headed brooches, should not be there at all. And if Catterick was already being settled by 450, or shortly thereafter, Anglian occupation might have been firmly consolidated by about 600. It follows that if the archaeological evidence has been correctly interpreted, then the Gododdin expedition was even more foolhardy than it has appeared hitherto. Parenthetically, it should be pointed out that Catterick is a mere 38 miles along Dere Street from the dense early Anglian settlement around York: a day's ride or two days' march. On the other hand, Edinburgh is 168 miles distant by the western route through Carlisle.

So we must begin to wonder whether the identification of Catraeth with Catterick Bridge is sound; or whether the *Gododdin* is to be regarded as a historical document at all. The first of these propositions is unacceptable, given the weight of linguistic authority in its favour. The second reminds us of the various detailed discrepancies which we have found between the poem and the archaeology of the later sixth and earlier seventh centuries as we know it at present: the two-way anachronism of torques and filigree; or the contrast between the gold of the poem and the silver of the archaeology.

At this point, it is necessary to grasp firmly the difference between historicity and authenticity; or for that matter, between historicity and literary merit. Indeed, on the second of these points, it might almost be said that the kind of imagination which fires a work of literature is out of place in a historical account. As for authenticity, it has been well argued that Aneirin was a real poet, and that the two versions of the *Gododdin* which have come down to us enable us to approach very closely to an authentic version of what Aneirin sang. Beyond that, the poem may give us the genuine flavour and ethos of the heroic society of the late sixth and seventh centuries: though here the argument may be somewhat circular, since our knowledge of that ethos is not wholly independent of the poem.[25]

To all this, the question of historicity is irrelevant. It does not matter whether Din Eidyn—which is attested in other sources—was the seat of Mynyddog Mwynfawr, who is otherwise unknown to us. It does not matter whether a war-band of three hundred, or three hundred and three or some other number of noble warriors went to Catterick Bridge or to some other Anglian settlement or stronghold. We might ask here, why then is Catraeth/Catterick so central to the poem, if it was not the objective of an expedition? The answer might be twofold: in general terms, that certain places acquired fame as battle sites, as the list of Arthur's battles shows; and more specifically, that its role as a late

[25] T. M. Charles-Edwards (1978).

fourth-century military base on the road north may well have made *Cataractonium* famous among the Gododdin. However that may be, the Men of the North fought vigorously and bravely, as did their Anglian opponents: the *Historia Brittonum* admits this. And both sides cherished precious artefacts, fine brooches and fine weapons; and not least, honour and nobility. The archaeologist can do a little to reveal the artefacts; and nothing at all to dim the nobility of those who cherished them.

Acknowledgements

My wife has contributed largely to the research and synthesis which underlie this paper. In addition, I have benefited from information and advice from many colleagues notably C. J. Arnold, V. I. Evison, H. B. Duncan, C. M. Hills, D. Longley, I. MacIvor, M. Nieke, J. S. Wacher and R. Warner. My warmest thanks are due to them all.

CHAPTER 17

Graves and Status in Bernicia[1]

1. INTRODUCTORY

It has long been a commonplace that, in Bernicia, Anglian graves are distinguished only by their scarcity and poverty. This was expressed most starkly by Hunter Blair in 1959. Assessing, in a mere footnote, 'the entire body' of early Anglo-Saxon material from Northumberland, he declared that it 'would be scarcely equivalent to the contents of six well-furnished graves from, for example, the Cambridge region'.[2]

Given the power of Bernicia to resist combined British attacks in the third quarter of the sixth century, and its even more remarkable expansion towards the end of the century under Æthelfrith,[3] the scarcity of pagan burials has presented an enigma. Various explanations have been proffered, some in historical terms, some looking rather to the hazards of archaeological discovery. Perhaps the settlers were indeed few in number. Perhaps the major Anglian settlement did not begin until the end of the pagan era, and hence furnished graves should not be expected; this explanation, however, leaves the paradox of the late sixth-century expansion. Perhaps the lack of gravel-digging,[4] or arable farming,[5] or other soil-disturbing mechanisms, has left pagan cemeteries largely undiscovered.

There may be an element of truth in each of these explanations. But it is the central purpose of this paper to argue that, in so far as they are addressed to the supposed poverty, as well as scarcity, of Anglian graves in Bernicia, they are misconceived. Bernician graves may be few, but they are frequently rich. Their quality first became evident in 1976, with the proper publication, after a lapse of a century, of the Darlington cemetery;[6] for here, in a cemetery of only six burials, there were two swords as well as rich jewellery. This prompted a reassessment of burials and cemeteries between the Tees and the Forth, which is offered to Nowell Myres as a token of gratitude for all his work on grave goods as a basis for settlement studies.[7]

2. THE GRADATION OF PAGAN GRAVES

The starting-point for the present discussion of Bernician graves is the common observation that there is a graded series among at least the weapon-bearing graves of the pagan English. At one extreme are graves which include not only weapons, but body armour as well: helmets and mail coats. These are so rare that they may be disregarded here. Next

---

[1] Originally published, under the title 'Quantity or quality: the Anglian graves of Bernicia' in V. I. Evison (1981), 168–86. The core of the essay was an O'Donnell Lecture, delivered in the University of Edinburgh on 21 April 1978.
[2] P. Hunter Blair (1959), 149, n. 1.
[3] J. N. L. Myres (1936), 422.
[4] D. W Harding (1976b), 44.
[5] M. J. Swanton (1973), 12.
[6] R. Miket and M. Pocock (1976).
[7] For other recent, less optimistic surveys, see R. J. Cramp (1970, 1983); D. W. Harding (1976b), 44.

are graves which contain a sword, and with it probably a scabbard, sword-harness fittings, and also perhaps a spear and a shield. Less well furnished are graves in which the only military gear is a spear, with or without a shield as well. At the bottom of the range are male graves (where the sex can be distinguished) which have only an iron knife and perhaps an iron belt buckle. These scarcely merit consideration as weapon-graves, but must be mentioned to complete the range.[8]

Without at present entering into questions of social stratification (below, Part 4, pp. 261–3), it can be accepted that this graded series marks differences in the value of the weaponry deposited in the grave, reckoned as a factor of the skill and effort needed for its manufacture. In terms of the labour theory of value, a sword-grave is rich; a grave with only a knife is poor; shield plus spear is richer than spear only. In broad terms, the gradations objectively determined in this way may be signalled by calling sword-graves alpha, spear-graves beta, and knife-graves gamma. In the present state of study, this is more helpful than numerical markers. In particular, it could lend itself to refinement: a grave with a sword, ornamented scabbard, jewelled hangings, and other weapons, might be alpha plus, whereas one with only a sword and poor scabbard fittings would be alpha minus.

It is also a commonplace that sword-graves are rare while spear-graves are common.[9] In some cemeteries swords are entirely lacking. A preliminary report on Bishopstone, Sussex, refers to 112 inhumations: 'weaponry in the graves included spears and three shield-bosses but no swords'.[10] At Snell's Corner, Hants, five graves yielded spears, but there were no swords.[11] A single sword is recorded at Finglesham, Kent, in a cemetery with two spear-graves: the sword-grave, G2, is a typical alpha burial, with a spear, shield, and elaborate belt-fittings.[12] At Holywell, Cambridgeshire, there were twenty spear-graves (a small majority also containing a shield), but only one sword-burial was found.[13] At Bergh Apton, Norfolk, there was only one sword in a cemetery with twelve spearmen.[14] Abingdon, Berkshire, exhibits two alpha minus deposits: swords accompanied with little other than scabbard fittings. In addition there were seventeen spear-graves, of which no fewer than nine lacked a shield (beta minus).[15] A variant on the alpha grave is suggested at Petersfinger, Wilts, where, in addition to eleven spear-greaves, there were three sword-graves, of which grave XXI contained an iron battle-axe as well.[16]

It is not considered worth attempting to quantify the gamma graves. Without other diagnostic features, a knife may belong to either a male or a female grave. It seems possible, too, that some burials found without grave goods may formerly have contained small iron knives which have disappeared through corrosion.

While the grading of male, weapon-bearing graves is simple and relatively objective, it is far more difficult to put forward a scheme for women's graves, because of the much wider range of objects in female burials. An iron knife or buckle, or two or three beads may well mark a gamma grave. But at what point in the proliferation of beads, brooches,

[8] There is a preliminary, more tentative statement in L. Alcock (1971; 1973), 291–2.
[9] M. J. Swanton (1973), 2–4; (1974).
[10] M. Bell (1977), 193
[11] G. M. Knocker (1958).
[12] S. E. Chadwick (1958).
[13] T. C. Lethbridge (1931), 1–45.
[14] B. Green and A. Rogerson (1978).
[15] E. T. Leeds and D. B. Harden (1936).
[16] E. T. Leeds and H. de S. Shortt (1953).

chatelaines, work-boxes, and so on do we place the change from beta to alpha? At Holywell, Cambridgeshire, Grave 11 contained, apparently, the body of a child accompanied by a gilt-bronze square-headed brooch; silver bracelets, pendants, and ring; bronze girdle-hangers, buckles, and other belt-fittings; two bronze bowls; beads of amber, crystal, glass, and jet; and an iron weaving batten. Lethbridge reasonably describes this as 'the finery of a young East Anglian lady'.[17] For comparable finery from Kent, we might turn to Finglesham grave D3. Here again was a weaving batten, described by Chadwick as 'clearly a wealthy woman's prerogative'.[18] In Finglesham D3 it was associated with a glass claw-beaker, fifty-two beads of glass and amber, three gold bracelets, five silver brooches further embellished with gilding and garnet inlay, an iron buckle plated with silver, and several minor objects. It would be impossible to grudge an alpha classification to either Holywell 11 or Finglesham D3.

Finglesham E2, with a silver-gilt great square-headed brooch, two other silver-gilt square-heads, a silver disc brooch with garnets, and other trinkets, might be considered alpha minus. So might Holywell 48, with two large and two small cruciform brooches and various beads and pendants; or Holywell 79, with three cruciforms, two small-long brooches, wrist-clasps, girdle hangers, and other miscellanea. At Petersfinger, it would be difficult to assign a grade higher than alpha minus to any female burial: from grave XXV came a gilt-bronze bow brooch, three gilt saucer brooches, two Roman coins, fifty-nine beads of amber, crystal and glass, a buckle, and odd rings, discs, and rods of bronze or iron. Finally, in the case of Abingdon, where two brooches and a string of beads are the height of female display, it is doubtful if any female graves merit alpha at all.

It may be thought that the argument so far has been founded on a very eclectic use of grave-associations. It should therefore be stressed that its basis was a wholly casual collection of cemetery reports, satisfying merely the two criteria that the report should be accessible, and that it should assign objects unequivocally to individual graves. The next part of the discussion is admittedly subjective, and probably tendentious as well. It is not essential to the overall argument of the paper, but it is included in the hope that it might stimulate or provoke some researcher with adequate resources of time to test it fully.

What is now claimed is that, if individual burials can be graded on an alpha-beta-gamma scheme, then so can whole cemeteries. Ideally this should be done by grading each burial, adjusting the grades to a points system, and averaging for the cemetery as a whole. Clearly this would be a lengthy procedure, certainly far more so than the scope of the present paper allows. On the other hand, it should lend itself to analysis by automated methods of information retrieval. For the present what has been done is to take the summary lists of grave goods from Wiltshire and Berkshire in Meaney's *Gazetteer*[19] and assign grades to the cemeteries. These two counties were chosen as representing, so far as any modern counties can, the heartland of pagan Saxon Wessex.

In the larger cemeteries, all three grades may be assigned if, for instance, there are a couple of sword-graves, many spear-burials, and some graves containing only a knife. Using summary lists, it is certain that the gamma element is massively underrepresented. It is also possible, since the presence of swords and rich jewellery stands out in the lists, that the alpha grade is overrepresented. With these warnings, the results may be tabulated.

[17] T. C. Lethbridge (1931), 9.
[18] S. E. Chadwick (1958), 32.
[19] A. L. Meaney (1964).

	Berks.	Wilts.	Total
alpha	8	9	17
beta	28	33	61
gamma	4	9	13

The figures for alpha and beta cemeteries seem consistent enough from one county to the other to give some credibility to the scheme. On the other hand, the ratio of alpha to beta, about 1:3.6, when compared with the sword to spear ratio in any one cemetery, demonstrates how far the alpha element is favoured by the method.

3. THE BERNICIAN GRAVES

With this information about the relative richness of southern English burials in the background, it is now possible to examine the Bernician graves in detail, and attempt to grade them. Two problems arise at the outset: one of definition, the other of the quality of our information.

Firstly, where are we to draw the boundaries of Bernicia? To the south, many distribution maps of the period coyly evade this issue by leaving a gap, roughly between the Tees and the Tyne, separating the names of Bernicia and Deira.[20] Sometimes it is suggested that this was a wilderness, barren of settlement and communications. For the present paper, however, Jackson's bold lead is followed, and the southern boundary of Bernicia is placed on the Tees.[21] On the north, at the very end of the pagan period, the siege and capture of Edinburgh *c.* AD 638 took Bernician power to the shores of the Firth of Forth.[22] Consistent with this, one of the finest, and also one of the latest, objects of filigree and garnet work comes from Dalmeny in West Lothian.

As for the quality of the information available about pagan burials in Bernicia, it scarcely needs saying that not a single cemetery has been reported to the standards considered normal for Wessex or East Anglia. For some of the major finds, the circumstances of discovery are totally unknown. An account of the richest cemetery, that at Darlington, has had to be pieced together from newspaper reports and auctioneers' catalogues.[23] Even the best-reported graves, those at Howick Heugh, were uncovered in quarrying operations; and though records were made during periodic visits by R. C. Bosanquet, it was only after his death that the cemetery and grave goods were written up by G. S. Keeney.[24] It is even more regrettable that in this case, where we can attribute objects to individual graves, the overall grade is gamma, with a few beta elements.

Given the inadequacy of our primary information about find circumstances, we might well feel little confidence in any conclusions to be drawn from it. Despite these reservations, it is worth listing the Bernician burials, and assigning grades to them. In the sequel, the graves are listed alphabetically, with a reference either to Meaney's *Gazetteer*,[25] or to fuller documentation.

[20] e.g. Ordnance Survey (1966).
[21] K. H. Jackson (1969), 7.
[22] P. Hunter Blair (1959); K. H. Jackson (1959).
[23] R. Miket and M. Pocock (1976).
[24] G. S. Keeney (1939).
[25] A. L. Meaney (1964).

BARRASFORD (NTB)   *alpha*
Secondary inhumation in barrow, with abundant grave goods, including a sword, and silver-ornamented shield boss.

Meaney, 198.

BENWELL (NTB)   *beta (? alpha)*
Probably one or more inhumations, with a cruciform and a square-headed brooch, also a glass vessel. If the latter is associated, then alpha would be appropriate.

Meaney, 198.

BOLDON (DRH)   *alpha*
Inhumation burial, with bronze buckle having three bosses ornamented with gold filigree and garnet carbuncles.[26] Although the buckle is the only object known from the grave, the use of gold and garnet argues for the alpha grade.

Meaney, 83.

CAPHEATON (NTB)   *alpha (?)*
Apparently many burials (perhaps not all of this date) secondary in a barrow, from which was also recovered a bronze hanging bowl with two out of three escutcheons present but detached. The hanging bowl suggests at least one alpha-grade burial.

Meaney, 198.

CASTLE EDEN (DRH)   *alpha*
Inhumation burial with a glass claw-beaker.[27] For alpha contexts for claw-beakers, compare Finglesham (KNT) grave D3[28] and Coombe (KNT).[29]

Meaney, 83.

CORBRIDGE (NTB)   *beta (perhaps alpha ?)*
Anglo-Saxon objects, potentially from inhumation burials, include two cruciform brooches (not strictly a pair, but apparently intended to be worn as such) and some beads.[30] There is also a mount for a sword-scabbard which, if it was indeed with an Anglian burial, implies an alpha element.

Meaney, 198.

CORNFORTH (DRH)   *beta*
Eight or nine skeletons in cists, two of them with iron spearheads, marking a beta element. The presence of a horse in one cist could even be interpreted as denoting an alpha grave, but this point is not pressed.

Meaney, 83.

DALMENY, WEST CRAIGIE FARM (WLO)   *alpha*
Some time before 1853, a pyramidal sword ornament was found on the land of West Craigie Farm, Dalmeny, West Lothian (not, as recent accounts claim, in Dalmeny

[26] G. Baldwin Brown (1915), 349, with pl. lxxi, 5.
[27] G. Baldwin Brown (1915), 484, with pl. cxxiv.
[28] S. E. Chadwick (1958), 12, with pl. iv, c.
[29] H. R. E. Davidson and L. Webster (1967), 21, with pl. ii.
[30] G. Baldwin Brown (1915), 811–12, with pl. clviii, 9.

churchyard, nor in Roxburghshire).[31] The pyramid, ornamented with gold filigree and plate garnets[32] was curiously overlooked by Baldwin Brown; this may partly account for claims that no pagan Anglo-Saxon jewellery has ever been found in northern Bernicia. Although we have no information about find circumstances, a rich warrior-grave seems the most likely occasion for the burial in the Lothians of this fine jewel. Certainly, the presence of a sword, scabbard, and harness may be inferred.[33]

DALMENY, HOUND POINT (WLO)   *beta (?)*

An inhumation burial in a cist produced a necklace of glass beads, with a centre-piece of Roman glass. Baldwin Brown seems unreasonably hesitant about an Anglian attribution,[34] while Laing even more unreasonably rejects it as 'not a pagan Saxon deposit, nor is the character in keeping with a Christian grave'.[35]

Meaney, 304.

DARLINGTON (DRH)   *alpha*

The full publication of the finds from this small inhumation cemetery by Miket and Pocock have amply demonstrated its alpha quality.[36] Because of the character of the records, it is not possible to attribute grave goods to individual burials. It is nonetheless clear that among six skeletons of both sexes, both adult and children's, there were two sword-bearing warriors, and perhaps one spearman. Two great square-headed brooches, two cruciforms, two small-longs, and two circular brooches are to be distributed among the womenfolk, implying at least one alpha-grade lady. A chatelaine may also symbolize matronly authority.

GALEWOOD (NTB)   *beta*

Apparently two inhumations, one a woman with a pot, two bronze rings, and a bead, the other male, with two iron spearheads.

Meaney, 198–9.

GREAT TOSSON (NTB)   *beta*

Secondary burials in a barrow, with a bronze buckle and an iron spearhead.

Meaney, 199.

HEPPLE (NTB)   *beta*

An uncertain number of burials found with knives, beads, toilet articles, a bronze chain: all very undistinguished.

Meaney, 199.

---

[31] *Proc. Soc. Antiq. Scotland* 1 (1851–4), 217–18. I am grateful to Mr. J. L. Davidson, Archaeology Branch, Ordnance Survey, for advice on the correct location.
[32] Ll. R. Laing (1973), 46; R. L. S. Bruce-Mitford (1974), 268, with pls. 86e, f, 87.
[33] H. R. E. Davidson (1962), 85–8.
[34] G. Baldwin Brown (1915).
[35] Ll. R. Laing (1973), 45–6.
[36] R. Miket and M. Pocock (1976).

Howick (NTB)   *gamma (beta?)*

Keeney's reconstitution of the evidence of burials and grave goods found in quarrying in 1928–30 demonstrated that they had come from a cemetery of about 15 burials.[37] The only common objects were iron knives which, together with three glass beads, would suggest a gamma grade for the cemetery. Only one burial is raised to the beta level by a spearhead; though an iron horse-bit, if it truly belongs with a burial, may hint at a higher grade.

The grades assigned above may now be tabulated as follows:

alpha	*alpha ?*	*beta*	*beta ?*	*gamma*
5	1	6	1	1

Even if we ignore the queried alpha and beta, the alpha:beta ratio of 5:6 is obviously dramatically different from the observed in Berkshire and Wiltshire. This point is reinforced by consideration of the ratio of sword to spear burials. If we infer that at Darlington there were two sword-burials and one spear-grave, and if we accept the presence of a sword at Dalmeny but not at Corbridge, then we have a 4:6 ratio. Now it can easily be objected that we are dealing with a small sample, and that these ratios could easily be upset by new discoveries. But before too much weight is given to this criticism, it can easily be calculated that to bring the Bernician ratio into line with that for Abingdon (2:17), the next twenty-eight weapon-burials in Bernicia would all have to produce spears, without a single sword. In other words, the number of spears would have to be multiplied nearly five times without any additional swords. Faced with the need for a numerical manipulation of this order, it can scarcely be objected that our Bernician sample is unusably small.

In brief: it can reasonably be inferred that pagan burials in Bernicia, though scant in number, are rich in quality compared with those of Wessex. It can certainly be demonstrated that the proportion of sword-burials to spear-burials is significantly higher. So far as the evidence of weapon-graves can take us, our picture of Wessex, and of East Anglia too, would be of a community of spearmen, with only a small leaven of swordsmen. But for Anglian Bernicia, we see relatively few warriors, and those as likely to be armed with a sword as with a spear. So far as the weapons go, this is the observed evidence: its implications, in terms of social patterns and settlement history, are another matter.

4. The Social Implications of Cemetery-Gradation

Although the pioneers of pagan Saxon archaeology, such as Faussett and Akerman,[38] do not seem to have concerned themselves with apparent differences in wealth between one grave or cemetery and another, it has long been accepted that weapon-graves reflect gradations of rank in early English society.[39] In particular, Davidson has shown that the cost of forging a sword, so well demonstrated by Anstee and Biek,[40] must imply that a sword-grave reflected great wealth, and the corresponding social status of the warrior with whom it was buried.[41] Anthropologically oriented prehistorians are, of course,

[37] G. S. Keeney (1939).
[38] B. Faussett (1773, but published 1856); J. Y. Akerman (1855).
[39] G. Baldwin Brown (1915), 196–7; 205–7.
[40] J. W. Anstee and L. Biek (1961).
[41] H. R. E. Davidson (1962), 211.

working towards similar equations between grave goods and social structure,[42] not always without opposition.[43] Fortunately, in the protohistoric field of pagan England, enough retrospective light is cast by the documents of early history for us to be reasonably certain, firstly, that society was stratified, and secondly, that there is some correlation between the status of the living and the equipment of the dead.

Both these propositions are implicit in poetic sources, and especially in *Beowulf.*[44] We may, however, have reservations, because the poet's picture of pagan society and its customs, although ultimately founded in fact, is none the less idealized or romanticized. Fortunately, no such doubts attach to those legal documents which bring wealth, status, and death into common focus, namely, wills and the payment of heriot on a warrior's death. Brooks has shown that the evidence of wills confirms that of law codes: by the late Saxon period, the payment due from a lesser thegn to his lord consisted of a horse with its gear, a helmet, a mail-coat, a sword, a spear, and a shield.[45] Some two centuries earlier, the capitularies of Charlemagne required a vassal to be equipped with a horse, sword, scramasax, lance, and shield; but the same sources likewise defined the arms of a free man as *scutum et lanceam*: shield and spear.[46] The capitularies reflect here the pattern of Germanic warrior society in the late eighth and early ninth centuries, and equally clearly, the furnishing of our alpha and beta graves two centuries earlier still.

The parallel between warrior status as determined by heriot payments and as reflected in grave goods can be stated even more precisely. Brooks quotes Stein (1967) for the German view that the heriot derived from the pagan practice of burying weapons in the graves of noble warriors, adding that 'the weapons found in the Alemannic aristocratic graves of the seventh and eighth centuries correspond particularly closely with the arms specified in medieval heriots'. In England 'it is certainly possible that the practice of paying a heriot of weapons and treasure to the lord from the goods of a dead noble follower emerged in England ... from the opportunities provided by the abandonment of pagan burial practices'.[47] Finally, we must note his view that 'the evidence of pagan Saxon graves strongly suggests that ... the ubiquitous spear and shield were the basic equipment of free men'.[48]

In sum, then, the documentary evidence encourages us to see a threefold division of the early Anglo-Saxons into thegns, *ceorls* or free warriors, and the unfree. This social stratification is represented in the grave furniture by the three classes of alpha, beta, and gamma graves.

Even if this picture is correct only in broad terms, it could ultimately provide a basis for assessing the relative numbers of the three classes in any one community, in so far as that community is represented by its cemetery. Already we can see in Wessex a society comprising a few sword-bearing thegns, probably underrepresented in the graves because of the practice of handing swords down from generation to generation;[49] a large mass of yeoman-warriors, the *ceorls*; and a substratum of the unfree, difficult to quantify at present

[42] For instance: J. A. Brown (1971); R. W. Chapman (1977); J. A. Tainter (1975); also D. L. Clarke and B. Chapman (1978), 140.

[43] P. J. Ucko (1969).

[44] R. J. Cramp (1957); P. Wormald (1978).

[45] N. P. Brooks (1978), 81.

[46] Ibid., 82–3.

[47] Ibid., 90–2.

[48] Ibid., 83.

[49] H. R. E. Davidson (1962), 118.

because of the povery of their graves. This view, derived from our analysis of the Wiltshire and Berkshire cemeteries, agrees reasonably with the picture of Wessex society which we gain, for instance, from the Wessex law codes and other documentary sources.

But if the arguments deployed here about the correlation of grave furniture with social status are reasonable, and if the analysis of the Bernician graves in Part 3 above is sound, then the social structure of Bernicia ought to be different from that of Wessex. Such a conclusion need not surprise us, for it is already implicit in Bede's account of the North-umbrian king's thegn, *minister regis*, Imma (HE, iv, 22).[50] Wounded and captured in a battle against the Mercians, Imma attempted to escape death by claiming to be not a soldier, *miles*, but a *ceorl* or yokel, *rusticus*, who was poor and recently married, and had merely come to the battlefield to bring supplies for the troops.

It is difficult to reconcile Bede's antithesis of peasant and soldier with the military obligations of the Wessex *ceorl* as set out, for instance, in Ine's Laws (Ine 51).[51] It is true that Finberg, while accepting that the *ceorl* was liable for military service, claims that 'the story of Imma shows conclusively that the husbandman's place was in the commissariat, not in the fighting line'.[52] Given that the Wessex *ceorl* was a freeman with military obligations, and that 'the bearing of arms was in Germanic society a symbol of legal freedom',[53] such an interpretation seems perverse. It is certainly impossible to reconcile with the presence of spears, and frequently shields as well, in the generality of Wessex male graves. Archaeological evidence and documentary sources concur in presenting the mass of Wessex peasants as warriors too.

But the contrast between *miles* and *rusticus*, soldier and husbandman, may be explained if we remember not only that Imma was a Northumbrian thegn, but also that our source, Bede, was Northumbrian, and a man of literally cloistered experience at that. If the high ratio of sword- to spear-graves in Bernicia really has social implications, then it must surely imply a society in which warrior-peasants were thin on the ground, and warrior-aristocrats relatively numerous. This is the social background which Bede's account of Imma requires in order to appear credible.

5. THE ANGLIAN ELEMENT IN BERNICIA

It is agreed that Anglian burials are scanty in Bernicia. In Part 3 it has been shown that, among the few graves, sword burials are commoner in relation to spear burials than is the case in Wessex. In Part 4, it is argued that this implies a different social structure too: one in which the class of spear-bearing freemen was unimportant as compared with the sword-bearing thegnly class. If, in this respect, the graves accurately reflect the character of Anglian society in Bernicia, then the further point may be advanced that in its social structure Anglian society must have differed little from the British society which it supplanted.

We have, of course, no cemetery evidence for the structure of British society, but there is at least helpful documentary evidence. The Welsh law books,[54] though strictly relevant only to early medieval Wales, have echoes in Northumbria which reveal the character of

[50] B. Colgrave and R. A. B. Mynors (1969), 400–5.
[51] D. Whitelock (1979), 404; N. P. Brooks (1971), 69.
[52] H. P. R. Finberg (1974), 68.
[53] N. P. Brooks (1978), 83.
[54] Most easily accessible in M. Richards (1954).

the pre-Anglian arrangements there.[55] By contrast, the *Gododdin* poem is absolutely relevant to Bernicia on the very eve of the Anglian takeover; if, that is, we can believe that its core is the authentic work of the poet Aneirin, composed in the decades around AD 600. The arguments in favour of this are not beyond question, but they have recently been strongly reaffirmed from a historian's point of view.[56]

The law books reveal a sharply tapered pyramid: at the top, the king; immediately below him, a small group of officials, and the rather larger *teulu*, the king's bodyguard or war-band;[57] and then, as a very broad base, the bondmen, tillers of the soil and suppliers of the services and renders in kind which supported king, *teulu*, and officials.[58] There is no sign here of the free, spear-bearing peasantry of Wessex.

Taken at face-value, the evidence of the *Gododdin* is in agreement, for the poem, itself a series of elegies on fallen warriors, incorporates the story of a force of only 300 warriors: the war-band of Mynyddog Mwynfawr of Edinburgh, augmented from other kingdoms for a special campaign. This small band consists principally, if not entirely, of mounted warriors, armed with swords and spears, we cannot say in what ratio. Jackson has argued, however, from general military probabilities, from one express mention of infantry, and from the fact that parts of the action at Catraeth were fought on foot, 'that "three hundred" means three hundred picked chiefs, each of whom would have with him a sufficient complement of supporting foot-soldiers'. He has suggested 'anything up to three thousand or more would perhaps be reasonable' for the whole army.[59]

Jackson's figure was rejected by Alcock,[60] partly on the basis of the social analysis advanced above, partly from a wider examination of the size of Dark Age armies. In reviewing Alcock 1971, Jackson modified his original figure: 'perhaps only two or three [retainers to each mounted noble], making the army total about 1,000, would be acceptable'.[61] On present evidence, the hypothesis that the mounted warrior aristocrats of the Gododdin were accompanied by unsung infantry retainers can neither be proved or disproved. What is certain is that, as a class, such men have left no evidence of their existence in the law codes. From other documentary evidence, Davies has concluded that in another British area, south-east Wales, 'the existence of untied completely free peasantry is neither demonstrable nor deniable'.[62]

The British evidence would seem, then, to point to a society in which free, weapon-bearing peasantry were not prominent. The Bernician graves indicate a similar social structure: one very different from pagan Wessex, and equally different from our general picture of Germanic society. Jolliffe showed long ago that the administrative arrangements of Northumbria owed much to British pre-Anglian organization.[63] Taken altogether, evidence of varied kinds suggests that a very few Anglian thegns, supported by a small number of retainers, took over the territory and organization of the British Votadini as a going concern.

---

[55] J. E. A. Jolliffe (1926); W. Rees (1963); W. E. Kapelle (1979); see also Chapter 4 above.

[56] K. H. Jackson (1969); D. N. Dumville (1978); T. M. Charles-Edwards (1978). But see also comments in Chapter 16 above.

[57] L. Alcock (1971; 1973), 324–5; Chapter 19 below.

[58] G. R. J. Jones (1972), 299 ff.

[59] K. H. Jackson (1969), 15.

[60] L. Alcock (1971; 1973), 336.

[61] K. H. Jackson (1973), 80.

[62] W. Davies (1978a), 47.

[63] J. E. A. Jolliffe (1926).

There are other pointers in the same direction. The 'E' recension of the Anglo-Saxon Chronicle, s.a. 547, describes Ida's building of Bamburgh in terms reminiscent of the fortification of a late Saxon *burh*: 'first enclosed with a stockade, and afterwards with a wall'.[64] This would seem to reflect a tenth- or eleventh-century source,[65] rather than a sixth-century one. Indeed, if Ida really had built Bamburgh, this would be highly remarkable, for we have no other evidence that the early English built fortified places.[66] On the other hand, *Historia Brittonum* provides us with a British name for Bamburgh: Din Guoaroy or some such.[67] This British, and therefore pre-Anglian, name, clearly implies a pre-Anglian *din* or fort. We may reasonably see Bamburgh, therefore, as a British promontory fort, which came into the possession of the Bernician dynasty, whether by gift or seizure, in the mid-sixth century. In other words, as a royal city (*urbs regia*) of Bernicia, Bamburgh results from the Anglian take-over of a British centre of power.

The same seems to be true of another Bernician royal site, the *villa regia . . . Adgefrin*, Yeavering. The entrance arrangements of the remarkable palisaded fort here—bulbous rampart terminals containing a rectangular timber structure—mark it as a Votadinian work, with antecedents in Harehope II, and probably Hogbridge, Peebleshire, as well.[68] On this evidence alone, it would be possible to postulate that the Bernician dynasty had taken over a British fortified political centre at Yeavering. This conclusion, already tenable before the full publication of the Yeavering excavations, has now been strongly reinforced by the very varied evidence of Bernician indebtedness to the Britons at Yeavering.[69] Moreover, the succession of royal or thegnly halls at Doon Hill, East Lothian, also argues for an Anglian take-over, perhaps by force, of a prestigious British site.[70]

Finally, there is a distinct probability that the Bernician Angles inherited from the Britons a major military technique: the use of cavalry. The earliest reference to a mounted force among the Anglo-Saxons appears to be in Eddius' *Life of Wilfrid*.[71] He tells us that, about AD 672, Ecgfrith of the Bernician dynasty, in the face of a Pictish rebellion, *statim equitatui exercitu praeparato . . . invasit*, 'having got together a cavalry force, immediately invaded'. I know of no earlier reference to the use of cavalry in battle among the Angles or their continental ancestors. On the other hand, as we have seen, mounted warriors formed the core, if not indeed the whole, of the army of Gododdin. It seems likely, therefore, that the Angles of Bernicia learned this new technique of warfare, which must have included the breeding and training of horses for battle, from the Britons. They may have done so, of course, by contact on the field of battle. But given the clear social implications of this expensive new technique,[72] it is altogether more probable that it was part of the overall package of social and administrative organization which they acquired from the Britons.

[64] J. Earle and C. Plummer (1892), 16–17.
[65] For which there are other arguments, as Professor D. Whitelock kindly informed me.
[66] L. Alcock (1978b); Chapter 15 above.
[67] K. H. Jackson (1963), 27–8.
[68] L. Alcock (1979b).
[69] B. Hope-Taylor (1977).
[70] N. Reynolds (1980).
[71] As B. Colgrave pointed out in 1927, 165; text, ibid., 40–3; but H. M. Chadwick (1907), 159, n. 1, took a less rigid line.
[72] N. P. Brooks (1978).

6. Epilogue

Parts 4 and 5 of this paper have taken us a long way from the original study of the Bernician graves, on an exploration of the sociological significance of grave-archaeology: a significance which is often hinted at,[73] but all too rarely pursued. It is no doubt appropriate that this exploration should have been attempted in an area of considerable interplay between German and Celt; for over the past two decades most of the progress in combining archaeology with varied documentary sources in order to write a richly-textured economic and social history has been made in Celtic areas. At a time, too, when a major survey of Anglo-Saxon archaeology[74] gives little weight to cemeteries and grave-goods, it may have been useful to reassert the historical potential of the traditional materials of pagan archaeology.

At the end of the journey, we are very close to Myres's position in 1936. He then wrote: 'in Bernicia a far greater proportion of the native lands were at first left for tributary British subjects of the new military aristocracy than was the case in those parts of Britain where the invaders were rather seeking habitable lands for themselves than to live on the rents of a dependent native population'.[75] This seems to represent very well the balance of Angle and Briton in Bernician society. To it we would only add that, increasingly, the evidence leads us to believe that the Anglian aristocracy took over the political, military, social, and economic arrangements of the Votadinian Britons as a going concern.

Postscript

Since this essay was written, much of relevance to the evidence and interpretations which it presents has appeared in P. Rahtz *et al.* (1980). Especially important is R. Miket's paper, 'A re-statement of evidence for Bernician Anglo-Saxon burials' (P. Rahtz *et al.* (1980), 289-305), which takes a far more pessimistic and negative attitude to the burial evidence, and goes on to question the current emphasis on British, rather than Anglian elements in the population of Bernicia.

For the problems of inferring social status from grave goods, see also J. Shephard, 'The social identity of the individual in isolated barrows and barrow cemeteries in Anglo-Saxon England', in B. C. Burnham and J. Kingsbury (eds) (1979), 47–9. E.-J. Pader's interesting discussion of symbolism, social relations and the interpretation of mortuary remains (1982) seems to me to be weakened by an excessively rigid theoretical stance, and by an apparent ignorance of the kind of documentary evidence deployed by N. P. Brooks (1978); see p. 262 above. Finally it should be noticed that R. Cramp has directly questioned the methodology of the present paper (1983, 269–70).

---

[73] E.g. A. L. Meaney and S. C. Hawkes (1970); P. V. Addyman (1976).
[74] D. M. Wilson (1976).
[75] J. N. L. Myres (1936), 422.

CHAPTER 18

Roman Britons and Pagan Saxons: an Archaeological Appraisal[1]

The *Anglo-Saxon Chronicle, sub anno* 457, says:

> Hengest and Aesc fought against the Britons at . . . Crayford and slew four thousand men, and the Britons forsook Kent and fled to London in great terror.

Again, *sub anno* 491, we read:

> Aelle and Cissa besieged Anderida and slew all the inhabitants; not even one Briton was left there.

And *sub anno* 508, dealing with Wessex, we find:

> Cerdic and Cynric slew a Welsh King and five thousand men with him.

Now, for all the difficulties of accepting the early annals of the *Chronicle* as an accurate historical record, entries like these do seem to embody a tradition that the settlement of the Anglo-Saxons in south-eastern Britain was accompanied by the expulsion or extermination of the native Britons. This judgement on the nature of the English settlement may perhaps be reinforced by an appeal to the writings of the monk Gildas. But it was not acceptable to the late Charles J. O'Donnell. He believed that the Britons largely survived, and that if you scratch an Englishman, you will find a Briton beneath the skin. He therefore endowed lectures with the fundamental purpose of uncovering, in the language, customs and population of England, the subcutaneous Celt.

In essaying this task I find myself in a situation of some irony. In 1965, reviewing some published O'Donnell lectures, I wrote: 'in our present state of ignorance and half-knowledge, more can be achieved by detailed discussions on a narrow front . . . [than by examining] the O'Donnell theme very broadly'. This, indeed, I profoundly believe. But the Board of Celtic Studies has placed on me the responsibility of being the first archaeologist to deliver O'Donnell lectures in the University of Wales; and this entails the further responsibility of surveying the potential archaeological evidence widely rather than digging deep in one small corner. It will be for other archaeologists in the future to survey special aspects of the O'Donnell field. We may hope that they will then take some of my sketches and elaborate, perfect, or erase them.

In essence, the O'Donnell lectures treat of the relations between Britons and English. An archaeologist must stress at once that the initial contacts between the Britons and the Germanic ancestors of the English lie back in the third century AD, when the Britons were romanized, and the contacts were mediated through Roman authority. This has the

---

[1] The University of Wales O'Donnell Lecture, 1965–6, originally printed in *Welsh History Review*, 3 (1966–7), 228–49. In preparing a printed version of this paper, I benefited from the advice and comments of my colleagues in University College, Cardiff, and of Professor C. F. C. Hawkes and Mrs S. C. Hawkes. I did, however, leave the paper largely as it was delivered, in the hope that the immediacy of the spoken word might compensate for the ineluctable ephemerality of any archaeological generalization.

advantage that the present enquiry can begin in a period about which archaeologists are competent to make some positive statements. The most striking evidence for ancestral Englishmen in Roman Britain is provided by the altars set up at Housesteads, on Hadrian's Wall, in honour of certain Germanic gods, by a unit of Frisian cavalry; for, despite Bede's neglect of them, the Frisians were certainly one of the Germanic peoples who contributed to the English stock. Similar dedications by the *numerus Hnaudifridi*— Notfried's Irregulars, like Cameron's Highlanders or Lovat's Scouts—reveal a German unit serving on the Wall under its own tribal leader perhaps as early as the third century. Such units must have become increasingly common in the following century, when the historian Ammianus tells us of a unit of Alamanni serving under their *rex*, Fraomarius. But by this time, large and wholly Roman military units were under German commanders. In the great disaster of 367, both the *comes maritimi tractus* and the *dux Britanniarum* were Germans.

There is other archaeological evidence for the use of Germanic troops to defend the province of Britain against her barbarian assailants. Pottery with strongly-marked Frisian characteristics occurs in cemeteries outside Roman forts and towns in eastern England, and it has been claimed that this marks the burial of German federates or allies, who had been recruited and settled by Roman authority. (The use of the technical term *foederati* is not, in fact, helpful here.) The evidence of this 'Anglo-Frisian' pottery may be supplemented by that of other urns which would be dated before AD 400 on the continent, and which likewise demonstrates the introduction of Germans to eastern Britain in some capacity or other before the end of the fourth century.

The case is further strengthened by the occurrence in Britain of late fourth-century buckles and belt fittings which have good parallels in Germanic warrior graves along the Rhineland frontier of the Roman Empire. In this country, these buckles occur mostly as strays, and it is at least curious that when they do occur in graves, with one exception the bodies are female; but then, the buckles from the English graves are normally unserviceable, and belong to a large class of broken Roman bronzes from Saxon burials which must be discussed later. We cannot doubt that the buckles and similar equipment represent a Germanic element in the troops under Roman command in the later fourth century; and we must therefore affirm that in the fourth, and indeed earlier, centuries German soldiers played a large part in defending the province of Britain, not only against other Germans, but also against the Irish and the Picts.

The next stage of our enquiry must be an examination of the state of the province of Britain in the fourth century; and in this the evidence of archaeology is paramount. The major element in the romanization of Britain was, of course, the towns. When all allowance has been made for the patchy nature of our evidence, especially where Roman towns can only be explored through post-medieval basements, it appears that the towns were flourishing in the fourth century. It is true that some public buildings were in decay, but not all. As for private houses, there is accumulating evidence for building and maintenance work throughout the century. And in the public sector, we now recognize that not only were town defences well maintained, but their effectiveness was drastically improved by the addition of bastions: that is, projecting platforms for artillery pieces. These presumably imply military detachments in the towns and they may partly account for the occurrence of Germanic buckles in urban contexts. We may conclude that the troubled conditions of the fourth century, and especially the great barbarian raid of 367, had given the towns a powerful new *raison d'être* as defensive centres.

Indeed, to a raiding party, whether Saxon, Pictish or Irish, there can have been no apparent difference between a town and a fort of the new Saxon Shore style; both had high walls with projecting bastions, discharging a hail of ballista bolts. In the *Notitia Galliarum* some towns are expressly called *castrum*—Castrum Uindonissense, Fort Uindonissa, for instance; and it is tempting to think that, if we had a similar document for Britain, we might find the same thing here. This may be relevant to the borrowing of the Latin word *castra*, or more probably *castrum*, into Anglo-Saxon as a normal word for 'town'. Philologists appear to have overlooked the fact that it is not a normal Latin word for town, and they have failed to consider why the Latin word for 'fort' or 'encampment' should have been applied to towns. We can now see that the architectural assimilation of forts and towns in the fourth century provides a possible explanation, and we may further suggest that the borrowing took place among ancestral Englishmen serving as garrisons in both Roman towns and forts.

In the countryside, the major romanized feature was the villa. This constitutes the most numerous class of Roman structure known to the archaeologist; it is also the worst-excavated and the least adequately published. Despite this, it seems safe to say that the fourth century saw the heyday of the villa in Britain. Not only were relatively modest establishments rebuilt at this time; it is now that the largest and most luxurious villas reach their apogee. Undoubtedly some villas may have suffered in the great raid of 367 and in other less-documented attacks, though the supposed evidence for this is not always simple to interpret. It is easy to picture raiders wantonly casting corpses down a well; more difficult to imagine them being so careless with coins; and altogether impossible to believe that they would have troubled to heave stone columns and capitals into the water. Evidence like this may refer rather to social upheavals at the end of the century than to barbarian raids; but whatever its explanation, it does not represent the general fate of villas in Britain. On other villas there are conflicting trends in the late fourth century: in some, the laying of new mosaic floors; in others, the breaking-up of floors in order to insert corn-drying kilns, marking clearly a degrading of the status of the room in question.

The farming system which the villas worked can no longer be described with confidence. Three different types of plough were in use by the fourth century; and two different forms of field were tilled, one the small, squarish, 'Celtic' field, the other a longer, narrower strip. But we cannot positively correlate either plough or field type with the villas. Nor is the relationship of the villas and other, less-romanized farms clear. It has been suggested that these so-called 'native farms' were the homes of the *coloni* or tenants of the villas; but the observed geographical distribution of romanized and unromanized farms does not lend weight to the hypothesis. Here, the lack of documents is a bar to a fuller understanding of the archaeological evidence. We can at least accept that there were *coloni* in Britain, and we may speculate that they were the progenitors, institutionally-speaking if in no other way, of the bondmen of British society in the fifth or later centuries. Perhaps the most positive result of recent archaeological work has been to emphasize that the Roman Britons, whether from villas or 'native' farms, were exploiting valley-bottom as well as down-land soils, and that much low-lying arable land was under cultivation. It may be suspected that by the fourth century AD the spectacular Celtic field systems of the downs were as marginal as they have since remained.

Whether they lived in country or in town, the inhabitants of Roman Britain enjoyed a rich variety of material possessions. Archaeologically, the most copious of these is the pottery: competent, serviceable vessels, aesthetically dull for the most part, but occasionally enlivened by animals and floral motifs in a free-flowing style. In this some have discerned the Celtic love of the curvilinear breaking out; others attribute it to the technical exigencies of barbotine work. It is at least certain that much of the pottery found here was manufactured in this country by a highly capitalized industry, geared to an economy in which commerce was well developed. We can be less certain of the place of manufacture of other goods and especially of the metalwork. The study of Romano-British ironwork is in its infancy; that of the ubiquitous trinkets of bronze is as yet unborn, except in its typological and art-historical aspects. When we find that the penannular brooch, a type which was perhaps invented in pre-Roman Britain, remained popular throughout the Roman period, we must believe that British craftsmen continued to make it. There are other undoubtedly British brooches—the dragonesque, for example— which show that in the early Roman period British craftsmen were competent in enamel and inlaid metalwork. But for want of technological studies, we do not know the range of techniques in the hands of British metalworkers in the fourth century, nor can we say with confidence which pieces are British and which are Gallo-Roman.

The way of life and material culture of the ancestral English in their continental homelands were, of course, quite different from what I have outlined in Roman Britain. They had, it is true, competent metalworkers producing a variety of tools, weapons and trinkets. But their pottery, hand-modelled rather than industrially-produced, was lump-ish in form and ornament. They too were farmers, both raising stock and tilling the land, but we no longer believe that they worked strip-fields with a heavy, wheeled plough. Their farmsteads were frequently spacious dwellings, as commodious as many of the smaller Roman villas, but they were ignorant of mortared masonry, and built entirely in timber. Finally, though they often lived in sizeable nucleated villages in their native lands, they did not live in towns. This is not to say that when they were brought into contact with civilization, they shunned towns and town-life. I find no evidence for this, nor for the belief that when they settled in Britain they avoided Roman towns through superstitious dread.

Having thus outlined the principal features of fourth-century Britain as they appear to an archaeologist, I should now enquire which of them continued into the fifth century, and were then accepted or rejected by the incoming Anglo-Saxons. But before I do so, I may perhaps be allowed a brief historical excursus. Our picture of the events of the fifth century has for too long been centred on Bede's concept of an *Adventus Saxonum* which was a major, catastrophic and datable event. Recently, it is true, this fire-and-slaughter picture has shown signs of crumbling, especially since the recognition that there were Germanic peoples in Britain in the fourth century and the first half of the fifth. Indeed, it has seemed possible that some of us might wish to replace the picture furnished by Bede, Gildas and the *Anglo-Saxon Chronicle* with one which might best be described as the English-without-tears picture. But now the fire-and-slaughter picture has been colourfully refurbished by the suggestion that the invasions of Kent, Sussex and Wessex, listed separately and serially in the *Anglo-Saxon Chronicle*, were really a single co-ordi-nated operation datable to the mid fifth century. We must, of course, admit that on technical, chronological grounds the *anno domini* dates of the fifth century in the *Chronicle* are valueless. This is a good reason for abandoning any attempt to use them to write narrative history, but it surely does not license us to shuffle events around to fit some preconceived pattern.

To my mind, we possess enough historical and quasi-historical notices to realize that the politico-military events of the fifth century were complex, but not enough to enable us to thread a path through the maze of that complexity. Two little-regarded facts seem to me to be curious and possibly significant. First, Zosimus at least thought that the end of Roman Britain came not with a whimper but a bang of revolt; whether inspired by political, social or religious motives matters not. Secondly, as late as the third generation of the fifth century, a nation which allegedly had become wholly dependent on Germanic troops for its defence was able to send a large war-band to Gaul to assist Anthemius, Augustus of the West, against the Visigoths. Taken together, these two facts could imply a greater degree of independence and vigour, both political and military, on the part of the Britons than we might infer from Gildas's groans.

From the problems of political history we must turn now to the archaeological evidence for the continuance into the fifth century of those elements of material culture which we discerned in the fourth. Here at once the very concept of continuity presents us with a problem. The question has been shrewdly asked: 'how anyone would "prove" the continuous existence of an English village which appears for the first time in a Saxon charter of the eighth century, reappears in Domesday Book 300 years later, and is then again lost to view until the thirteenth century'. An answer to this might be that between the eighth and thirteenth centuries there was no major change in population or language, and therefore no reason to expect discontinuity, and every reason to assume continuity. If, therefore, the name of a village remains the same—allowing for inevitable linguistic evolution—then we can accept that the village was continuously occupied. But these arguments will not see us through the period of our present interest. The salient fact of that period is that over a large area of Britain the language was changed from British to English; and this change was accompanied, or indeed brought about, by a change in population which may have been on a major scale; I say 'may', because the scale of that change of population is one of the matters which might be discussed within my present terms of reference. At any rate, considering, firstly, that there was some change in the population of England in the fifth century, and, secondly, that the material culture of the English in their continental homelands was markedly different from that of the Roman Britons, we have no need to expect cultural continuity, and no right to assume it. It becomes a subject for discussion and, perhaps, proof.

But here we find two different approaches to the idea of continuity, almost indeed two different meanings for the word. There appears to be a school of local historians and historical geographers which is prepared to postulate continuity not merely of settlement, but even of social and administrative arrangements, if, within an area a mile or so across, they find some Roman building, and also a medieval court or manor-house; or if they find a pre-Roman hill-fort within five miles of some medieval territorial centre. Indeed, the social arrangements which facilitated the building of Stonehenge in the early second millennium BC have been detected in the manorial organization of the second millennium AD. To the archaeologist, however, the word 'continuity' implies something altogether more precise, more particular, more contiguous. For the fifth century both the concept and the fact are splendidly exemplified at Dorchester-on-Thames.

Dorchester-on-Thames was a small Romano-British town, perhaps founded on a pre-Roman Belgic site. Sections cut across the defences display a history characteristic of many such towns: an originally open settlement was embanked in the late second century; the bank was reinforced with a stone facing-wall in the late third century, and artillery bastions may have been added after AD 360. But it is to a small area-excavation in the interior of the town that we turn for evidence of continuity in the fifth century and beyond. The evidence takes three forms: continuity of the find-sequence, of building activity, and of town layout. In terms of finds, a coin hoard of Honorius and Arcadius takes us into the fifth century. Characteristic Anglo-Frisian pottery, found lying over a Roman street, may be dated around the middle of the century, while certain hybrid vessels, Anglo-Frisian in form but more Roman in ware, should also belong to this time. The following century is represented by vessels which have parallels elsewhere in Oxfordshire, datable, by their association with brooches, to the second half of the sixth century. Less closely datable pottery of 'middle Saxon' type carries us into the period of the Conversion, when Dorchester was the site of the first Wessex bishopric.

In terms of building activity, the early fifth century saw the erection of a characteristic Roman building, rectangular in plan, with mortared stone footings supporting a timbered superstructure. Since a roughly-cobbled yard outside the building overlay a very worn coin datable to AD 394–5, it is possible to assign the construction of the building to the years 400–25. Such a timbered house, set on a stone sleeper wall, might well have survived for several generations before another building, Saxon in character and wholly of timber, was laid across its ruins. Meanwhile, however, to the north of the late Roman building, a characteristically Saxon *Grubenhaus* or semi-subterranean building was constructed. The precise nature of this is difficult to reconstruct, but since its principal feature was a stratified series of hearths and ovens, it was probably a kitchen or bakery for some adjacent surface structure. From the latest floor and the destruction level of this *Grubenhaus* came the pottery which has already been mentioned as datable to the later sixth century. The inference is, then, that the first use of this building goes back into the early sixth century, perhaps overlapping that of the late Roman building. Last of all, a large rectangular building of timber was laid across the filled-in *Grubenhaus*; this must date to the middle or late Saxon period.

Finally, continuity of civic layout. The late Roman building stands alongside one of the north–south streets of the town. The *Grubenhaus* was entered by a crude flight of steps leading down from the edge of that street. As for the later Saxon timber building, one row of the posts which supported the roof was dug through the metalling of the road; but since the building itself was aligned at right angles to it, it is clear that the road was still in being, even if building frontages were not being maintained.

Now it should be emphasized that, taken separately, the site of the late Roman building and that of the *Grubenhaus* would never have suggested any degree of continuity. In terms of stratification, we should note that humus immediately overlies the footings of the Roman building, as well as the Saxon structures. But when we take the whole assemblage of evidence, there can be no doubt at all that at Dorchester-on-Thames we have continuity of occupation from the fourth through the fifth into later centuries. The shrinkage of the town to a village, which has ultimately made possible the area-excavation in the interior, is part of its later history. Dorchester was the first Roman town where the presence of Germanic troops under Roman command was recognized archaeologically, and it is tempting to believe that it was these troops who eased the transition from Roman Britain to Saxon England, and made continuity of settlement possible. However that may be, Dorchester provides a touchstone for the critical assay of the evidence from other Roman towns.

It can be said at once that no other town produces quite the range of evidence of Dorchester; but Canterbury and Verulamium come close to it. At Canterbury, for instance, there is a number of *Grubenhäuser*, and also pottery of Anglo-Frisian type, which perhaps suggest the presence of Germanic troops in the fifth century. Pottery and burials of the later fifth and sixth centuries, from around the town, suggest further continuity of occupation. The scale of this is difficult to judge, however, because of the restricted nature of research and publication. It has, indeed, been argued that there can have been no continuity of civic control, because the Roman street-plan was lost. It is curious, however, to notice that while the modern street-plan does not agree with the Roman street-grid, it is nonetheless in reasonable conformity with the orientation of the principal known Roman public building, the theatre. Finally, we should note Bede's statement that in the late sixth century Queen Bertha was worshipping in 'a church built of old in honour of S. Martin while yet the Romans inhabited Britain'. Fragments of this church have been recognized; and though a recent authority would regard them as 'probably of sub-Roman or early Anglo-Saxon rather than of Roman construction', there is no technical reason why this should be so, unless indeed the dedication itself is put in evidence. If we accept Bede's authority over a question where it is likely to be reliable, then we have evidence that a building erected before AD 400 was still serviceable around AD 600.

This point, that structures of mortared brick and stone are built to be durable, has not normally commended itself to Romano-British archaeologists, but it has recently been made in connection with Verulamium. Here a sizeable mansion, erected as late as AD 370, was lavishly remodelled as late as 390 or 400; further, more mundane modifications must take us into the fifth century. At some date now unascertainable, but at any rate well after 400, the mansion was demolished and a large hall built upon its site. Ultimately, this too was demolished and a wooden pipe-line laid across the area. This complicated sequence argues that building activity was continuing well down the fifth century, while the last phase, the water-pipe, argues for a continuance of romanized civic traditions. Elsewhere in the town, we may believe that other private houses built in the fourth century lasted for a century or more. It is noteworthy that this is happening in a town where there is no evidence for Germanic troops. Moreover, there are no early cemeteries betokening settlement in its vicinity. This may argue that the *municipium* of Verulamium had successfully looked to its own defence.

For other towns the evidence is far less cogent, but this may be due as much to the destruction of post-Roman levels by medieval or later pits and buildings, or to restricted or incompetent excavation, as to lack of occupation in the late fifth or sixth centuries. At Winchester, timber buildings with cobbled floors were built over the Roman streets sometime between the fifth and tenth centuries and they are taken as implying a breakdown of civic control. At Silchester, painstaking search through the relics of old excavations has produced a very few objects of the fifth to seventh centuries, some British and others Saxon; but they are too few to tell a story.

But if, in some of the Roman towns of eastern and midland England, we find evidence for the breakdown of civic control, or a lack of evidence of continuous occupation through the fifth and sixth centuries, we should now notice that these phenomena should not necessarily be attributed to Germanic raids or to the supposed barbarian dread of towns. For similar phenomena can be observed in western Britain, beyond the range of early English settlement, and even in Wales. It is now well established that from about AD 470 the lands around the Irish Sea—Ireland, Wales, south-west England and south-west Scotland—were importing very distinctive pottery from the eastern Mediterranean. None of this has yet been recognized in extensive excavations at Caerwent or at

Cirencester. This implies that by the end of the fifth century, neither of these towns was functioning as a commercial centre. It is, therefore, no surprise that in each case the Roman street-plan broke down save for the continuance of through roads linking the principal gates, or rather the principal gaps through the defences. It may be that for general economic reasons we ought to expect a collapse of urban life and organization in the fifth century; and if this is so, the evidence for continuity at Dorchester-on-Thames, Canterbury and Verulamium becomes all the more striking.

One other piece of evidence has been used to suggest that the towns formed a particularly tough element in the politico-military situation of the fifth century. About a score of Romano-British town names survived to form at least an element in the modern place-name. On the other hand, except for the special case of Canterbury, none of the names of the tribes which had been administered from the cities survived as post-Roman town names, and in England only the Cantii survived even as a regional name. This is in striking contrast to Gaul, where the tribal names regularly become the city names. This shows clearly that in England, the political organization of the *civitas* did not persist; and it should be noted in passing that even in Wales, only the Deceangli and the Demetae survived as the political units of Tegeingl and Dyfed. By contrast, the towns themselves seem to have been more resistant. But there is another way of looking at this. The political organization of a *civitas* existed essentially in the realm of ideas; when it collapsed it would leave no tangible relics, but would vanish utterly. But a Roman town, even with its civic organization gone, its buildings largely in ruins, its population reduced to half-a-dozen families, would remain for centuries as a landmark, a place requiring a name; and what more natural than that enquiring Anglo-Saxons should learn and adopt the British name? So we should be very cautious in the conclusions that we draw from the survival of Roman city names.

Other archaeological remains have, however, been put in evidence for the survival of the political organization of the *civitas*: namely, a number of defensive or boundary dykes. Now it is common ground that at Bokerly Dyke, south-west of Salisbury, a dyke system was first established about 325, and was later thrown into a defensive posture in the great barbarian raid of 367, and again at the very end of the fourth century or the beginning of the fifth. In East Anglia the evidence for the date of the well-known group of dykes is less clear cut, but the balance of probability suggests that some of them were dug under Roman authority at the very end of the fourth century and were already silted up by the late fifth century. Thus, neither Bokerly nor the East Anglian dykes are relevant to our immediate discussion. For possible dyke-building by a post-Roman political authority, we must turn to the area north-west of Silchester, where it has been argued that a series of dykes defended the post-Roman successor of the *civitas Atrebatum* against early English settlement in the Upper Thames Valley, and screened Silchester against movement between Dorchester-on-Thames and the Salisbury region. But it should be noticed that none of these dykes has been satisfactorily dated by excavation; that it is now recognized that dykes were built in pre-Roman Britain as well as in the period under discussion; and that though the Silchester Grim's Bank appears to rest its flank on a Roman road, this is as likely to reflect a fourth-century date, on the analogy of Bokerly Dyke, as one in the late fifth century.

Finally, as another possible example of a British community retaining into the late fifth century the authority to organize a labour force and undertake a sizeable military work, we may notice the suggestion that East Wansdyke was a creation of Ambrosius

Aurelianus, designed to cover the Amesbury region against danger from the Upper Thames—against those very Germanic troops under Roman command whom we have already seen at Dorchester-on-Thames. The author of this interpretation of East Wansdyke advances it as only one of three possibilities, with the caveat that 'the premises on which a historical proof can rest are not at present among the facts before us'.

From the towns and the political units associated with them we turn to the countryside, where, as has recently been stressed, the greater part of the population of Roman Britain and Saxon England lived and worked. One way to seek evidence for the continuity of rural settlement might be to examine the earliest levels of deserted medieval villages, and the latest levels of the Romano-British settlements associated with the so-called 'Celtic' fields, since these are both types of monument which are readily identifiable on the ground. Occupation in the fifth and sixth centuries could thus be bracketed between earlier and later occupations. The results of an enquiry on these lines are that pagan Saxon and later material is virtually unknown on the settlements with 'Celtic' fields; while of the many deserted medieval villages which have been systematically examined over the last dozen years, only three have produced significant quantities of Roman material. At first sight, this appears fatal to any idea of a general continuity of rural settlement. But it is noteworthy that very few of the deserted medieval villages so far excavated have produced material earlier than the twelfth century. This suggests at once that the deserted villages represent an expansion of the area of cultivation and settlement in the twelfth century. Of necessity, therefore, they can tell us little or nothing about Dark Age settlements. In that sense they were marginal, as indeed the Romano-British settlements with 'Celtic' fields were marginal in the fourth century. They cannot really assist our enquiry, one way or the other.

Evidence from the villas is no more satisfactory. A few, especially in western England, have yielded the buckles and other military equipment attributable to Germanic troops of the late fourth and early fifth centuries. It is more difficult to understand the institutional relations between such troops and the villas than those between the troops and the towns. But whatever the relationship may have been, there is no evidence in the form, say of late fifth-century brooches or pagan Saxon pottery, that German officers succeeded Romano-British landlords as proprietors of the villas. It is sometimes urged that the evidence is defective because the late levels of villas have been ploughed away, or have been badly excavated by archaeologists eager to get down to solid walls and mosaic floors. But it is difficult to believe that all the cultural detritus of a late fifth-century occupation could have been destroyed or overlooked; if metalwork of around 400 has survived, why not that from around 500, if it ever existed on the villas? But if we believe that villa-houses were no longer occupied in England in the late fifth century, this is not necessarily due to the nasty habits of the English settlers. For none of the villas so far excavated in south-western England or Wales has produced that east Mediterranean pottery which has already been mentioned. This is good evidence that even in areas unaffected by English settlement, the villa type of dwelling had been abandoned by AD 450, whether for economic reasons or because of peasant revolts.

Here it must be admitted that to say that the villa-houses, and the settlements associated with 'Celtic' fields, were no longer occupied by AD 450 is not at all the same thing as to say that 'Celtic' fields and villa fields (if they differed) were similarly abandoned, to revert to thorns and ultimately to forest. In the case of the 'Celtic' fields on the chalk downs, it is likely that they have been continuously grazed ever since they ceased to be tilled. Less clear is the case of the villa-estates and the fields not on the downs. Two small pieces of evidence may be helpful here, provided that their fragmentary nature is remembered. At Great Wymondley (Herts.), the medieval open-field system was laid out on a Roman road, which may merely have provided a convenient boundary centuries after the Roman period; it also surrounded a Roman villa, but this may be a coincidence; and most striking of all, traces of the Roman system of centuriation have been discerned in the layout of the medieval strips. Then, at Upton (Glos.), recent excavations have suggested that a medieval boundary wall which separates a croft from arable land is on the same line as that between a Roman occupation site and its associated arable. Compared with concrete evidence like this, the attempt to correlate the area or boundaries of the Roman villa at Withington (Glos.) with those of the subsequent Saxon estate fails for vagueness. In the last analysis, it seems, the argument rests on Saxon Withington having well-defined natural boundaries on three sides, which might earlier have provided boundaries for the villa. Even if we accept this, it is clear that it may be an example of geographic features producing like effects in different periods, rather than of organic continuity. And whatever continuity may be postulated at Withington, it is certain that its south-western neighbour, Chedworth, was completely buried in woodland at the time of its discovery in 1864.

We may assert, then, that the land around some villas was abandoned to forest; we may deny the possibility of showing that any Romano-British farm-estate was taken over as a working unit by pagan Saxon settlers. But equally we cannot support the ideas that those settlers colonized uncleared forest; chose the sites for their villages with regard to a common zone of tolerance between neighbours, but without regard to earlier settlements and clearances; and pioneered the clearance of forest, the ploughing of heavy soils, and the settlement of valley-bottoms. These ideas are both popular and authoritatively supported; but they fail for a number of reasons. Firstly, even if we believe that there was a wholesale extermination of Britons by Saxons, it is difficult to believe that forest had grown up everywhere over ruined British villages and derelict fields before the Saxons began to settle. Secondly, the earliest generations of the English could not have pioneered the clearance of heavy forest and of heavy clay soils; we know little enough about their agricultural equipment, and that principally from continental sources, but we cannot believe that it was superior to that of the Roman Britons. Thirdly, in any case, the cultivation of suitable valley soils had already begun before AD 400. This is now well established in the valleys of the Welland and the Warwickshire Avon, both areas of early English settlement. Finally, in Cheshire and Shropshire, a study of the progress of woodland clearance has made it possible to determine certain nuclear areas of early deforestation; it is there that the early Anglian place-names are largely found, and it is there too that the Celtic place-names cluster. This strongly suggests that that Anglian settlers moved into areas already cleared and cultivated by the Britons.

There is at first sight a paradox here. We cannot find pagan Saxon villages or farmsteads on top of Romano-British villages. Yet we deny that the pagan Saxons revolutionized the pattern of settlement of rural England. The paradox may be resolved if we accept the possibility that a substantial number of late Roman and early Anglo-Saxon villages lie under modern villages which have been continuously occupied since the cultivation of the valley bottoms began. Inevitably, we can expect to find only the most fragmentary traces of such hypothetical early occupation. How far we are prepared to extrapolate from such fragments as may occur will probably depend not on the evidence itself but on preconceived hypotheses about the nature of the English settlements.

If ambiguity still rules over the field of settlement studies, the position is no better in that of material culture and handicrafts. Even in western Britain, there seems to have been a catastrophic decline in material culture in the fifth century and later. This decline is almost measurable in terms of iron production, as witnessed by the relative quantities of iron slag found on Roman and post-Roman sites. Deficient in quantitative terms, the culture of the sub-Roman Britons is nebulous in quality too, save for some fine metalwork, which is mostly of the sixth century. The absence of any rich, clearly defined material culture can be demonstrated most strikingly in Brittany. It is widely accepted that Brittany was settled on a massive scale by migrants from south-west Britain in the late fifth or sixth century. But it is quite impossible, in the museums of Brittany, to point to the relics of these settlers. Either there never was a folk-movement to Armorica, or the Britons had no distinguishable material culture to transmit, whether across the sea or to the English settlers at home. Despite this, some interesting hints can be obtained from the handicrafts of pottery and metalworking.

It is obvious that the hand-modelled, lumpish pots in which the Anglo-Saxons placed the ashes of their dead have little in common with the highly competent, wheel-thrown vessels which were readily available to the Britons of the fourth century. But it is also recognized that mass-produced pottery was not available to the Britons of the mid fifth century, presumably because the pottery industry itself had collapsed. In default of wheel-thrown pots, it has been suggested that the sub-Roman Britons used hand-model-led vessels, which in their shapes represent a degeneration from popular Roman forms. But these sub-Roman vessels have only been reported very occasionally, and even their chronological position has not been certain. Buried in the four volumes of excavations at Richborough (Kent), however, is the information that many examples of just such hand-modelled jars were found in the top soil. They also occur at Richborough in significant numbers in pits along with fragments of fourth-century wheel-thrown vessels. It is incon-ceivable that these hand-modelled vessels can be contemporary with the manufacture of the wheel-thrown wares; altogether more likely that the latter represent a few pieces surviving in use after the collapse of the Roman pottery industry, at a time when local needs were being met by the degenerate hand-modelled jars. These latter, then, do represent a sub-Roman pottery industry. Furthermore, though the shapes may be too simple to be diagnostic, we cannot ignore the fact that very similar vessels occur in pagan Saxon cemeteries such as Lackford (Suffolk).

The pottery known as Romano-Saxon may also reflect some cultural interchange between Briton and Saxon. It is common ground that Romano-Saxon pottery occurs in the fourth century in just those parts of eastern Britain where we believe that Germanic troops were stationed; and that it is certainly a product of the Romano-British pottery industry. But the ornament on the pots—dimples, bosses and incised diagonal lines—is considered to be alien to wheel-thrown pottery, whereas it is very common on hand-modelled pagan Saxon urns. It is, therefore, considered that the ornament is a Germanic fashion and that the vessels were manufactured by Romano-British potters to meet the established taste of German customers. Now it might be thought a little unlikely that the mass-production of a higher material culture should thus adapt itself to barbarian taste; but the real difficulty lies in demonstrating a significant taste for dimples and so on in the continental homelands before the earliest Romano-Saxon pottery in England. On present evidence, it seems more likely that the ornament was invented by British potters in the late third and fourth centuries; and that, through the subsequent settlement of Germanic troops in eastern Britain, it was eventually transmitted to free Germany as the latest in civilized taste. If we accept this view, we have here an example of a British element in the material culture of the English in the strictest O'Donnell terms. Moreover, Romano-Saxon pottery would fall into line with other well-known instances of the adoption of Roman art forms in the Barbarian north.

It is generally accepted in the field of metalwork, for instance, that certain provincial Roman ornamental techniques and motifs were received and then transformed by Germanic craftsmen: notably chip-carving, and the use of more-or-less realistic animals, especially on the edges of brooches and buckles or as formalized friezes. Such animals occur in England in the late fifth century, and so do chip-carved spirals with a very Celtic look; but it seems that the line of transmission was not directly from Romano-British to pagan Saxon art, but rather from late Gallo-Roman, or even late Antique, metalwork to south Scandinavia and north Germany, and thence to England.

One form of brooch is, however, so characteristically British, even Celtic, that when it appears in Saxon contexts we must believe it comes from a British source: namely, the penannular brooch. But there were various ways in which such brooches could reach Saxon hands, and thence Saxon graves, to be discovered by the archaeologist. Some may represent the acquisition of Romano-British trinket-boxes, either as simple loot or in association with British women, whether acquired by force or by lawful marriage. Others, perhaps of fifth-century manufacture, may have been obtained from British craftsmen in unanglicized areas, again as loot or perhaps by purchase; or they may be the work of British craftsmen surviving in areas largely settled by Anglo-Saxons. Archaeology cannot distinguish between these alternatives. It has, indeed, recently been noted that one particular type of penannular brooch preponderates in Anglo-Saxon graves in eastern England, in almost precisely the same area in which this type predominated in the pre-Roman and Roman periods. This is taken as implying that the type was made by Saxons. But this is surely the opposite of any reasonable inference, and it is altogether more likely that British craftsmen were continuing to make these brooches for a patronage that was becoming increasingly anglicized.

The whole question of British craftsmen surviving in the east has indeed to be handled with great care, for we now see that several classes of jewellery which were once believed to exemplify such survival are really too late to do so. But even if we accept the Gildasian blood-and-slaughter concept of the English settlement in all its rigours, it seems inherently unlikely that no Romano-British craftsmen would have been spared to serve new masters. So when we find features in admittedly Germanic metalwork which are unique to England, it is natural to ask what there was in England to create such uniqueness; natural also to wonder whether the answer might lie in some use of British craftsmen. For instance, a very distinctive group of buckles, with ornament inlaid in silver wire, was used along the Rhine, and then introduced to England perhaps around the waists of Frankish warriors. But the English series of these inlaid buckles has a greater range of ornamental techniques, and a more elaborate repertory of designs, than its continental counterpart, and it should therefore represent development in this country. When we consider that the inlaid-wire technique, though rare, was not unknown in Roman Britain and, further, that the distinctive motifs of the English buckles include very

Roman or Celtic cables and spirals, we may wonder whether British craftsmen played some part in the development.

Another case may be provided by the spectacular silver quoit brooches and related jewellery of south-east England. Admittedly, quoit brooches, like penannular ones, have been found on the Continent, but their scarcity there serves to emphasize that both are characteristic of this island. It can also be affirmed that the essentially British form—the penannular—was taken up in the quoit and related brooches, even if their ornament can no longer be derived convincingly from Roman Britain. But when the English quoit brooches are reviewed against the wider field of Germanic metalwork in the fifth and sixth centuries, it is their individuality and their superlative craftsmanship which stand out. Does this reflect some survival of British skills among eclectic craftsmen, willing to use both British and Germanic forms, techniques and ornaments in the service of Germanic masters?

Finally, there is the evidence of pagan Saxon burials and cemeteries, of which much has been made in the past. Anglo-Saxon graves have been found in Romano-British cemeteries, or adjacent to them, but the evidence is slight and scattered and difficult to evaluate. It has also been suggested that some pagan cemeteries contain skeletons whose slightness, compared with the supposed robustness of the Anglo-Saxons, proclaims that they are the bones of Roman Britons, who had become sufficiently integrated in early English communities to share their burial rites. But the use of skeletal material to determine nationality is not nowadays in fashion, and the current view is that we cannot suggest Romano-British traits on biological grounds alone. Some graves, however, contain Roman coins or Romano-British trinkets, and here, at first sight, it seems likely that it was the descendants of Roman Britons, the rightful possessors of Romano-British heirlooms, who were buried in them. But when we bear in mind what has already been said about the possible ways in which penannular brooches may have come into Saxon hands, it is clear that the case is not so simple. And there is another complication. A significant proportion of these Roman trinkets belong not to the generation immediately before AD 400, but to the third, second or even first centuries. It is difficult to believe that these really are heirlooms, and it seems more probable that they had been dug up by the pagan Saxons from Roman towns or villas, or even from burials. Such an idea is repugnant to us; but the practice of exhuming cremation urns of the third millennium BC for modern household use is well attested in Baluchistan. And the case in fifth-century England is clinched when we find urns of the pre-Roman iron age, in an almost intact state, in a Saxon grave. These could not possibly have survived in a Belgic and later romanized household down to the sixth or seventh century AD; they can only have been dug up. It is not perhaps surprising, in these circumstances, that many of the Roman trinkets in Saxon graves were useless, with their pins or other functional parts missing. But this does make it difficult to understand why they were placed in the graves; and it also renders them unhelpful for any discussion of Romano-British survival.

To a predominantly non-archaeological audience, much of what I have said must have appeared at best ambiguous, at worst starkly negative. The reasons for this lie, I submit, partly with the archaeologist, partly with the period. For the historian, it seems, a happening in the past only becomes an historical event or fact if it can be fitted into an interpretation which historians find significant. But for an archaeologist, a piece of pottery remains a pot-sherd even if it cannot be fitted into a complete vessel, or made to bear witness of ancient trade or invasion. The first duty of the archaeologist is to conserve and respect such bits and pieces of the past as have survived the myriad forces of destruction. Now the fifth century is full of bits and pieces of the past, of history and legend and saga, of settlement- and grave- and art-archaeology. And from these bits and pieces it is not difficult to select those which fit a significant interpretation—provided we bring that interpretation to the facts, and use it as a sieve or filter in selecting them. But to sieve the facts is neither to conserve nor to respect them. Indeed, I would maintain that the fragmentation of the evidence, its obscurity, its contradictoriness, its complexity, is part of the very texture of fifth-century Britain, as it would have appeared to a contemporary, and as it should appear to us. So the archaeologist, by adding to that contradictoriness and complexity, is giving to our picture of the period a new verisimilitude.

Postscript

The original printed version of this essay had no footnotes, and was supported merely by a brief collection of references. No attempt has been made to furnish full documentation here, in part because the paper had served as a preliminary sketch for parts of *Arthur's Britain*, which was written only four years later. Much of the archaeological evidence deployed here, both Roman and Saxon, will therefore be found in an expanded form, and adequately referenced, in that work.[2] Inevitably, however, the discussion has progressed over the last dozen years; and while it would be inappropriate in the present context to offer an extensive bibliography, it seems none the less worth drawing attention to a few key works.

A broad survey of the problems of *The end of Roman Britain* is presented in the proceedings of a conference with that title, edited by P. J. Casey (1979a). Much of the debate turns on the fate of the towns, and here J. Wacher (1974) brings together the scattered archaeological information on which historical interpretations must be based. At present, the most challenging interpretation is a provocative paper by R. Reece (1980) in which he claims that 'the towns of Roman Britain had gone by 350', replaced essentially by administrative villages; and that by the fifth century there was little *romanitas* left in Britain to be swept away by 'a few boatloads of unorganized Anglo-Saxons'. At a more detailed level, we may see, as the outstanding recent contribution to our knowledge of late Roman towns, the excavations of P. A. Barker on the baths basilica at Wroxeter. There, a building of classical form, but built in timber not stone, may have formed the centre-piece of an estate which would well fit Reece's model (P. A. Barker, 1981).

Turning from the Romans to the Anglo-Saxons, a general survey of *The archaeology of the Anglo-Saxons* was edited by D. M. Wilson (1976). This is somewhat weak on the early, pagan archaeology, and much of it is therefore irrelevant here; but M. Biddle's discussion of towns addresses itself critically to the problems of continuity.

A comprehensive review of the archaeology of the pagan period was presented by C. Hills (1979) in a paper which is especially critical of the significance of the supposed Germanic military buckles.

The pottery of the Anglo-Saxons has always been regarded as crucial for our understanding of their settlement of England. Here a major interpretative monograph by J. N.L. Myres (1969) was subsequently supported by his corpus of the pottery (1977). These both need reading, however, in the light of reviews that are critical of Myres's methodology, for instance by D. Kidd (1976) and T. M. Dickinson (1978).

---

[2] L. Alcock (1971, 1973).

Much important research at regional level has recently appeared, notably by B. N. Eagles on Humberside (1979), by M. G. Welch on Sussex (1983), and at a lesser level by various authors on Essex (ed. D. G. Buckley 1980) and Kent (ed. P. E. Leach 1982). At present, the impression given by much of this work is that the evidence for pagan Saxon settlement in the early fifth century is significantly slighter, and that for the later fifth century much stronger, than appeared in the 1960s. Correspondingly, it is now more difficult to find points of contact between Germans settled in Roman contexts and by Roman authority, and Saxons of the wholly post-Roman folk colonization.

Historical sources also have a large part to play in our interpretation of these problems. In two papers, respectively on the evidence of Gildas and that of Bede and the Anglo-Saxon Chronicle, P. Sims-Williams (1983a; 1983b) gives admirably balanced examples of the modern critical approach. Altogether more credulous in their analysis of the written sources are the various writings of E. A. Thompson, culminating in his idiosyncratic account of St Germanus of Auxerre and the end of Roman Britain (1984).

Finally, two strongly contrasting recent surveys should be mentioned. C. J. Arnold provides a deliberately revisionist account of the transition from Roman Britain to Saxon England (1984). His sub-title, 'An archaeological study', proclaims his intention to write 'pure' archaeology, in a prehistoric mode, rejecting altogether the evidence of written sources and the interpretative problems which they entail. In sharp distinction, J. Campbell (ed. 1982) and his co-authors write as historians who have sympathy for the archaeological evidence, and some knowledge of it. The result is both richer and more convincing than Arnold's.

Part Five:
Synthesis

CHAPTER 19

Economy, Society and Warfare[1]

THE ECONOMY OF THE BRITONS AND THEIR ENEMIES

Despite detailed differences in the material cultures of the Britons and their enemies, whether Celtic or Germanic, these essentially barbarian peoples shared one cultural trait: the pursuit of warfare as a major activity of society. This was as true of the Britons of the sixth century AD as of the Anglo-Saxons or the *Scotti*. In this, of course, there was a great contrast with Romano-British society, which even in the fourth century was largely organized for peaceful pursuits. It cannot be disputed that war was a central element in the Arthurian situation, and no account of Arthur's Britain could be considered complete without an analysis of the character of warfare in the period. As a preliminary to that analysis, the structure of the society and economy from which it drew its strength must be lightly sketched.

The basic economy of the various peoples active in Britain in our period was the same: mixed farming, supplemented with cottage industries and a little trade, but lacking currency. So far as the Britons are concerned, the evidence has been most fully worked out in Wales, where both verbal and material evidence have been used to revolutionize our picture of early Welsh—and by implication early British—economy and the social structure erected upon it.[2] The former view was that the early Welsh had been meat-eating, bread-scorning cowherds, who roamed the Cambrian mountains without settled abodes or any fixed pattern of land-holding—in a phrase, 'footloose Celtic cowboys'.[3] This view was maintained firstly by a biased selection from the observations made by early medieval writers, and secondly by ignoring the limitations of archaeological evidence for arable farming, and arguing then from the negative evidence. It is now certain that the Britons of our period were grinding corn, and it seems possible that at Pant-y-saer and at Gwithian we even have the fields in which they grew it. In this case archaeology can only supplement the clear proof provided by the Welsh Laws for the importance of both grain and bread in the economy. The importance of animal husbandry, and especially the raising of cattle, is equally undeniable, and it is now clear that we must think in terms of unspecialized mixed farming.

A similar statement can now be made about the *Scotti*, on the basis both of archaeological finds from raths and crannogs, and of the actual siting of the raths

---

[1] This chapter was originally published as Chapter 11 of my *Arthur's Britain: history and archaeology AD 367–634* (Penguin Books, 1971; 1973). In that work, it served to pull together, in a general synthesis, aspects of the barbarian peoples whose archaeology had been covered in detail in the preceding chapters. As one student's synoptic interpretation, it provides an equally valid rounding off for the various sub-themes of the present work, as well as a convenient summary of the major theme. I have therefore left it unaltered, except for some recent references, and some minor editorial emendations in the interests of consistency of presentation.

[2] The pioneering work has been by G. R. J. Jones (1961); (1965); (1972). For a sketch of the archaeology in relation to economy and social structure: L. Alcock (1965b), and Chapters 2–4 above.

[3] The phrase is from S. Piggott (1958), 25.

themselves.[4] Where this has been studied in relation to the distribution of different qualities of soil, it appears that the rath-builders favoured the best farming land. Since this must have put the raths at risk from latter-day agricultural activities, their survival in tens of thousands appears all the more remarkable. In excavated raths the best proof of arable farming is provided by occasional ploughshares or coulters of iron (Fig. 19.1), which imply the use of a heavy plough. Such shares and coulters are indeed rare, and so are sickles which might have been used for reaping corn or cutting hay. But broken objects of iron can be reforged so easily that no argument can be based on their scarcity. On the

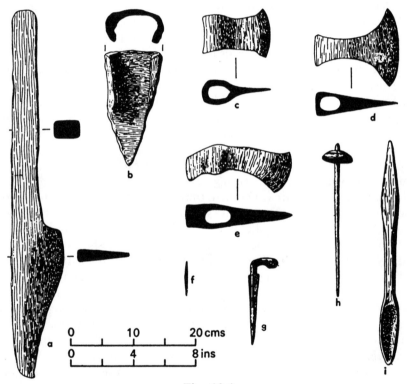

Fig. 19.1.
Iron tools and implements: *a* plough-coulter, White Fort, Co. Down; *b* ploughshare, Dundrum Castle, Co. Down; *c* axe, Buiston Crannog, Ayrshire; *d* axe, perhaps a weapon rather than a tool, from a warrior-grave at Petersfinger, Wiltshire; *e* axe-hammer, Cadbury–Camelot, Somerset; *f* awl, possibly for leather-working, Buiston; *g* spring from a barrel padlock, Buiston; *h* iron spindle and bone whorl, Sutton Courtenay, Berkshire; *i* spoon bit, Buiston.
For Buiston: R. Munro (1882), 190–239; Cadbury: L. Alcock (1972a); Dundrum: Archaeol. Survey Co. Down (Belfast 1966), fig. 79.1; Petersfinger: E. T. Leeds and H. de S. Shortt (1953); Sutton Courtenay: E. T. Leeds (1947), pl. xxii; White Fort: D. M. Waterman (1956).

[4] V. B. Proudfoot (1961). For the important discovery of water mills of our period in Ireland, see M. G. L. Baillie (1982), 175–96.

other hand the abundance of hand-mills makes it certain that corn was being ground, and occasionally the kilns in which it was dried have also been excavated. Alongside the evidence for cereal-growing must be set the enormous amounts of animal bones recovered from both crannogs and raths. Clearly the raising of cattle, pigs and sheep (in that order of frequency) was a major activity of the farmer. But it is not possible, either in Britain or Ireland, to estimate the relative importance of arable and pasture.

When we turn to the Anglo-Saxons we find that no systematic analysis of their economy in the settlement period has yet been worked out.[5] This is partly because so few domestic sites are known and because it is permissible to doubt whether an excavated village like Sutton Courtenay is truly representative. The archaeological evidence for small-time sheep-rearers and weavers of homespun is impossible to reconcile with continental evidence for prosperous mixed farming among the ancestral English. At the same time it is impossible to doubt that the large-scale exploitation of the arable potential of lowland England, which was fully established by the eleventh century, had its beginnings in the seventh, sixth and fifth centuries, if not actually in Roman Britain. Certainly the literary evidence from late Saxon England is in favour once again of mixed farming.

All these communities of farmers, British, Irish and English, supported craftsmen at two levels. The higher of these was represented by the jeweller and the armourer, the maker of fine swords and rare helmets. Such craftsmen are not likely to have been found at village level, or in the humbler raths. The literary evidence suggests that they were peripatetic, seeking the patronage of chiefs and princes. Indeed, the Welsh poem *Culhwch and Olwen* ranks 'a craftsman bearing his craft' along with the 'son of a rightful prince' in terms of the welcome he might expect at a royal court. Apart from lay patrons, of course, the bronze- or gold-smith might seek employment in a monastery, to make vessels for the service of the church as well as ornamented book-covers, reliquaries and other religious objects. Consistent with this, the sites which produce copious evidence for the manufacture of fine metalwork—crucibles, moulds, scrap bronze and glass, 'sketch-pads' and so on—are either monasteries like Nendrum, royal sites like Lagore or Garranes, or forts like Garryduff I, Mote of Mark and Dinas Powys where the total evidence argues for a high social status.

The lower level of craftsmanship is represented by cottage or village industries. It is reasonable to believe that these included the production of iron tools and implements for farming and other crafts, but no smithies have been found by excavation. The principal evidence is in fact for textile production. Both British and Irish sites have yielded highly polished stones which may have served as linen-smoothers. Whorls for spinning wool are common and bone and iron spindles also occur occasionally (Fig. 19.1). Anglo-Saxon villages, and even isolated houses like that at Bourton-on-the-Water, have produced evidence for upright looms in the form of clay loom-weights which are sometimes associated with the post-holes of the loom itself. Iron awls and heavy needles suggest that leather goods—vessels, clothes and shoes—were also made domestically. Potting was no doubt another home industry in those areas—Ulster, Cornwall and pagan England— where native as opposed to imported pottery was in use. It may however be questioned whether the more elaborate Anglo-Saxon cinerary urns were made in the home, rather than by specialized potters. Certainly in East Anglia in the later sixth century pots bearing similar designs and even identical stamped ornaments were buried in several

---

[5] But see now P. J. Fowler (1981).

cemeteries. The implication is that these vessels had all been made by the same potter, who was working not to meet immediate local needs but to sell to a market.

This is virtually the only evidence that we have for internal trade in our period, and it is important to determine its scale. About 90 per cent of the vessels made by the so-called 'Illington/Lackford' potter are found within a radius of eight miles—a day's walk to market and back. Within the framework of the farming economy this was probably the limit of trade, or indeed of movement at all, except for certain necessities with a naturally limited distribution like salt and iron. When we move from the level of the village and farm to that of court and monastery the range of trade widens at once. The raw materials required for fine jewellery are of restricted occurrence in nature—tin and gold extremely so, copper and silver (derived from lead) less restricted. So the very fact that these materials were used implies a trade in metals, and suggests also the existence of specialized communities engaged in extracting and refining the ores. But this last suggestion should not be given too much weight, for the Dinas Powys evidence demonstrates that some jewellery was made by melting down the trinkets of other peoples or earlier times. A trade in scrap metal remains indisputable of course, but a trade in finished products cannot be proved incontrovertibly. Even when closely similar jewels are found in different cemeteries, we may be dealing with the movement of people—craftsmen, brides, hostages, or even whole nations—rather than with commercial activity.

External trade, by contrast, ranged over quite surprising distances. In western Britain and Ireland this is best reflected by the imported pottery, of which Class D comes from western Gaul, while Classes A and B come from the east Mediterranean and north Africa. The millefiori glass used for ornamenting brooches and religious objects found at princely sites like Dinas Powys and Garranes probably originated in Alexandria. The extent of external trade among the Anglo-Saxons is no less remarkable. Even if we make an exception of the Byzantine silverware from the Sutton Hoo ship-burial, the range of imports extends to Africa and Asia for bronze bowls, ivory, lapis lazuli and above all garnets. But however impressive these imports are in geographical terms, their real economic significance is far more questionable. We have already seen that the commerce between the Celtic West on the one hand and Gaul and the Mediterranean on the other was at best sporadic (above, pp. 89–92). We have also surmised that the church played a large part in its organization, but we can scarcely even speculate about how the Anglo-Saxons arranged to import quantities of garnet or lapis. In the case of the less common exotic objects, it is probable that they came as bribes, loot, dowries, diplomatic gifts, or in other ways which had no commercial aspect.

It should be remembered here that trade, whether internal or external, was hampered by the lack of conventional means of exchange. From the mid-fourth to the late seventh century the economy of these islands was a natural one, and the use of currency was unknown. This at least is the archaeological evidence, for it is impossible to imagine that the Sutton Hoo coins had ever circulated in this country, and no others have been found. Commerce was therefore a matter of barter and personal negotiation—perhaps a dozen eggs for one of the Illington-Lackford potter's urns, or a cow with calf for the Pant-y-saer silver penannular brooch. There is indeed a little evidence from Wales that cattle provided a standard of value. But the archaeological and numismatic evidence may not be the whole story here. In the very first English law code, the Laws of Æthelberht of Kent, promulgated early in the seventh century, the penalties are regularly quoted in shillings or in *sceattas*, the *sceat* being one twentieth of a shilling. Moreover, the very lukewarm account of trade given in the preceding paragraphs needs to be read in the light of Bede's description of seventh-century London as a 'market for many peoples coming thither by land and sea', *ipsa multorum emporium populorum terra marique venientium*.

HEROIC SOCIETY[6]

Among all the peoples of Arthur's Britain, the basic economy of mixed farming and cottage industry supported a social pyramid of which the apex was a warrior king. Wherever the evidence is available, the institution of kingship is seen to have deep ancestral roots. The pre-Roman Britons had certainly been ruled by kings—or occasionally queens—and though the institution was rapidly suppressed after the Roman Conquest, it is likely that a folk-memory of it persisted to inspire political developments in the fifth and later centuries. Classical writers, especially Caesar and Tacitus, make it clear that one function of British kings and queens was to lead their people on the battlefield. Tacitus is also our chief witness for political arrangements among the early Germans.[7] His epigrammatic style tends to obscure rather than elucidate the complexities of the institution, but it seems that the Germans of the first century AD recognized both kings chosen from a royal stock and war-leaders chosen for their valour and military skill. It seems probable that under the stress of folk-movement and land-seizure these two aspects of leadership coalesced. For the prehistoric Irish and Picts there is no comparable evidence, but kingship was certainly well developed among them when they appear on the historical scene. One curious exception to these generalizations must be noted among the Old- or continental Saxons, who even in Bede's day had no king, only a number of co-equal rulers from whom a temporary leader was chosen in time of war.

It may be that this last arrangement lies behind the title of *ealdorman* which the *Anglo-Saxon Chronicle* bestows on the two Saxon leaders Cerdic and Cynric. In other words, among their own people they may well have been co-rulers before they ventured forth to found the dynasty of Wessex. Only of these two is the term *ealdorman*, or any other constitutional expression used, and we are in fact generally ignorant of the personal status of the men who established dynasties in England. It is true that they normally trace their descent from the god Woden, and this may imply that they were members of various divinely recognized royal families, but it is also possible that the genealogies are post-conquest fabrications designed to put the seal of divinity on *de facto* rulers. In the west, however, Eochaid mac Artchorp of the Dési was of royal stock, for two of his brothers ruled in succession in Ireland. Eochaid was probably a cadet of the family, who went adventuring with his personal following and gained a kingdom in Dyfed through the invitation of the Romans. For the original status of men like Cunedda we have no early evidence, but we need not doubt that north of the Antonine Wall, and perhaps even south to Hadrian's Wall, the prehistoric roots of kingship had been strengthened by Roman cultivation.[8]

But we cannot invoke such ancestral kingship to explain the emergence of British kings in the former civil zone of Roman Britain. Whatever construction we place on the events of AD 407–10 we have still to explain the emergence of the *superbus tyrannus* of Gildas out of

---

[6] The basic survey is H. M. Chadwick (1912). There is little recent work on heroic society in Britain (as opposed to heroic literature); and the word is absent from the indexes of recent general studies. But for relevant hints, see P. Wormald (1978); J. Campbell (1979b); W. Davies (1982), 51–2; 68–71.

[7] E. A. Thompson (1965); J. M. Wallace-Hadrill (1971).

[8] L. Alcock (1979b), 135–6.

the framework of Roman civil administration. Our only clue to the constitutional processes involved is the word *tyrannus* itself. At its simplest it means merely 'ruler', then by
extension, 'one who rules despotically'. This scarcely seems appropriate to the *superbus
tyrannus*, who shared the decision to invite in the Anglo-Saxons with a council: *tum omnes
consiliarii una cum superbo tyranno caecantur*, 'all the counsellors together with the chief ruler
were blinded', as Gildas puts it. The most likely meaning is in fact 'usurper', for the word
is used in this sense by Greek writers of the fourth and fifth centuries AD, and Gildas
himself uses it of Magnus Maximus. The probability is, then, that the *superbus tyrannus* of
the mid-fifth century was following in the tradition of Maximus in the late fourth and of
Marcus, Gratian and Constantine III in 406–7. Finally, the kings of Gildas's own day
were *tyranni* in his eyes either because they were the creation of usurpers like Maximus and
Vortigern, or because they had seized by force their small territories.[9]

The adjective *superbus* may indicate that among the Britons, as was certainly the case
among the English and the Irish, kingship was not the simple and absolute institution
which it became in the Middle Ages. The *superbus tyrannus* was perhaps the 'high king' or
'supreme ruler', with the implication that there were also lesser kings. The dynasty of
Gwynedd claimed a special position among British kings and it may well be that when
Cadwaladr is said to be *regnante apud Brittones*, 'ruling among the Britons', or when his
grandfather Cadfan is described as *opinatis[s]imus omnium regum*, 'most renowned of all
kings', they are being accorded the same kind of supremacy as the *superbus tyrannus* had
enjoyed nearly two centuries earlier. One the other hand the rulers of Rheged or Strathclyde can scarcely be described as sub-kings. For men in that position we must look to the
three British *cyninges*, Conmail, Condidan and Farinmail, slain at the battle of Dyrham in
577. It may be no more than a coincidence that their deaths led to the English capture of
the three towns of Cirencester, Gloucester and Bath. But it is worth recalling that it was to
the towns that Honorius remitted the responsibility for defence in 410, and that the
archaeological evidence suggests the presence in the towns of military forces which might
serve as the instruments for local seizures of power. The men in the best position to profit
by this were the magistrates. A sixth-century inscription from Penmachno shows that the
office was still in existence then, and leaves the thought that the three men who appeared
as *cyninges* to the Saxons might have been *magistratus* to their fellow Britons.

Whatever the case among the Britons, it is clear that the English used the term *cyning* to
describe more than one grade in a constitutional hierarchy. When in 626 Edwin of
Northumbria undertook an expedition against Wessex in retaliation for an attempt to
assassinate him, he slew five 'kings' as well as many of the people. But Cwichelm, the king
responsible for the assassination attempt, survived to be baptized in 636. It seems likely
therefore that Edwin's victims were mere under-kings, the kind of men who are described
as *sub-regulus* in Latin documents of the seventh century. Above them in the hierarchy
come the rulers of the individual English kingdoms. They in turn frequently share their
rule with a son or other member of the royal stock. Finally, at the head of the system stand
those rare kings on whom, in the entry for 829, the *Anglo-Saxon Chronicle* bestowed the title
Bretwalda, 'ruler of Britain'. The *Chronicle* list of these supreme rulers is based on Bede's
account of the kings who had held *imperium* over the English. The first four of these—Ælle
of Sussex, Ceawlin of Wessex, Æthelberht of Kent and Rædwald of East Anglia—exer-
cised sway south of the Humber only, but they were then followed by three Northumbrian

---

[9] For a recent discussion, K. H. Jackson (1982).

rulers, Edwin, Oswald and Oswiu, who claimed supremacy over all the inhabitants of Britain, both Britons and English, excluding Kent. It will be recalled that Edwin's assertion of this suzerainty provoked the hostility of both Penda of Mercia and Cadwallon of Gwynedd, while Cadwallon's challenge to Northumbria was ultimately fatal to himself.[10]

This reminds us that the claim to *imperium* was both asserted and denied by military might, and we must therefore examine the military role of kingship. But before we do, it is pertinent to ask how the institution and its activities, whether civil or military, were paid for. To a limited extent, of course, warfare was financed out of loot. The Laws of Hywel Dda show that a British king took a third share of spoil, and they set out elaborate arrangements for its division. To give a concrete example:

> If a king's body-guard takes spoil, the chief of the body-guard receives the share of two men, and any animal which he shall choose from the third of the king.

But loot must always have been a precarious source of income, and it is clear that the main support of the king was an elaborate system of tributes, food-rents, and obligatory service. Again, it is worth quoting the Welsh Laws:

> From the bondmen the king is to have packhorses in his hosting, and from every bond township he has a man and a horse with axes for constructing his strongholds, and they are to be at the king's expense.

Although such arrangements for the exaction of military service are most fully set out in the Welsh Laws they were obviously not confined to the Britons. A Dalriadan document, though obscure in general, makes it clear that among the *Scotti* households were organized into hosts or musters three hundred or seven hundred strong, with sea musters of 'twice seven benches to each twenty houses'.[11] Likewise when Bede, describing Edwin's conquest of Anglesey and Man, describes these islands in terms of 960 and more than 300 households respectively, he is referring to an assessment for the purpose of levying tribute.

The Laws of Hywel also list in great detail the food-gifts owed to the king by both bondmen and free, even to the extent of prescribing 'each loaf as broad as from the elbow to the wrist', or 'a tub of butter three hand-breadths across and three in depth', or 'a sow three fingers thick in her hams'. It is declared: 'The township is to bring all these [and many other items] to the king and to light a fire three days and three nights for him.' What is not clear here is whether the king and his court had come to the township in the first instance—in other words whether the court was static or peripatetic, that is to say moving from township to township eating up the food-rents of each in turn. This was certainly the later medieval pattern among both kings and nobles. Apart from winter and spring food-gifts, four were due in summer, and this may mean that the court visited each township six times during the year. It is at least certain that the bodyguard and some of the court officials were entitled to 'a circuit' or to be billeted on the bondmen, while others received specified food when travelling on the king's business. In early English society the *villae regiae* or *regales*, 'royal townships', probably functioned as centres for a peripatetic court to which tribute in kind would be brought. Bede mentions three in Edwin's reign alone, by the river Derwent, at Yeavering, and at *Campodonum* near Dewsbury.

Returning now to the military role of kingship, we find that it was customary, though

---

[10] For a recent discussion of the title *Bretwalda*, see P. Wormald (1983).
[11] J. Bannerman (1974).

not invariable, that the king should lead the muster or hostings whether it was to another kingdom or in defence of his own. As the Laws of Hywel Dda state:

> Once every year the king is to have a hosting along with him from his country to a border country; always however when it may be necessary a host is to attend him in his own country.

And in the early years of the *Anglo-Saxon Chronicle* the most frequent class of entry runs: 'In this year Hengest and Æsc—or Ælle, or Cerdic and Cynric, or Ceawlin and Cutha—fought against the Britons.' We can be sure that this is not just an elliptical expression for 'the hosts of Hengist or Ælle or whoever' because of the frequency with which the kings of the period met their death on the battlefield. On the other hand, the account of the battle of *Degsastan* given in the northern recension of the *Chronicle* suggests that even when a ruler is mentioned in relation to a specific campaign or battle, he may not have taken part personally. The opening sentence for the year 603 is 'Aedan, king of the Scots, fought along with the people of Dal Riada against Æthelfrith, king of the Northumbrians ...' But it seems certain that Æthelfrith was not himself involved in the battle, for the entry concludes 'Hering, son of Hussa, led the army'. Hering was of the royal stock, for his father is mentioned in the 'Northern British History' and appears as Æthelfrith's predecessor in the Northumbrian king-list. Moreover, Æthelfrith's brother Theodbald was killed with all his own force at the battle, so the royal family was well represented. If we find the absence of the king himself surprising, we should recall that the most renowned of British battles, the defeat of the men of Gododdin at *Catraeth*, was also fought without the personal leadership of the king who had instigated it, Mynyddog Mwynfawr of *Din Eidyn*, Edinburgh.

Some of the warriors celebrated in the Gododdin's elegiac stanzas were certainly of royal descent, and the terse *Chronicle* account of *Degsastan* demonstrates the military function of the royal family even more clearly. In the Laws of Hywel, 'the chief of the bodyguard is to be a son of the king or his nephew'. The bodyguard or personal war-band, *comitatus* attendants, in Latin, *heorð-geneatas*, hearth-companions in English and *teulu*, family, in Welsh, represents the layer immediately below the royal stock in a highly stratified society. It seems likely that among the Britons and their various enemies there was an aristocracy both of birth and of service to the king. The rates of *wergild*, blood-price (below, p. 294), laid down in the early English laws reveal that there were grades even within the aristocracy, and show us too that some but not all of the nobility were great landowners. These are the men whom we expect to find buried with sword, shield and spear and jewelled belt-fittings (Fig. 19.2), while their wives have elaborate jewel suites, and symbols of matronhood like chatelaines and weaving-swords or beaters. In the north and west they are presumably the builders of small fortified homesteads, especially the raths of Ireland and some of the duns of western Scotland.

Beneath the nobility were various classes of freemen. Perhaps the clearest group is that of men who had some craft, skill or mystery, the *aes dána*, men of art, of Irish society. One of the triads of the Welsh Laws is significant here, because it both sets limits within the hierarchy and hints at the possibility of social advancement:

> Three arts which a bondman cannot teach his son without the consent of his lord: clerkship and smithcraft and bardism; for if the lord be passive until the clerk be tonsured or the smith enter his smithy or a bard graduate, he can never enslave them after that.

Apart from these specialists, who must always have been few, it would be reasonable to expect that the largest class of freemen would have been that of yeoman farmers or peasant proprietors. But it is not easy to detect such men in Celtic society, where there is no evidence

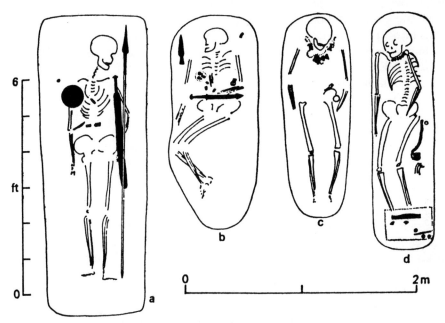

Fig. 19.2.

Four characteristic Anglo-Saxon graves: *a* Petersfinger, Wiltshire, grave 20, warrior
with sword and spear at left side, belt-fittings and knife at waist, shield at right
shoulder, other minor objects; *b* Shudy Camps, Cambridgeshire, grave 36, warrior
with spear, battle-knife (*seax*) hanging from elaborate harness including a pouch, knife
and strike-a-light near waist, rim-binding of wooden cup above left shoulder;
c Holywell Row, Suffolk, grave 37, woman with string of 150 amber and 8 glass beads
round neck and through bows of two elaborate small-long brooches and a cruciform
brooch, iron knife and bronze pin with other trinkets (perhaps in a bag) at left hip;
d Burwell, Cambridgeshire, grave 121, woman with collar of silver pendants, bronze
work-box suspended by chain, food-offering of lamb-chops, wooden box at feet
containing bone comb, chalk beads or whorls and other oddments.
For Burwell and Holywell Row: T. C. Lethbridge (1931); Shudy Camps: T. C.
Lethbridge (1936); Petersfinger: E. T. Leeds and H. de S. Shortt (1953).

for common soldiery who were free but not noble. Among the Anglo-Saxons, this class is
represented by the *ceorl*, no mean person as his *wergild* shows. Among the pagan graves the
ceorl is presumably represented by a large class of burials which are accompanied only by
an iron spear, or possibly a spear and simple shield. If this correlation is correct, then the
ceorl was a warrior as well as a farmer. A clause in a late seventh-century Wessex law does
indeed assign military duties to the *ceorl*, but this is difficult to reconcile with a story told
by Bede in which a Northumbrian king's thegn, *minister regis*, escapes death on the
battlefield by pretending to be *rusticus*, not *miles*, a yokel, not a warrior.

Just as British society seems to lack anyone corresponding to the *ceorl* in his military
capacity, so too there appears to be no class of free farmers, and the British equivalent of
the *ceorl* as tiller of the soil was in fact a bondman. The Welsh Laws give no systematic
account of this class, but none the less they make it clear that the bondman, or settlement

of bondmen, owed considerable services and food-gifts to the king as well as lodging the bodyguard and court officials. We have seen that the bondman could not learn a craft without his lord's permission, and he was in effect bound to his fields. A detailed study of bond townships in Gwynedd has shown that in compensation they occupied the best farming land. All the available evidence suggests that the tilling of the soil by nucleated settlements of bondmen was the main basis of the British economy and the real source of the king's wealth. Below the bondmen in the hierarchy were the slaves, probably not a large class in British society, but all too numerous among the Anglo-Saxons even after the conversion. Capture in war and failure to meet legal obligations were among the causes which could reduce even a king's thegn to slavery, and Bede makes it clear that the slave-trade was one aspect of commerce between England and the Continent.

One other social group, the religious, should be mentioned briefly. Whatever ritual functions the king performed in pagan society, whether Celtic or Germanic, there was certainly also a priesthood. Bede tells how Coifi, chief of the Northumbrian priests, violated his own temple at the time of the conversion, and simultaneously broke the taboos which forbade a priest to carry arms or to ride a stallion. After the conversion, it was necessary to fit the church into the framework of society. Both the English and Welsh laws show how this was done without disturbing too much a pre-Christian system in which violence or sexual irregularity were not sins but offences demanding compensation. It was also necessary to provide for the church in the physical sense by grants of land and other endowments. Presumably it was by royal gift that a number of forts were converted into monastic enclosures: Reculver and Burgh Castle in England, Caer Gybi in Wales, Nendrum in Ireland, are all instances of this. The church made repayment by praying for the king and his army. When Æthelfrith found the monks of Bangor-on-Dee praying for the Britons at the battle of Chester, he ordered that they should be slain first, on the grounds that 'although they do not bear arms they fight against us with their hostile prayers.'

It was not in fact the sanctions of the church which held together or controlled the barbarian societies of Arthur's Britain. The major controlling element was the duty of the kindred, on the one hand to protect and if necessary to avenge its members, on the other hand to make compensation to other kin-groups on behalf of its own delinquents. In primitive conditions the responsibility of the kin was given teeth by the blood-feud, which could be incurred even by slaying a man on the battlefield. In our period, the self-perpetuating feud was being replaced by a system of blood-payments such as *wergild* and *manbot* in English, *galanas* and *sarhad* in Welsh. Traces of the blood-feud linger in Bede, but the weight of the church's influence was obviously in favour of non-violent compensation for offences. Bede relates with great approval how, after Ælfwine, the younger brother of the Northumbrian king Ecgfrith, had been killed in battle with the Mercians, Archbishop Theodore arranged that no more human lives were given for the dead man, but that a money compensation was accepted instead; as a result, there was then a long period of peace between the two kingdoms.

The various nations of Arthur's Britain were barbarian in the technical sense that they lacked urban civilization. Their societies were also heroic in the technical sense that martial valour was the principal virtue of the leading social class, and that society, economy and both spirtual and material culture were all directed towards the main-tenance of warfare as major activity. But the warrior noble was distinguished by other characteristics as well as by valour. The king's thegn who tried to pass himself off as a yokel was ultimately betrayed 'by his countenance, his deportment and his conversation', *ex vultu et habitu et sermonibus eius.* The warriors of Gododdin, however fierce in battle, were liberal in gifts, civil to suppliants, gentle, even bashful, in the presence of maidens. If we were to seek the spirit of the age, we need not look further than the elegy of Gorthyn son of Urfai: 'a hundred men bore away his harsh warning from battle yet he provided song at the New Year Feast.'

WEAPONS, TACTICS AND STRATEGY

We turn now to the technical aspects of warfare in Arthur's Britain. Our sources of information are many, and of very varied worth. First of course we have the actual weapons and armour, which are abundant in pagan Saxon graves. Then from the late seventh century on we have pictures of warriors and occasionally battle scenes drawn in illuminated manuscripts or carved on stones or even on a whale-ivory casket. The value of these pictures is in fact highly suspect, for some are certainly based on Mediterranean book illustrations, and depict Roman or Byzantine methods of warfare. The verbal evidence includes battle poetry, at once stylized and elegiac; terse but often factual statements in annals and chronicles; and longer accounts from the pens of well-informed but cloistered writers like Bede. Field monuments, both forts and dykes, provide certain clues for the archaeologist. All these forms of evidence have to be examined in the light of a general interpretation of politico-military developments among the barbarian peoples in the post-Roman centuries. In turn they help to create and modify that general interpretation.

It is simplest to begin with the individual warrior and his equipment. The principal weapons of the period were the spear, the sword and the shield, which are only rarely supplemented by the axe. In pagan Saxon graves swords are relatively uncommon and when they occur they are normally accompanied by other weapons and military gear, in short, by a rich grave assemblage. It is reasonable to conclude from this that the sword was confined to the nobility. This is very likely if we accept the calculation that, in terms of modern values, there was at least £250 worth of workmanship in a sword. The Saxon sword had a long, parallel-sided blade and sharply tapering point, no true hilt guard and only a light pommel.[12] Its length overall, around 3 ft., relates it to the long iron sword of the pre-Roman Celts. This had been wielded both by them and by Roman auxiliary troops as a cavalry weapon, but among the English the longsword was used entirely for fighting on foot. The Britons also used swords, but we have no evidence of their form. In *Y Gododdin* references to sword-strokes or blades are less frequent than those to spears, suggesting that for the British forces, as for the Saxon, the sword was not the common weapon. In Ireland again we find parallel-sided sword blades, but they are markedly smaller than the Saxon examples, ranging from about 14 in. to not more than 26 in. at the largest (Fig. 19.3).[13]

Single-edged swords or military knives are also found in Saxon graves and Irish crannogs, and a passing reference in *Y Gododdin* suggests that the Britons used them too. *Seax*, the word for knife, is considered to have given the Saxons their tribal name, but despite this, knives suitable for battle are not often found in the graves. In the Arthurian period war-knives had a narrow blade from about 12 to 20 in. long, and it was only after AD 600 that the blade became first broader and then longer as well. The Irish examples have either long tapered blades or parallel-sided ones in a comparable range of sizes.

---

[12] H. R. E. Davidson (1962); J. W. Anstee and L. Biek (1961).
[13] E. Rynne (1966), (1981); J. P. Mallory (1981).

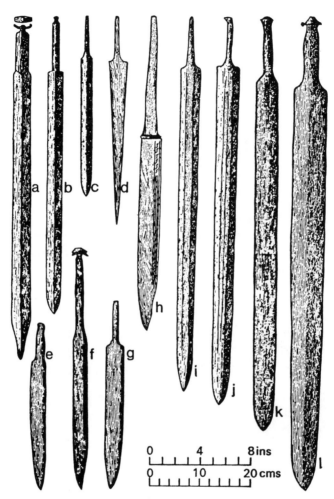

Fig. 19.3.

Anglo-Saxon and Irish swords: *a, b, c* Irish double-edged swords, Lagore crannog, Co.
Meath; *d, g* single-edged swords, Lagore; *e seax*, Burwell, Cambridgeshire, grave 47;
f seax, Shudy Camps, Cambridgeshire, grave 36 (see Fig. 19.2); *h seax*, Northolt,
Middlesex; *i, j* Saxon double-edged swords, Abingdon, Berkshire, graves 49 and 42;
k, l Saxon swords, Croydon, Surrey.

For Abingdon, E. T. Leeds and D. B. Harden (1936); Burwell: T. C. Lethbridge
(1931); Croydon: G. B. Brown (1915), vol. 3 pls. xxv and xxvii; Lagore: H. O'N.
Hencken (1950); Northolt: V. I. Evison in J. G. Hurst (1961); Shudy Camps: T. C.
Lethbridge (1936).

Occasionally both the longsword and the knife are found in graves in positions showing
that they were slung at the hip (Fig. 19.2).

The spear (Fig. 19.4) was by far the commonest weapon among the barbarians—
indeed, a single spear is the minimum equipment of a warrior-grave. We are really
dealing here with three separate weapons, which cannot always be distinguished one from
another on the basis of the metal parts which the archaeologist finds. The javelin is for

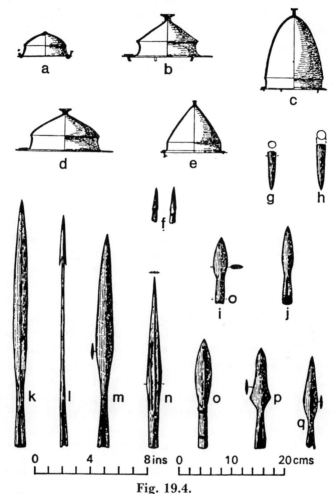

Fig. 19.4.

Anglo-Saxon, British and Irish weapons: *a* Irish shield-boss, Lagore; *b, d* Saxon shield-bosses, Petersfinger, graves 20 (see Fig. 19.2) and 7; *c* Saxon 'sugar-loaf' boss, Lowbury Hill, Berkshire; *e* Saxon boss, Alton, Hampshire; *f* arrow-heads, Buiston crannog, Ayrshire; *g, m* Saxon spearhead and ferrule, Petersfinger, grave 20; *h* Irish spear-ferrule, Lagore; *i* Irish spearhead, Garryduff, Co. Cork; *j* British, Irish or Pictish spearhead, Dunadd, Argyll; *k* Saxon spearhead, Snell's Corner, Hampshire, grave S 14; *l* angon, Abingdon, Berkshire, grave 69; *n* Irish ribbed spearhead, Ballinderry Crannog no. 2, Co. Offaly; *o* British spearhead, Buiston; *p, q* Saxon spearheads, Petersfinger, graves 27 and 6.

For Abingdon: E. T. Leeds and D. B. Harden (1936); Alton and Lowbury Hill: V. I. Evison (1963); Ballinderry: H. O'N. Hencken (1942); Buiston: R. Munro (1882); Dunadd: D. Christison and J. Anderson (1905); Garryduff: M. J. O'Kelly (1962); Lagore: H. O'N. Hencken (1950); Petersfinger: E. T. Leeds and H. de S. Shortt (1953); Snell's Corner: G. M. Knocker (1958).

throwing, and it is sometimes thought that small spearheads, around six inches long or less, are from javelins. They are found occasionally among both the English and the Irish, and there are also British references to throwing-spears. A hand-held spear, used with a thrusting motion, is either a cavalry lance or an infantry pike. In pagan graves we find angular, leaf-shaped or long tapered blades, exceptionally up to 16 in. long. The shaft has normally decayed, but sometimes a soil-stain, or the presence of an iron ferrule in line with the head, shows that the overall length of a pike may have been 7 ft. (Fig. 19.2). In pre-Viking Ireland there are also leaf-shaped or long tapered pike blades which occasionally exceed 12 in. A British spearhead, with a heavy leaf-shaped blade $8\frac{1}{2}$ in. long is known from Buiston, but it is impossible to know whether this is from a lance, a javelin, or even a pike. Two further comments are needed on the ubiquity of spears. First, many though by no means all the spears in pagan graves are wrought very simply, so they cannot have been costly weapons. Second, the spear is a hunting weapon as well as a martial one, and a necessary defence for swineherd and cowherd in lands where bears, wolves and boars roamed wild.

Certain highly specialized weapons occur only rarely in pagan graves. The angon has a short head which may be barbed, a long slender iron shaft, and a short socket, all in one piece, with an overall length of about 2 ft. Married to the socket is a wooden shaft which may add a further 6 ft. The ancestor of the angon is the Roman legionary *pilum* or throwing-spear, which was designed to penetrate the enemy shield and then bend, so that its weight bore the shield down immediately before the legion charged. Angons occur in the Nydam and Thorsbjerg bog deposits, and also in Germanic warrior-graves of the fifth and later centuries. A few have been found in England, and their presence in royal graves at Sutton Hoo and Taplow suggests that they were prestige weapons. Also rare in this country is the *francisca* or throwing axe, which is considered characteristic of the Franks on the Continent. The distribution of *franciscas* in this country may also denote a Frankish element, for they are relatively common in Kent. They are, however, also known from Saxon areas including Essex, Sussex and Wiltshire. The hand-held axe is even more rare, though its occasional presence with a sword or other military gear shows that a simple woodman's axe might also rank as a prestige weapon.

Another potential weapon, the bow and arrow, seems not to have been used for military purposes. It was certainly known to the Germanic peoples, for arrows occur in large numbers in the Thorsbjerg and Nydam bog deposits, accompanied by bows 5 ft. long— true long-bows, in fact. Arrow-heads are certainly found in graves of the fourth and later centuries on the Continent, especially in the Frankish area. In England, however, only six occurrences are known, mostly in cemeteries in Kent and the Isle of Wight which display other Frankish influences. The probability that the bow and arrow was in fact widely known is shown by an incident in the Whitby *Life of Saint Gregory;* which tells how Paulinus, after preaching to Edwin of Northumbria, was mocked by a crow, which was promptly shot by one of Paulinus' servants. In other words, bows were certainly ready to hand but perhaps only as hunting weapons. This would be consistent with the absence of bows and arrows from both warrior-graves and battle poems. On the other hand, Buiston crannog yielded two arrows with heavy pyramidal heads which would undoubtedly have been described as *ballista* bolts had they been found in a Roman context.

Against this array of offensive weapons the principal defence was the shield (Fig. 19.4). This is common even in the simplest warrior-graves which otherwise contain only a spear. The principal traces left by the shield are its iron fittings: a hand-grip and a circular, domed or conical boss. In our period the boss of the English shield is commonly 5 to 6 in. in diameter and stands 3 to 6 in. high. This reminds us that among the Germans, at least from the first century AD, the shield with its protruding boss was an offensive as well as defensive weapon, one which could be thrust with devastating effect into the face of an enemy. Other parts of the Saxon shield are not well preserved, but from stains in the ground, and odd residues of wood and leather it can be inferred that the main part, the orb, was circular and either flat or concave. It might be up to 2 ft. 9 in. in diameter, and a quarter of an inch thick, made up of leather-covered plywood.[14] Copious references in the poetry make it clear that the Britons also used shields, but no remains have been discovered. From Ireland come rare shield bosses, scarcely more than 4 in. in diameter and 2 in. high. This is consistent with the undeveloped form of Irish swords, and it reminds us of the small circular targes depicted in the Book of Kells.

The question of body armour is exceptionally difficult. The manufacture of ring mail was known to both the Celts and the Germans independently of Roman influences. Cuirasses of chain mail were present in Britain in the Roman army, they were included among the loot or bribes in the Danish bog deposits, and they may well have passed to the Picts, the Scots and the Britons in the same way. Fragments of mail are known from the royal or princely Anglian burials at Sutton Hoo and Benty Grange, but not from other graves, so it is reasonable to conclude that mail armour was worn only by the very highest rank in the Anglo-Saxon armies. In contrast, the impression has been created that British warriors regularly wore armour, including coats of mail. This hypothesis is based on two words which we find used in *Y Gododdin*. The first is *seirch*, which has been translated 'armour' or 'harness'. It is probably derived from the Latin *sarcia*, 'rigging' of a ship, and if this is so then it refers to the leather straps of horse- or sword-harness. The more important word, regularly translated as 'mail-coat', is *lluric*, which certainly comes from Latin *lorica*. Now *lorica* is used for any form of protective device, including the breastwork of a fortification, but more particularly it means a leather cuirass. It also occurs in combinations like *lorica squamata*, 'cuirass of scale armour', or *lorica hamata*, 'cuirass of ring-mail', but without the qualifying adjective it means simply a protective leather jerkin. *Lluric* should mean the same, and if it does then the Gododdin warriors wore simple cuirasses of leather.[15] The Anglo-Saxon analogy would suggest nevertheless that their principal commanders may have worn chainmail.

The helmet was as rare as mail-armour. In fact, the only graves in which helmets have been found are the two already mentioned for their mail, the seventh-century royal burials of Sutton Hoo and Benty Grange. The remains of the Benty Grange helmet consist merely of a framework of iron bands which, according to the excavator, bore traces of plates of horn. The crown of the helmet was surmounted by a wrought-iron boar. The Sutton Hoo helmet was of iron, ornamented with silver inlays, cloisonné garnets, and tinned bronze panels with designs of god and heroes. It had a visor, a neck-guard and hinged cheek-pieces, and its dimensions showed that it must have been heavily padded to fit the warrior's head. Its elaboration argues that it was intended as a parade piece rather than for use in combat. There is indeed no evidence that either the Anglo-Saxons or the Britons wore helmets on the field of battle.[16]

[14] The view that the orb was of plywood is rejected by H. Härke (1981).

[15] For a very different interpretation, see K. H. Jackson (1969), 32.

[16] I now consider this statement to be too strong. It is highly likely that the well-known battle-scene from Aberlemno (Angus) churchyard shows a mounted warrior wearing a helmet of Anglian type.

It has already been pointed out that some iron spearheads might come from either infantry pikes or cavalry lances. Any discussion of the weapons and equipment of the individual warrior must therefore involve the question of whether or not he was mounted. It is notorious that some of the Germanic barbarians were cavalrymen, and much—perhaps too much—has been made of the defeat of the infantry legions by Gothic cavalry at Adrianople in AD 378. But there is no evidence that the Germanic peoples who assaulted Britain—Angles, Saxons, Jutes, Franks, Frisians or others—were horsemen. Consistent with this is the almost complete absence of horse-harness from pagan burials. On the other hand, *Y Gododdin* has enough references to horses to make it clear that the British warriors did use them, and the question arises, how? Did they ride to the field of battle and then fight dismounted as the late Saxons and their Viking opponents certainly did? Or did they actually fight from horseback, either as a disciplined body sweeping the Saxon infantry away with a massed charge, or in some more irregular manner? It is not easy to see any clear or convincing tactical picture in the Gododdin elegies (below, pp. 306–7), but for what they are worth they suggest that the last of these alternatives is correct. Thus we hear of Bleiddig, son of Eli, that 'on the day of combat he would do feats of arms, riding his white steed.' Even more telling is the verse in praise of Marchlew: 'he showered spears in fight from his bounding, wide-coursing [horse].'

The picture which emerges from this and other references to horses in *Y Gododdin* is certainly not one of disciplined cavalry charges. It has even been doubted whether the horsemen of the time, lacking stirrups, could withstand the shock of riding a footsoldier down with a lance.[17] Too much weight should not be given to this suggestion, for a long series of Greek and Roman funerary monuments going back to around 400 BC depict a stirrup-less lancer riding down an infantryman. None the less, our clearest reference in *Y Gododdin*, the Marchlew verse, shows the spear as a missile, not a lance. The thrown spear, together with the sword wielded from horseback, would have suited the spirit of heroic warfare, with its emphasis on individual feats of arms rather than on disciplined common action. It may also be suggested that such weapon-play harks back to the ancestral Celtic cavalry of pre-Roman Britain and Gaul, rather than to military models derived from the Romans.

Having equipped the warrior, we may now inquire into the size and organization of the army of which he was a member. To judge from the casualty figures which the *Anglo-Saxon Chronicle* gives the armies of the Britons were numbered in thousands: 4,000 Britons (or 'four troops' in some versions) were slain at *Creacanford* in 456; 5,000 were killed with their king Natanleod in 508; and in 614 Cynegils and Cwichelm slew over 2,000 Britons at *Beandun*. These figures are almost certainly quite misleading.[18] It is notorious that even in modern warfare claims about enemy slain or aircraft shot down may add up to more than the entire hostile force. In medieval battle accounts too it is well known that when chroniclers' figures for combatants can be tested against actual payments to troops, they may be found to exaggerate by a factor of ten or even fifty. Fortunately we have some very specific figures to control our ideas on the armies of Arthur's Britain. The Laws of Ine of Wessex in the late seventh century defined three grades of raiding party or robber band: up to seven men were thieves, from seven to thirty-five constituted a band, but above three dozen was an army, *here* in Old English. Obviously this was a minimum figure. But when

---

[17] L. White (1962.
[18] P H. Sawyer (1962); (1971), has a parallel discussion of the size of Viking armies.

in 786 Cyneheard, brother of the dispossessed Wessex ruler Sigeberht, tried in turn to overthrow king Cynewulf, his following amounted to eighty-five men, and this was almost enough to capture the kingdom.

Figures like these make the *Chronicle* accounts of the actual immigrant bands seem entirely reasonable. Hengist and Horsa in 449, Ælle and his three sons in 477, and the West Saxons in 514, are all said to have come in three ships. It might be thought that 'three' was a conventional poetic number but for the fact that Cerdic and Cynric in 495 are said to have had five ships, and Port, Bieda and Maegla in 501 two only. But even if we are dealing with conventionalized, even partly fictional accounts, we can at least be sure that we have here the right order of magnitude: two to five ship's companies, perhaps one hundred to two hundred and fifty men. 'Three times fifty men passed over in the fleet with the sons of Erc,' says the *Senchus Fer n Alban* of Dalriada. This same document attributes to the three principal districts of Dalriada an armed muster of twelve (or possibly fifteen— the figures are corrupt) hundred men, and a sea muster of about one thousand 'rowing benches'. If their armed forces were on this scale, it becomes possible to understand how the Scots were able to accept losses of three hundred and three in a victorious battle against the Pictish *Miathi*. The figure itself has a poetic ring, but since our source, Adomnan, is sympathetic to Dalriada there is no reason to suspect that he has exaggerated the losses.

It is in the light of all these examples that we must consider the size of the army which set out from Edinburgh, *Din Eidyn* (Fig. 16.7), to attack the kingdom of Deira at the battle of *Catraeth*, Catterick: the army of the Gododdin. In the poem this force is repeatedly said to have numbered three hundred, though there is also a variation which puts it at three hundred and sixty three. These figures are clearly poetic conventions, the latter being three hundreds and three score and three. We therefore cannot know the exact size of the army, but assuming that *Y Gododdin* is narrating an historical event we can at least ask whether this is the right order of size. On the basis of the Dalriadan evidence we might think not, for a force that was no more numerous than the Dalriadan casualties in a single battle could scarcely have hoped to achieve anything against an established Anglian kingdom. But when we consider how close Cyneheard came to winning the throne of Wessex with a force of less than a hundred, it seems not at all impossible that the Guotodin warriors, given three times that number, might have overthrown the Deiran dynasty if they had enjoyed the luck of battle. Attempts to expand the numbers of the British force by any significant factor depend on the assumption that the mounted nobility was accompanied by a much larger body of footsoldiers who were ignoble and therefore unsung. But it is difficult to see in the social structure of the Britons any large class of ignoble but free-born men who had the right and the responsibility to bear arms. There is one other strict control over our estimates for the size of British and Anglo-Saxon armies. The best calculation for the field army of Roman Britain in about AD 400 puts it at not more than 6,000 troops. In the face of this it is impossible to believe that any of the dozen or so successor-kingdoms could have raised a force of a thousand men.[19]

The organization of these small armies was on a highly personal basis. Its nucleus was the war-band or bodyguard of the king or of a great lord. At the battle of *Degsastan* the king's brother Theodbald was slain 'with all his troop'. There is an echo here of the irregular units of the Roman army, recruited from the barbarians and serving under their

[19] See also the discussion of the size of the Gododdin army in Chapter 17.

own tribal chiefs—the *numerus Hnaudifridi*, for instance. But there is an even stronger echo of the *comitatus*, 'band of companions', which Tacitus described in his account of the Germans of the first century AD. Essentially this was a group of warriors, not necessarily all from the same tribe, who attached themselves voluntarily to a leader of repute in return for arms, food, a share of the booty, and perhaps a permanent grant of land. This institution was of course Celtic as well as Germanic, British as well as Anglo-Saxon. *Y Gododdin* says of Gorthyn, son of Urfai, that 'his gifts and his fame brought visiting throngs', and it is implicit that the 'throngs' were of young warriors who wished to fight under Gorthyn's leadership. In fact the Gododdin army was the *comitatus* of Mynyddog of *Din Eidyn*. It is interesting to notice that Gorthyn had come to Edinburgh from Gwynedd along with other Venedotian soldiers, and that there were also warriors from Elmet and from Pictland in Mynyddog's army. These men should not be thought of as mercenaries, but rather as adventurous young men who offered their military skill to any prince who would reward them with fine weapons, gold rings, mead, feasting and the praise of bards.

But though part of the *comitatus* might be recruited from outside a kingdom in this way, there is no doubt that in our period its kernel was the royal family itself. It was not only his gifts and his fame that brought visiting throngs to Gorthyn, but the fact that 'he was son of a rightful king'. In the Laws of Hywel Dda 'the chief of the bodyguard is to be a son of the king or his nephew'. We have already seen one of Æthelfrith's brothers, Theodbald, killed with his troop at *Degsastan*, and the Northumbrian army was led to battle by another member of the royal family, Hering, son of Æthelfrith's predecessor Hussa. This is not to say that the royal kin would or could have provided the whole of the war-band, even when kinship was reckoned to six or seven degrees. Part at least must have been recruited from the nobility, whether of birth or of service, within or without the kingdom or the tribal territory. But however they were recruited, they were bound to their lord to the death, as numerous contemporary witnesses reveal. The Gododdin band provides one example, Theodbald's troop another. All save one of Cynewulf's companions were slain in 786, and on the following day there was only a single survivor from the *comitatus* of the pretender Cyneheard.

Our next concern must be the kind of military activity in which these armies engaged. We should look at this first from a geographical point of view—where were battles fought, what strategic ideas can be discerned, and so on. No very clear picture emerges before about AD 600, because many of the early battle sites in the *Anglo-Saxon Chronicle* cannot be identified and because the kingdoms themselves were still undefined. The only reasonable generalization is that battles were fought at relatively short range, and mostly within the area that was to crystallize out as a kingdom. The clearest example of this is provided by Wessex in the 570s, when the places captured ranged from Limbury in the east in 571 to Bath in the west in 577, a total crow-distance of ninety miles. The seventh century immediately presents us with a markedly increased range of military operations but this is a reflection of the greater detail of our sources rather than of any revolution in the mobility of armies. We can therefore reasonably infer that a sixth-century army would have been capable of similar movements.

Some concrete examples may be calculated on the assumption that the attacking army set out from the capital or principal stronghold of its own kingdom, though in fact we are never told this in the sources (Fig. 19.5). The century opens, then, with Aedan mac Gabran's army moving from the Dalriadic fortress of Dunadd to a defeat at Dawston (*Degsastan*) in Liddesdale: 120 crow-miles, but a considerably longer journey if it was

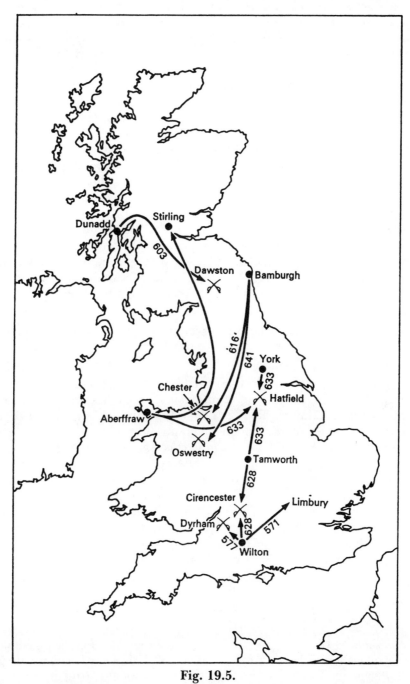

Fig. 19.5.
Map: some historically documented campaigns of the later sixth and seventh centuries

done overland all the way. In 616 Æthelfrith, victor of Dawston, led an army 175 crow-miles from his capital of Bamburgh to Chester to defeat Selim, son of Cynan Garwyn on the borders of Powys. In 633 Edwin was slain at Hatfield Chase only thirty miles from his own capital at York, but sixty-five from Penda's chief centre at Tamworth, and 145 from Cadwallon's principal seat at Aberffraw. Within two years, Cadwallon himself had been killed even further from home, at Denisesburna in the heart of Northumbria. But the most remarkable campaign is that recorded in the 'Northern British History', in which the kings of the Britons went on an expedition with Penda of Mercia against Oswy of Northumbria 'as far as the city called Iudeu', which is probably Stirling.[20] This is 250 miles from Tamworth and about 280 from Aberffraw by way of Chester. Apart from the mobility of seventh-century armies, a further fact is demonstrated by these campaigns. Battles frequently occur near the frontier of the kingdom which is being attacked, but Cadwallon's death at Denisesburna shows that this was not invariably so. And if the place of Oswald's death has been correctly identified as Oswestry, this was on the western, not the eastern boundary of Mercia as might have been expected. It follows that we cannot necessarily infer where frontiers lay from the evidence of battlesites.

Before we inquire further into the strategic ideas of the period, we must examine the motives which inspired a resort to arms in Arthur's Britain. It has frequently been supposed that territorial aggrandizement was a principal motive, but we should not assume without discussion and proof that the policies of a sixth-century barbarian king were the same as those of a post-Renaissance monarch. It has been said of pre-Viking Ireland that

> all wars followed a curiously ritual pattern ... hedged around with taboos ... one did not annex the enemy's territory [nor] dethrone the sacred tribal dynasty; one refrained from attacking a number of 'neutral zones' [including] the monastic settlements.[21]

This hypothesis of ritual, taboo-bound war can be refuted at several points. For instance, it can be proved that the plundering of an enemy's churches and monasteries was a regular feature of pre-Viking warfare in Ireland.[22] Again, the mid-eighth-century folk-tale, 'The Expulsion of the Dessi', though it contains numerous mythical elements, has a genuine historical situation as its core. A compact is made between the Dessi and Oengus mac Nadfraich of Cashel to drive the men of Ossory off their tribal land; after a series of defeats the Dessi are helped to victory by the magic of their druids; 'thereupon the Dessi divide those lands into four parts'. In short, one of the motives of warfare in Ireland could be to 'annex the enemy's territory', contrary to the hypothesis of ritual war outlined above. Nevertheless the very fact that the hypothesis has been put forward demonstrates that we must produce evidence for the causes of war in our period and not simply assume that they are ones familiar to us in the field of post-Machiavellian power politics.

For a start, we should make an analytical distinction between personal reasons and reasons of state, with the caution that in a heroic society this may well be a distinction without a difference. The personal motives of the individual warrior are well set out in *Y Gododdin*:

> When my comrade was struck, he struck others, there was no insult he would put up with. Steady in guarding the ford, he was glad when he bore off the honoured portion in the palace [i.e. a picked portion of meat as a recognized reward at the feast after battle].

[20] Crucial discussion of the identification, and of the significance of the campaign: K. H. Jackson (1963), 35–8. Defence of the identification, K. H. Jackson (1981).

[21] D. A. Binchy (1962).

[22] A. T. Lucas (1967).

and again: 'he slew a great host to win reputation, the son of Nwython slew a hundred princes wearing gold torques so that he might be celebrated.' Ambitions such as these are the driving force of heroic society, and granted the personal nature of kingship, they would have appealed as readily to the king as to any of his lords. And in the realm of ideas, the king would have the further inspiring goal of overlordship over neighbouring rulers.

Apart from these ideal motives, there were of course solid material gains from war. The first of these was loot, expressed most simply in terms of cattle driven in from border countries. Cattle-raiding was endemic in later centuries in Ireland, and there is every reason to project it back into our period and earlier.[23] The Laws of Hywel Dda made provision for the king to take a hosting every year to a border country, and regulated in detail the division of the spoil, which was thought of entirely in terms of cattle. It has been suggested that cattle-raiding was an exciting sport for the young men which did not necessarily breed internecine strife. But there are reasonable analogies here with the better documented sports of horse-raiding among the Blackfoot Indians, or camel-raiding among the Bedu.[24] The purpose in all cases is to take animals, not lives; but if a raiding party is opposed, homicide may result, with all that it entails in blood-feud and vengeance. As it happens, cattle-raiding was more socially acceptable among the Irish, and probably the Britons too, than horse-raiding among the Blackfoot. An extension of the policy of raiding for cattle and other spoil was that of ravaging alien territory in order to exact tribute or, more crudely expressed, to extort bribes. This policy had been well tried against the Roman empire, and it was continued between the various peoples and kingdoms of these islands in the fifth and later centuries. Gildas's description of the Saxon revolt suggests that it had been actuated by motives like these, rather than by any intention of land-taking.

It is nevertheless clear that another objective in warfare might be the extermination, expulsion or subjugation of a native people in order to occupy their territory. The case of the Dessi and the men of Ossory has already been cited. Similarly Cunedda and his sons—a short-hand statement for his war-band—expelled the *Scotti* from Gwynedd and then took over that territory. It should be observed however that there is no reason to think that this particular operation involved either a folk-movement from Manau to Gwynedd, or the extermination and expulsion of the peasant masses. The bondmen merely exchanged one set of masters for another. Likewise, when the *Historia Brittonum* tells us that Edwin of Northumbria took possession of Elmet and drove out Ceretic the king of that district, there is no reason to think that anyone was affected beyond the king and his war-band. It is not in fact easy to assess the evidence for Anglo-Saxon action against the Britons. For centuries the *Anglo-Saxon Chronicle* is full of items about the Britons being slaughtered or put to flight, in terms which seem significantly different from the accounts of battles between one English king and another in the same source. It is almost as though there is an element of literary convention about the record of battles against the Britons. And when we find Bede praising Æthelfrith because of the lands which he had brought under English control, 'having killed off or subjugated the natives', we should also remember that he compared Æthelfrith to Saul and regarded him as an agent of divine retribution on the faithless or heretic Britons. Given the nature of our sources, it is impossible to arrive at an objective assessment of the extent to which the

[23] A. T. Lucas (1958).

[24] Blackfoot Indians: J. C. Ewers (1958), accessible in P. Bohannan (1967). Bedu: first-hand account in W. Thesiger (1959).

Britons were removed, by slaughter or expulsion, from the lands which fell to the English kingdoms.

Land-taking is, of course, an understandable motive of state. But it seems necessary to conclude this survey of the occasions of war in Arthur's Britain with some more examples of the personal character of politics. In 626 there was war between Northumbria and Wessex because of Cwichelm's attempt to have Edwin assassinated. We are not told the reasons for the attempt, but it may be permissible to recall the assassination of Urien of Rheged, which was arranged by his fellow-Briton Morcant out of jealousy. Was it likewise personal jealousy of the success of Æthelfrith of Northumbria, or was it reasons of state, justifiable fear of an expanding neighbour, which caused Aedan mac Gabran to send an army against him? Again we may ask whether it was a clash of personalities or a matter of politics that led Æthelfrith to threaten war against Rædwald of East Anglia for harbouring the refugee Edwin. Whatever the motive, the outcome was in fact that Æthelfrith lost his life and Edwin was set on the Northumbrian throne by Rædwald. A clear-cut case is noted in the middle of the seventh century, when Cenwealh was driven from the throne of Wessex by Penda of Mercia because he had repudiated his wife who was Penda's sister. Surveying the records as a whole, and remembering that they are necessarily incomplete, we cannot escape the impression that war between kings, of whatever nation, was a normal state of affairs; that war was what kingship and nobility were about; and that no further reason of state was required: 'Once every year the king is to have a hosting to a border country.'

If this is so, it is perhaps unreasonable to look for any clear-cut strategic ideas in the warfare of the time. Rædwald's defeat of Æthelfrith is a classic example of a pre-emptive strike. Having been threatened by Æthelfrith, Rædwald raised a large force and overthrew him before he had had time to muster his whole army. The battles of Dyrham in 577 and Chester in 616 have both been seen as strategic moves, respectively by Wessex and Northumbria, to divide the British kingdoms which opposed them. Given our total ignorance of affairs west of the Pennines there is no evidence to support this interpretation of the battle of Chester, and despite Æthelfrith's success there, it appears to have been a hazardous move to operate so far from his main centre of power. Dyrham should be seen simply as a westward expansion from the Wessex heartland, comparable with the eastern expansion along the Chilterns in 571, rather than as part of a strategic plan. On the whole, politics and strategy in the sixth and seventh centuries might be summed up in these terms: every other kingdom, Christian or heathen, English, British, Pictish or Scottish, might be a potential ally, but was certainly an enemy, to be hit whenever the opportunity offered.

It is not easy to say much of contemporary tactics. The chronicles and annals are normally too terse, while Bede is obsessed with the triumph of the small armies of righteousness against the legions of evil. We are left with the colourful details of the battle poetry, but there is good reason to suspect the evidence offered by that genre. The heroic poetry of the *Iliad* appears to offer circumstantial accounts of personal combat, but a detailed study has shown that these by no means exhaust the possible combinations of events in man-to-man encounters.[25] The inference is that battle poetry, far from providing accurate and comprehensive descriptions of the incidents of battle, is a highly stylized medium, bound by set formulas, and to that extent it is a very limited witness. In British

[25] B. Fenik (1968).

battle poems, the emphasis is mostly on personal feats of arms, and on the prowess with spear or sword of the individual warrior. The battle of *Catraeth* has an incoherent, untidy look, which is no doubt realistic enough for close-locked combat, but which blurs any tactical plan or scheme of co-operative action. *Y Gododdin* has, it is true, many apparent references to tactical matters: to vans and wings, to arrays and battle-pens, to plans and designs. But these cannot be used as a basis for writing a sensible account of British weapon-handling and tactics. They fail because they are too stylized, or too vague, or even, in some critical cases, because scholars of equal competence cannot agree on a translation.[26]

Two tactical moves can be discerned more clearly. The first is the dawn attack, which is mentioned repeatedly in *Y Gododdin*, and also in an interpolated verse which tells not of *Catraeth*, but of the battle at Strathcarron, near Falkirk, in 642. Similarly, at the battle of *Denisesburna* Oswald advanced against Cadwallon *incipiente diluculo*, 'as dawn was breaking'. It is not known whether these dawn actions were preceded by night marches of any length, and it is unlikely that they were, given the difficulty of such a manoeuvre. The second tactic is the defence of river-lines, with the consequence that battles frequently take place at fords. One of the Gododdin warriors is praised because he was 'steady in guarding the ford'. Out of the handful of poems reliably attributed to the sixth-century poet Taliesin, one describes a hard-fought battle at a river-crossing in the unidentified Gwen Ystrat. Out of the dozen battles attributed to Arthur in the *Historia Brittonum*, no less than seven were fought at rivers. Whether or not the *Historia Brittonum* is a reliable source here for the historical Arthur, the fact remains that its compiler, or the bard whose battle poem lies behind it, regarded river-lines as the most obvious place for battles to take place. It has been claimed that at fords even a small force of British horsemen would enjoy a great advantage over Anglo-Saxon infantry. This is to ignore the fact that many of the earliest English victories, as reported in the *Anglo-Saxon Chronicle*, were also won at river-crossings.[27]

The emphasis on river battles has as its corollary that warfare was open and mobile, and that strongholds or prepared positions played no great part in it. This makes the rare attacks on fortified places all the more interesting. We have already dismissed the suggestion that Badon was fought at a hill-fort, for this has no support in the earliest accounts of the battle. But the pre-Roman hill-forts of Old Sarum, *Searoburh* in English, and Barbury Castle, *Beranbyrig*, were the scenes of battle between the Britons on the one hand and Cynric and Ceawlin of Wessex on the other in the 550s. The cryptic entries of the *Chronicle* conceal whether or not the engagements took place near the hill-forts, or actually in them, and if the latter, whether the Britons or Saxons were the defenders. Nor is there archaeological evidence to show whether either place had been comprehensively refortified like Cadbury–Camelot, or reoccupied with a minimum of refurbishing like Castle Dore. Altogether more remarkable is the *Chronicle* entry for AD 491:

> 491. Aelle and Cissa besieged Andredes ceaster and slew all who were in there. Not one Briton was left alive.

Andredes ceaster is certainly the Saxon Shore fort of Anderida or Pevensey. We have no idea whether the Britons who were slain formed a regular garrison, or were mere civilian refugees seeking the protection of long-abandoned walls. The fact remains that the main

---

[26] Throughout the preceding section, all references to the evidence of the Gododdin poem should be read in the light of Chapter 16, and of the very different conclusions of K. H. Jackson (1969).

[27] For a fuller discussion of this and the following paragraph, see Chapter 15.

defences would have been substantially intact at the time, and Pevensey would be a formidable obstacle to infantry assault even today.

Another example of an English force beseiging a British army within a Roman fortification is provided by Osric king of Deira who, as Bede says, rashly besieged Cadwallon in an unlocated fortified town. British sieges and attacks on strongholds are also known. According to the 'Northern British History', Urien of Rheged shut up Theodric of Northumbria for three days and nights on the island of Metcaud, Lindisfarne. Here there is no suggestion of a fortified position, and indeed there is little evidence that the Anglo-Saxons made use of prepared strongholds. But if *Catraeth* is correctly identified with Catterick Bridge, *Cataractonium*, then this was a Roman town which had grown up on the site of an original fort. If this is the place referred to when Gwawrddur 'glutted black ravens on the wall of the fort', then that wall was stone-built, $7\frac{1}{2}$ ft thick, and enclosed eighteen acres. There is no reason to suppose that it was in ruins by AD 600. One other stronghold can certainly be attributed to the English of Northumbria: Bamburgh. The northern recension of the *Anglo-Saxon Chronicle* attributes the building of this to Ida, who founded the Anglian dynasty of Bernicia in 547, and states: 'It was enclosed with a hedge and later with a wall.' But the *Historia Brittonum* says that Æthelfrith gave *Dinguoaroy* to his wife Bebba, and from her it took its name, that is *Bebbanburh*, Bamburgh. The question immediately arises, if Ida was responsible for building Bamburgh, why had it a British name, which is what *Dinguoaroy* clearly is. There seems to be a strong possibility that Ida took over a pre-existing British promontory fort, and used it first as a beach-head and subsequently as the citadel of his kingdom.

Whether this was so or not, Bamburgh is the only certain instance of a fortified place used by the early English.[28] But among the Celtic peoples such strongholds were normal, and we must now examine their role in warfare. In Ireland they played an important part as is demonstrated by the frequent references to battles, sieges and burnings at *duns*, that is, at ring-forts, in the contemporary annals. These are supplemented by St Columba's prophecy of a battle in Dun Cethirn, on Sconce Hill near Coleraine: '*in hac vicina munitione Cethirni belligerantes committent bellum*'. In the British sources, by contrast, notices of attacks on strongholds are rare. Except for the rampart of the Roman town of *Cataractonium*, *Catraeth*, there are none in the battle poetry. In the list of Arthur's battles, the ninth was '*in urbe Legionis*', the Roman fortress of Chester or Caerleon; the eighth was '*in castello Guinnion*', an unidentified site which sounds like a Roman auxiliary fort; and the eleventh, if we accept one group of manuscripts and one interpretation of these, may have been at the auxiliary fort of High Rochester. Two points emerge quite clearly. First, the dearth of references to strongholds helps to reinforce the view that warfare was essentially open, and that its major incidents were not sieges and assaults on fortifications but battles at river-crossings. Second, none of the strongholds listed above is known to have been a British fort, whereas those which can be identified for certain are Roman fortifications, whether urban or military.

There is an obvious causal connection between the absence of attacks on British fortifications and the relative weakness of the known defensive works. These often consist of a feeble wall, set, however, in a position of natural strength. There is also a clear relationship between the social structure of the time and the small area of most of these

---

[28] To this I would now add the Northumbrian royal *urbs* of Dunbar which, like Bamburgh, utilized a British stronghold (Fig. 13.11).

forts. Sites like Castle Dore, Chûn, Dinas Powys and Dunadd are essentially defended homesteads, suitable for a prince and his war-band, together with his personal retainers, servants and craftsmen.[29] They contrast with the medium and large hill-forts, enclosing more than three acres, which comprise nearly a half of the pre-Roman forts of southern Britain. These presumably protected social units at the level of the clan or tribe. The contrast is starkest in the case of Garn Boduan, where the post-Roman work, less than half an acre in size, was set within the decayed ramparts of an Iron-Age fort twenty-eight acres in extent (Fig. 19.6). Sometime between the first and the sixth centuries AD there was a social revolution marked by the change in the unit of defence from the tribe as a whole to the chief and his warrior-band. It may be that the abandonment of the thirty-acre tribal capital of Traprain Law in the early fifth century marks the precise moment of that change. If these generalizations are sound, they emphasize the unusual character of Cadbury–Camelot among British strongholds, in terms both of the strength of its post-Roman refortification and of its large extent. It seems unlikely that this eighteen-acre fort

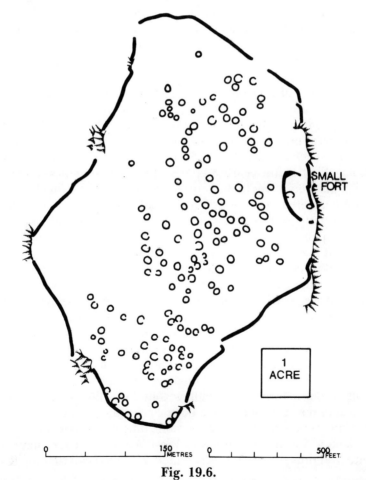

Fig. 19.6.
Plan of Garn Boduan hill-fort, with the later small fort on the summit of the hill

[29] These comments should now be read in the light of Chapter 10.

was intended as a prince's defended homestead, and it is unthinkable that it was a tribal centre on the pre-Roman model. It seems most likely to have served as the base for an army that was large by the standards of the time. This might have been recruited widely like the Gododdin host, or might have combined the war-bands of several kingdoms for the defence of southern and western Britain against Saxons on the south coast and in the Thames valley. Within our present framework of knowledge, it seems plain enough that Cadbury–Camelot played some special part in the warfare of southern Britain in the late fifth and sixth centuries.[30]

We turn finally to the most difficult of all problems in the military archaeology of the late Roman and post-Roman centuries: that of the 'dykes'. It is known that in the fourth century an imperial estate in north Dorset was defended by Bokerly Dyke, a rock-cut ditch and upcast bank.[31] There were three structural phases, of which the second was a response to the great barbarian raid of 367, while the last is dated to the early fifth century. In Cambridgeshire there are several similar dykes which may also have been built in the late fourth century, though it is fair to stress that over the last fifty years their supposed date has fluctuated from the pre-Roman Iron Age to the mid seventh century AD.[32] If, however, we accept a late Roman date for them, then the crossings through the Cambridgeshire dykes may have been manned by troops from the Saxon Shore forts as ambuscades against raiding parties. The greatest of all the dykes attributed to our period is *Wodnesdic*, Wansdyke, which ran from near Savernake Forest in Wiltshire to Maes Knoll in Somerset, with a fifteen-mile gap in the middle. Excavation has shown that the dyke is late Roman or later, while its very name, 'Woden's Dyke', shows that it was in existence before the conversion of Wessex in the 630s. All else about its history is conjecture. It is disputed for a start whether the two separate halves, East and West Wansdyke, are part of the same scheme. East Wansdyke may have been a defensive frontier for the Britons of Salisbury Plain against early Saxon settlers in the Thames valley; or it may be a creation of the Saxons themselves in the course of some internal struggle. West Wansdyke may likewise be interpreted in terms of Wessex politics, or it may be a British defence thrown up after the battle of Dyrham in 577. In that case, it would be part of that same scheme of British response to Dyrham as we have already seen in the second phase of the sixth-century gate at Cadbury–Camelot.

There is at present no evidence to help us decide between these hypotheses, but even if there were we would still be left with the tactical problem: how were the dykes used? We have already noticed the possibility that the Cambridgeshire dykes were used to ambush raiding parties. This seems reasonable granted first that the raiders were encumbered by loot, cattle and captives and were thereby compelled to use the crossings through the dykes; and second, that the posse of the defenders was highly mobile. But these conditions would not apply if the Wansdyke were intended as a defence against military operations other than raiding parties. It is difficult to believe that the infantry of Wessex, whether attacking Britons or fellow-Saxons, would have found the ditch and bank an insuperable obstacle. They would not, therefore, have been constrained to use the gaps through the dyke, where they might be ambushed. At the same time it is impossible that the ten miles of East Wansdyke and the thirteen miles of West Wansdyke could have been manned continuously either in time or space. It is pertinent here to recall that the Roman walls of

---

[30] These arguments are further considered in Chapters 12 and 13.
[31] P. A. Rahtz (1961).
[32] T. C. Lethbridge (1958).

northern Britain, which presumably provided the inspiration for these unsophisticated copies, were dependent for their success on a permanently manned barrier, supplemented by garrisoned forts to front and rear. There were no such permanent garrisons along Wansdyke. It is of course typical of our period that one of its major archaeological monuments should defy attempts to date it, to set it in its political context, or to understand its tactical function.[33]

[33] The best critical account of Wansdyke is still J. N. L. Myres (1964).

Bibliography

Addyman, P. V., 1972. 'The Anglo-Saxon house', *Anglo-Saxon Engl.*, 1, 273–307.

Addyman, P. V., 1976. 'Archaeology and Anglo-Saxon society', in Sieveking *et al.* (1976), pp. 309–22.

Akerman, J. Y., 1855. *Remains of pagan Saxondom* (London).

Alcock, L., 1960a. 'Castell Odo: an embanked settlement on Mynydd Ystum, near Aberdaron, Caernarvonshire', *Archaeol. Cambrensis*, 109, 78–135.

Alcock, L., 1960b. 'Dark age objects of Irish origin from the Lesser Garth Cave, Glamorgan', *Bull. Board Celt. Studies*, 18, 221–7.

Alcock, L., 1960c. 'Post-Roman sherds from Longbury Bank cave, Penally, Pemb.', *Bull. Board Celt. Studies*, 18, 77–8.

Alcock, L., 1963a. *Dinas Powys, an iron age, dark age and early medieval settlement in Glamorgan* (Cardiff).

Alcock, L., 1963b. 'Pottery and settlement in Wales and the Marches, AD 400–700', in Foster and Alcock (1963), pp. 281–302.

Alcock, L., 1965a. 'Hillforts in Wales and the Marches', *Antiquity*, 39, 184–95.

Alcock, L., 1965b. 'Some reflections on early Welsh society and economy', *Welsh Hist. Rev.*, 2, 1–7.

Alcock, L., 1966. 'Castle Tower, Penmaen: a Norman ring-work in Glamorgan,' *Antiq. J.*, 46, 178–210.

Alcock, L., 1967a. 'By South Cadbury is that Camelot ...', *Antiquity*, 41, 50–3.

Alcock, L., 1967b. 'A reconnaissance excavation at South Cadbury Castle, Somerset', *Antiq. J.*, 47, 70–6.

Alcock, L., 1967c. 'Excavations at Degannwy Castle, Caernarvonshire, 1961–6', *Archaeol. J.*, 124, 190–201.

Alcock, L., 1968a. 'Cadbury Castle, 1967', *Antiquity*, 42, 47–51.

Alcock, L., 1968b. 'Excavations at South Cadbury Castle, 1967: a summary report', *Antiq. J.*, 48, 6–17.

Alcock, L., 1969a. 'South Cadbury excavations, 1968', *Antiquity*, 43, 52–6.

Alcock, L., 1969b. 'Excavations at South Cadbury Castle, 1968: a summary report', *Antiq. J.*, 49, 30–40.

Alcock, L., 1970a. 'South Cadbury excavations, 1969', *Antiquity*, 44, 46–9.

Alcock, L., 1970b. 'Excavations at South Cadbury Castle, 1969: a summary report', *Antiq. J.*, 50, 14–25.

Alcock, L., 1970c. 'Was there an Irish Sea culture-province in the dark ages?, in Moore (1970), pp. 55–65.

Alcock, L., 1971. 'Excavations at South Cadbury Castle, 1970: a summary report', *Antiq. J.*, 51, 1–7.

Alcock, L., 1971; 1973. *Arthur's Britain* (London).

Alcock, L., 1972a. *'By South Cadbury is that Camelot ...'*, (London).

Alcock, L., 1972b. 'Excavations at Cadbury-Camelot, 1966–70', *Antiquity*, 46, 29–38.

Alcock, L., 1976. 'A multi-disciplinary chronology for Alt Clut, Castle Rock, Dumbarton', *Proc. Soc. Antiq. Scot.*, 107, 103–13.

Alcock, L., 1978a. *Excavations at Dundurn, St Fillans, Perthshire, 1976–77* (Glasgow).

Alcock, L., 1978b. 'Her ... gefeaht wiþ Walas: aspects of the warfare of Saxons and Britons', *Bull. Board Celt. Studies*, 27, 413–24.

Alcock, L., 1979a. *Excavations at Dun Ollaigh, Oban, Argyll, 1978* (Glasgow).

Alcock, L., 1979b. 'The north Britons, the Picts and the Scots', in Casey (1979a), pp. 134–42.

Alcock, L., 1980a. 'Refortified or newly fortified? The chronology of Dinas Powys', *Antiquity*, 54, 231–2.

Alcock, L., 1980b. 'The Cadbury Castle sequence in the first millennium BC', *Bull. Board Celt. Studies*, 28, 656–718.

Alcock, L., 1980c. '*Populi bestiales Pictorum feroci animo*: a survey of Pictish settlement archaeology', in Hanson & Keppie (1980), pp. 61–95.

Alcock, L., 1981a. 'Early historic fortifications in Scotland', in Guilbert (1981), pp. 150–80.

Alcock, L., 1981b. 'Early historic fortifications of Scotland', *Current Archaeology*, No. 79, 230–6.

Alcock, L., 1981c. 'Quantity or quality: the Anglian graves of Bernicia', in Evison (1981), 168–85.

Alcock, L., 1982. 'Cadbury-Camelot: a fifteen-year perspective', *Proc. Brit. Acad.*, 68, 355–88.

Alcock, L., 1983. 'Gwŷr y Gogledd: an archaeological appraisal', *Archaeol. Cambrensis*, 132, 1–18.

Alcock, L. & Jones, G. R. J., 1962. 'Settlement patterns in Celtic Britain', *Antiquity*, 36, 51–5.

Anderson, A. O. & M. O., 1961. *Adomnan's Life of Columba* (London and Edinburgh).

Anderson, M. O., 1973; 1980. *Kings and Kingship in early Scotland* (Edinburgh).

Andrew, C. K. C., 1949. *Archaeol. Newsletter* 2, 7, 111. Report of Exeter conference.

Anstee, J. W. & Biek, L., 1961. 'A study in pattern welding', *Medieval Archaeol.*, 5, 71–93.

Applebaum, S., 1954. 'The agriculture of the British early iron age', *Proc. Prehist. Soc.*, 20, 103–14.

Arnold, C. J., 1984. *Roman Britain to Saxon England* (London).

ASC. *The Anglo-Saxon Chronicle*, Garmonsway, G. N. trans. 1953; Whitelock, D. *et al*. trans. 1961.

Astill, G. & Lobb, S., 1982, 'Sampling a Saxon settlement site: Wraysbury, Berks., 1980', *Medieval Archaeol.*, 26, 138–42.

Baillie, M. G. L., 1982. *Tree-ring dating and archaeology* (London).

Bannerman, J., 1974. *Studies in the history of Dalriada* (Edinburgh).

Barker, G., 1978. 'Dry bones? Economic studies and historical archaeology in Italy', in H. McK. Blake, T. W. Potter and D. B. Whitehouse (eds.), *Papers in Italian Archaeology I: the Lancaster Seminar* (Oxford), pp. 35–49.

Barker, P. (ed.), 1981. *Wroxeter Roman City Excavations 1966–80*, Dept. of Environment.

Barnes, I., n.d. but *c.* 1982. The analysis and recreation of bronzes and brass mould residues, in T. Bryce & J. Tate (eds.), *The laboratories of the National Museum of Antiquities of Scotland* Vol. 2 (Edinburgh).

Barrow, G. W. S., 1973. *The Kingdom of the Scots* (London).

Bartrum, P., 1949. Some studies in early Welsh history, *Trans. Hon. Soc. Cymmrodorion*, (1948), 279–302.

Bass, G. F., 1982. The pottery, in Bass and van Doorninck, (1982), 155–88.

Bass, G. F. & van Doorninck, F. H., 1982. *Yassi Ada, a seventh-century Byzantine shipwreck* (College Station, Texas).

Battiscombe, C. F. (ed.), 1956. *The relics of St. Cuthbert* (Durham).

Bell, M., 1977. 'Excavations at Bishopstone', *Sussex Archaeol. Collections*, 115.

Bersu, G., 1940. 'Excavations at Little Woodbury', *Proc. Prehist. Soc.*, 6, 30–111.

Biddle, M., 1962. 'The deserted medieval village of Seacourt, Berkshire', *Oxoniensia*, 26/27, 70–201.

Binchy, D. A., 1962. 'The passing of the old order', *Proc. International Congress Celt. Stud. Dublin 1959* (Dublin), 119–32.

Binford, L. R., 1978. *Nunamiut ethnoarchaeology* (New York).

Binford, L. R., 1983. *In pursuit of the past* (London).

Bohannan, P. (ed.), 1967. *Law and warfare: studies in the anthropology of conflict* (New York).

Bonney, D. J., 1973. 'The pagan Saxon period, *c.* 500–*c.* 700', in Crittall (1973).

Boon, G. C., 1957. *Roman Silchester* (London).

Boon, G. C., 1958. 'A note on the Byzantine Æ coins said to have been found at Caerwent', *Bull. Board Celt. Studies*, 17, 316–19.

Boon, G. C., 1975. 'Segontium fifty years on: 1, a Roman stave of larchwood and other unpublished finds mainly of organic materials, together with a note on late barracks', *Archaeol. Cambrensis*, 124, 52–67.

Boon, G. C., 1976. 'Segontium fifty years on: II, the coins', *Archaeol. Cambrensis*, 125, 40–79.

Borius, R. (ed.), 1965. *Constance de Lyon: vie de Saint Germain d'Auxerre*, Sources chrétiennes No. 112 (Paris).

Bourdillon, J. & Coy, J., 1980. 'The animal bones', in P. Holdsworth, *Excavations at Melbourne Street, Southampton, 1971–76* (London), pp. 79–121.

Bradley, R., 1971. 'Artifact density in the interpretation of timber buildings', *Antiquity*, 45, 222–4.

Brahmer, M., Helsztynski, S. & Krzyzandowski, J. (eds.), 1966. *Studies in language and literature in honour of Margaret Schlauch* (Warsaw).

Breese, C. E., 1930. 'The fort of Dinas Emrys', *Archaeol. Cambrensis*, 85, 342–54.

Bromwich, R. & Brinley Jones, R., 1978. *Astudiaethau ar yr Hengerdd* (Cardiff).

Brooke, G. C., 1932. English coins (London).

Brooks, N. P., 1971. 'The development of military obligations in eighth- and ninth-century England', in Clemoes and Hughes (1971), pp. 69–84.

Brooks, N. P., 1978. 'Arms, status and warfare in late-Saxon England', in D. Hill (ed.), *Ethelred the Unready* (Oxford), 81–103.

Brothwell, D. & Higgs, E. (eds.), 1969. *Science in Archaeology* (London).

Brown, G. B., 1903–30. *The arts in early England*, 6 vols., (London).

Brown, J. A. (ed.), 1971. *Approaches to the social dimensions of mortuary practices*, Memoirs of the Society for American Archaeology, 25.

Bruce-Mitford, R. L. S., 1974. *Aspects of Anglo-Saxon archaeology, Sutton Hoo and other discoveries* (London).

Buckley, D. G. (ed.), 1980. *Archaeology in Essex to* AD *1500* (London).

Bulleid, A. & Gray, H. St. G., 1911, 1917. *The Glastonbury Lake Village*, 2 vols., (Taunton).

Bu'Lock, J. D., 1956. 'Early christian memorial formulae', *Archaeol. Cambrensis*, 105, 133–41.

Bu'Lock, J. D., 1960. 'Vortigern and the Pillar of Eliseg', *Antiquity*, 34, 49–53.

Burnham, B. C. & Kingsbury, J. (eds.), 1979. *Space, hierarchy and society* (Oxford).

Burrow, I. C. G., 1973. 'Tintagel—some problems', *Scot. Archaeol. Forum*, 5, 99–103.

Burrow, I. C. G., 1979. 'Roman material from hill-forts', in Casey (1979a), 212–29.

Burrow, I. C. G., 1981a. *Hillforts and hill-top settlement in Somerset in the first to eighth centuries* AD (Oxford).

Burrow, I. C. G., 1981b. 'Hill-forts after the iron age: the relevance of surface fieldwork', in Guilbert (1981), 122–149.

Calkin, J. B., 1955. 'Kimmeridge coal-money: the Romano-British shale armlet industry', *Proc. Dorset Nat. Hist. Archaeol. Soc.*, 75, 45–71.

Camden, W., 1586. *Britannia*.

Campbell, A. (ed. and trans.), 1962. *Chronicon Aethelweardi. The Chronicle of Aethelweard* (London).

Campbell, E. *et al.*, 1984. 'E ware and Aquitaine—a reconsideration of the petrological evidence,' *Scottish Archaeol. Rev.*, 3. i, 35–41.

Campbell, J., 1979a. 'Bede's words for places', in Sawyer (1979), pp. 34–54.

Campbell, J., 1979b. 'Bede's *reges* and *principes*', *Jarrow Lecture*.

Campbell, J. (ed.), 1982. *The Anglo-Saxons* (Oxford).

Casey, P. J., 1971. 'Excavations at Brecon Gaer, 1970', *Archaeol. Cambrensis*, 120, 91–101.

Casey, P. J. (ed.), 1979a. *The end of Roman Britain* (Oxford).

Casey, P. J., 1979b. 'Magnus Maximus in Britain: a reappraisal', in Casey (1979a), pp. 66–79.

Chadwick, H. M., 1907. *The origin of the English nation* (Cambridge).

Chadwick, H. M., 1912. *The heroic age* (Cambridge).

Chadwick, H. M., 1954; 1959. 'The foundation of the early British Kingdoms', in Chadwick, N. K. (1954; 1959), pp. 47–60.

Chadwick, N. K. (ed.), 1954; 1959. *Studies in early British history* (Cambridge).

Chadwick, N. K. (ed.), 1963. *Celt and Saxon* (Cambridge).

Chadwick, S. E., 1958. 'The Anglo-Saxon cemetery at Finglesham, Kent: a reconsideration', *Medieval Archaeol.*, 2, 1–71.

Champion, T., 1978. 'Strategies for sampling a Saxon settlement: a retrospective view of Chalton', in Cherry, Gamble, Shennon (1978), 207–28.

Chaney, W. A., 1970. *The cult of Kingship in Anglo-Saxon England* (Manchester).

Chaplin, R. E., 1971. *The study of animal bones from archaeological sites* (London).

Chaplin, R. E., 1975. Comments on Professor Alcock's paper, in Evans *et al.* (1975), 123.

Chapman, J. C. & Mytum, H. C. (eds.), 1983. *Settlement in north Britain 1000 BC–1000 AD* (Oxford).

Chapman, R. W., 1977. 'Burial practices: an area of mutual interest', in Spriggs (1977), pp. 19–34.

Charles, B. G., 1934. *Old Norse relations with Wales* (Cardiff).

Charles-Edwards, T. M., 1970. 'The date of the four branches of the Mabinogi', *Trans. Hon. Soc. Cymmrodorion*, 263–80.

Charles-Edwards, T. M., 1972. 'Kinship, status and the origins of the hide', *Past and Present*, 56, 3–33.

Charles-Edwards, T. M., 1978. 'The authenticity of the *Gododdin*: an historian's view', in Bromwich and Jones (1978), pp. 44–71.

Cherry, I. F., Gamble, C. & Shennan, S. (eds.), 1978. *Sampling in contemporary British Archaeology* (Oxford).

Christison, D. & Anderson, J., 1905. 'Report on the Society's excavations of forts on the Poltalloch estate, Argyll in 1904–5', *Proc. Soc. Antiq. Scot.*, 39, 259–322.

Christlein, R., 1971. 'Anzeichen von Fibelproduktion in der völkerwanderungszeitlichen Siedlung Runder Berg bei Urath', *Archäologisches Korrespondenzblatt*, 1, 47–9.

Clarke, D. L. & Chapman, B., 1978. *Analytical Archaeology* 2nd ed. (London).

Clark, J. G. D., 1939. *Archaeology & Society* (London).

Clark, J. G. D., 1947. 'Sheep and swine in the husbandry of prehistoric Europe,' *Antiquity*, 21, 122–36.

Clemoes, P. (ed.), 1959. *The Anglo-Saxons* (London).

Clemoes, P. & Hughes, K. (eds.), 1971. *England before the Conquest*, studies in primary sources presented to Dorothy Whitelock (Cambridge).

Close-Brooks, J., forthcoming. Excavations at Clatchard Craig.

Clutton-Brock, J., 1976. 'The animal resources', in Wilson (1976), pp. 373–92.

Coles, J. M. & Simpson, D. D. A. (eds.), 1968. *Studies in Ancient Europe* (Leicester).

Colgrave, B. (ed. and trans.), 1927. *The Life of Bishop Wilfrid by Eddius Stephanus* (Cambridge).

Colgrave, B. & Mynors, R. A. B. (eds. and trans), 1969. *Historia Ecclesiastica Gentis Anglorum* (Oxford).

Collingwood, W. G., 1908. Report on an exploration of the Romano-British settlement at Ewe Close, Crosby Ravensworth, *Trans. Cumberland and Westmoreland Antiq. Archaeol. Soc.*, NS 8, 355–68.

Collins, A. E. P., 1955. 'Excavations in Lough Faughan crannog, Co. Down, 1951–2', *Ulster J. Archaeol.*, 18, 45–82.

Cowie, T. G., 1978. 'Excavations at the Catstane, Midlothian 1977', *Proc. Soc. Antiq. Scot.*, 109, 166–201.

Coy, J., 1980. 'The animal bones', in J. Haslam, 'A Middle Saxon iron smelting site at Ramsbury, Wiltshire', *Medieval Archaeol.*, 24, 41–51.

Cramp, R. J., 1957. '*Beowulf* and archaeology', *Medieval Archaeol.*, 1, 57–77.

Cramp, R. J., 1970. 'The Anglo-Saxon period', in Dewdney (1970), pp. 199–206.

Cramp, R. J., 1983. 'Anglo-Saxon settlement', in Chapman & Mytum (1983), pp. 263–98.

Craw, J. H., 1930. 'Excavations at Dunadd and at other sites on the Poltalloch Estates, Argyll', *Proc. Soc. Antiq. Scot.*, 64, 111–27.

Crawford, O. G. S., 1952. 'Cerdic's landing place', *Antiquity*, 26, 193–200.

Crittall, E. (ed.), 1973, *A history of Wiltshire*, vol. 1. pt. 2 (London).

Crofts, C. B., 1955. 'Maen Castle, Sennen: The excavations', *Proc. West Cornwall Field Club*, 1 pt. 3, 98–115.

Cross, J. E., 1971. 'The ethic of war in old English', in Clemoes & Hughes (1971), pp. 269–282.

Cunliffe, B. W., 1969. *Roman Bath* (London).

Cunliffe, B. W., 1975. *Excavations at Porchester Castle, vol. 1, Roman* (London).

Cunliffe, B. W., 1976. *Excavations at Porchester Castle, vol. 2, Saxon* (London).

Cunliffe, B. W., 1983. 'Earth's grip holds them', in Hartley & Wacher (1983), pp. 67–83.

Curle, A. O., 1905. 'Fortifications on Ruberslaw', *Proc. Soc. Antiq. Scot.*, 39, 219–32.

Curle, A. O., 1914. 'Report on the excavation in September 1913 of a vitrified fort at Rockcliffe, Dalbeattie, known as the Mote of Mark', *Proc. Soc. Antiq. Scot.*, 48, 125–68.

Curle, C. L., 1982. *Pictish and Norse finds from the Brough of Birsay 1934–74* (Edinburgh).

Curwen, E. C., 1937. Querns, *Antiquity*, 11, 133–51.

Davidson, H. R. E., 1962. *The sword in Anglo-Saxon England; its archaeology and literature* (Oxford).

Davidson, H. R. E. & Webster, L., 1967. The Anglo-Saxon burial at Coombe, Woodnesborough, Kent, *Medieval Archaeol.*, 11, 1–41.

Davies, J. L., 1983. 'Coinage and settlement in Roman Wales and the Marches: some observations', *Archaeol. Cambrensis*, 132, 78–94.

Davies, J. L., Hague, D. B. & Hogg, A. H. A., 1971. 'The hut-settlement on Gateholm, Pembrokeshire', *Archaeol. Cambrensis*, 120, 102–110.

Davies, W., 1978a. *An early Welsh microcosm* (London).

Davies, W., 1978b. 'Land and power in early medieval Wales', *Past and Present*, 81, 1–23.

Davies, W., 1979a. 'Roman settlements and post-Roman estates in south-east Wales', in Casey (1979a), pp. 153–73.

Davies, W., 1979b. *The Llandaff Charters* (Aberystwyth).

Davies, W., 1982. *Wales in the early middle ages* (Leicester).

Davies, W., 1983. 'A historian's view of Celtic archaeology', in Hinton (1983), pp. 67–73.

Dawes, E. & Baynes, N. H., 1948. *Three Byzantine saints* (Oxford).

DEB *De Excidio Britonum*, see Winterbottom (1978).

Descriptio Kambriae, see Dimock, J. F. (1868).

Dewdney, J. C. (ed.), 1970. *Durham County with Teeside* (Durham).

Dickinson, T. M., 1978. 'Post-Roman and pagan Anglo-Saxon', *Archaeol. J.*, 135, 332–44.

Dillon, M., 1977. 'The Irish settlements in Wales', *Celtica*, 12, 1–11.

Dimock, J. F. (ed.), 1868. *Giraldi Cambrensis opera VI: Itinerarium Kambriae et Descriptio Kambriae* (Rolls series, London).

Doherty, C., 1980. 'Exchange and trade in early medieval Ireland', *J. Roy. Soc. Antiq. Ireland*, 110, 67–89.

Dolley, R. H. M., 1957. 'The emergency mint of Cadbury', *Brit. Numis. J.*, 28, 99–105.

Dolley, R. H. M. (ed.), 1961. *Anglo-Saxon Coins* (London).

Dolley, R. H. M. & Metcalf, D. M., 1961. 'The reform of the English coinage under Eadgar', in Dolley (1961), pp. 136–68.

Dumville, D. N., 1976. 'Nennius and the *Historia Brittonum*', *Studia Celtica* 10/11, 78–95.

Dumville, D. N., 1977a. 'On the North British section of the Historia Brittonum', *Welsh Hist. Rev.*, 8, 345–54.

Dumville, D. N. 1977b. 'Sub-Roman Britain: history and legend', *History*, 62, 173–92.

Dumville, D. N., 1978. 'Palaeographical considerations in the dating of early Welsh verse', *Bull. Board Celt. Studies*, 27, 246–51.

Eagles, B. N., 1979. *The Anglo-Saxon settlement of Humberside* (Oxford).

Earle, J. & Plummer, C., 1892, 1899. *Two of the Saxon Chronicles Parallel*, 2 vols., (Oxford).

ECMW, *Early Christian Monuments of Wales*, see Nash-Williams (1950).

Edel, D., 1983. 'The catalogue in *Culhwch and Olwen* and Insular Celtic learning', *Bull. Board Celt. Studies*, 30, 253–67.

Edwards, J. G., 1929. *Hywel Dda and the Welsh Lawbrooks* (Bangor).

Edwards, N. *et al.*, 1984. 'The archaeology of early medieval Wales: conference summary', *Bull. Board Celt. Studies*, 31, 319–29.

Ekwall, E., 1936. *The concise Oxford dictionary of English place-names* (Oxford).

Ellison, A., 1980. 'Natives, Romans and Christians on West Hill, Uley', in Rodwell (1980), pp. 305–28.

Ellmers, D., 1978. 'Shipping on the Rhine during the Roman period: the pictorial evidence', in Taylor & Cleere (1978), pp. 1–14.

Emanuel, H. D., 1967. *The Latin texts of the Welsh laws* (Cardiff).

EPNS, English Place-Name Society.

Evans, J. G., Limbrey, S. & Cleere, H. (eds.), 1975. *The effect of Man on the Landscape: the Highland zone* (London).

Evans, J. G. & Rhys, J., 1893. *The Book of Llan Dâv* (Oxford).

Evison, V. I., 1961. In Hurst, J. G., 'The kitchen area of Northolt manor, Middlesex', *Medieval Archaeol.*, 5, 226–30.

Evison, V. I., 1963. 'Sugar-loaf shield bosses', *Antiq. J.*, 43, 38–96.

Evison, V. I., (ed.), 1981. *Angles, Saxons and Jutes* (Oxford).

Ewbank, J. M. *et al.*, 1964. 'Sheep in the Iron Age: a method of Study', *Proc. Prehist. Soc.*, 30, 423–6.

Ewers, J. C., 1958. *The Blackfeet* (Oklahoma).

Fairhurst, H., 1939. 'The galleried dun at Kildonan Bay, Kintyre', *Proc. Soc. Antiq. Scot.*, 75, 185–208.

Fanning, T., 1983. 'Some aspects of the bronze ringed pin in Scotland', in A. O'Connor & D. V. Clarke, *From the Stone Age to the 'Forty-five* (Edinburgh), pp. 324–42.

Farrell, A. W., Penny, S. & Jope, E. M., 1975. 'The Broighter boat: a reassessment', *Irish Archaeol. Research Forum*, II.2, 15–28.

Faussett, B., 1773. *Inventorium Sepulchrale: an account of some antiquities dug up … in Kent from AD 1757 to AD 1773* (London, published 1856).

Fenik, B., 1968. *Typical battle scenes in the Iliad* (Wiesbaden).

Finberg, H. P. R. (ed.), 1972. *The agrarian history of England and Wales, Vol. I–II, AD 43-1042.* (Cambridge).

Finberg, H. P. R., 1974. *The formation of England, 550–1042* (London).

Firth, R., 1927. 'Maori hill-forts', *Antiquity*, 1, 66–78.

Forde-Johnston, J., 1976. *Hill-forts of the Iron Age in England and Wales* (Liverpool).

Foster, I. Ll., 1969. 'Presidential address: Wales and north Britain', *Archaeol. Cambrensis*, 118, 1–16.

Foster, I. Ll. & Alcock, L. (eds.), 1963. *Culture and environment* (London).

Fowler, E., 1960. 'The origins and development of the penannular brooch in Europe', *Proc. Prehist. Soc.*, 26, 149–77.

Fowler, P. J., 1971. 'Hill-forts, AD 400–700', in Hill and Jesson (1971), pp. 203–13.

Fowler, P. J. (ed.), 1972. *Archaeology and the landscape* (London).

Fowler, P. J., 1981. 'Farming in the Anglo-Saxon landscape: an archaeologist's review', *Anglo-Saxon Engl.*, 9, 263–80.

Fowler, P. J., Gardner, K. S. & Rahtz, P. A., 1970. *Cadbury Congresbury, Somerset 1968, an introductory report* (Bristol).

Fox, A., 1946. 'Early Christian period, 1. Settlement sites and other remains', in Nash-Williams (1946), pp. 105–22.

Fox, A., 1952. 'Hill-slope forts and related earthworks in south-west England and south Wales', *Archaeological J.*, 109, 1–22.

Fox, C. and A., 1934. 'Forts and farms on Margam Mountain, Glamorgan', *Antiquity*, 8, 395–413.

Fox, C. & Dickins, B., 1950. *The early cultures of north-west Europe* (Cambridge).

Frere, S. S., 1961. 'Excavations at Verulamium, 1960', *Antiq. J.*, 41, 72–83.

Fulford, M., 1978. 'The interpretation of Britain's late Roman trade: the scope of medieval historical and archaeological analogy', in Taylor & Cleere (1978), pp. 59–69.

Gamble, C., 1978. 'Optimizing information from studies of faunal remains', in Cherry *et al.* (1978), pp. 321–53.

Gardner, W. & Savory, H. N., 1964. *Dinorben, a hill-fort occupied in early iron age and Roman times* (Cardiff).

Garmonsway, G. N. trans., 1953. *The Anglo-Saxon Chronicle* (Everyman edn., London).

Gelling, P. S. & Stanford, S. C., 1967. 'Dark Age pottery or Iron age ovens?', *Trans. Proc. Birmingham Archaeol. Soc.*, 82, 77–91.

Gerriets, M., 1983. 'Economy and society: clientship according to the Irish laws', *Cambridge Medieval Celtic Studies*, 6, 43–61.

Gilbert, J. M., 1976. 'Crossbows on Pictish stones', *Proc. Soc. Antiq. Scot.*, 107, 316–7.

Gildas, see Winterbottom (1978).

Gillies, W., 1981. 'The craftsman in early Celtic literature', *Scot. Archaeol. Forum*, 11, 70–85.

Graham-Campbell, J., 1981. 'The bell and the mould', in Reece (1981), pp. 23–5.

Graham-Campbell, J., Close-Brooks, J. & Laing, L., 1976. 'The Mote of Mark and Celtic interlace', *Antiquity*, 50, 48–53.

Grant, A., 1975. 'The animal bones', in Cunliffe (1975), pp. 378–408.

Grant, A., 1976. 'The animal bones', in Cunliffe (1976), pp. 262–87.

Grant, I. F., 1961. *Highland folk ways* (London).

Gray, H. St. G., 1913. 'Trial excavations at Cadbury Castle, S. Somerset, 1913', *Somerset Archaeol. Natur. Hist. Soc.*, 59, 1–24.

Green, C., 1963. *Sutton Hoo: the excavation of a royal ship-burial* (London).

Green, B. & Rogerson, A., 1978. *The Anglo-Saxon cemetery at Bergh Apton, Norfolk: Catalogue*, East Anglian Archaeology Report 7, Gressenhall.

Gresham, C. A., 1965. Review of *Dinas Powys*, *Antiq. J.*, 45, 127–8.

Grierson, P., 1959. 'Commerce in the dark ages: a critique of the evidence', *Trans. Roy. Hist. Soc. 5th series*, 9, 123–40.

Grimes, W. F., 1951. *The Prehistory of Wales* (2nd edition by H. N. Savory), (Cardiff).

Guilbert, G., 1979. 'Dinorben 1977–8', *Current Archaeology*, No. 65, 182–8.

Guilbert, G. 1980. 'Dinorben C14 dates', *Current Archaeology*, No. 70, 336–8.

Guilbert, G. (ed.), 1981. *Hill-fort studies: Essays for A. H. A. Hogg* (Leicester).

Guthrie, A., 1969. 'Excavation of a settlement at Goldherring, Sancreed, 1958–61', *Cornish Archaeol.*, 8, 5–39.

Hanson, W. S. & Keppie, L. J. F. (eds.), 1980. *Roman Frontier Studies 1979*, (Oxford).

Harden, D. B. (ed.), 1956a. *Dark Age Britain* (London).

Harden, D. B., 1956b. 'Glass vessels in Britain and Ireland, AD 400–1000', in Harden (1956a), pp. 132–67.

Harding, D. W. (ed.), 1976a. *Hill-forts, later prehistoric earthworks in Britain and Ireland* (London).

Harding, D. W. (ed.), 1976b. *Archaeology in the North*.

Harfield, M., 1962. 'Cadbury Castle', *Somerset Archaeol. Natur. Hist. Soc.*, 106, 62–5.

Härke, H., 1981. 'Anglo-Saxon laminated shields at Petersfinger: a myth', *Medieval Archaeol.*, 25, 141–4.

Harris, W., 1773. 'Observations on the *Julia Strata* and on the Roman stations, forts and camps in the counties of Monmouth, Brecknock, Carmarthen and Glamorgan', *Archaeologia*, 2, 1–24.

Hartley, B. & Wacher, J. (eds.), 1983. *Rome and her northern provinces* (Gloucester).

Hawkes, C. F. C., 1947. 'Britons, Romans and Saxons round Salisbury and in Cranborne Chase', *Archaeol. J.*, 104, 27–81.

Hawkes, C. F. C. & Hull, M. R., 1947. *Camulodunum* (Oxford).

Hawkes, S. C. & Dunning, G. C., 1961. 'Soldiers and settlers in Britain, fourth to fifth century: with a catalogue of animal-ornamented buckles and related belt-fittings', *Medieval Archaeol.*, 5, 1–70.

Hayes, J. W., 1972. *Late Roman pottery* (London).

Hayes, J. W., 1980. *Supplement to late Roman pottery* (London).

HE Bede, *Historia Ecclesiastica Gentis Anglorum*, Colgrave, B. & Mynors, R. A. B. (eds.) (1969).

Hencken, H. O'N., 1936. 'Ballinderry Crannog, No. 1', *Proc. Roy. Ir. Acad.*, 43, Section C, 103–239.

Hencken, H. O'N., 1938. *Cahercommaun: a stone fort in County Clare*, extra volume Roy. Soc. Antiq. Ir.

Hencken, H. O'N., 1942. 'Ballinderry Crannog, No. 2', *Proc. Roy. Ir. Acad.*, 47, section C, 1–76.

Hencken, H. O'N., 1950. 'Lagore Crannog: an Irish royal residence of the 7th to 10th centuries AD', *Proc. Roy. Irish Acad.*, 53, Section C, 1–247.

Henry, F., 1956. 'Irish enamels of the Dark Ages and their relations to the cloisonné techniques', in Harden (1956a), pp. 71–88.

Hensel, W., 1969. 'Fortifications en bois de l'Europe orientale', *Château Gaillard 4, Gand 1968*, 71–136.

Higgs, E. S. (ed.), 1972. *Papers in economic prehistory* (Cambridge).

Higgs, E. S. & White, J. P., 1963. 'Autumn killing', *Antiquity*, 37, 282–9.

Hill, D. & Jesson, M. (eds.), 1971. *The iron-age and its hill-forts* (Southampton).

Hills, C., 1979. 'The archaeology of Anglo-Saxon England in the pagan period: a review', *Anglo-Saxon England*, 8, 297–329.

Hinton, D. A. (ed.), 1983. *25 years of medieval archaeology* (Sheffield).

Hirst, S. and Rahtz, P., 1976. *Liddington Castle, Wiltshire, England, 1976*, duplicated note.

Hodges, R., 1982. *Dark Age economics: the origins of towns and trade AD 600–1000* (London).

Hodges, R. & Whitehouse, D., 1983. *Mohammed, Charlemagne & the origins of Europe: archaeology and the Pirenne thesis* (London).

Hodgkin, R. H., 1935. *A history of the Anglo-Saxons*, 2 vols., (London).

Hodgson, G. W. I., 1983. 'The animal remains from medieval sites within three burghs on the eastern Scottish seaboard', in V. B. Proudfoot, *Site, environment and economy* (Oxford), pp. 3–32.

Hogg, A. H. A., 1957. 'A fortified round hut at Carreg-y-Llam, near Nevin', *Archaeol. Cambrensis*, 106, 46–55.

Hogg, A. H. A., 1960. 'Garn Boduan and Tre'r Ceiri', *Archaeol. J.*, 117, 1–39.

Hogg, A. H. A., 1972. 'Cerdic and the Cloven Way again', *Antiquity*, 46, 222–3.

Hogg, A. H. A., 1974. 'The Llantwit Major villa: a reconsideration of the evidence', *Britannia*, 5, 225–50.

Hogg, A. H. A., 1979. *British hill-forts: an index* (Oxford).

Hope-Taylor, B., 1965. Review of *Dinas Powys, Medieval Archaeol.*, 9, 223–4.

Hope-Taylor, B., 1966. 'Bamburgh', *Univ. Durham Gazette*, 8, 11–12.

Hope-Taylor, B., 1977. *Yeavering: an Anglo-British centre of early Northumbria* (London).

Hope-Taylor, B., 1980. 'Balbridie and Doon Hill', *Current Archaeol.*, No. 72, 18–19.

Hoskins, W. G., 1960. *The westward expansion of Wessex*, Dept. of English Local History, University of Leicester, Occasional Papers 13.

Howell, M., 1966. 'A soil conductivity meter', *Archaeometry*, 9, 20–3.

Hughes, K., 1972. *Early Christian Ireland: introduction to the sources* (London).

Hughes, K., 1980. *Celtic Britain in the Early Middle Ages* (Woodbridge).

Hunter Blair, P., 1954; 1959. 'The Bernicians and their northern frontier', in Chadwick, N.K., (1954; 1959), pp. 137–72.

Hunter Blair, P., 1963. 'Some observations on the *Historia Regum* attributed to Symeon of Durham', in Chadwick, N.K. (1963), pp. 63–118.

Jackson, D. A. & Ambrose, T. M., 1978. 'Excavations at Wakerley, *Britannia*, 9, 115–242.

Jackson, K. H., 1945. 'Once again Arthur's battles', *Modern Philology*, 63, 44–57.

Jackson, K. H., 1950. 'Notes on the Ogam inscriptions of southern Britain', in Fox and Dickins (1950), pp. 197–213.

Jackson, K. H., 1955. 'The Britons in southern Scotland', *Antiquity*, 29, 77–88.

Jackson, K. H., 1958. 'The site of Mount Badon ', *J. Celt. Stud.*, 2, 152–5.

Jackson, K. H., 1959. 'Edinburgh and the Anglian occupation of Lothian', in Clemoes (1959), pp. 34–42.

Jackson, K. H., 1963. 'On the Northern British Section in Nennius', in Chadwick, N.K. (1963), pp. 20–62.

Jackson, K. H. (trans.), 1969. *The Gododdin* (Edinburgh).

Jackson, K. H., 1973. Review of Alcock 1971, *Antiquity*, 47, 80–1.

Jackson, K. H., 1981. '*Varia I*: Bede's *urbs Giudi*: Stirling or Cramond?', *Cambridge Medieval Celtic Studies*, 2, 1–8.

Jackson, K. H., 1982. '*Varia II*: Gildas and the names of the British Princes', *Cambridge Medieval Celtic Studies*, 3, 30–40.

James, E., 1982. 'Ireland and western Gaul in the Merovingian period', in Whitelock *et al.* (1982), pp. 362–86.

James, H. & Williams, G., 1982. 'Rural settlement in Roman Dyfed', in Miles (1982), pp. 289–312.

Johnson, N. & Rose, P., 1982. 'Settlement in Cornwall—an illustrated discussion', in Miles (1982), pp. 151–207.

Jolliffe, J. E. A., 1926. 'Northumbrian Institutions', *Engl. Hist. Rev.*, 41, 1–42.

Jones, A. H. M., 1964. *The later Roman Empire*, 3 vols., (Oxford).

Jones, G. & Jones, T. (trans.), 1949. *The Mabinogion*, Everyman edn., (London).

Jones, G. R. J., 1960. 'The pattern of settlement on the Welsh border', *Agricultural Hist. Rev.*, 8, 66–81.

Jones, G. R. J., 1961. 'Settlement patterns in Anglo-Saxon England', *Antiquity*, 35, 221–32.

Jones, G. R. J., 1963. 'The tribal system in Wales: a re-assessment in the light of settlement studies', *Welsh Hist. Rev.*, 1, 111–32.

Jones, G. R. J., 1965. 'The distribution of bond settlements in north-west Wales', *Welsh Hist. Rev.*, 2, 19–36.

Jones, G. R. J., 1967. Review of *Dinas Powys*, *Welsh Hist. Rev.*, 3, 75–6.

Jones, G. R. J., 1972. 'Post-Roman Wales', in Finberg (1972), pp. 279–382.

Jones, G. R. J., 1976. 'Multiple estates and early settlements', in Sawyer (1976), pp. 15–40.

(Alcock, L.) & Jones, G. R. J., 1962. 'Settlement patterns in Celtic Britain', *Antiquity*, 36, 51–5.

Jones, M. (ed.), 1983. *Integrating the subsistence economy* (Oxford).

Jones, T., 1964. 'The early evolution of the legend of Arthur', *Nottingham Medieval Stud.*, 8, 3–21.

Jones, T., 1966. 'A sixteenth-century version of the Arthurian cave legend', in Brahmer *et al.* (1966), pp. 175–85.

Jones, T., 1972. Review of Alcock 1971, *Studia Celtica*, 7, 184–6.

Jope, E. M. (ed.), 1961. *Studies in building history* (London).

Jope, M., 1962. 'The animal remains', in Biddle, (1962), pp. 197–201.

Kapelle, W. E., 1979. *The Norman Conquest of the North* (London).

Keeney, G. S., 1939. 'A pagan Anglian cemetery at Howick, Northumberland', *Archaeol. Aeliana*, 4th series, 16, 120–8.

Kent, J. P. C., 1961. 'From Roman Britain to Saxon England', in Dolley (1961), pp. 1–22.

Kent, J. P. C., 1979. 'The end of Roman Britain: the literary and numismatic evidence reviewed', in Casey (1979a), pp. 15–27.

Kidd, D., 1976. Review of J. N. L. Myres & W. H. Southern, *The Anglo-Saxon cremation cemetery at Sancton, Medieval Archaeol.*, 20, 202–4.

Kilbride-Jones, H. E., 1980a. *Celtic craftsmanship in bronze,* (London).

Kilbride-Jones, H. E., 1980b. *Zoomorphic penannular brooches* (London).

King, A., 1978. 'A comparative survey of bone assemblages from Roman sites in Britain', *Bulletin, University of London Inst. Archaeol.*, 15, 207–32.

Knocker, G. M., 1958. 'Early burials and an Anglo-Saxon cemetery at Snell's Corner, near Horndean, Hampshire', *Proc. Hants. Fld. Club Archaeol. Soc.*, 19, 117–70.

Krusch, B. & Levison, W. (eds.), 1920. *Passiones vitaeque sanctorum aevi Merovingici* (Hanover and London).

Laing, Ll. R., 1969. 'Timber halls in dark age Britain—some problems', *Trans. Dumfriesshire Galloway Natur. Hist. Antiq. Soc.* 3rd series, 46, 110–27.

Laing, Ll. R., 1973. 'The Angles in Scotland and the Mote of Mark', *Trans. Dumfriesshire Galloway Natur. Hist. Antiq. Soc.* 3rd series, 50, 37–52.

Laing, Ll. R., 1975a. 'The Mote of Mark and the origins of Celtic interlace', *Antiquity*, 49, 98–108.

Laing, Ll. R., 1975b. *Settlement types in post-Roman Scotland* (Oxford).

Lamm, K., 1980. 'Early medieval metalworking on Helgö in central Sweden', in Oddy (1980), pp. 97–116.

Lamond, E. & Cunningham, W., 1890. *Walter of Henley's Husbandry* (London).

Lane, A., 1984. 'Some Pictish problems at Dunadd', in J. G. P. Friell and W. G. Watson, *Pictish Studies* (Oxford), pp. 43–62.

Lane, F. C., 1974. 'Progrés technologique et productivité dans les transport maritimes de la fin du Moyen Age au début des temps modernes', *Revue Historique*, 510, 278–9.

Lasko, P., 1956. 'The comb', in Battiscombe (1956), pp. 336–55.

Lauwerier, R. C. G. M., 1983. 'Pigs, piglets and determining the season of slaughtering', *J. Archaeol. Science*, 10, 483–8.

Lawlor, H. C., 1925. *The monastery of Saint Mochaoi of Nendrum* (Belfast).

Leach, P. E. (ed.), 1982. *Archaeology in Kent to AD 1500* (London).

Leeds, E. T., 1927. 'Excavations at Chûn Castle in Penwith, Cornwall', *Archaeologia*, 76, 205–40.

Leeds, E. T., 1931. 'Excavations at Chûn Castle in Penwith, Cornwall' (Second Report), *Archaeologia*, 81, 33–42.

Leeds, E. T., 1947. 'A Saxon village near Sutton Courtenay, Berkshire', *Archaeologia*, 92, 79–94.

Leeds, E. T., 1949. *Corpus of great square-headed brooches* (Oxford).

Leeds, E. T. & Harden, D. B., 1936. *The Anglo-Saxon cemetery at Abingdon, Berkshire* (Oxford).

Leeds, E. T. & Pocock, M., 1971. 'A survey of the Anglo-Saxon cruciform brooches of florid type', *Medieval Archaeol.*, 15, 13–36.

Leeds, E. T. & Shortt, H. de S., 1953. *An Anglo-Saxon cemetery at Petersfinger, near Salisbury, Wilts.* (Salisbury).

Lethbridge, T. C., 1931. *Recent excavations in Anglo-Saxon cemeteries in Cambridgeshire and Suffolk,* Cambridge Antiq. Soc. Quarto Publications, n.s.3.

Lethbridge, T. C., 1936. *A cemetery at Shudy Camps, Cambridgeshire,* Cambridge Antiq. Soc. Quarto Publications n.s. 5.

Lethbridge, T. C., 1956. 'The Anglo-Saxon settlement in eastern England', in Harden (1956a), pp. 112–22.

Lethbridge, T. C., 1958. 'The riddle of the dykes', *Proc. Cambridge Antiq. Soc.*, 51, 1–5.

Levison, W., 1920. *Vita Germani auctore Constantio,* in Krusch and Levison (1920).

Lewis, H. (ed.), 1963. *Angles and Britons, O'Donnell lectures* (Cardiff).

LHD *The Laws of Hywel Dda*, see Richards, M. (1954).

Lloyd, J. E., 1911; 1939. *A History of Wales* (London).

Longley, D., 1982. 'The date of the Mote of Mark', *Antiquity*, 56, 132–4.

Lucas, A. T., 1958. 'Cattle in ancient and medieval Irish society', *O'Connell School union record 1937–58*.

Lucas, A. T., 1967. 'The plundering and burning of churches in Ireland, 7th to 16th century', in Rynne (1967), pp. 172–229.

Lynn, C. J., 1978. 'Early Christian period domestic structures: a change from round to rectangular plans?', *Irish Archaeol. Research Forum*, 5, 29–46.

The Mabinogion, see Jones, G. & Jones, T.

McCormick, F., 1983. 'Dairying and beef production in Early Christian Ireland: the faunal evidence', in T. Reeves-Smyth & F. Hammond (eds.), *Landscape archaeology in Ireland* (Oxford), pp. 253–67.

McGrail, S., 1976. 'Problems in Irish nautical archaeology', *Irish Archaeol. Research Forum*, III. 1, 21–31.

McGrail, S., 1980. 'Ships, shipwrights and seamen', in J. Graham-Campbell (ed.), *The Viking world* (London), pp. 36–63.

MacGregor, A. G., 1985. *Bone, antler, ivory and horn: the technology of skeletal materials since the Roman period* (London).

MacGregor, A. G. & Currey, J. D., 1983. 'Mechanical properties as conditioning factors in the bone and antler industry of the 3rd to the 13th century AD', *J. Archaeol. Science*, 10, 71–7.

MacQueen, J., 1955. 'Yvain, Ewen, and Owain ap Urien', *Trans. Dumfriesshire Galloway Natur. Hist. Antiq. Soc.* 3rd ser., 33, 107–31.

Maguire, D. J., 1983. 'The identification of agricultural activity, using pollen analysis', in Jones, M. (1983), pp. 5–18.

Mallory, J. P., 1981. 'The sword of the Ulster cycle', in B. G. Scott (ed.), *Studies on early Ireland*, pp. 99–114.

Maltby, M., 1979. *Faunal studies on urban sites: the animal bones from Exeter 1971–1975*, in *Exeter archaeological reports Vol. 2*, (Sheffield).

Manning, W. H., 1964. 'The plough in Roman Britain', *J. Roman Stud.*, 54, 54–65.

Manning, W. H. & Scott, I. R., 1979. 'Roman timber military gateways', *Britannia*, 10, 19–62.

Mattingly, H., Sydenham, E. A., *et al.*, 1923. *Roman Imperial Coinage* (London).

Meaney, A. L., 1964. *A gazetteer of early Anglo-Saxon burial sites* (London).

Meaney, A. L. & Hawkes, S. C., 1970. *The Anglo-Saxon cemeteries at Winnal*, Society for Medieval Archaeology Monograph series: No. 4, London.

Megaw, J. V. S. (ed.), 1976. *To illustrate the monuments. Essays on archaeology presented to Stuart Piggott* (London).

Meyer, K., 1896. 'Early relations between Gael and Brython', *Trans. Hon. Soc. Cymmrodorion*, 55–86.

Meyer, K., 1900. 'The expulsion of the Dessi', *Y Cymmrodor*, 14, 101–35.

Miket, R., 1980. 'A re-statement of evidence for Bernician Anglo-Saxon burials', in Rahtz *et al.*, (1980), pp. 289–305.

Miket, R. & Pocock, M., 1976. 'An Anglo-Saxon cemetery at Greenbank, Darlington', *Medieval Archaeol.*, 20, 62–74.

Mildenberger, G., 1959. *Die germanischen Funde der Völkerwanderungszeit in Sachsen* (Dresden).

Miles, D. (ed.), 1982. *The Romano-British countryside, studies in rural settlement and economy* (Oxford).

Miles, H. *et al.*, 1977. 'Excavations at Killibury hill-fort, Egloshayle 1975–6', *Cornish Archaeol.*, 16, 89–121.

Miles, H. and T., 1973. 'Excavations at Trethurgy, St Austell, interim report', *Cornish Archaeol.*, 12, 25–9.

Miller, M., 1976a. 'The relative and absolute publication dates of Gildas's *De Excidio* in medieval scholarship', *Bull. Board Celt. Studies*, 26, 169–74.

Miller, M., 1976b 'Date-guessing and pedigrees', *Studia Celtica*, 10/11, 96–109.

Miller, M., 1978a. 'Date-guessing and Dyfed', *Studia Celtica*, 12/13, 33–61.

Miller, M., 1978b. 'The foundation legend of Gwynedd in the Latin texts', *Bull. Board Celt. Studies*, 27, 515–32.

Miller, M., 1979. *The Saints of Gwynedd* (Woodbridge).

Miller, M., 1980. 'Royal Pedigrees of the insular dark ages: a progress report', *Hist. in Africa*, 7, 201–24.

Mitchell, A., 1880. *The past in the present* (Edinburgh).

Moore, D. (ed.), 1970. *The Irish Sea Province in Archaeology and History*, (Cambrian Archaeological Association, Cardiff).

Morgan, W. Ll., 1920. 'Presidential address: the classification of camps and earthworks', *Archaeol. Cambrensis*, 75, 201–23.

Moritz, L. A., 1958. *Grain-mills and flour in classical antiquity* (Oxford).

Morris, E. L., 1981. 'Ceramic exchange in western Britain: a preliminary view', in H. Howard & E. L. Morris (eds.), *Production and distribution: a ceramic viewpoint* (Oxford), pp. 67–81.

Morris, J., 1963. Review of Chadwick, N. K. (ed.), *Studies in the early British church, Welsh Hist. Rev.*, 1, 229–32.

Morris, J., (ed. & trans.), 1980. *Nennius: British History and the Welsh Annals* (London).

Morris-Jones, J., 1918. 'Taliesin', *Y Cymmrodor*, 28.

Moss, R. J., 1927. 'A chemical examination of crucibles', *Proc. Roy. Irish Acad.*, 37, Section C, 175–93.

Munro, R., 1882. *Ancient Scottish Lake-Dwellings or Crannogs* (Edinburgh).

Musson, C. R., 1968. 'A geophysical survey at South Cadbury Castle, Somerset, using the Howell soil "conductivity" anomaly detector', *Prospezioni Archaeologiche*, 3, 115–21.

Musson, C. R., 1976. 'Excavations at the Breiddin 1969–1973', in Harding (1976a), pp. 293–302.

Myres, J. N. L., 1936. Book V of Collingwood, R. G. and Myres, J. N. L., *Roman Britain and the English Settlements* (Oxford).

Myres, J. N. L., 1964. 'Wansdyke and the origin of Wessex', in Trevor-Roper (1964), pp. 1–29.

Myres, J. N. L., 1969. *Anglo-Saxon pottery and the settlement of England* (Oxford).

Myres, J. N. L., 1977. *A corpus of Anglo-Saxon pottery of the pagan period* (Cambridge).

Mytum, H. C., 1982. 'Rural settlement of the Roman period in north and east Wales', in Miles (1982), 313–35.

Nash-Williams, V. E., 1930. 'Further excavations at Caerwent, Monmouthshire, 1923–5', *Archaeologia*, 80, 229–88.

Nash-Williams, V. E., 1946. *A hundred years of Welsh archaeology: Cambrian Archaeological Association Centenary Volume 1846–1946* (Gloucester, n.d.).

Nash-Williams, V. E., 1950. *The early Christian monuments of Wales* (Cardiff).

Nash-Williams, V. E., 1953. 'The forum-and-basilica and public baths of the Roman town of *Venta Silurum*', *Bull. Board Celt. Studies*, 15, 81–98.

Nash-Williams, V. E., 1954. *The Roman frontier in Wales* (Cardiff).

Nieke, M. R., 1983. 'Settlement patterns in the first millennium AD: a case study of the island of Islay', in Chapman & Mytum (1983), pp. 299–325.

Noddle, B. A., 1975. 'A comparison of the animal bones from medieval sites in southern Britain', in A. T. Clason (ed.), *Archaeolzoological Studies* (Amsterdam), pp. 248–60.

Noddle, B. A., 1983. 'Size and shape, time and place: skeletal variations in cattle and sheep', in Jones, M. (1983), pp. 211–38.

O'Connor, T. P., 1984. *Selected groups of bones from Skeldergate and Walmgate* (London).

ÓCorráin, D., 1980. Review of Bannerman (1974), *Celtica*, 13, 168–82.

Oddy, W. A. (ed.), 1980. *Aspects of early metallurgy* (London).

O'Kelly, M. J., 1952. 'St Gobnet's House, Ballyvourney, Co. Cork', *J. Cork Hist. Archaeol. Soc.*, 57, 18–40.

O'Kelly, M. J., 1962. 'Two ring-forts at Garryduff, Co. Cork', *Proc. Roy. Irish Acad.*, 63, Section C, 17–125.

O'Leary, T. J., 1981. 'Excavations at Upper Borough Walls, Bath, 1980', *Medieval Archaeol.*, 25, 1–30.

O'Meadhra, U., 1979. *Early Christian, Viking and Romanesque art motif-pieces from Ireland* (Stockholm).

O'Neil, B. H. St. J., 1935. 'Coins and archaeology in Britain', *Archaeol. J.*, 92, 64–80.

O'Neil, B. H. St. J., 1937. 'Excavations at Breiddin hill camp, Mont. 1933–5', *Archaeol. Cambrensis*, 92, 86–128.

O'Rahilly, T. F., 1946. *Early Irish History and Mythology* (Dublin).

Ordnance Survey, 1966. *Map of Britain in the dark ages* (Chessington).

Ordnance Survey, 1973. *Britain before the Norman Conquest* (Southampton).

Ó Ríordáin, S. P., 1942. 'The excavation of a large earthen ring-fort at Garranes, Co. Cork', *Proc. Roy. Irish Acad.*, 47, Section C, 77–150.

Ó Ríordáin, S. P., 1949. 'Lough Gur excavations: Carraig Aille and the "Spectacles",' *Proc. Roy. Irish Acad.*, 52, Section C, 39–111.

Ó Ríordáin, S. P. & Hartnett, P. J., 1943. 'The excavation of Ballycatteen Fort, Co. Cork', *Proc. Roy. Irish Acad.*, 49, Section C, 1–43.

Orme, B., 1981. *Anthropology for archaeologists: an introduction* (London).

Oschinsky, D., 1971. *Walter of Henley* (Oxford).

Owen, A., 1841. *Ancient Laws and Institutes of Wales* (London).

Padel, O. J., 1981. 'Tintagel—an alternative view', in Thomas (1981), pp. 28–9.

Pader, E.-J., 1982. *Symbolism, social relations and the interpretation of mortuary remains* (Oxford).

Page, W., 1906. *Victoria History of the County of Devon* I, (London).

Payne, S., 1972a. 'Partial recovery and sample bias: the results of some sieving experiments', in Higgs (1972), pp. 49–64..

Payne, S., 1972b. 'On the interpretation of bone samples from archaeological sites', in Higgs (1972), pp. 65–82.

Peacock, D. P. S., 1978. 'The Rhine and the problem of Gaulish wine in Roman Britain', in Taylor & Cleere (1978), pp. 49–51.

Peacock, D. P. S. & Thomas, A. C., 1967. 'Class E imported post-Roman pottery: a suggested origin', *Cornish Archaeol.*, 6, 35–46.

Pearce, S. (ed.), 1982. *The early church in Western Britain and Ireland* (Oxford).

Phillimore, E., 1888. 'The *Annales Cambriae* and old Welsh Genealogies from Harleian MS 3859', *Y Cymmrodor*, 9, 141–93.

Phillips, C. W., 1934. 'The excavation of a hut group at Pant-y-Saer in the parish of Llanfair-Mathafarn-Eithaf, Anglesey', *Archaeol. Cambrensis*, 89, 1–36.

Pickford, C. E., 1969. 'Camelot', *Bibliographical Bull. International Arthurian Soc.*, 21, 158–9.

Pierce, T. Jones, 1963; 1972. 'Social and historical aspects of the Welsh Laws', *Welsh Hist. Rev.*, special number, 33–49, and in *Medieval Welsh Society*.

Pierce, T. Jones, 1972. *Medieval Welsh Society: selected essays*, (ed.), J. B. Smith (Cardiff).

Piggott, S., 1958. 'Native economies and the Roman occupation of north Britain', in Richmond (1958), pp. 1–27.

Playne, G. F., 1876. 'On the ancient camps of Gloucestershire', *Proc. Cotteswold Naturalists' Field Club*, 6 (1871–6), 202–46.

Pocock, M., 1970. 'A note on two early Anglo-Saxon brooches', *Yorkshire Archaeol. J.*, 42, 407–9.

Pocock, M., 1971. 'A buckle-plate and three Anglian brooches from Catterick', *Yorkshire Archaeol. J.*, 43, 187–8.

Pollard, S. H. M., 1966. 'Neolithic and dark age settlements on High Peak, Sidmouth, Devon', *Proc. Devon Archaeol. Soc.*, 23, 35–59.

Proudfoot, V. B., 1961. 'The economy of the Irish rath', *Medieval Archaeol.*, 5, 94–122.

Rackham, J., 1983. 'Faunal sample to subsistence economy: some problems in reconstruction', in Jones, M. (1983), pp. 251–77.

Radford, C. A. R., 1935. 'Tintagel: the castle and Celtic monastery', *Antiq. J.*, 15, 401–19.

Radford, C. A. R., 1951. 'Report on the excavations at Castle Dore', *J. Roy. Inst. Cornwall*, N.S.1 appendix.

Radford, C. A. R., 1956. 'Imported pottery found at Tintagel, Cornwall', in Harden (1956a), pp. 59–70.

Radford, C. A. R., 1957. 'The Saxon house', *Medieval Archaeol.*, 1, 27–38.

Radford, C. A. R., 1958. 'Vortigern', *Antiquity*, 32, 19–24.

Radfort, C. A. R., 1967. 'The early church in Strathclyde and Galloway', *Medieval Archaeol.*, 11, 105–26.

Radford, C. A. R., 1978. 'The pre-Conquest boroughs of England', *Proc. Brit. Acad.*, 64, 131–53.

Radford, C. A. R. & Cox, J. S., 1955. 'Cadbury Castle, South Cadbury', *Proc. Somerset Archaeol. Natur. Hist. Soc.*, 99–100, 106–13.

Rahtz, P. A., 1961. 'An excavation on Bokerley Dyke, 1958', *Archaeol. J.*, 118, 65–99.

Rahtz, P. A., 1963. 'The Saxon and medieval palaces at Cheddar, Somerset', *Medieval Archaeol.*, 6–7, 53–66.

Rahtz, P. A., 1971. 'Castle Dore—a reappraisal of the post-Roman structures', *Cornish Archaeol.*, 10, 49–54.

Rahtz, P. A., 1976. 'Buildings and rural settlement', in Wilson (1976), pp. 49–98.

Rahtz, P. A., Dickinson, T. & Watt, L. (eds.), 1980. *Anglo-Saxon cemeteries 1979* (Oxford).

Rahtz, P. A. & Fowler, P., 1972. 'Somerset AD 400–700', in Fowler (1972), pp. 187–221.

Ralston, I. B. M., 1980. 'The Green Castle and the promontory forts of north-east Scotland', *Scot. Archaeol. Forum*, 10, 27–40.

RCAHMS, 1971. *Argyll, an inventory of the ancient monuments, Vol. I, Kintyre* (Edinburgh).

RCAHMW, 1937. *An inventory of the ancient monuments in Anglesey* (London).

RCAHMW, 1956–1964. *An inventory of the ancient monuments in Caernarvonshire*, Vol. I, East (1956); Vol. II, Central (1960); Vol. III, West (1964), London.

RCAHMW, 1976. *An inventory of the ancient monuments in Glamorgan*, Vol. I, pt. 2, The Iron Age and Roman occupation; pt. 3, The Early Christian period.

Reece, R., 1980. 'Town and country: the end of Roman Britain', *World archaeology*, 12:1, 77–92.

Reece, R., 1981. *Excavations in Iona 1964 to 1974* (London).

Rees, W., 1963. 'Survivals of Ancient Celtic customs in Medieval England', in Lewis (1963), pp. 148–68.

Reynolds, J. M., 1966. 'Legal and constitutional problems', in J. S. Wacher, (ed.), *The civitas capitals of Roman Britain* (Leicester), pp. 70–5.

Reynolds, N., 1980. 'Dark age timber halls and the background to excavation at Balbridie', *Scot. Archaeol. Forum*, 10, 41–60.

RIC, 1923. *Roman Imperial Coinage*, (eds.) Mattingly, H., Sydenham, E. A. *et al.*, (London).

Richards, M., (trans.), 1954. *The Laws of Hywel Dda (the Book of Blegywryd)* (Liverpool).

Richards, M., 1960. 'The Irish settlements in south-west Wales', *J. Roy. Soc. Antiq. Ir.*, 90, 133–62.

Richards, M. 1971. 'Places and persons of the early Welsh church', *Welsh Hist. Rev.*, 5, 333–49.

Richards, M., 1973. 'The Lichfield Gospels (Book of St Chad)', *National Library Wales J.*, 18, 135–46.

Richmond, I. A., (ed.), 1958. *Roman and native in north Britain* (Edinburgh).

Richmond, I. A., 1961. 'Roman timber buildings', in Jope (1961), pp. 15–26.

Richmond, I. A., 1968. *Hod Hill* (London).

Rigoir, J., 1968. 'Les sigillées paléochrétiennes grises et orangées', *Gallia*, 26, 177–244.

Rigoir, J. & Y. & Meffre, J.-F., 1973. 'Les derivées paléochrétiennes du groupe atlantique', *Gallia*, 31, 207–64.

Rigold, S., 1969. 'Recent investigations into the earliest defences of Carisbrooke Castle, Isle of Wight', in Taylor (1969), pp. 128–38.

Ritchie, J. N. G., 1971. 'Iron age finds from Dùn an Fheurain, Gallanach, Argyll', *Proc. Soc. Antiq. Scot.*, 103, 100–12.

Rivet, A. L. F., 1958. *Town and country in Roman Britain* (London).

Rivet, A. L. F., 1971. 'Hill-forts in action', in Hill & Jesson (1971), pp. 189–202.

Rodwell, W. (ed.), 1980. *Temples, churches and religion: recent research in Roman Britain* (Oxford).

Ross, A., 1967. *Pagan Celtic Britain* (London).

Ryder, M. L., 1983. 'Milk products', in Jones, M. (1983), pp. 239–50.

Rynne, E., 1966. 'The impact of the Vikings on Irish weapons', *Proc. 6th International Congress Pre- & Protohistoric Sciences*, 181–5.

Rynne, E. (ed.), 1967. *North Munster Studies* (Limerick).

Rynne, E., 1981. 'A classification of pre-Viking Irish iron swords', in B. G. Scott (ed.), *Studies on early Ireland*, 93–7.

Rynne, E. and MacEoin, G., 1978. 'The Craggaunowen crannog; gangway and gatetower', *North Munster Antiq. J.*, 20, 47–56.

Salin, E., 1950–9. *La civilisation mérovingienne*, 4 vols., (Paris).

Saunders, C., 1972. 'The excavations at Grambla, Wendron, 1972, interim report', *Cornish Archaeol.*, 11, 50–2.

Savory, H. N., 1956. 'Some sub-Romano-British brooches from south Wales', in Harden (1956a), pp. 40–58.

Savory, H. N., 1960. 'Excavations at Dinas Emrys, Beddgelert, Caernarvonshire, 1954–56', *Archaeol. Cambrensis*, 109, 13–77.

Savory, H. N., 1964. Review of *Dinas Powys*, *Archaeol. Cambrensis*, 113, 184–5.

Savory, H. N., 1976. 'Welsh hill-forts: a reappraisal of recent research', in Harding (1976a), pp. 237–91.

Sawyer, P. H., 1962; 1971. *The age of the Vikings* (London).

Sawyer, P. H., (ed.), 1976. *Medieval settlement: continuity and change* (London).

Sawyer, P. H., 1977. 'Kings and merchants', in Sawyer and Wood (1977), pp. 139–58.

Sawyer, P. H. & Wood, I. N., (eds.), 1977. *Early medieval kingship* (Leeds).

Seller, T. J., 1982. 'Bone material', in Curle (1982), pp. 132–8.

Shephard, J., 1979. 'The social identity of the individual in isolated barrows and barrow cemeteries in Anglo-Saxon England', in Burnham and Kingsbury (1979), pp. 47–79.

Sieveking, G. de G., Longworth, I. H. & Wilson, K. E. (eds.), 1976, *Problems in economic and social archaeology* (London).

Silver, I. A., 1969. 'The ageing of domestic animals', in Brothwell and Higgs (1969), pp. 283–302.

Sims-Williams, P., 1982. Review of W. Davies, *The Llandaff Charters*, *J. Eccles. Hist.*, 33, 124–9.

Sims-Williams, P., 1983a. 'Gildas and the Anglo-Saxons', *Cambridge Medieval Celt. Stud.*, 6, 1–30.

Sims-Williams, P., 1983b. 'The settlement of England in Bede and the *Chronicle*', *Anglo-Saxon Engl.*, 12, 1–41.

Smail, R. C., 1956. *Crusading Warfare (1097–1193)* (Cambridge).

Smith, A. H., 1956. *English place-name elements*, English Place-Name Society 25–6, (Cambridge).

Smith, J., 1919. 'Excavation of the forts of Castlehill, Aitnock and Coalhill, Ayrshire', *Proc. Soc. Antiq. Scot.*, 53, 123–34.

Smith, J. T., 1963. 'Romano-British aisled houses', *Archaeol. J.*, 120, 1–30.

Smith, P. & Hague, D. B., 1958. 'Ty-Draw', *Archaeol. Cambrensis*, 107, 109–20.

Spratling, M. G., 1970a. 'The Smiths of South Cadbury', *Current Archaeol.*, No. 18, 188–91.

Spratling, M. G., 1970b. 'Bronze shield mount', *Antiq. J.*, 50, 21–2.

Spriggs, M., (ed.), 1977. *Archaeology and Anthropology: Areas of mutual interest* (Oxford).

Steer, K. A. & Bannerman, J. W. M., 1977. *Late medieval monumental sculpture in the West Highlands* (Edinburgh).

Stenton, F. M., 1943. *Anglo-Saxon England* (Oxford).

Stevenson, R. B. K., 1949. 'The nuclear fort of Dalmahoy, Midlothian, and other dark age capitals', *Proc. Soc. Antiq. Scot.*, 83, 186–98.

Stevenson, R. B. K., 1955. 'Pins and the chronology of brochs', *Proc. Prehist. Soc.*, 21, 282–94.

Stevenson, R. B. K., 1972. 'Note on mould from Craig Phadrig', in A. Small & M. B. Cottam, *Craig Phadrig* (Dundee), pp. 49–51.

Stevenson, R. B. K., 1974. 'The Hunterston brooch and its significance', *Medieval Archaeol.*, 18, 16–42.

Stevenson, R. B. K., 1976. 'The earlier metalwork of Pictland', in Megaw (1976), pp. 245–51.

Storrie, J., 1894. 'Roman iron-making at Ely race-course', *Cardiff Nat. Soc. Trans.* (1894), 38–9.

Stukeley, W., 1776. *Itinerarium curiosum*, 2nd ed.

Swanton, M. J., 1973. *The spearheads of the Anglo-Saxon settlements* (London).

Swanton, M. J., 1974. *Pagan Anglo-Saxon spear-types* (Oxford).

Swindells, N. & Laing, Ll., 1980. 'Metalworking at the Mote of Mark, Kirkcudbright in the 6th–7th centuries AD', in Oddy (1980), pp. 121–8.

Tainter, J. A., 1975. 'Social inference and mortuary practices: an experiment in numerical classification', *World Archaeol.*, 7, 1–15.

Taylor, A. J. ed., 1969. *Château Gaillard European Castle Studies* 3, (Chichester).

Taylor, J. du P. & Cleere, H. (eds.), 1978. *Roman shipping and trade: Britain and the Rhine provinces* (London).

Thesiger, W., 1959. *Arabian Sands* (London).

Thomas, A. C., 1956. 'Evidence for post-Roman occupation of Chûn Castle, Cornwall', *Antiq. J.*, 36, 75–8.

Thomas, A. C., 1958. *Gwithian, Ten Years' work, 1949–58* (Gwithian).

Thomas, A. C., 1959. 'Imported pottery in Dark-Age western Britain', *Medieval Archaeol.*, 3, 89–111.

Thomas, A. C., 1968. 'Grass-marked pottery in Cornwall', in Coles & Simpson (1968), pp. 311–31.

Thomas, A. C., 1971. *The early Christian archaeology of north Britain* (Glasgow).

Thomas, A. C., 1972. 'The Irish settlements in post-Roman western Britain: a survey of the evidence', *J. Roy. Inst. Cornwall*, N.S.6, 251–74.

Thomas, A. C., 1981. *A provisional list of imported pottery in post-Roman western Britain and Ireland* (Redruth).

Thomas, A. C., 1982. 'East and West: Tintagel, Mediterranean imports and the early insular church', in Pearce (1982), pp. 17–24.

Thompson, E. A., 1965. *The early Germans* (Oxford).

Thompson, E. A., 1977. 'Britain AD 406–410', *Britannia*, 8, 303–18.

Thompson, E. A., 1984. *Saint Germanus of Auxerre and the end of Roman Britain* (Woodbridge).

Toynbee, J. M. C., 1953. 'Christianity in Roman Britain', *J. Brit. Archaeol. Ass.*, 3rd ser., 16, 1–24.

Trevor-Roper, H. R. (ed.), 1964. *Studies in British History, presented to Sir Keith Feiling* (London).

Trow-Smith, R., 1957. *A history of British livestock husbandry to 1770* (London).

Tylecote, R. F., 1959. 'An early medieval iron-smelting site in Weardale', *J. Iron Steel Inst.*, 192, 26–34.

Tylecote, R. F., 1962. *Metallurgy in archaeology* (London).

Ucko, P. J., 1969. 'Ethnography and archaeological interpretation of funerary remains', *World Archaeol.*, 1, 262–80.

Unger, R. W., 1980. *The ship in the medieval economy 600–1600* (London).

Uslar, R.v., 1964. *Studien zu frühgeschichtlichen Befestigungen zwischen Nordsee und Alpen* (Köln).

Vayda, A. P., 1970. *Maori Warfare* (Wellington, New Zealand).

VC *Vita Columbae*, see Anderson A. O. & M. O. (1961).

VW *The Life of Bishop Wilfrid by Eddius Stephanus*, B. Colgrave, (ed. and trans), (1927).

Wacher, J. S., 1971. 'Yorkshire towns in the fourth century', in R. M. Butler, *Soldier and civilian in Roman Yorkshire* (Leicester), pp. 165–77.

Wacher, J. 1974. *The towns of Roman Britain* (London).

Wade-Evans, A. W., 1938. *Nennius's 'History of the Britons'* (London).

Wade-Evans, A. W., 1944. *Vitae Sanctorum Britanniae et Genealogiae* (Cardiff).

Wainwright, G. J., 1967. *Coygan Camp* (Cardiff).

Wall, J. C., 1906. Ancient Earthworks, in Page (1906).

Wallace-Hadrill, J. M., 1971. *Early Germanic Kingship in England and on the Continent* (Oxford).

Walter of Henley, see Lamond & Cunningham (1890).

Walton, J., 1957. The Skye house, *Antiquity*, 31, 155–62.

Warner, R., 1979. 'The Clogher yellow layer', *Ceramics*, 3, 37–40.

Waterman, D. M., 1956. 'The excavation of a house and souterrain at White Fort, Drumaroad, Co. Down', *Ulster J. Archaeol.*, 19, 73–86.

Waterman, D. M., 1958. 'Excavations at Ballyfounder Rath, Co. Down', *Ulster J. Archaeol.*, 21, 39–61.

Watson, J. P. N., 1978. The interpretation of epiphyseal fusion data', in D. R. Brothwell, K. D. Thomas & J. Clutton-Brock, *Research problems in zooarchaeology* (London), pp. 97–101.

Webster, L. E., 1973. 'Catterick, North Riding, Yorkshire, Medieval Britain in 1972', *Medieval Archaeol.*, 17, 150.

Webster, L. E., 1977. 'Liddington Castle, Wiltshire, Medieval Britain in 1976', *Medieval Archaeol.*, 21, 214.

Welch, M. G., 1971. 'Late Romans and Saxons in Sussex', *Britannia*, 2, 232–7.

Welch, M. G., 1983. *Early Anglo-Saxon Sussex* (Oxford).

Welsh History Review, 1963. *The Welsh Laws*.

Wheeler, R. E. M., 1925. *Prehistoric and Roman Wales* (Oxford).

Wheeler, R. E. M., 1943. *Maiden Castle (Dorset)* (London).

Wheeler, R. E. M., 1952. 'Earthwork since Hadrian Allcroft', *Archaeol. J.*, 106: *Memorial Volume to Sir Alfred Clapham*, pp. 62–82.

Wheeler, R. E. M. & T. V., 1932. *Excavation of the prehistoric, Roman and post-Roman site in Lydney Park, Gloucestershire* (London).

White, L., 1962. *Medieval technology and social change* (Oxford).

White, R. B., 1978. 'New light on the origin of the Kingdom of Gwynedd', in Bromwich & Brinley Jones (1978), pp. 350–5.

White, R. B., 1980. 'Excavations at Aberffraw, Anglesey, 1973 and 1974', *Bull. Board Celt. Studies*, 28, 319–42.

Whitelock, D. ed., 1979. *English historical documents c. 500–1042*, 2nd edn, (London).

Whitelock, D. with Douglas, D. C. & Tucker, S. I., 1961. *The Anglo-Saxon chronicle: a revised translation* (London).

Whitelock, D., McKitterick, R. and Dumville, D. N. (eds.), 1982. *Ireland in early medieval Europe* (Cambridge).

Wild, J. P., 1963. 'The *Byrrus Britannicus*', *Antiquity*, 37, 193–202.

Williams, A., 1952. 'Clegyr Boia, St Davids, Pemb.: excavation in 1943', *Archaeol. Cambrensis*, 102, 20–47.

Williams, G., 1950. *The Rent that's due to Love: a selection of Welsh poems* (London).

Williams, J., 1971. 'Tynron Doon, Dumfriesshire: a history of the site with notes on the finds 1924–67', *Trans. Dumfriesshire Galloway Natur. Hist. Antiq. Soc.* 3rd Series, 48, 106–17.

Williams, J. E. Caerwyn, 1968. *The poems of Taliesin* (Dublin).

Wilson, B., Grigson, C. & Payne, S., (eds.), 1982. *Ageing and sexing animal bones from archaeological sites* (Oxford).

Wilson, D. M. (ed.), 1976. *The archaeology of Anglo-Saxon England* (London).

Wilson, D. R., 1972. 'Roman Britain in 1971', *Britannia* 3, 299–351.

Winterbottom, M., 1978. *Gildas: The ruin of Britain and other works* (London).

Wormald, P., 1978. 'Bede, "Beowulf" and the conversion of the Anglo-Saxon aristocracy', in R. T. Farrell, *Bede and Anglo-Saxon England* (Oxford), pp. 32–95.

Wormald, P., 1983. 'Bede, the *Bretwaldas* and the origins of the *gens Anglorum*', in P. Wormald, *Ideal and reality in Frankish and Anglo-Saxon Society* (Oxford), pp. 99–129.

Wynne, E. J. & Tylecote, R. F., 1958. 'An experimental investigation into primitive iron-smelting technique', *J. Iron Steel Inst.*, 190, 339–48.

Young, C. J., 1983. 'The lower enclosure at Carisbrooke Castle, Isle of Wight', in Hartley & Wacher (1983), pp. 290–301.

Young, H. W., 1891. 'Notes on the ramparts of Burghead', *Proc. Soc. Antiq. Scot.*, 25, 435–47.

Young, H. W., 1893. 'Notes on further excavations at Burghead', *Proc. Soc. Antiq. Scot.*, 27, 86–91.

Index